THE CONSTRUCTION OF FORMAL SPECIFICATIONS
An Introduction to the Model-Based and Algebraic Approaches

THE LIBRARY

University of U

12

02

D0543199

THE McGRAW-HILL INTERNATIONAL SERIES IN SOFTWARE ENGINEERING

Consulting Editor

Professor D. Ince
The Open University

Titles in this Series

THE CONSTRUCTION OF FORMAL SPECIFICATIONS
An Introduction to the Model-Based and Algebraic Approaches

J.G. Turner
University of Westminster

T.L. McCluskey
University of Huddersfield
Formerly of the City University, London

McGRAW-HILL BOOK COMPANY

London • New York • St Louis • San Francisco • Auckland • Bogotá • Caracas
Lisbon • Madrid • Mexico • Milan • Montreal • New Delhi • Panama • Paris
San Juan • São Paulo • Singapore • Sydney • Tokyo • Toronto

100330932
005.1 XX
TUR

Published by
McGRAW-HILL Book Company Europe
Shoppenhangers Road, Maidenhead, Berkshire, SL6 2QL, England
Telephone 0628 23432
Fax 0628 770224

British Library Cataloguing in Publication Data
Turner, John
    Construction of Formal Specifications: Introduction to the Model-based and Algebraic
    Approaches. – (McGraw-Hill International Series in Software Engineering)
    I. Title   II. McCluskey, T. Lee   III. Series 005.1

    ISBN 0-07-707735-0

Library of Congress Cataloging-in-Publication Data
Turner, John,
    The construction of formal specifications: an introduction to the model-based and algebraic
    approaches/John Turner, T. Lee McCluskey.
       p.   cm.—(The McGraw-Hill international series in software engineering)
       Includes bibliographical references and index.
       ISBN 0-07-707735-0
       1. Software engineering.   I. McCluskey, T. Lee,   II. Title.   III. Series.
    QA76.758.T86 1994   93-31699
      005.1'2—dc20   CIP

Copyright © 1994 McGraw-Hill International (UK) Limited. All rights reserved. No part of this publication may be reproduced, stored in a retrieval system, or transmitted, in any form or by any means, electronic, mechanical, photocopying, recording, or otherwise, without the prior permission of McGraw-Hill International (UK) Limited, with the exception of material entered and executed on a computer system for the reader's own use.

12345CUP97654

Typeset by Interprint Limited, Valletta, Malta.
Printed and bound in Great Britain
at the University Press, Cambridge.

CONTENTS

AIMS OF THE BOOK

This book aims to introduce the reader to the field of formal specification. It should enable the reader to understand the role and nature of formal specifications of computer programs, and to develop skills at creating such specifications. We have endeavoured to make the book educational in nature, rather than a training guide to one particular notation or another.

The book has been written with the following objectives in mind. It should show the reader how to:

- *Construct* specifications; books on formal methods do not generally contain adequate explanations of how a specifier goes about constructing specifications. They tend to present a specification as a *fait accompli*; the specification itself may be well documented, but the process of arriving at it is not.
- Write formal specifications of sequential programs in *both* the algebraic and model-based styles. Also, several of the specifications in the book are developed in both styles: this helps the reader understand the differences between the two approaches, and leads to a greater understanding of formal specification itself.
- *Prototype* the specifications once they have been created. The emphasis on prototyping rather than program development means that specifications can be validated without the specifier having to work through complicated refinement procedures.

We have tried to write the book in an intuitive and accessible fashion. Formal methods have been slow to be adopted, and one reason is that books on the subject are inaccessible to students and practitioners alike. We have tried to pitch the book at a level that assumes only a standard background in logic, mathematics, and programming.

THE READERSHIP

This book is intended to be a coursebook on formal specification for use in universities and colleges, and as a self-tutor for computing professionals. Most degree schemes in computer related disciplines now have material on formal specification/methods in the second or third year of their undergraduate courses: we hope this book will contribute to providing an understanding and feel for formal specification in general (rather than simply developing specification-writing skills alone). Although a study of the two different kinds of specification methods covered by this book should provide the reader with a balanced view of the area, we have tried to make it possible to study them separately. Thus, it is possible for a reader to study VDM in the first part of the book alone, or alternatively, starting at Chapter 8, learn about the algebraic approach to specification.

As a pre-condition to reading this book, we expect the background of the reader to include some programming, discrete mathematics, and logic. Also, some experience in logic programming is essential for a full understanding of Chapter 7, which uses Prolog as the prototyping language for VDM.

STRUCTURE OF THE BOOK

While Chapters 1 and 2 serve as an introduction and as a mathematical refresher, respectively, Chapters 3, 4, 5, and 6 cover *model-based* specification using VDM, and Chapter 7 introduces the reader to prototyping VDM in Prolog. Chapters 8 to 13 cover the algebraic approach to specification. Chapter 14 contains a case study of a neural network, specified using both styles, and the book is rounded off with a discussion of both styles in Chapter 15. Appendix 1 contains a full listing of the prototype derived from the case study in Chapter 6, while Appendix 2 contains prototypes derived from the algebraic specifications. Finally, we provide a glossary of terms used in algebraic specifications.

The particular choice of ordering of the two specification styles (with VDM first) was made on the basis of our experience in teaching the material: students find the algebraic style harder to grasp. With its underlying mathematical foundation in the area of category theory, it is hardly surprising that students often have difficulty when first meeting the algebraic approach: we have intentionally provided a more detailed exposition of it in order to overcome this problem.

Finally, a note on the notations and conventions used in the text. In the case of VDM, we use the now standard notation employed by Jones (1990) (full reference is given at the end of Chapter 1).

In the case of the algebraic approach, sort and operation names, axioms and the completed specifications themselves are presented in a serif typewriter face. Identifiers used in the text to denote the specifications are presented in a sans serif typeface.

J.G. Turner
T.L. McCluskey

1

INTRODUCTION TO FORMAL SPECIFICATION

1.1 A FIRST SPECIFICATION LANGUAGE

Imagine the following situation. You have learned your first programming language, and written many programs in it. Happily you have given them to a program compiler which translates the programs to a form that is executable. Let us assume the compiler (compiler 'A') is one that checks a program's syntax first before proceeding onto the language translation stage. In the past, on the basis of its syntax analysis, it has always proceeded in one of two ways:

- Either it asserts the syntax of your program is correct and proceeds to the language translation stage, displaying:

  Starting program compilation..
  ⇒ program parsed correctly: yes
  ⇒ starting translation stage
  ....

- Or it aborts, displaying the syntax errors that have occurred:

  Starting program compilation..
  ⇒ program parsed correctly: no

  ** compilation aborted **
  Syntax error in line ....

Then one day something changes. Instead of making a definitive yes or no answer at the first stage, it makes the reply:

Starting program compilation..
⇒program parsed correctly: maybe...

The compiler has checked your program's syntax and answered that it *may be* correct! The syntax of a programming language is generally very complex; and this is an answer you might expect from a person—but not from a compiler.

Of course this never happens, but why? The answer is that the programming language syntax you are using has been defined *precisely*—a string of characters representing a program either belongs in the language or it does not. There is no maybe, no buts, no perhaps. The compiler has been written to embody this precise syntax definition, so that it will answer yes when your program conforms to it or no when your program does not.

Returning to our hypothetical compilation session, imagine that, rather than replying with 'maybe', the compiler aborts, finding syntax errors in your program. Disgruntled, you decide to turn to another compiler (compiler 'B') which was also written to compile programs for the same language. This time, when you input the same program file, compiler 'B' returns:

Starting program compilation..
⇒ program parsed correctly: yes
⇒ starting translation stage

. . . .

Now you are faced with two compilers, supposedly for the same programming language, which give conflicting answers!

Of course, this should never happen (and rarely does). Why? The reason is that the programming language syntax has been defined in an *unambiguous* way, so that any compiler that embodies this definition conforms to a unique interpretation. Also, the definition will most probably be written in a standard, compiler-independent form that allows us to decide which compiler is wrong, in the event of disagreement.

Hence, this precise, unambiguous definition of the syntax is very important for the writers of the compiler. How is it written? One way is to specify syntax using a graphical medium such as 'Syntax Charts', where graphs are used to convey the content of a language. The standard symbolic way of defining the syntax of a programming language, however, is to use a *grammar*, typically the extended Backus–Naur form, known as EBNF. The EBNF gives us a general notation for specifying languages, and therefore is sometimes called a 'metalanguage' (meaning 'a language used to describe another language'). It should be familiar even to novice programmers as it is used in many introductory books on computer languages. In fact, since its introduction in the sixties, it has enjoyed widespread use within computer science for a number of reasons which we shall explore shortly.

A fragment of the language definition of Pascal using EBNF is:

Program → 'PROGRAM' Declarative_part Statement_part'.'

Statement_part → '*BEGIN*' *Statement* {*Statement*} '*END*'

Declarative_part → ['*CONST*' *Constant_definition* {*Constant_definition*}]
　　　　　　　　['*VAR*' *Variable_declaration* {*Variable_declaration*}]

Symbols such as '→', '[', ']', '{' and '}' are part of the EBNF specification language itself, while letters quoted are those that appear in an actual program, and words in italics stand for syntactic structures which are defined elsewhere in the specification. The fragment consists of three rules, each rule having the same meaning as its corresponding Syntax Chart in Fig. 1.1. The first rule states that a program must begin with the word '*PROGRAM*' and end with a full stop, and whatever comes in between is specified by rules starting with '*Declarative_part*' and '*Statement_part*'. The other two rules, therefore, follow on, and the detail of the correct internal structure of a Pascal program emerges.

Program

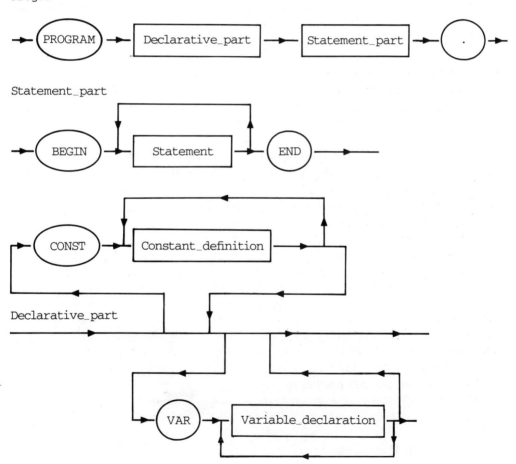

Figure 1.1 Syntax Charts corresponding to Pascal syntax rules.

One uses the EBNF to specify language syntax in a *generative* fashion. Every syntactically correct program in the language being defined can be generated using the rules, starting at a special word (here '*Program*'). We can use the rules in a precise manner to rewrite the special symbol into a full program; hence:

Program

rewrites by the first rule to

'*PROGRAM*' *Declarative_part Statement_part* '.'

which rewrites by the second rule to

'*PROGRAM*' *Declarative_part* '*BEGIN*' *Statement* {*Statement*} '*END*'

and so on until an actual program. In this manner, a language definition written in EBNF specifies precisely and unambiguously every legal element of the language. *EBNF is in fact a formal specification language.*

Exercise 1.1

(a) Look for syntax definitions of programming, database and operating system languages in books and manuals that train the reader how to use those languages. What sort of convention is used to give language syntax definitions? How precise are these definitions?

(b) EBNF may provide us with a notation for writing good language specifications, but it does not guarantee it. For example, we may legally write the rules:

bill → *ben*
ben → *bill*

Start with the word *bill*:

bill

this rewrites to

ben

by the first rule, and *ben* rewrites to

bill

by the second. This rewrites to

ben

and so on. Since there are no other rules with which to rewrite *bill* or *ben*, we cannot avoid generating a never-ending series of rewrites. This may be easy to spot in our contrived example, but in the midst of hundreds of rules, nonterminating rewrite loops may be more difficult to spot. Can you think of any other rules or rule forms in an EBNF definition that may be pointless or superfluous?

1.2 WHAT IS A SOFTWARE SPECIFICATION?

A general dictionary definition of specification would run something like:

A specification is a detail of design or materials for work to be undertaken.

For example, in the field of mechanical engineering this might be a set of technical drawings, complete with dimensions, tolerances, parts lists and so on. In Britain this type of specification would have to be produced to the *British Standard* BS308.

As an exercise, you might like to form your own opinion before reading on as to what others have defined a software specification to be. Here then are some of the textbook definitions that have been given in the past:

1. A specification describes WHAT a program does, a design describes HOW the program does it, and documentation describes WHY it does it.
2. A specification is a document that forms a contract between the customer and the designer.
3. Specification is the second phase in the 'staged' model of software development, which consists of: requirements; specification; design; implementation; testing; maintenance.
4. A specification is a document by which we can judge the correctness of an implementation.

All these are consistent views of the nature of a specification. Read in isolation, they are simplistic, and to attempt a better answer we must provide some background to the question 'What is a software specification?'.

In the context of software engineering, there are several acknowledged phases that developers may pass through on route to a final, fully operational implementation, as suggested by the third definition above. The *feasibility* stage, in fact, is usually the first, in which the question being raised is 'does a problem admit a computationally feasible solution?', or more specifically 'does a problem allow a computationally feasible solution within the time, money, equipment and any other resource constraints that may be present?'.

Assuming a computational solution is feasible, one has to capture the requirements of the solution. This is a bit like restating the problem, but at this stage it is probably phrased in a language that is problem oriented, and one that the 'customers' can understand. If the customers are part of a business enterprise then the requirement phase may involve both a capture of the current system (which could be a payroll, accounting, or bookings system, for example) as well as a statement of the new system's requirements. If the customers are the software developers themselves, as is often the case with technical or system software, an explicit requirement phase might not even occur.

The next step, provided the requirements are agreed upon, is to attempt to *construct* a *system model* that satisfies these requirements. In the case of a commercial system, the system model may then be an evolution of the old system. The fundamental change here is from a form that is *assertive* (what you want) to one that is *constructive* (how you will get it). The problem, initially expressed as a set of requirements, is turned into a solution in the form of a system model. The first model will be necessarily abstract, and will carry through many of the requirements as properties and constraints on the model. Nevertheless, it will embody some commitments to structuring of the final implementation, and include some computational concepts (such as *input/output* and *data flow*). In other words, what we have is a top-level design.

So what has happened to the specification? Have we missed out a stage? The answer is that specification is *not* really a particular stage in software development; eliciting requirements and transforming these into a design may involve 'specification' at various stages. Some staged models of software development do include the phases 'requirements specification' and 'design specification' to emphasize this point. The requirements refer to needs, the design to models that should satisfy the needs—a specification can be a precise statement of the needs or even of the model to be constructed to fulfil them.

In this text you may sometimes find the word 'definition' used interchangeably with specification. This is not surprising since a 'definition' is something that is supposed to be *precise* and *complete*, two of the qualities we desire for software specifications. Also, there must be something whole and integrated about a specification—it must be more than just a piecemeal restatement of the requirements. In essence, it should form a 'theory' of which designs are possible models. It should also have a major characteristic of a good theory—one should be able to use it to *predict* the final system's behaviour. This means that the specification should pin things down that hitherto had been left open, and should throw up incompletenesses in the requirements.

Our discussion has led to an answer, which, it must be said, is more an *ideal* than a definition:

> A specification is a precise, unambiguous and complete statement of the requirements of a system (or program or process), written in such a way that it can be used to predict how the system will behave.

Exercises for discussion

(a) In Sec. 1.1 we asserted that EBNF was a specification language, but an EBNF specification defines a language, not a system. Discuss the connection between the specification of a program and of a language. (*Hint*: consider the set of inputs to a program as making up a language.)

(b) Consider the following documents. Discuss whether they fit any or all of the definitions of specification given above (you will have to generalize the definitions to cope with nonsoftware domains). If they do, say what they could be specifications of:
   (i) Your waist and inside leg measurements.
   (ii) A cooking recipe.
   (iii) A programming coursework description.
   (iv) The dimensions, weight, power, top speed and acceleration of a new car.

(v) A piece of pseudocode for a program.

(vi) A body of rules stating the separation standards of a collection of aircraft that are flying over the Atlantic at any point in time.

(c) Discuss whether any/all the 'definitions' of specification given are precise and complete!

1.3 WHAT IS A FORMAL SPECIFICATION?

We asserted at the end of Sec. 1.1 that EBNF was a formal specification language (FSL). What makes EBNF a good FSL (for specifying programming language syntax) is that it helps us write specifications of language syntax that satisfy certain criteria, such as *precision*. In the absence of any other rules, starting with '*Program* →', the EBNF fragment in Sec. 1.1 states precisely that any program conforming to it *must* start with the letters '*PROGRAM*' and end with a full stop, exactly what we expect of every Pascal program.

EBNF also satisfies other criteria that we look for in an FSL. It is:

- *Unambiguous*—a definition can be read in only one way; a decision as to whether a phrase is correct syntax is not open to different interpretations.
- *Standard*—the notation is generally acceptable and widely used.
- *Implementation independent*—the definition is independent of any program that embodies it.
- *Formally manipulatable*—the definition can be reasoned with using precise manipulations. EBNF is based on the idea of 'rewrite' rules that form a mathematical system.
- *Well founded*—there is a whole area of theory on which grammars are based (recall EBNF is a form of grammar). Also, various types of grammar have a strong correspondence with abstract computing machines.

Other qualities of a syntax specification that EBNF encourages are as follows (note that EBNF itself does not *guarantee* these qualities):

- *Abstract*—the notation encourages a user to write definitions that are concise, in other words they use the minimum amount of detail to say exactly *what* is in a target language, and nothing more.
- *Structured*—the definition can be built up compositely, and the structure of the definition can be used to reflect the meaning of the language syntax being defined.

These properties are all necessary in an FSL, but there are more. The reason EBNF cannot be called a general FSL is that it is not expressive enough to specify every sequential algorithm. In fact, EBNF cannot even capture the full syntax definitions of most programming languages: it cannot completely capture the *context-sensitive* parts of the Pascal language, such as the restriction that any variable name used in an expression must have been previously defined. None the less, it has still proved useful for the particular application of language syntax definition.

The two styles of formal specification language used in this book are general: they can be used to specify arbitrary, sequential computer programs, not just language syntax. Hence, an additional property we require of an FSL is as follows:

- It must be *expressive* enough to be able to specify any piece of (sequential) software.

Finally, EBNF does not highlight that we require the property of *consistency* in specifications. This is because it only allows a user to say what is correct language syntax: one cannot use EBNF to say what is *not* correct syntax. A specification is inconsistent if two parts of it are contradictory with each other. Naturally, we want to avoid writing specifications that are inconsistent, but in a large, realistic application this might not be easy.

Through our analysis of what has made EBNF a good FSL, we are now in a position to build on our earlier definition of 'specification' by summarizing the particular properties of an FSL:

- The characteristics of an FSL are that it is expressive enough for general computation, is well founded in mathematics, and encourages the development of precise, predictive, well-structured, self-consistent and complete specifications.

An apparent disadvantage of FSLs We have not yet exhausted our list of desirable qualities of an FSL. There is one quality of a specification language on which all FSLs do not seem to score too well, and the reason that there are graphical forms of EBNF such as Syntax Charts provides a clue to the nature of this quality.

Specifications should provide a *communication medium* between the developers, and the customers and 'end users' of the proposed system. If the specification is to be viewed as some sort of contract, then the customers and end users will need to perform validation on it.

Unfortunately, FSLs tend to be highly mathematical, and here lies the problem. There are approaches to overcome this, however:

- The specification could be accompanied by enough natural language description that one could gain an understanding of it by simply reading the text.
- The specification could be transformed to a 'validation form' that is easily understandable (as Syntax Charts could be used as a validation form for EBNF). This transformation should preferably be automatic, to minimize the possibility of error introduction.
- The specification could be *animated* by transforming it to a working prototype. Again, the transformation should preferably be automatic for the reason given above.

The first approach shall be used in this book, although in Chapters 7 and 13 we explore the third approach.

1.4 THE SCOPE OF THIS BOOK

This book covers only a certain aspect of specification in software engineering, roughly summed up as the 'functional specification of sequential software'. Other entities that a specification may have to address are:

- Hardware—what computers are required.
- Performance—what size memory is required and what kind of processing speed.

Both these are beyond the scope of this book, as is the specification of concurrent (rather than sequential) processes.

Also, this book is *not* meant as a training manual or handbook in one FSL or another (and this is one reason why we do not include EBNF descriptions of the FSLs we use!). Indeed, the two languages in which we write specifications are not exhaustively detailed. The parts of these languages that were not needed for our purposes were left out.

On the other hand, the book is meant to introduce the reader to the important concepts in formal specification, to give a feel for the whole area, and to provide some basic skills in specification construction. To this end, we have included:

- FSLs from two differing specification styles: the specification language used in the first half of the book (VDM) is of the *model-based* style, while the language used in the second half of the book is of the *algebraic* style. This should give the reader a broad view of the subject.
- Interesting case studies, particularly the *neural network* and *automated planner* case studies of Chapters 14 and 6 respectively.

1.5 SUMMARY

Ideally, a formal specification should be a precise, consistent, unambiguous, complete, and implementation independent statement. One should be able to reason about its properties and predict the behaviour of the system it specifies. It should be written in a formal specification language that supports these properties, is mathematically well-founded and provides syntactic structures (e.g., functions, modules) on which we can build up or decompose a complex specification.

EBNF is seen as a successful formal specification language, although its use is limited to language syntax definition.

2

MATHEMATICAL STRUCTURES FOR FORMAL SPECIFICATION

2.1 INTRODUCTION

In this chapter, we provide a brief review of some standard results from the theory of sets, mappings and relations and look at the concept of binary operations. This chapter will furnish the necessary mathematical framework for the formal approaches to specification that are to be examined in this book. The formal concepts are explained with the help of a number of examples from applications in software engineering. This chapter can be skipped by readers familiar with sets, functions and relations. To start, we give a brief introduction to sets and mappings.

2.2 SETS

A *set* is any collection of objects, and each object in the collection is called an *element* of the set. We write $x \in X$ to indicate that x is an element of the set X while the notation $x \notin X$ means that x is *not* an element of the set X.

2.2.1 Terminology

It is customary to reserve certain symbols for the frequently occurring sets:

- $\mathbb{N}$ denotes the set of *natural numbers* 0, 1, 2, 3,... so that $5 \in \mathbb{N}$ but $-1 \notin \mathbb{N}$. Note that we follow the usual practice in computer science of including the value 0 in the set of natural numbers, unlike mathematics where the set of natural numbers describes the set of positive integers 1, 2, 3,... .

- $\mathbb{Z}$ denotes the set of all *integers*, ..., -2, -1, 0, 1, 2, 3, ... ($\mathbb{Z}$ comes from the German *Zahl* meaning *number*).
- $\mathbb{Q}$ denotes the set of all *rational numbers*, that is fractions of the form $\frac{m}{n}$ where $m \in \mathbb{Z}$, $n \in \mathbb{N}$ and $n \neq 0$. ($\mathbb{Q}$ stands for *quotient*.) Examples of rational numbers are $\frac{1}{3}$, $\frac{5}{2}$, $\frac{-4}{8}$.
- $\mathbb{R}$ denotes the set of all *real numbers* such as $\sqrt{2}$, -12.341, 0.05.
- $\mathbb{B}$ denotes the set of *Boolean* values and consists of the two elements *true* and *false*.

Sets can be specified by listing their elements *explicitly* and enclosing them within braces (curly brackets). For example, we can write the Boolean set $\mathbb{B}$ as

$$\mathbb{B} = \{true, \ false\}$$

A set can also be specified *implicitly* by means of some common characteristic property P of its elements. We write

$$X = \{x \mid x \text{ has property } P\}$$

for the set X of all elements x having the property P. As an example, the set X of values x such that x is a natural number that is greater than or equal to 4 and less than or equal to 7 is written

$$X = \{x \mid x \in \mathbb{N} \text{ and } 4 \leqslant x \leqslant 7\}$$

The vertical bar '|' in such an implicit definition is read as 'such that' or 'where'. The colon ':' is also used for this purpose but since the colon is used in VDM with a different meaning, we will use the vertical bar symbol '|'.

The set $\{x \in \mathbb{R} \mid 2x^2 - 5x + 2 = 0\}$ describes the set of solutions of the quadratic equation $2x^2 - 5x + 2 = 0$, which produces the set $\{0.5, 2\}$, whereas the set $\{x \in \mathbb{N} \mid 2x^2 - 5x + 2 = 0\}$ is the *singleton* set $\{2\}$ (since the root 0.5 is not a natural number).

2.2.2 Subsets

Let A and B denote arbitrary sets. If each element of A is also an element of B, then A is called a *subset* of B and we write $A \subseteq B$ or equivalently $\forall x \in A : x \in B$. Thus

$$\mathbb{N} \subseteq \mathbb{Z}; \quad \mathbb{Z} \subseteq \mathbb{Q}; \quad \mathbb{Q} \subseteq \mathbb{R}$$

If $A = \{0, 1, 3, 4\}$, $B = \{3, 4\}$, then all of the following statements are true

$$\{3\} \subseteq A; \quad \{3\} \subseteq B; \quad B \subseteq A; \quad A \subseteq A; \quad B \subseteq B$$

Note that for any set A, $A \subseteq A$ is true. It should be noted that the symbol '$\subset$' is sometimes used to denote the subset although we will use '$\subset$' to denote a *proper* subset. This is explained further in Sec. 2.2.6.

2.2.3 Equality

If $A \subseteq B$ and $B \subseteq A$, then A and B are said to be *equal* and we write $A = B$. In other words two sets A and B are equal if every element of A is an element of B and also if every element of B is an element of A. Thus two sets are equal if they consist of the same elements. For example if $A = \{0, 2, 3, 8\}$ and $B = \{3, 2, 8, 0\}$ then $A = B$. Note that duplicate elements are not allowed and that the order in which the elements is given is unimportant.

Given the set A where

$$A = \{x \mid x \in \mathbb{N}, x \text{ is odd and } x^2 < 10\}$$

and the set B where

$$B = \{t \mid t \in \mathbb{N} \text{ and } 3 \text{ is exactly divisible by } t\}$$

then $A = B = \{1, 3\}$.

2.2.4 Intersection

Let A and B denote sets, then the *intersection* of A and B, written $A \cap B$, is the set of those elements that belong to *both* A and B. Hence

$$A \cap B = \{x \mid x \in A \quad \text{and} \quad x \in B\}$$

For example, if $A = \{1, 2, 4, 5, 10, 12\}$ and $B = \{2, 5, 7, 11, 12\}$, then

$$A \cap B = \{2, 5, 12\}$$

If A is the collection of positive integers less than 50 that are divisible by 6 and B is the collection of positive integers less than 60 that are divisible by 8, then $A \cap B = \{24, 48\}$, that is the set of integers less than 50 that are divisible both by 6 and by 8.

2.2.5 Union

Let A and B denote sets, then the *union* of A and B, written $A \cup B$ is the set of elements that belong to A or to B or to both. Hence

$$A \cup B = \{x \mid \text{either } x \in A \quad \text{or} \quad x \in B\}$$

An immediate consequence of this definition for set union is that, for any set S, it follows that $S \cup S = S$. Also if $A \subset B$, then $A \cup B = B$. As an example, if A and B are as defined in the example above then

$$A \cup B = \{6, 8, 12, 16, 18, 24, 30, 32, 36, 40, 42, 48, 56\}$$

As another example, if $S=\{a, b, d, m\}$ and $T=\{b, g, k, m, s\}$, then

$$S \cup T = \{a, b, d, g, k, m, s\}$$

2.2.6 Null or empty set

The *empty set* or *null set* denoted by $\emptyset$ or by $\{\}$ is the set that contains no elements. For example $\{x \mid x \in \mathbb{N} \text{ and } 2x=1\}=\emptyset$. As a further example, if $A=\{1, 2, 4\}$ and $B=\{3, 5, 9, 10\}$ then $A \cap B = \emptyset$ (A and B have no elements in common).

Note that for any given set A, then $\emptyset \subseteq A$, that is the empty set is a subset of any set A. Furthermore, if $A \subseteq B$, $A \neq \emptyset$ and $A \neq B$, then A is called a *proper* subset of B. It is important to remember that we use '$\subset$' to denote a *proper* subset and '$\subseteq$' for the more general subset relation.

A word of caution here—do not confuse the empty set $\emptyset$ with the set $\{0\}$ which denotes the nonempty set consisting of the single element *zero*.

2.2.7 Disjoint sets

The sets A and B are *disjoint* if they have no elements in common, that is $A \cap B = \emptyset$. For example, if $A=\{-3, -1, 1, 3, 5\}$ and $B=\{-2, 0, 2, 4\}$, then $A \cap B = \emptyset$.

2.2.8 Cardinality and finite sets

A set is a *finite set* if it contains a finite number of elements. A set that is not finite is called an *infinite set*. $\mathbb{N}$, $\mathbb{Z}$, $\mathbb{Q}$, $\mathbb{R}$ are examples of infinite sets whereas $\mathbb{B}$ is finite.

Let A be a finite set, then the number of *distinct* elements of A is called the *cardinality* of A and is denoted by $|A|$ or $card(A)$. The cardinality of $\mathbb{B}=\{true, false\}$ is 2 while the cardinality of $\{2, 2, 4, 6, 6\}$ is 3. Note that $|\emptyset|=0$ and $|\{0\}|=1$.

2.2.9 Power set

Given a set A, then the *power set* of A is the set of all subsets of A including the empty set and the set A itself. It is denoted by $\mathscr{P}(A)$. If A has cardinality n, then the power set will contain 2^n elements. For example, if $A=\{1, 2, 3\}$ then the power set derived from A is the set

$$\mathscr{P}(A)=\{\emptyset, \{1\}, \{2\}, \{3\}, \{1,2\}, \{1,3\}, \{2,3\}, \{1,2,3\}\}$$

2.2.10 Set difference

Let A and B denote sets, then the *difference* of A and B, written $A \backslash B$ is the set of those elements which belong to A but which do not belong to B. Hence

$$A \backslash B = \{x \mid x \in A \quad \text{and} \quad x \notin B\}$$

so that if $A=\{0, 1, 2, 4, 6, 9, 10\}$ and $B=\{1, 4, 8, 9, 12\}$, then $A \backslash B = \{0, 2, 6, 10\}$ whereas $B \backslash A = \{8, 12\}$.

2.2.11 Associativity and commutativity

It can be shown that for any sets A, B, C

1. $A \cup (B \cup C) = (A \cup B) \cup C$
2. $A \cup B = B \cup A$

Result 1 expresses the fact that the union operation '$\cup$' is *associative* and so enables result 1 to be written as $A \cup B \cup C$ without ambiguity, while result 2 states that the union operation is *commutative*. It can be shown that the operation of set intersection '$\cap$' is also both associative and commutative.

Not all set operations are associative and/or commutative. In the case of the set difference operation, as the example demonstrates, the difference operation is not commutative, that is $A \backslash B \neq B \backslash A$. It is also easily verified that the difference operation is not associative either, that is $A \backslash (B \backslash C) \neq (A \backslash B) \backslash C$.

These concepts of associativity and commutativity are of fundamental importance in mathematics. The familiar operations of addition and multiplication over the real numbers are both associative and commutative.

2.3 CARTESIAN PRODUCT AND TUPLES

Let X and Y denote sets, then the set of all ordered pairs (x, y) with $x \in X$, $y \in Y$ is called the *Cartesian product* of X and Y and is written $X \times Y$. The Cartesian product $X \times X$ is often denoted by X^2. This definition can be extended: if $X_1, X_2, \ldots, X_n$ are sets, then the set of all *n-tuples* $(x_1, x_2, \ldots, x_n)$ where $x_1 \in X_1, x_2 \in X_2, \ldots, x_n \in X_n$ is the Cartesian product of $X_1, X_2, \ldots, X_n$ and is written $X_1 \times X_2 \times \ldots \times X_n$.

As an example, consider the Cartesian product of the set of natural numbers and the set of Boolean values. The Cartesian product is then the set of *all* ordered pairs of the form (n, b) where $n \in \mathbb{N}$ and $b \in \mathbb{B}$, and is written $\mathbb{N} \times \mathbb{B}$. Typical members of $\mathbb{N} \times \mathbb{B}$ include $(3, true)$; $(5, true)$; $(9, false)$; $(3, false)$.

The concept of a Cartesian product may be more clearly understood by considering the following situation. Suppose a young child is given a list of natural numbers, e.g. 3, 5, 9, 8, 2,... and has to state whether or not they are *odd*. Suppose further that the child is required to submit the answers at a computer terminal by typing in successive natural number, Boolean value pairs, for example '3 true'; '5 true'; '8 false'; '2 true';... and that after each pair is entered the system responds with an appropriate message: 'Your answer is correct' or 'Your answer is wrong!' A Boolean-valued Pascal function is_correct_pair and its use in a program that will accomplish this task is shown in Fig. 2.1.

The built-in Boolean function odd(n) returns *true* if n is *odd* and *false* if n is *even*. The formal parameter list n : natural; b : boolean in the function declaration states that the function will accept as valid input any *ordered pair* whose first element is a natural number and whose second element is a Boolean value. The *set* of *all* such ordered pairs, which we express mathematically as $\mathbb{N} \times \mathbb{B}$ is therefore simply the collection of all valid input tuples for the function and delineates precisely the set of all syntactically legal input value pairs to the function is_correct_pair.

```
type
  natural = 0 .. maxint; (* largest integer value the machine can hold *)

  function is_correct_pair(n : natural; b : boolean) : boolean;
  begin
    is_correct_pair := (odd(n) = b)
  end; (* is_correct_pair *)

(* main program fragment *)

read(n, b); (* assuming an implementation that reads Boolean variables! *)
if is_correct_pair(n, b) then
  writeln('Your answer is correct')
else
  writeln('Your answer is wrong!')
```

Figure 2.1   Pascal program for the Cartesian product.

2.4 MAPPINGS

Two sets may be related to each other in a variety of ways. One important type of relation is the *mapping* of one set to another.

To introduce this idea, consider the set U of all authorized users of a mainframe machine. User $u \in U$ has a user-number which we suppose is a positive integer which we can denote by $a(u)$. For instance if *John Smith* is an authorized user (and so is a member of the set U) and has user-number 2136, then we can write $a(John\ Smith) = 2136$. We observe that, in general, each element $u \in U$ will give rise to a specific and unique element $a(u) \in \mathbb{N}$. This relationship is an instance of a *mapping* of U to $\mathbb{N}$, where in this example a is the user-number mapping. Formally, we use the notation

$$a : U \rightarrow \mathbb{N}$$

to mean that a is a mapping (or map) of U to $\mathbb{N}$. The above notation also defines a *signature* for the mapping.

The application of mappings is one of the most commonly used techniques in formal specification methodologies and indeed the concept of mappings plays a key role in computer science with wide-ranging applications. One way to think of a mapping f is to treat it as a function that takes an input and transforms this input into an output, so that symbolically

$$f(input) = output$$

In this context, a Pascal compiler can be thought of as a function that takes a high-level source program as input and transforms it into the corresponding object program (the output). One essential characteristic of this mapping is the *uniqueness* of the output.

On a more concrete level, the use of finite maps such as finite sets of (*index, value*) or (*key, value*) pairs underlies the implementation of such data structures as arrays, hash-tables, keyed files and colour look-up tables. Mappings also play a crucial role in *operating systems*, for example dynamic address translation mechanisms need to maintain *address translation maps* illustrating which virtual storage locations are currently in real storage and exactly where they are.

2.4.1 Relations and mappings

Let X and Y denote sets, then a *relation* between X and Y (or a relation from X into Y) is any subset S of $X \times Y$ with $x \in X$ and $y \in Y$. Hence, a relation between X and Y is a collection S of tuples (ordered pairs) (x, y). The notion of a *mapping* involves relations of a special type.

A mapping $a: X \rightarrow Y$ from a set X into a set Y is a relation from X into Y such that each element of the first set X is related to exactly one element of the second set Y. We sometimes denote the element $y \in Y$ by $y = a(x)$. The terms *function* and *transformation* are often used as synonyms for *mapping*, while the term *map* is widely used in computer science to describe a function between finite sets.

We can denote a mapping in one of several ways. For example, the mapping $f: \mathbb{R} \rightarrow \mathbb{R}$ defined by $f(x) = 4x + 3$ in familiar mathematical notation is an alternative but more usual description of

$$f = \{(x, 4x + 3) \mid x \in \mathbb{R}\}$$

As another example, if $A = \{1, 2, 3, 4\}$, $B = \{a, b, c, d\}$ and $m: A \rightarrow B$ is the mapping defined by

$$m(1) = a, \quad m(2) = b, \quad m(3) = c, \quad m(4) = d$$

then we can express the mapping m as either a set of tuples (ordered pairs)

$$m = \{(1, a), (2, b), (3, c), (4, d)\}$$

or the set

$$m = \{1 \mapsto a, 2 \mapsto b, 3 \mapsto c, 4 \mapsto d\}$$

2.4.2 Domain and range

Let $a: X \rightarrow Y$ be a mapping. The set X is called the *domain* of a and Y is called the *range* or *codomain* of a.

2.4.3 Composition of mappings

Let $a: X \rightarrow Y$ and $b: Y \rightarrow Z$ be mappings. The *composition* of a and b, written $b \circ a$, is a mapping from X into Z. The mapping $b \circ a: X \rightarrow Z$ is defined by

$$(b \circ a)x = b(a(x))$$

that is the mapping that results from *first* applying a and then applying b. Note that the composition of a and b is defined only if the range of a is identical with the domain of b, that is only if a and b are *compatible*.

As an example, suppose $X=\{1,\ 2,\ 3\}$, $Y=\{p,\ q,\ r\}$, $Z=\{-5,\ -6,\ -7\}$ and the mappings $a: X \rightarrow Y$ and $b: Y \rightarrow Z$ are given by

$$a=\{1\mapsto p,\ 2\mapsto q,\ 3\mapsto r\}$$
$$b=\{p\mapsto -5,\ q\mapsto -6,\ r\mapsto -7\}$$

then the composite mapping $b \circ a: X \rightarrow Z$ is given by

$$b \circ a: X \rightarrow Z=\{1\mapsto -5,\ 2\mapsto -6,\ 3\mapsto -7\}$$

2.4.4 Mappings and PASCAL

The ideas of *domain*, *range* and *Cartesian product* should be familiar to the Pascal programmer in the context of function subprograms. For example, the header for a Pascal function to find the average of two real numbers

```
FUNCTION average(number1, number2 : REAL) : REAL ;
```

describes a function with domain $\mathbb{R} \times \mathbb{R}$ and range $\mathbb{R}$, which we can express as

```
average : ℝ × ℝ → ℝ
```

2.5 TYPES OF MAPPING

Mappings can be classified into a number of different types: injective, surjective, bijective, and total and partial. These are considered in the following subsections.

2.5.1 Injective

The mapping $a: X \rightarrow Y$ is called *injective* or *one–one* if for each $y \in Y$ there exists *at most* one $x \in X$ such that $a(x)=y$. (Note that no such x may exist.) Another way of saying that a is injective is $a(x)=a(x')$ implies $x=x'$ where $x, x' \in X$. A graphical representation of an injective mapping is shown in Fig. 2.2.

2.5.2 Surjective

The mapping $a: X \rightarrow Y$ is called *surjective* or *onto* if for each $y \in Y$ there exists *at least* one $x \in X$ such that $a(x)=y$. This type of mapping is illustrated in Fig. 2.3.

2.5.3 Bijective

A mapping that is both injective and surjective is called *bijective* or *one-to-one* and such a mapping is illustrated in Fig. 2.4. For such mappings, there is a one-to-one correspondence between the members of X and Y.

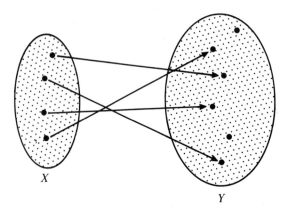

Figure 2.2 An *injective* mapping *a*: $X \to Y$ (not *surjective*).

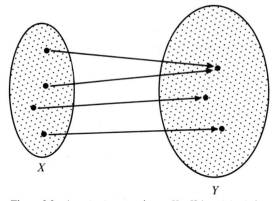

Figure 2.3 A *surjective* mapping *a*: $X \to Y$ (not *injective*).

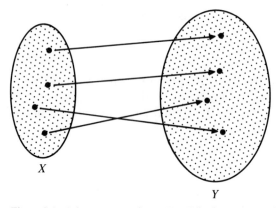

Figure 2.4 A *bijective* mapping *a*: $X \to Y$ (both *injective* and *surjective*).

2.5.4 Total and partial

If a mapping *a*: $X \to Y$ is defined for *every* $x \in X$, then the mapping *a* is said to be *total*. The mappings illustrated in Figs 2.2, 2.3 and 2.4 are all total (that is every element in X maps to an element in Y). If a mapping *a* is *not* defined for all $x \in X$, then the mapping *a* is said to be *partial*. Expressed another way, we can say that a mapping *a* is partial if not all possible inputs have a defined output. An example of a partial mapping is illustrated in Fig. 2.5. This mapping is partial since there are elements in *X* that are not mapped to a corresponding value in *Y*.

We should emphasize again that we treat mappings as single-valued, that is, for any mapping $a: X \rightarrow Y$, we assume that, for any $x \in X$, there is *at most one* $y \in Y$ such that $y = a(x)$. This is an essential property for computer science applications since, for example, it would be most undesirable for an array element to have two distinct values.

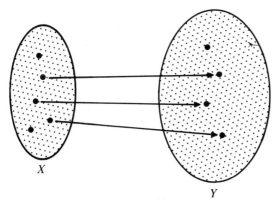

Figure 2.5 Example of a *partial* mapping.

Note also that the terminology is by no means standard in this area. In mathematics, functions (mappings) are, by definition, total, that is for each $x \in X$ there is a *unique* $y \in Y$ such that $x \mapsto y$. In computer science applications however, the function (mapping) *a* from *X* to *Y* is usually defined by stating that *a* maps an element from *X* onto *at most* one element of *Y*. Hence, there is no necessity for every member of *X* to be mapped to a member of *Y*.

2.5.5 Two examples of mappings

In order to capture the various concepts associated with mappings and to summarize, it will be helpful to look briefly at two examples of mappings.

Consider first a class of 25 students who sit an examination where marks are awarded in the range 0 to 100. If we denote the set of student names by *S* and the set of possible marks by *M* (so that *M* will be the set $\{m \mid m \in \mathbb{N}, \ 0 \leqslant m \leqslant 100\}$), then the 'examinations-results-list' constitutes a *total* mapping since *every* student has an examination mark and that mark is unique. We can write this mapping as

examination-results-list: $S \rightarrow M$

If every student whose name appears in *S* sat the examination, the mapping is *total*. Note that not every possible examination mark will appear on the results list because there are 101 possible marks but only 25 students. Hence, for each mark $m \in M$, it is *not* the case that there is *at least one* student of name $s \in S$ who has attained that mark and so the mapping is not *surjective*. If it transpired that each of the 25 students achieved a *different* mark in the examination, then the mapping would be *injective* (since for each $m \in M$, there is *at most* one $s \in S$ with that mark).

Suppose now that there are 200 students taking the examination and that each of the 101 possible marks has been scored. In this situation, for each mark, there is *at least* one student who has achieved that mark and so now the mapping is *surjective*. The mapping is not *injective*, however, since at least one mark will have been scored by two or more students. In the (unlikely) event of 101 students taking the examination and each scoring a different mark, the resulting mapping would be *bijective* (both *injective* and *surjective*) and we would have a one-to-one correspondence between the set of student names and the set of examination marks.

As a second example, consider a simple memory manager in an operating system. The *heap* contains memory available to applications programs and the space in the heap zone is subdivided into a number of contiguous blocks, say $0, \ldots, h_N$. Each block in the zone is either allocated to a user or is free. The *storage manager* is responsible for recording which blocks are currently owned by which user. If we denote the set of user-names by U and the set of blocks by H (so that H will be the set $\{m \mid m \in \mathbb{N}, \, 0 \leqslant m \leqslant h_N\}$), then the storage manager constitutes a mapping from the set of block numbers to the set of users, which we can express as

$$storage\text{-}manager\colon H \to U$$

Note that this constitutes a *partial* mapping in the situation where one or more blocks are not owned by any user. Also, since, in general, some users may not own any blocks while other users may own several, the mapping will be neither *surjective* nor *injective*.

2.6 BINARY RELATIONS

We recall that the Cartesian product of two sets $A \times B$ is the set of *all* ordered pairs (a, b) with $a \in A$ and $b \in B$. A subset of the Cartesian product is called a *relation* or *binary relation* on the two sets.

It follows that if $\mathfrak{R}$ is a relation defined over the sets A and B, then, for any *given* ordered pair $(a, b) \in A \times B$, that ordered pair will or will not belong to $\mathfrak{R}$. If (a, b) *does* belong to $\mathfrak{R}$, that is $(a, b) \in \mathfrak{R}$, then we write $a \, \mathfrak{R} \, b$. This notation is used to stress the fact that, when $(a, b) \in \mathfrak{R}$, a relationship exists between a and b. If the sets A and B are the same, then a relation $\mathfrak{R}$ is a subset of $A \times A$ and we say that $\mathfrak{R}$ is a relation on A.

As an example of a *relation*, suppose that *John* knows PASCAL, *Lee* knows FORTRAN, *Barbara* knows C and *Pauline* knows COBOL. If we let P denote the set of people, so that

$$P = \{John, \, Lee, \, Pauline, \, Barbara\}$$

and D denote the set of computer languages

$$D = \{C, \, COBOL, \, FORTRAN, \, PASCAL\}$$

we can then express who knows which language in terms of a relation K where

$$K = \{(John, \, PASCAL), \, (Lee, \, FORTRAN), \, (Barbara, \, C), \, (Pauline, \, COBOL)\}$$

In this example, $p\,K\,d$ represents the relation 'person p knows computer language d'. We can also express this relation formally using set notation

$$K = \{(p, d) \mid \text{person } p \text{ knows computer language } d\}$$

Note that the Cartesian product $P \times D$ contains sixteen ordered pairs and that K is a subset containing four of those pairs.

The following are all examples of relations on the set of integers $\mathbb{Z}$

1. $\{(x, y) \mid x > y\}$
2. $\{(x, y) \mid y = x^2\}$
3. $\{(x, y) \mid 2x + 3y = 1\}$

2.6.1 Equivalence relation

Let A be a set, then a subset $\mathfrak{R}$ of $A \times A$ is called an *equivalence relation* on A if the following properties all hold:

1. $(a, a) \in \mathfrak{R}$, $a \in A$ — *reflexive law*
2. If $(a, b) \in \mathfrak{R}$ then $(b, a) \in \mathfrak{R}$ — *symmetric law*
3. If $(a, b) \in \mathfrak{R}$ and $(b, c) \in \mathfrak{R}$ then $(a, c) \in \mathfrak{R}$ — *transitive law*

The reflexive property states that all objects are equivalent to themselves, while the symmetric property states that if a is equivalent to b then b is equivalent to a. The transitive property states that objects that are equivalent to the same object are equivalent to one another.

These conditions can also be written, using a different notation,

1. $a\,\mathfrak{R}\,a \quad \forall a \in A$
2. $a\,\mathfrak{R}\,b \Rightarrow b\,\mathfrak{R}\,a \quad \forall a, b \in A$
3. $a\,\mathfrak{R}\,b$ and $b\,\mathfrak{R}\,c \Rightarrow a\,\mathfrak{R}\,c \quad \forall a, b, c \in A$

where the symbol $\forall$ denotes the universal quantifier 'for all'.

As an example, consider a high-level block-structured programming language like Pascal, and let D denote the set of all declared identifiers in a Pascal program, then 'is declared in the same block as' constitutes an equivalence relation, while 'is declared in a block which encloses' is not an equivalence relation since property 2 does not hold in the second example.

As a further example, consider *aliased variables*. If two or more variables denote the same memory address, the variables are called *aliases* of one another. The ANSI version of Fortran allows aliased variables to be introduced by means of the aptly named nonexecutable EQUIVALENCE statement which declares that two or more variables in a program refer to the same memory location. As an example, the statement

```
EQUIVALENCE (T1,T2), (INDEX, JCOUNT, LOOPVAR)
```

instructs the compiler that the variables T1 and T2 share one memory location and that INDEX, JCOUNT, and LOOPVAR are to share another.

If $\mathscr{A}$ denotes the relation '*is an alias of*', then $\mathscr{A}$ constitutes an equivalence relation over the set of all program variables *V*. We can express the elements of the relation as

T1 $\mathscr{A}$ T2
INDEX $\mathscr{A}$ JCOUNT, INDEX $\mathscr{A}$ LOOPVAR, JCOUNT $\mathscr{A}$ LOOPVAR

We say that the set of all program variables *V* is *partitioned* by the equivalence relation $\mathscr{A}$. The set of all variables in *V* that are aliases of each other constitute what is called an *equivalence class* so that {T1, T2} and {INDEX, JCOUNT, LOOPVAR} constitute two separate equivalence classes. These ideas of partitioning and equivalence classes are formalized in the following definitions.

2.6.2 Partitions and equivalence classes

Let *A* denote a set. A *partition* of *A* is a family of nonempty subsets of *A* such that each element of *A* belongs to exactly one member of the family. In other words, a partition of a set *A* is a collection of nonoverlapping, nonempty subsets of *A* whose union is the set *A*.

If $\mathfrak{R}$ is an equivalence relation on the set *A*, then the set of all elements in *A* equivalent to a given element x_0 is called an *equivalence class*

$$A_0 = \{a \in A \mid a \cong x_0\}$$

2.6.3 Partial ordering

Another important type of relation on a set *A* is a *partial ordering*. A relation $\mathfrak{R}$ on a set *A* is called a *partial ordering* or *partial-ordering relation* if the following three properties all hold:

1. $(a, a) \in \mathfrak{R}$ — *reflexive law*
2. If $(a, b) \in \mathfrak{R}$ and $(b, c) \in \mathfrak{R}$ then $(a, c) \in \mathfrak{R}$ — *transitive law*
3. If $(a, b) \in \mathfrak{R}$ and $(b, a) \in \mathfrak{R}$ then $a = b$ — *antisymmetric law*

The reflexive and transitive properties are the same as those for an equivalence relation. However, a partial ordering is characterized by the antisymmetric property 3 which says that whenever $a \mathfrak{R} b$ and $b \mathfrak{R} a$, then $a = b$.

Such a partial order is also referred to as a *weak* partial-order. A *weak* partial-order is characterized by the *reflexivity* property, that is the statement $a \mathfrak{R} a$ is always true. On the other hand, a *strong* partial-order is characterized by the properties of *irreflexivity* and *transitivity*, that is

1. *not* $(a, a) \in \mathfrak{R}$ — *irreflexive property*
2. if $(a, b) \in \mathfrak{R}$ and $(b, c) \in \mathfrak{R}$ then $(a, c) \in \mathfrak{R}$ — *transitive property*

A set on which there is a partial ordering is called a *partially-ordered set* or *poset*. Some examples should help to clarify these ideas.

2.6.4 Examples of partially ordered sets

Consider firstly the set $A = \{1, 2, 3, 4\}$, then the relation $\Re$ on A defined by $a \, \Re \, b$ if $a \leqslant b$ is a partial order. The Cartesian product $A \times A$ contains 16 members and the above relation is specified by the subset

$$\{(1, 1), (1, 2), (1, 3), (1, 4), (2, 2), (2, 3), (2, 4), (3, 3), (3, 4), (4, 4)\}$$

We can show that the relation $\Re$ is a partial ordering by proving that the above properties 1, 2 and 3 all hold.

For 1, we observe that for any $a \in A$, then $a \leqslant a$. For 2, we note that if $a \leqslant b$ and $b \leqslant c$, where a, b, $c \in A$, it follows that $a \leqslant c$. For 3, if $a \leqslant b$ and $b \leqslant a$, then these two inequalities can only be satisfied if $a = b$. The three properties are satisfied so that the relation $\Re$ does indeed constitute a partial ordering on the set A. In fact, the above relation $\Re$ will constitute a partial ordering on the entire set of integers $\mathbb{Z}$.

As a second example, let A denote the set of courses offered by a college for a computer science degree. If we define the relation $\Re$ on A by $a \, \Re \, b$ if a and b are the same courses or if course a is a prerequisite for course b (that is, course a must have been studied before course b is started), then the relation $\Re$ makes A into a partially-ordered set.

Another example of a partial ordering that arises in the real world is the building of a new house in which there are certain tasks such as digging the foundations, laying the floor, etc., which must be completed before other phases of the construction such as erecting walls and building the roof can be undertaken. If the set of tasks that must be undertaken in building a house is denoted by A, we can define a relation $\Re$ on A by $a \, \Re \, b$ where a, $b \in A$ if a, b denote the same task or if task a must be completed before the start of task b. In this manner, we impose an order on the elements of A and so make it into a poset. Those with a knowledge of operational research will recognize this poset as a *PERT network* (the acronym PERT stands for 'Project Evaluation and Review Technique').

In general, if A is a set and the relation $\Re$ on A is a partial order (partial-ordering relation), then the pair or *tuple* $(A, \Re)$ is called a *partially-ordered set* or *poset*.

2.6.5 Total ordering

A *total ordering* is a special type of *partial ordering* defined as follows. Suppose $(A, \Re)$ is a poset (that is A is a set and the relation $\Re$ on A is a partial-ordering relation on A), then the set A is said to be *totally ordered* if for all a, $b \in A$, either $a \, \Re \, b$ or $b \, \Re \, a$. In this situation, $\Re$ is said to be a *total order*.

Some further examples should help to consolidate these ideas. Suppose A is the set $\{1, 2, 3, 4\}$ and that the relation $\Re$ on A is defined by $a \, \Re \, b$, that is by 'a divides exactly into b'. It follows that:

$$\Re = \{(1, 1), (1, 2), (1, 3), (1, 4), (2, 2), (2, 4), (3, 3), (4, 4)\}$$

is a partial order and $(A, \Re)$ is a poset. Note that this partial order is *not* a total order since, for example, when a is 2 and b is 3, neither 2 divides exactly into 3 nor 3 divides exactly into 2 (that is neither $(2, 3)$ nor $(3, 2) \in \Re$).

On the other hand, if the set A is as above and $\Re$ is defined by $a \Re b$ if $a \leqslant b$, then the relation $\Re$ is a *total order*. The elements of $\Re$ from above are

$$\Re = \{(1, 1), (1, 2), (1, 3), (1, 4), (2, 2), (2, 3), (2, 4), (3, 3), (3, 4), (4, 4)\}$$

and we see that, for *all* values a and $b \in A$, either $a \Re b$ or $b \Re a \in \Re$.

2.7 BINARY OPERATIONS

Let S denote a nonempty set, then the total mapping $m: S \times S \to S$ is called a *binary operation* on S. In other words, a binary operation is a rule that assigns to each ordered pair of elements of S a unique element of S. In spite of the fact that a binary operation is a mapping, it is common practice to use symbols rather than letters to name them and the most commonly used symbol is $*$.

If $*$ is a binary operation on a set S and $a, b \in S$, then there are three common ways of representing the image of the pair (a, b), namely:

1. $a * b$ (*infix*)
2. $ab*$ (*postfix*)
3. $*ab$ (*prefix*)

2.7.1 Unary operations

Some operations, such as the *negation* of numbers or the logical *not*, are *unary operations*, not binary operations. We can formally define a unary operation as a mapping $u: S \to S$, that is, it is a rule that assigns to each element of S a unique element of S.

2.7.2 Common properties or attributes of operations

Let S denote any set and let $*$ denote a binary operation on S, then there are a number of properties that a single binary operation *may* possess

1. $*$ is *associative* if $(a * b) * c = a * (b * c)$ for all $a, b, c \in S$.
2. $*$ is *commutative* if $a * b = b * a$ for all $a, b \in S$.
3. $*$ has an *identity* if there exists an element $e \in S$ such that $a * e = e * a = a$ for all $a \in S$.
4. $*$ has the *inverse* property if for each $a \in S$ there exists an element $b \in S$ such that $a * b = b * a = e$. The element b is called the *inverse* of a.

2.7.3 Closure

If $*$ is a binary operation on a non-empty set S and $T \subseteq S$, we say that T is *closed* under $*$ (or *relative* to $*$) if $a, b \in T$ implies that $a * b \in T$. In other words, when you operate upon elements of T with the binary operation $*$, you cannot obtain any new elements that are outside of T.

A few simple examples should clarify this definition. Consider the binary operation of addition on the natural numbers $\mathbb{N}$, then we say that $\mathbb{N}$ is *closed under addition* since the sum of two natural numbers is itself a natural number. Similarly, $\mathbb{N}$ is closed under multiplication. However, $\mathbb{N}$ is *not* closed under subtraction since $1 - 2$ is not a natural number. If we consider the operation of subtraction on the integers $\mathbb{Z}$, then, in this case, $\mathbb{Z}$ is *closed under subtraction.*

2.8 OPERATION TYPES

It should be noted that in the definitions above we have assumed that $*$ is an *infix* binary operation, although the definitions could have been expressed in terms of *prefix* ($*ab$) or *postfix* ($ab*$) notation. Prefix *unary* operations include negation ($- \_$) and logical not ($\neg\_$), while postfix unary operations include factorial ($\_!$) or inverse ($\_{}^{-1}$) and the underscore character $\_$ denotes the position of the argument(s). Two other types are *outfix*, such as the absolute value ($|\_|$), and *distfix* (or *mixfix*), such as in the selection function if_then_else_.

2.9 BAGS AND LISTS

There are two further discrete mathematical structures that complement the set, map and product or tuple structures already discussed, *bags* and *sequences* (*lists*). All of these structures provide fundamental models in the constructive approach to specification.

2.9.1 Bags

Bags are unordered collections of data items and although, like sets, the order of enumeration of the elements is unimportant, unlike sets, repeated elements are included in a bag, so that if $B_1 = \langle 1, 2, 5, 10 \rangle$, $B_2 = \langle 5, 10, 2, 1 \rangle$, $B_3 = \langle 1, 1, 2, 5, 10 \rangle$ then $B_1 = B_2$ but $B_1 \neq B_3$ and $B_2 \neq B_3$.

2.9.2 Lists

Often it is important to place objects in some sort of order, according to some property or they may be sorted in compliance with some key, for example. A *list* or *sequence* is used to describe such a collection of elements. Unlike a set, the elements of a list are totally ordered. The empty list, which contains no elements, is usually denoted by [ ], while nonempty lists are characterized by having a *head* and a *tail*. For example, given the list $L = [2, 3, 6, 6, 9, 10]$ whose elements belong to the natural numbers, then the head of L is the natural number 2 and the tail of L is the list $[3, 6, 6, 9, 10]$.

To conclude this chapter, we look at proving results using a method known as *mathematical induction*.

2.10 MATHEMATICAL INDUCTION

A powerful proof technique, which will be used later in VDM (Chapter 5) and in the algebraic approach to specification (Chapter 12), is *mathematical induction*. Induction can be used to establish properties about natural numbers, such as proving that the result of finding the sum of the first n natural numbers is $n(n + 1)/2$.

The proof that some general result S_n holds for all natural numbers n is first established by showing that the result is true for some *base* case (say $n = 1$). Then *assuming* S_n is true, if it can be shown that the truth of S_n implies the truth of S_{n+1} (that is $S_n \Rightarrow S_{n+1}$), then the proof that S_n holds is established. The inductive proof proceeds by observing that since S_1 is true (the base case), so is S_2; then since S_2 is true, so is S_3, and so on.

For the example above, we will use mathematical induction to show that the sum S_n of the first n natural numbers is equal to $n(n+1)/2$, that is

$$1 + 2 + \cdots + (n-1) + n = \frac{n(n+1)}{2}$$

The proof that $S_n = n(n+1)/2$ proceeds by first using the formula to *deduce* the sum of one term of the series. From the formula, the sum of one term is S_1 which evaluates to 1. This value is correct and so the base case is established.

Now assume that S_n is true and see what happens when we add the next term $n+1$ to the series. The sum to $n+1$ terms is given by $S_n + (n+1) = n(n+1)/2 + (n+1)$. This expression can be simplified to $(n+1)(n+2)/2$. We can write this result as

$$\frac{(n+1)((n+1)+1)}{2}$$

which is immediately seen to be the formula S_n with n replaced by $n+1$, that is S_{n+1}. Hence, if S_n is true so is S_{n+1} and the truth of the assertion has been established through induction. A more detailed treatment of many of the concepts discussed in this chapter can be found in Doerr and Levasseur (1985) and Wiitala (1987).

2.11 SUMMARY

- This chapter introduces much of the necessary mathematics used in the subsequent chapters.
- The discrete mathematical structures introduced include sets, bags, lists, tuples, the Cartesian product, mappings, relations and equivalence classes.
- Partial and total orderings over a set are discussed and the principle of proof by mathematical induction is introduced.
- These mathematical concepts are illustrated by using examples oriented towards software engineering applications.

ADDITIONAL PROBLEMS

2.1 If $A = \{c, o, m, p, u, t, i, n, g\}$ and $B = \{c, o, m, p, i, l, e, r\}$ are sets of single letter symbols, find:
  (a) $A \cup B$
  (b) $A \cap B$
  (c) $A \backslash B$
  (d) $B \backslash A$
  (e) $|A|$
  (f) $|B|$
  (g) $(A \backslash B) \cup (B \backslash A)$

     (h) $(A \backslash B) \cap (B \backslash A)$

     (i) $(A \backslash B) \backslash (B \backslash A)$

2.2 Repeat Prob. 2.1 if $A = \{1, 2, 4, 9, 12, 18, 21\}$ and $B = \{2, 3, 15, 18\}$. If, further, $C = \{5, 6, 9\}$, verify that:

     (a) $(A \cup B) \cup C = A \cup (B \cup C)$

     (b) $(A \cap B) \cap C = A \cap (B \cap C)$

     (c) $A \cup (B \cap C) = (A \cup B) \cap (A \cup C)$

     (d) $A \cap (B \cup C) = (A \cap B) \cup (A \cap C)$

2.3 If $U = \{1, 3, 5, 7, 9, 11, 13\}$ what are the cardinalities of U and the power set $\mathscr{P}(U)$?

2.4 Let $U = \{1, 2, 3, 4, 5, 6, 7, 8, 9\}$, $A = \{x \in U \mid x^2 \text{ is odd}\}$ and $B = \{x \in U \mid x + 1 \text{ is a multiple of } 3\}$. List the elements of the following sets:

     (a) A

     (b) B

     (c) $A \cap B$

2.5 If $A = \{\texttt{pascal}, \texttt{modula-2}, \texttt{basic}, \texttt{ada}, \texttt{c}\}$ and $B = \{\texttt{unix}, \texttt{ms-dos}, \texttt{vms}, \texttt{cp/m}\}$, list the elements of the following sets:

     (a) $A \times B$

     (b) $B \times A$

     (c) $A \times A$

     (d) $B \times B$

2.6 If $A = \{1, 2, 3, 4, 5\}$ and $B = \{1, 2, 3, 4\}$, list the elements of the following sets:

     (a) $A \times A$

     (b) $B \times B$

     (c) $A \times B$

     (d) $B \times A$

2.7 If $A = \{\text{a}, \text{b}, \text{c}\}$, find the power set $\mathscr{P}(A)$ of A. Hence find $\mathscr{P}(A) \times \mathscr{P}(A)$ and determine its cardinality.

2.8 Let P denote the set of positive integers, that is the set $\{1, 2, 3, 4, \ldots\}$. For each relation r defined over P, determine which of the specified ordered pairs belongs to r.

     (a) $x \, r \, y$ iff $y = x$; $(1, 1), (5, 5), (3, 2), (2, 3), (6, 6), (1, 2)$

     (b) $x \, r \, y$ iff $x = y^2$; $(1, 1), (2, 1), (4, 2), (2, 4), (9, 4), (9, 3)$

     (c) $x \, r \, y$ iff $y > x$; $(1, 1), (1, 2), (2, 1), (2, 2), (4, 2), (1, 8)$

     (d) $x \, r \, y$ iff 'y is divisible by x with no remainder'; $(1, 1), (1, 2), (2, 1), (2, 6), (6, 3), (3, 6)$ where *iff* stands for 'if and only if'.

2.9 Consider the two relations r and s defined over $T \times T$ where T is the set $\{1, 4, 7, 10\}$ and

$$x \, r \, y \quad \text{iff} \quad y = x + 3$$
$$x \, s \, y \quad \text{iff} \quad x \leqslant y$$

     List the ordered pairs (2-tuples) for each of the relations r and s.

2.10 Three lecturers *John*, *Lee* and *Ann* intend to teach a combined programming course in the languages Ada, Modula-2 and C. *John* has experience of Ada, *Lee* has experience of Modula-2, and *Ann* has experience of all three languages.

     (a) Let T denote the set of (three) lecturers, L the set of languages and p the relation 'has experience of the language'. Specify this relation as a set of ordered pairs.

(b) Two machines are available for the programming course: one has the software to support Modula-2 and Ada and the other supports C. Find a composite relation to describe which lecturer can use which machine for his/her part of the programming course.

2.11   Let $A=\{1, 2, 3, 4, 5\}$ and let r, s and t be relations defined over $A \times A$ where:

$$r=\{(1, 1), (1, 2), (2, 2), (2, 3), (3, 3), (3, 4), (4, 4), (4, 5), (5, 5), (5, 1)\}$$
$$s=\{(1, 1), (1, 2), (1, 4), (2, 1), (2, 2), (2, 4), (3, 3), (4, 1), (4, 2), (4, 4), (5, 5)\}$$
$$t=\{(1, 1), (1, 2), (2, 2), (3, 2), (3, 3), (4, 4), (5, 1), (5, 2), (5, 3), (5, 4), (5, 5)\}$$

(a) Which of these relations is an *equivalence relation* and list its *equivalence classes*?
(b) Which of these relations is a *partial ordering*?

2.12   Investigate whether the following relations are equivalence relations and/or partial orderings over $S \times S$ where S is the set of students in a given class.
(a) $x\,r\,y$ iff student x and student y have the same overall coursework grade.
(b) $x\,r\,y$ iff student x is smaller in height than student y.

2.13   Which of the following are injective (one–one), surjective (onto), or both (bijective)?
(a) $f_1: \mathbb{R} \to \mathbb{R}$ defined by $f_1(x)=x^3+x$
(b) $f_2: \mathbb{Z} \to \mathbb{Z}$ defined by $f_2(x)=1-x$
(c) $f_3: \mathbb{N} \times \mathbb{N} \to \mathbb{N}$ defined by $f_3(m, n)=2m+3n$
(d) $f_4: \mathbb{N} \to \mathbb{N}$ defined by $f_4(n)=n^2+n$
(e) $f_5: \mathbb{N} \to \mathbb{N} \times \mathbb{N}$ defined by $f_5(n)=(n, n+1)$

2.14   Show that the even integers are closed under multiplication and addition whereas the odd integers are closed under multiplication but not closed under addition.

2.15   Show that the set of positive multiples of 3 is closed under both addition and multiplication.

2.16   Let M denote any set and let $*$ be any operation on M that is associative and commutative. If a and b are elements of M, prove that

$$(a * b) * (a * b) = (a * a) * (b * b)$$

Furthermore, if a and b are *idempotent* elements, that is $a * a = a$ and $b * b = b$, deduce that

$$a * b * a * b = a * b$$

2.17   Mappings can be combined with the *overwrite* (or *update*) operator†. This operator takes two mappings as operands and produces a mapping as a result. Where a domain element appears in both mappings, the range element in the second operand has priority in the resultant mapping. If there is no duplication of domain elements, then mappings are simply combined to produce the result. For example, if

$$m1 = \{A \mapsto 1, \quad C \mapsto 3, \quad D \mapsto 2, \quad E \mapsto 5\}$$
$$m2 = \{B \mapsto 4, \quad C \mapsto 5, \quad E \mapsto 8\}$$

then

$$m1 \dagger m2 = \{A \mapsto 1, \quad B \mapsto 4, \quad C \mapsto 5, \quad D \mapsto 2, \quad E \mapsto 8\}$$
$$m2 \dagger m1 = \{A \mapsto 1, \quad B \mapsto 4, \quad C \mapsto 3, \quad D \mapsto 2, \quad E \mapsto 5\}$$

This idea of *map overwrite* is often used in computer science; for example, if we have a table of *user-name, password* entries such as

$$\{\text{Lee} \mapsto \text{'planner', John} \mapsto \text{'syzygy', Ann} \mapsto \text{'maths'}\}$$

and John wants to update his password to 'plasma', then this is expressed by

$$\{\text{Lee} \mapsto \text{'planner', John} \mapsto \text{'syzygy', Ann} \mapsto \text{'maths'}\} \dagger \{\text{John} \mapsto \text{'plasma'}\}$$

which produces the mapping

$$\{\text{Lee} \mapsto \text{'planner', John} \mapsto \text{'plasma', Ann} \mapsto \text{'maths'}\}$$

If

$$m1 = \{z1 \mapsto 2, \quad z2 \mapsto 4, \quad z3 \mapsto 6, \quad z4 \mapsto 8\}$$

and

$$m2 = \{z1 \mapsto 8, \quad z2 \mapsto 2, \quad z3 \mapsto 2, \quad z4 \mapsto 6\}$$

show that:
(a) $m1 \dagger m2 = m2$
(b) $m2 \dagger m1 = m1$

FURTHER READING

Of the many books that cover concepts in discrete mathematics, two are particularly recommended. An added bonus is that both introduce propositional and predicate logic with a more comprehensive account of predicate logic being given in Stephen Wiitala's book.

Doerr, A. and Levasseur, K. (1989) *Applied Discrete Structures for Computer Science*, Science Research Associates Inc., Pergamon, Chicago, IL.
Wiitala, S.A. (1987) *Discrete Mathematics—A Unified Approach*, McGraw-Hill, New York.

One additional book which is highly recommended and has the advantage that it includes an accessible introduction to algebras is:

Stanat, D.F. and McAllister, D.F. (1977) *Discrete Mathematics in Computer Science*, Prentice-Hall, Englewood Cliffs, NJ.

3

INTRODUCTION TO MODEL-BASED SPECIFICATION USING VDM

3.1 INTRODUCTION

To be able to write a formal specification we must first have a *formal specification language*, just as in writing a program we need first to choose a programming language. There are a variety of very different programming languages, and, likewise, specification languages differ. The specifications written in Chapters 3 through to 7 will be written in a standard specification language called VDM-SL. The type of specification built in VDM-SL is called *model-based* or *constructive*. Advocates of this approach maintain that the requirements of a system are best captured by creating a system model, then defining how a typical state of the model changes under the effect of operations. This has led to the approach also being termed *state-based*. In fact, the model-based approach to specification offers two distinct features:

- The means of creating an abstract system state using a collection of precisely defined data structures. These are discrete mathematical objects (all of which were introduced in Chapter 2), complete with a set of laws governing their behaviour, founded on set theory.
- The means of specifying operations implicitly in terms of properties to be achieved, using pre- and post-conditions that are composed of logical formulae.

VDM-SL is the standard specification language for VDM, which is itself a *software development method* (VDM stands for Vienna Development Method, and SL stands for specification language). We use the specification language only, since this is the main topic of the book, but for brevity we will drop the 'SL', and refer to the specification language simply as VDM. Over the years the specification notation has changed considerably, as can be witnessed by consulting Jones's publications in Jones (1979, 1986, 1990). These books led the way to the now standard notation, used in Jones (1990), which we shall also use in this book. VDM can be viewed as giving a framework for the construction of specifications, one that provides a very useful structure for the specifier to follow, implicitly suggesting a method for developing specifications. This framework will be presented in Section 3.5, while in the first part of this chapter the reader will learn how to specify a problem using some simple logic and familiar mathematical abstractions such as sets.

We will introduce the language of VDM as necessary, mainly through examples rather than formal definitions. Although more detailed examples will be developed in the following chapters, this book does not exhaustively cover the whole of the VDM language and indeed some of the more advanced and controversial features are left out completely.

3.2 THE IMPLICIT SPECIFICATION OF OPERATIONS

We define an *operation* to be a process that is input with a predetermined number of values, and outputs a single value. (A VDM operation may also access and change a *system state*, but we will delay discussion of this idea until later in the chapter.) These values are represented or held by parameters, and each parameter is given its own type which denotes the range of values it can hold. Note that this VDM definition of an operation is a generalization of the mathematical definition given in Sec. 2.7.

The specification of an operation defines the relationship between its input and output values, without necessarily resorting to any algorithmic details. To prepare the reader to write specifications in VDM, we first consider some simple but concrete examples of operations specified by formalizing conditions on their input and output parameters. The general form for writing operations is to start them with a heading, listing the operation's identifier, followed by its input and output parameters. On the lines following the heading, we write the pre-condition and the post-condition, summarized as follows:

> *operation-identifier (input parameters) output parameters*
> *pre-condition*
> *post-condition*

Note that:

- The pre- and post-conditions are logical conditions which can be evaluated to true or false after an operation's parameters have been supplied with values.
- Types for the parameters appear immediately after each parameter, in a similar fashion to parameter declarations in a Pascal procedure heading. One can think of a parameter's type as a kind of pre-condition, since an operation does not make sense if it is supplied with a value for a parameter that does not satisfy the type definition.
- Each VDM operation's identifier will be put in capital letters throughout this book.

It is sometimes useful to think of an operation in VDM as a specification for a program's procedure that has the same heading. To execute the procedure that implements an operation, under a particular parameter binding (that is an assignment of values, of the correct type, to parameters), the pre-condition must evaluate to true; for the procedure to be a correct implementation under the same binding, the post-condition must evaluate to true whenever the pre-condition is true and the procedure has been executed.

We will initially explore this specification method using simple operations with numeric input and output parameters. Conditions will be restricted (for the time being) to logic formulae containing only parameters, constants, primitive functions and logical connectives. In the examples below, we denote parameters of type *integer* with the symbol $\mathbb{Z}$, and those of type *natural number* with $\mathbb{N}$ as introduced in Chapter 2.

3.2.1 Examples of implicit specifications

1. An operation that is not supplied as a built-in primitive in the standard Pascal programming language is the *exponent*, and programmers must supply their own implementation. The specification in the format introduced above is:

   EXPONENT $(x: \mathbb{Z},\ n: \mathbb{N})\ y: \mathbb{Z}$
   pre *true*
   post $y = x^n$

   EXPONENT has two input parameters, x and n, and one output parameter, y. The post-condition is made up of the simple predicate '$=$' and use is made of the familiar mathematical power function, assumed to be a primitive in our specification language.
2. The integer square root of a number x is defined as that number whose square is less than or equal to x, but when incremented and squared, is greater than x. The specification can be concisely written:

   INT_SQR $(x: \mathbb{N})\ z: \mathbb{N}$
   pre $x \geqslant 1$
   post $(z^2 \leqslant x) \wedge (x < (z+1)^2)$

   In the operation *INT_SQR*, the pre-condition restricts input parameter x's value to be greater than or equal to 1. The output value held by z is implicitly defined, in that it is the value that makes the logical expression in the post-condition true.
3. Two functions that are primitive to Pascal, *MOD* and *DIV*, can be implicitly specified using similar specifications. Both take two arguments, x and y; *DIV* returns d, the integer value of y/x (rounded down), while *MOD* returns m, the remainder. Here is the full specification of *MOD*:

   MOD $(x,\ y: \mathbb{N})\ m: \mathbb{N}$
   pre $(x > 0) \wedge (y > 0)$
   post $\exists d \in \mathbb{Z} \cdot (y = d \times x + m) \wedge (0 \leqslant m) \wedge (m < x)$

These examples emphasize some important concepts:

- The post-conditions contain the *relationship* between input and output parameters. Later we will investigate more sophisticated post-conditions which refer to data in an external system state as well as data held in parameters.
- Conditions are logical formulae, for example, the post-conditions in Example 2 is a conjunction of two predicates. They contain primitive functions (for example, $+$, $\times$, power) and predicates (for example, $>$, $<$, $=$), which are 'built-in' to VDM.

The output parameter in the operations (for example, z in Example 2) has its values prescribed implicitly, without any clue as to what algorithm will be used in an implementation. They are thus examples of *implicit* specifications, since the post-conditions do not have an algorithmic interpretation; put simply, this means we cannot automatically compute the output(s) from the post-condition, given a value for each input (not surprisingly, since the post-condition must be a logical formula). Suppressing these algorithmic details is considered a useful form of abstraction.

In fact, in VDM these examples could have been specified *explicitly*, and such a specification takes the form of an executable function. Using an *explicit function definition* the output parameter's value may be computed. We shall cover explicit function definitions later, in Chapter 5.

3.2.2 The logical condition

Pre- and post-conditions, as well as other constructions we shall meet later, take the form of 'logical conditions' or 'logical formulae'. Technically, they could also be described as 'well-formed formulae in enriched first-order logic', but we will use the shorter name here. Given values for any parameters they contain, logical conditions will always evaluate to *true* or *false*. A logical condition we want to evaluate to *true* is called an *assertion*.

The following logical connectives, negation and quantifiers are used:

- $\wedge$ meaning 'and'
- $\vee$ meaning 'or'
- $\Leftrightarrow$ meaning 'if and only if'
- $\Rightarrow$ meaning 'implies'
- $\forall$ is a quantifier meaning 'for all'
- $\exists$ is a quantifier meaning 'there exists'
- $\neg$ meaning 'it is not the case that'

In proofs we may also take the liberty of using the symbol '$\Rightarrow$' to relate steps of the proof, as well as using it within the logical conditions. Also, VDM allows the striking through of some common predicates as a shorthand for negation (for instance, $x \neq y$ means $\neg (x = y)$).

To understand logical conditions one must be aware of all the syntax classes involved, and what symbols belong to each. A logical condition contains one or more predicates. Predicates are joined by logical connectives, possibly surrounded by quantifiers, and may contain functions, parameters, constants and quantified variables. In Section 3.2.1, Example 2, the symbols in the conditions can be categorized into syntax classes as follows:

- logical connectives: $\wedge$
- predicates: $\leqslant, <, \geqslant$
- primitive functions: $+$, *squared*
- constants: 1
- parameters: x, z

The predicates, functions and constants present in conditions will obviously depend on the data type of the parameters—in the three examples above these types were $\mathbb{N}$ or $\mathbb{Z}$.

Exercises 3.1

(a) Write down the syntax class for each of the symbols in the pre- and post-conditions of Examples 1 and 3.
(b) Specify the *DIV* procedure mentioned in Example 3.
(c) Using the pre- and post-condition format, try to formalize the specification of a procedure that outputs the maximum of three numbers.

3.2.3 Reasoning with pre- and post-conditions

A prime motivation for formalizing specifications is so that one can reason about them formally as well as informally. In Section 3.2.1, Example 2, for instance, it is not obvious that the integer square root, z, is actually unique—it may be possible that some positive integer x has more than one positive square root!

We can argue informally that this is not the case, or we can give a step-by-step proof, as follows: assume that given a value for input parameter x, there are two possible output values for z, called a and b, both satisfying the post-condition. To prove z's value is unique, we will show that $a=b$ must be true. From the post-condition, after execution of *INT_SQR*, we have:

$$a^2 \leqslant x < (a+1)^2 \tag{3.1}$$

and

$$b^2 \leqslant x < (b+1)^2 \tag{3.2}$$

Now we can prove a and b must denote the same value as follows. Since a and b are named arbitrarily, we can start by assuming that a is greater than or equal to b:

$$b \leqslant a \tag{3.3}$$

we can extract from (3.1)

$$a^2 \leqslant x \tag{3.4}$$

and from (3.2) and (3.4)

$$a^2 \leqslant x < (b+1)^2 \tag{3.5}$$

from (3.5) and the properties of inequality, we have:

$$a^2 < (b+1)^2 \tag{3.6}$$

$$\Rightarrow a < (b+1) \tag{3.7}$$

$$\Rightarrow a \leqslant b \tag{3.8}$$

Using (3.8) and (3.3) we have

$$a = b \tag{3.9}$$

Notice how properties of the data type (which was $\mathbb{N}$ in the proof above) were used in each step of the proof. Later we will encounter more examples of reasoning about specifications, sometimes formal and sometimes informal. Invariably we will draw on assertions taken from pre- and post-conditions, and use properties of the data type concerned.

Exercise 3.2 Paraphrase the formal proof given above in natural language to produce an 'informal argument' that the output parameter z's value is unique.

3.3 INTRODUCTION TO VDM DATA TYPES

The use of numbers and their associated primitive functions in the examples above was for illustrative purposes only. Less simple applications require a well defined, expressive specification language—one that allows the user to build problem-oriented, structured models.

VDM allows the creation of such models via user-defined types. Complex models can be built up hierarchically from primitives, and there is a similarity here with modern programming languages, which also allow the construction of user-defined types. The difference is that VDM data structures are *abstract* in the sense of not being influenced by computer storage or implementation details, but rather being based around mathematics and logic.

VDM has 'built-in' four well-defined and expressive data structures: *Sets, Composites, Sequences* and *Maps*. To introduce these data types we will describe the type Set, and some of its associated predicates in Sec. 3.3.2. First, we present the standard primitive types allowed in VDM. As a convention the names of all data types will start with a capital letter.

3.3.1 The primitive types

The main primitive types in VDM are:

- Boolean–denoted by '$\mathbb{B}$' and given by the set {*true, false*}
- Natural—denoted by '$\mathbb{N}$' and given by the values, 0, 1, 2, 3, 4, 5, 6, 7, ...
- Integer—denoted by '$\mathbb{Z}$' and given by the values
  $... -5, -4, -3, -2, -1, 0, 1, 2, 3, 4, 5, ...$
- Real—denoted by '$\mathbb{R}$' and given by the real numbers.

These types were previously introduced as sets in Sec. 2.2.1. Creating a new type in VDM is similar to creating one in a Pascal-like programming language; the format:

type name = type expression

is used. If we want to create a type that consists of a few named constants, this can be done using VDM's bar operator, written '|'. For example:

$Colours =$ GREEN | BLUE | RED

$Written\_numbers =$ ONE | TWO | THREE | FOUR

$Week\_days =$ MONDAY | TUESDAY | WEDNESDAY | THURSDAY | FRIDAY

$Going =$ GOOD | GOOD_TO_SOFT | SOFT

An unspecified collection of constants or identifiers is denoted by the type *Token*. A parameter of type *Token*, therefore, takes values that are constants or identifiers (written as strings of characters, and usually put in a 'small capital' font, as above).

3.3.2 The set type

Sets were introduced as mathematical abstractions in Chapter 2; nevertheless, we remind the reader here of their defining characteristics, while considering them from a computational standpoint. In VDM, a set is a data structure composed of a collection of distinct instances of some *base type*. Each of these instances is called an *element* (or sometimes *member*) of the set. For instance, taking the base type to be $\mathbb{N}$, then some example sets written in the VDM syntax are as follows:

$\{1, 4, 9, 16, 25, 36, 49, 64, 81\}$

$\{1, 3, 5, 7, 9, 11\}$

$\{\}$ (called the *empty set*)

Note that the ordering of elements when a set is written down makes *no* difference. For example

$\{1, 4, 9, 16, 25, 36, 49, 64, 81\}$
$\{9, 4, 1, 16, 25, 36, 49, 64, 81\}$
$\{36, 49, 64, 81, 1, 4, 9, 16, 25\}$

all represent the *same* set. As with the integer type, sets have well-defined primitive functions and predicates, first introduced in Sec. 2.2. A selection of these that we will use in this book is as follows:

- '$\in$' (which reads 'is an element of') is a two-place predicate that evaluates to *true* or *false* when supplied with two argument values. It is *true* if its first argument is a member of its second (set) argument. For example:

  $9 \in \{1, 4, 9, 16, 25, 36, 49, 64, 81\} = true$
  $42 \in \{1, 4, 9, 16, 25, 36, 49, 64, 81\} = false$

- '∪' (which reads 'union') is a function that takes two sets and evaluates to the set containing all the elements in either set. For example:

$$\{1, 4, 9, 16\} \cup \{1, 2, 4, 6, 9\} = \{1, 4, 9, 16, 2, 6\}$$
$$\{4, 9, 16, 25, 36\} \cup \{1, 2, 4, 6\} = \{4, 6, 9, 16, 25, 36, 1, 2\}$$

- '∩' (which reads 'intersection') is a function that takes two sets and evaluates to the set containing all the elements in both sets. For example:

$$\{1, 4, 9, 16\} \cap \{1, 2, 4, 6, 9\} = \{1, 4, 9\}$$
$$\{4, 9, 16, 25, 36\} \cap \{1, 2, 4, 6\} = \{4\}$$

- '\' is a function that takes two sets and returns the set difference. This means that when applied to two sets '\' returns the set containing all the elements that appear in the first set but not in the second. For example:

$$\{1, 4, 9, 16\} \setminus \{1, 2, 4, 6, 9\} = \{16\}$$
$$\{4, 9, 16, 25, 36\} \setminus \{1, 2, 4, 6\} = \{9, 16, 25, 36\}$$

The suffix -set after a type T denotes a Set type with T as the base type. Thus the expression '$\mathbb{N}$-set' denotes the type whose elements are *sets* of natural numbers; all the sets used in the examples above are in fact instances of this type. Other examples follow:

$\{1, -4, 9, -16, 2, -6\}$ is a value of the type $\mathbb{Z}$-set

$\{\{1, 4, 9\}, \{2, 1\}\}$ is a value of the type ($\mathbb{N}$-set)-set

Any type that has -set as a suffix has the empty set, $\{\}$, as an instance.

3.3.3 Worked example using sets

Using pre- and post-conditions, specify an operation that inputs a number n and a set X, and returns *true* if n is in the set, and *false* otherwise.

Answer The heading of the operation is straightforward, simply a listing of the input and output parameters in the VDM style:

$IS\_IN\_SET(n: \mathbb{N}, X: \mathbb{N}\text{-set})\ b: \mathbb{B}$

Next to consider is the post-condition: to construct this we need do little more than formalize the question, that is we want the Boolean parameter b to output:

true if $n \in X$

false if $n \notin X$

This can be summed up by the logical condition:

$$(n \in X \Rightarrow b = true) \land (n \notin X \Rightarrow b = false)$$

or as a shorter alternative:

$$b \Leftrightarrow (n \in X)$$

which reads 'b is true if and only if n is an element of X'.

Finally, we deal with the pre-condition: we must consider whether there are any bindings (legal values) of the input parameters for which the operation would be undefined. At this stage it is a good idea to consider 'boundary' or extreme values of the data types associated with the input parameters, such as 0 and $\{\}$. In this example, all legal values of the inputs will give a post-condition that can be satisfied: in other words, a value for the output parameter b can be determined whatever the input values. Hence the pre-condition is written simply as *true*. Our final version of the operation is:

IS_IN_SET $(n: \mathbb{N}, X : \mathbb{N}\text{-set})$ $b: \mathbb{B}$
pre *true*
post $b \Leftrightarrow n \in X$

The pre-condition is used to record restrictions on the use of operations: if the input values do not make the pre-condition *true*, then the operation cannot be used in that particular instance. In the IS_IN_SET example, the pre-condition is literally the value '*true*', hence the operation should be defined for any input values.

Exercise 3.3

(a) Write down examples of the types $\mathbb{B}$-set and ($\mathbb{B}$-set)-set. How many distinct values has the type $\mathbb{B}$-set?
(b) Using pre- and post-conditions, specify an operation that inputs a set of numbers and outputs the maximum of that set.
(c) The Set is a data structure in Pascal. By consulting a textbook or manual, compare the mathematical concept of a set and Pascal's Set type.

3.3.4 Implicit definition of sets

It is often useful to be able to define a set implicitly by stating a logical condition that an element must satisfy to be a member of that set (see Sec. 2.2.1). The first two examples in Sec. 3.3.2:

$\{1, 4, 9, 16, 25, 36, 49, 64, 81\}$
$\{1, 3, 5, 7, 9, 11\}$

could be redefined thus (assuming predicate *odd* has already been defined):

$$\{x^2 \mid x \in \mathbb{N} \cdot x \leqslant 9 \wedge x > 0\}$$

$$\{x \mid x \in \mathbb{N} \cdot odd(x) \wedge x \leqslant 11 \wedge x > 0\}$$

where the bar '|' means 'such that', and the expression before the dot '·' binds the variable(s) to range through a type. The bar symbol is overloaded in VDM as we have already seen, it is also used in type expressions. On the right-hand side of the bar is a formula that the parameter on the left-hand side of the bar must satisfy if it is to represent a value of the defined set. In VDM, this is called *set comprehension*. In the first example, the values of x satisfying the formula on the right-hand side of the bar are:

$$\{1, 2, 3, 4, 5, 6, 7, 8, 9\}$$

but the occurrence of x^2 before the bar means that all the members must be operated on by the squared function, resulting in the set:

$$\{1, 4, 9, 16, 25, 36, 49, 64, 81\}$$

3.4 CREATING VDM STATES

Up to now we have considered operations specified wholly in terms of data values passed in and out of them via parameters. Parameters may be assigned arbitrary data types, and this form of specification is theoretically sufficient although somewhat unrealistic for all computing applications.

A model-based approach to forming a specification involves capturing the central object or objects in an application with a well-fitting data structure. In information systems applications, for example, the central object might be a library system or some other large database; in compiler applications it may be a symbol table (see Chapter 4), while in automatic planning applications it may be a partially completed plan (see Chapter 6). It seems unnatural to use parameters as the sole means of allowing operations to access and manipulate this kind of data, because the whole object would have to be represented by input parameters whenever any part of it was needed by an operation.

This central object is called the system state, and instances of it are called *states*. Often an operation may only need to access or change a small part of the state; all other parts of the state are implicitly assumed to be unchanged. VDM allows operations to perform such actions by treating the state as a global data type, and by allowing operations to have 'read' and 'write' permissions on various parts of this state.

3.4.1 An example using an external state

As an introductory example to the idea of a state, let us assume we have to specify a system that keeps a record of houses up for sale in an estate agent's computer system. User-defined types in VDM can be constructed as in modern programming languages, and (sparing the details) we will assume that we have created the data type *Address*. Let our simplified system state of the houses for sale be a Set with base type *Address*. In VDM, this type, called *Houses_for_sale*, may be declared as:

$$Houses\_for\_sale = Address\text{-set}$$

As new houses are put onto the market and others sold, the state will change. A typical operation on this state would be one to delete an address of a house that had just been sold. The specification of operation *DELETE_HOUSE* would be as follows:

DELETE_HOUSE(addr: Address)
ext wr *hs*: *Houses_for_sale*
pre *addr* ∈ *hs*
post $hs = \overleftarrow{hs} \setminus \{addr\}$

In constructing this operation we use a similar procedure to the worked example of Sec. 3.3.3, the main difference being that *DELETE_HOUSE* accesses and changes the system state represented by values of *Houses_for_sale* via the local variable *hs*. The expression ext wr stands for 'external write', and means that the operation is accessing an external, overwritable part (or in this case the whole) of the system state. In particular, note that in the post-condition we need to refer to the *input state hs* as well as the output state, so that we can relate the two. Since the input state is somewhat foreign in the post-condition (which is supposed to be a condition on the output) in VDM it is decorated with a hook. For VDM operations:

- The pre-condition, written after pre, is a logical condition that in its most general form relates input parameters and the input state. Sometimes, as in the *IS_IN_SET* example, it may simply be '*true*'.
- The post-condition, written after post, is a logical condition which, in its most general form, relates input and output parameters and input and output states. Variable(s) representing the *input state* within the post-condition are decorated with a hook.

In the *DELETE_HOUSE* example, *hs* represents the input state in the pre-condition; in the post-condition, *hs* represents the output state, whereas $\overleftarrow{hs}$ represents the input state.

Figure 3.1 gives a pictorial view of a typical VDM operation. The output state and parameter values are a set of values that make the post-condition true. Cases where no output values satisfy the post-condition, or more than one distinct set of values do, will be dealt with later in the chapter.

An operation that accesses, but does not change the state, is *IS_ON_MARKET*. It is a Boolean operation that checks whether a particular address is up for sale:

IS_ON_MARKET(addr: Address) b: 𝔹
ext rd *hs*: *Houses_for_sale*
pre *true*
post *b* ⇔ *addr* ∈ *hs*

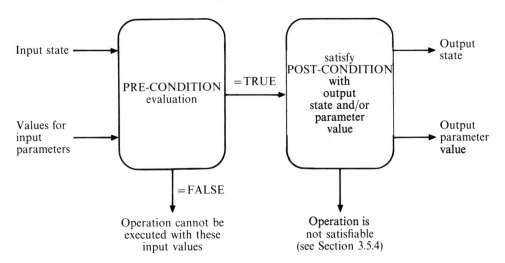

Figure 3.1   General form of a VDM operation.

The expression ext rd means that the operation is accessing an external, readable part of the system state which cannot be changed by the operation. The post-condition ensures that the output parameter *b* takes the same Boolean value as the expression *addr ∈ hs*. Note that there is no need for a hook over *hs* since the state represented by *hs* does not change.

Exercise 3.4 Write an operation similar to *DELETE_HOUSE* that adds a new address to the system, that is it puts a house up for sale.

3.4.2 Composites

VDM states are usually made up from the second data-structuring facility we will now introduce. The *Composite type* resembles the record structure in Pascal-like languages, and is used when data of different types need to be structured together. The estate agent's database needs to contain more than one distinct set of houses, and we shall see in the next section how this can be modelled using a composite type. As another example, consider an *Address* type: it can be created using the composition of different types representing street number, street name, post code, etc.

One syntax for the Composite type is to write the name of the Composite type we are creating, followed by a list of component variables, each followed by their type. This general form looks like:

$$type\_name :: component\_name : component\_type_1$$

$$...$$

$$...$$

$$component\_name : component\_type_n$$

Component types can be any primitive or predefined type—they can even be themselves composites. As another example, consider creating a 3-D co-ordinate type for the space $\mathbb{N}^3$, called *Co_ordinate*. The type definition would be:

> *Co_ordinate*:: *xaxis*: $\mathbb{N}$
> *yaxis*: $\mathbb{N}$
> *zaxis*: $\mathbb{N}$

Values of the Composite types are often referred to as 'records'. They are represented using a *make* or constructor function. This takes values of the components as arguments (in the order used in the definition of the Composite type) and creates a value of the type. The letters *mk-* are placed with the composite type name which is followed by the component values in brackets. Here are some examples of values of the Composite type *Co_ordinate*:

> *mk-Co_ordinate*(0, 0, 0)
> *mk-Co_ordinate*(1, 2, 3)
> *mk-Co_ordinate*(11, 42, 333)

The '*mk*' operator constructs composites but we also need to access or select their individual components. In VDM, component names are used as selector functions, returning the value in their slot. These selectors can be written with a prefix function syntax, or after a dot extension. Thus we can write:

> *xaxis*(*mk-Co_ordinate*(1, 2, 3))
> *zaxis*(*mk-Co_ordinate*(11, 42, 333))
> *yaxis*(*mk-Co_ordinate*(1, 2, 3))

or

> *mk-Co_ordinate*(1, 2, 3).*xaxis*
> *mk-Co_ordinate*(11, 42, 333).*zaxis*
> *mk-Co_ordinate*(1, 2, 3).*yaxis*

but in both cases the expressions' values are the same. We will adopt the dot extension syntax, as it may be more familiar to those who have programmed in a high-level language. The values obtained from these expressions are:

> *mk-Co_ordinate*(1, 2, 3).*xaxis* = 1
> *mk-Co_ordinate*(11, 42, 333).*zaxis* = 333
> *mk-Co_ordinate*(1, 2, 3).*yaxis* = 2

Exercise 3.5

(a) Consider an example data model representing the states of a lift travelling between three floors:

> *floors* = ONE | TWO | THREE

lift_positions = ONE | BETWEEN_ONE_AND_TWO | TWO | BETWEEN_TWO_AND_THREE | THREE

lift_status:: *position*   : *lift_positions*
         goal_position: *floors*
         direction   : UP | DOWN | STATIONARY

The lift status when the lift is going up to floor three having just left floor two is represented by:

mk-lift_status(BETWEEN_TWO_AND_THREE, THREE, UP)

Write down the lift status when:
 (i) The lift is going down to floor one having just left floor two
 (ii) The lift is stationary at floor one.
(b) In VDM, sets can be used to denote types, particularly subrange types. Thus if we wanted a type *Day* to represent the numbered days in a month, we could declare it thus:

$$Day = \{1, ..., 31\}$$

Design composite structures to represent:

(a) Someone's date of birth
(b) Someone's address, including street name and street number

3.5 A SYSTEMATIC APPROACH TO THE CONSTRUCTION OF VDM SPECIFICATIONS

It is useful for the purposes of learning how to write formal specifications to break down the process into steps. In VDM we can separate out the construction and development of a specification into five steps. The steps are: *creation of a system state, construction of data type invariants, modelling of the system's operations, discharging proof obligations* and *specification refinement*, and are outlined in Secs 3.5.1 through to 3.5.5. We have already encountered two of these: creation of a system state and operations on the state. Although the phases are related (in particular, the first two phases, which may be performed at the same time), we will use them both to separate out our description of VDM, and also as a means by which we can create specifications. An estate agent's database will be used as a running example.

3.5.1 First step: creation of a system state

In this first step, one constructs a data model of the target system out of primitive types and built-in data structures, such as Sets and Composites. This model can be viewed as a user-defined data type and implicitly defines the universe of possible states that the target system could be in during execution. Each state corresponds therefore to a value of the data model.

In more complex applications (such as in the case study of Chapter 6), it may be that the data model cannot be immediately decomposed into built-in data structures. In this case we have to decompose the data model S into a composite of component data types less complex than S. Each of these components can then be modelled with simpler user-defined types, which themselves may be specified in a similar fashion to S. We shall return to this subject of *building blocks* in Chapter 5, but it will be enough for the purposes of this chapter to assume that S is simple enough to be modelled immediately by built-in data structures.

In Section 3.4 we used the *local* variable name *hs* to refer to the state of the data type *Houses_for_sale* inside the operation *DELETE_HOUSE*. On the other hand, if the state has many components that operations may access separately, then we can declare *global* variables to represent those parts of the state that operations can access by direct reference to the variable name. This is done by encapsulating the state variables in a special kind of composite definition written as follows (here state, of and end are literals that actually appear in the VDM definition):

state *state_name* of
    component_name: *component_type*$_1$
    ...
    ...
    component_name: *component_type*$_n$
end

A typical composite state value would have the form $mk\text{-}state\_name(x_1, ..., x_n)$, where $x_1, ..., x_n$ are values of type $component\_type_1, ..., component\_type_n$ respectively.

Running example   In the estate agent example of Sec. 3.4, a typical system state is a set of addresses. To make the estate agent's model more sophisticated, we will require that the system holds an address in one of two modes: 'for sale' and 'under offer' (the latter means that an offer has been made upon the property and has been informally accepted). A data model pairs up two Address sets, creating a composite state called *Db* for the database. The two component names are *forsale*, and *underoffer*, as follows:

state *Db* of
    forsale   : *Address*-set
    underoffer: *Address*-set
end

Making the simplifying assumption that *Address* is a Composite as follows:

Address:: *street*   : *Token*
        house_no: $\mathbb{N}$

then a simple state of this database, with two houses for sale and none under offer, would be:

$mk\text{-}Db(\{mk\text{-}Address(\text{STRAND}, 62), mk\text{-}Address(\text{WHITEHALL}, 26)\}, \{ \})$

3.5.2 Second step: construction of data-type invariants

The desired system state may have relationships between its components that have to be fixed throughout its execution lifetime; or some of the component's structures may have to have their range tailored to fit the problem. This is akin to the idea of user-defined types in programming, and integrity constraints in databases.[1] In many applications we would like to record explicit assumptions about the properties and relationships of the data: VDM allows us to do this by defining a logical condition on the component data types of the state, or on the whole state itself, which restricts the values of these types.

This is done by presenting a definition of the following form after the state (or data type) declaration it refers to:

inv $exp \triangleq condition$

where:

- *exp* is an expression consisting of variables used to represent each of the state components, possibly bound together with a *make* constructor. If the state or data type on which the invariant is being written has a single component, then *exp* may be a single variable representing a typical value.
- $\triangleq$ means 'is defined as'. It is also used to explicitly define VDM functions (see Chapter 5).
- *condition* is the invariant; it is the logical condition that, given values of the correct type for the variables in *exp*, will evaluate to *true* or *false*. It must evaluate to *true* for all valid instances of the state.

An invariant can be designed for the system state or a data type, but if it is a condition on the system state then it can be included in the state composite definition, being written under the state variable declarations. Figure 3.2 shows pictorially how it restricts the set of all states to that subset of states that makes the invariant's condition true.

As a simple example, if we wanted a state representing someone's age in years, then we could declare it as follows:

state *Person_age* of
    $n: \mathbb{N}$
    inv $n \triangleq n \leqslant 130$
end

The type declaration defines the states (values) of *Person_age* to be natural numbers— clearly there are many unnatural age values here! The invariant restricts the possible states of *Person_age* to be natural numbers below 131. It therefore embodies the assumption that people do not live any longer. States satisfying the invariant are sometimes called *valid* states, and the data type invariant defines the set of all valid states. Invariants can be thought of as global conditions on states. For instance, they could be explicitly added (using the logical and '$\wedge$') to all operations' pre-conditions on the input state and all

---

[1] In Date (1990), an integrity constraint is defined as 'a *condition* that all correct states of the database are required to satisfy'—which is essentially the meaning of a data-type invariant.

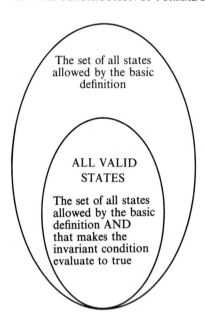

Figure 3.2   The effect of the data type invariant on states.

post-conditions on the output state. An important consequence is that we must demonstrate that the invariants are not violated by the operators that we specify (see
Sec. 3.5.4).

When creating a system state, one may have to choose between different representations. As well as recording assumptions that operations should not violate, the size of the
invariant is said to be a good measure of the suitability of the data representation: a
complex invariant suggests that the representation is not apt for the problem. The reason
for this is quite simple—a small invariant means that the assumptions about the problem
are recorded implicitly in the initial choice of data structure, which by definition makes the
representation a more natural choice.

Running example   One invariant for *Db* that immediately springs to mind is that 'no
house should be both for sale and under offer at the same time'. This would help stop
unscrupulous agents trying to obtain a better offer on a property, even though one has
been verbally accepted. This restriction can be captured by the invariant given below in
our extended definition of the state:

state *Db* of
    forsale: *Address*-set
    underoffer: *Address*-set
    inv *mk-Db*(*forsale*, *underoffer*) $\triangleq$ *forsale* $\cap$ *underoffer* = { }
end

The invariant declares that the intersection of the *forsale* and *underoffer* components of the database must be empty. Consider the following estate agent's database:

$mk\text{-}Db(\{mk\text{-}Address(\text{STRAND}, 62), mk\text{-}Address(\text{WHITEHALL}, 26)\},$
$\{mk\text{-}Address(\text{WHITEHALL}, 26)\})$

Clearly, the two sets making up this state have a nonempty intersection, and so it does not satisfy the invariant. It therefore represents an invalid state of the database.

3.5.3 Third step: modelling of the system's operations

The operations on the system state may now be specified by considering what is required in terms of pre- and post-conditions. An operation is given a name, a collection of input and output parameters, and access permissions to parts of the system model identified by state variables. A typical form for an operation that changes (possibly part of) the state is then:

$OP\_NAME(i: inputs)\ o: output$
ext wr $s: state\_type$
pre $pre\text{-}op(i, s)$
post $post\text{-}op(i, \overleftarrow{s}, o, s)$

In general, pre-conditions involve input parameters and input state variables, and post-conditions additionally may involve output parameter and output state variables. Here, we use the phrase '*i: inputs*' as shorthand for a list of zero, one, or more input parameters, paired with their data type name. Similarly, '*o: output*' is shorthand for zero or one output parameters. Finally, the state variable *s* could be split up into several variables having read or write access to various parts of the system state, as shown in the running example below.

Operations are *not* allowed to 'call' or reference other user-defined operations that access the system state. Inclusion of other operator names in operator conditions is not therefore permitted. Otherwise, the effect on the state would be opaque (it could be rather like a string of nested procedure calls in programming, where each procedure was dependent on and updated a global data structure—the overall effect would be very difficult to predict!). If a post-condition is large or too complex it can however be factored out for simplicity, by the use of *user-defined functions and types*. This facility will be addressed later, in Chapter 5, where the need for these functions will be established.

Finally, it is possible to specify operations whose post-conditions may be made true by more than one output state. We will deal with this eventuality in Sec. 3.5.4.

Running example An operation that changes both parts of the state is called *MAKE-OFFER*. It needs an input parameter *addr* to hold the value of the address on which an offer has been made, but no values are output and therefore no output parameter is needed. The operation will remove *addr* from those houses up for sale, and place it in those under offer; hence it will access and change both parts of the state. In this case the operation's heading is as follows:

$MAKEOFFER(addr: Address)$
ext wr *forsale*: *Address*-set
    wr *underoffer*: *Address*-set

The pre-condition of the operation needs to check that *addr*'s value is contained in the database. The post-condition should express the property required of the output state, that *addr* has been removed from *forsale* and is now in *underoffer*. Hence, the completed operation is:

$MAKEOFFER(addr: Address)$
ext wr *forsale*: *Address*-set
    wr *underoffer*: *Address*-set
pre *addr* ∈ *forsale*
post *forsale* = $\overleftarrow{forsale}$ \ {*addr*} ∧ *underoffer* = $\overleftarrow{underoffer}$ ∪ {*addr*}

3.5.4 Fourth step: discharging proof obligations

Errors in specifications fall roughly into two areas: syntactic errors and semantic errors. Syntactic errors manifest themselves in incorrect lexicon, type inconsistencies and incorrect syntactic structure (for example, giving a function the wrong number or type of arguments). On the other hand, semantic errors in the specification—imprecisely known as 'logical' errors—generally take the form of omissions in the conditions of operations and inconsistencies between data-type invariants and operations.

In trying to eliminate errors from specifications, *software tools* are important. Formal specifications are written in formal languages, that is they have, like programming languages, precise syntax. Syntax checking tools are available for all serious formal specification languages including VDM. They are essential, particularly for creating large specifications. Anyone who has written a non-trivial program can testify to the fact that many syntax errors will arise, often repeatedly, before the program is made syntactically correct. Syntax checking tools in formal specifications perform a similar function, in that they can pick up on lexical errors, type mismatching, and incorrect syntactic structure (and it is another advantage of *formalization* that they exist).

It is the process of *discharging proof obligations* that helps to throw up semantic or logical errors. Tools, sometimes called *proof assistants*, are also becoming available to help in the process of discharging proof obligations, and these complement syntax checkers. The need for these tools will be seen in Sec. 3.6, where we describe the proof obligations in formal logic.

Satisfiability   Proof obligations are assertions that sum up the checks a developer should make at various stages of software development to give assurance that specifications and designs are self-consistent. Although they are a general concept, in VDM we describe proof obligations at the specification stage as assertions that sum up *satisfiability*. The specification of an operation is satisfiable if it is possible to find an implementation (an algorithm) that satisfies the operation. An algorithm satisfies an operation if, given any system state and/or input parameter values that make its pre-condition true, the algorithm eventually produces an output state and/or output parameter value that make the post-condition evaluate to true.

Discharging proof obligations means we have to argue, using the specification as a base, that these assertions are correct for every operation we create. This process also makes the developer think deeply about the specification, consequently attaining a much better, coherent understanding of it. Also, once the obligations have been discharged, it results in a much greater confidence in the validity of the specification.

In some cases, especially where data types have been tailored with invariants, it may not be obvious that the specification is satisfiable. Even simple specifications that do not access an external state may be problematic: for example, we might give the following operation as the answer to Exercise 3.3(b):

$MAX\_IN(s: \mathbb{N}\text{-set})\ m: \mathbb{N}$
pre *true*
post $m \in s \wedge \forall i \in s \cdot i \leqslant m$

This operation is not satisfiable: the post-condition is not achievable by any algorithm if the input parameter's value is taken to be the empty set, that is $s = \{\ \}$. In this case, $m \in s$ is always false, and so the post-condition could not be true. The following is a correct version:

$MAX\_IN(s: \mathbb{N}\text{-set})\ m: \mathbb{N}$
pre $s \neq \{\ \}$
post $m \in s \wedge \forall i \in s \cdot i \leqslant m$

Given this new post-condition, there is always a value of m that makes it evaluate to true, no matter what value of s is input. Hence, the process of discharging proof obligations can throw up unforeseen errors in a specification, as in the erroneous version of MAX_IN above.

In summary, an operation is satisfiable if:

- *For every possible valid input state and/or every possible legal input parameter value(s) that satisfy the pre-condition, it is possible to compute a valid output state and/or a legal output parameter value that makes the post-condition true.*

As we have seen an operator may not involve input or output parameters, or may not change the state. In these special cases the definition will be adapted accordingly.

Traditionally, the satisfiability condition is broken down into the following two proof obligations which deal specifically with operations that change an external state (consideration of the state invariant makes satisfiability hard to prove, and breaking it into a two-step process makes it easier to test each VDM operation):

1. For every possible valid input state and every possible legal input parameter value(s) that satisfy the pre-condition, prove an output state can be computed regardless of whether it satisfies the state invariant.
2. Prove that all output states are valid (that is they satisfy the state invariant).

Condition 1 asserts that, provided the invariants and the pre-conditions are made true by an arbitrary binding for the input state and input parameters, the post-condition, ignoring invariants on the output state, can be met.

Condition 2 then deals with the invariant on the output state—it asserts that an operation should never leave the system in an *inconsistent* state. This means proving that, for every input state that makes the invariant true, the action of the operation, provided its pre-conditions have been met, outputs a state that also makes the invariant true.

In fact, condition 2 goes further; we have tentatively assumed that only one output state can satisfy the post-condition. Post-conditions can be written, however, which may be satisfied by more than one output state, and in this sense they form a *nondeterministic* operator specification. Condition 2 is strong in that it asserts that all (not just at least one of) these output states must be valid. Nondeterministic operations are used in Chapter 6, and they prove a useful form of abstraction when we do not want an overcommitment to choice. Proving uniqueness of an output state is not, therefore, necessarily part of the proof obligation process (although it may be desirable).

Running example To check that *MAKEOFFER* can be satisfied, we will use the two-stage process. First, we make conditions 1 and 2 specific to this particular operation:

1. for any possible nonintersecting address sets, *forsale* and *underoffer*, and any address *addr* that is a member of *forsale*, prove that an output state can always be computed.
2. Provided an output state can be computed that satisfies the post-condition

$$forsale = \overleftarrow{forsale} \setminus \{addr\} \wedge underoffer = \overleftarrow{underoffer} \cup \{addr\}$$

prove it is necessarily valid.

No matter what address sets the input state components of *forsale* and *underoffer* represent, and what the value of *addr* is, the post-condition certainly admits an output state. This is so because both set difference and set union are always defined when their arguments are valid VDM sets, and the equality in the post-condition gives directly the output state values. Hence condition 1 is true.

To argue that 2 is true, we note that the state invariant on the input state, which is made up of the sets $\overleftarrow{forsale}$ and $\overleftarrow{underoffer}$, asserts that they do not intersect. For the output state (represented by *forsale* and *underoffer*) to be invalid, one or more elements must be added to the input sets. Only one element, *addr*, is effectively added to the input state component $\overleftarrow{underoffer}$. On the other hand, the same element is taken out of $\overleftarrow{forsale}$ to give the output state component *forsale*. Therefore, the output state component sets, *forsale* and *underoffer*, also have an empty intersection and so satisfy the state invariant.

Note:

- This example of discharging proof obligations was straightforward, because the post-condition of the operation read virtually as an assignment statement (although it must be stressed strongly that equality is a logic relation). More complex conditions and state invariants may require a higher degree of formality, and in Sec. 3.6 we will describe how this can be achieved.

- The output state of *MAKEOFFER* is unique, because set difference and set union always give a unique answer. Thus, not only does there always exist a valid output state, but it is also unique.

3.5.5 Fifth step: specification refinement

The final phase in the methodology is generally the most difficult. Once a top-level specification has been produced, tuned to the requirements, and proof obligations discharged, we may have to refine both the operations and the system state into a correct implementation.

The abstract mathematical data types used in the specification are not normally implementable in a general purpose programming language, and in any case may be grossly inefficient representations. As well as this, an operation's implicit, abstract post-condition needs to be refined into an explicit algorithm that satisfies it.

In this book we are interested in the first four phases of this methodology, and we will essentially leave out the last phase: instead of describing specification refinement, we will consider only specification prototyping, for the following reasons:

- We are interested in specification construction rather than program design; the development of programs from specifications is an area that itself has books devoted to it (see, for instance, Backhouse (1986)).
- The field of data and operation refinement is very controversial: correctness proofs involved in refinement are very complex even for small applications, although the methods behind them are well understood. Automated ways of translating specifications into programs are a subject of current research.
- We devote part of the book to prototyping, which is itself a way of producing a faithful, though usually inefficient, implementation. Specification prototyping will be addressed in Chapter 7, for VDM, and Chapter 13, for the algebraic approach.

3.6 FORMAL PROOF OBLIGATIONS

We have seen in Sec. 3.5.4 how proof obligations can be discharged informally, and often this will be enough to give the developer a sufficient depth of understanding to iron out logical errors, leading to a better specification. One advantage of using a formalism to capture the system state and its operations, however, is that we can also formalize the proof obligations.

First, we will show how the satisfiability condition can be turned into an assertion about a VDM operation, using the general form for an operation given in Sec. 3.5.3. Then, from this assertion, we will derive formalizations of proof obligations (1) and (2) from Sec. 3.5.4.

For a given operation, let s_i represent the input state, s_o the output state, i an input parameter and o an output parameter (for the moment we assume for simplicity that the operation has one input and one output parameter). Then the first part of the satisfiability condition:

'For every possible valid input state and/or every possible legal input parameter value(s), that satisfy the pre-condition...'

translates to:

$$\forall s_i, i \cdot pre\text{-}op(i, s_i)$$

The second part of the satisfiability condition for an operation:

'it is possible to compute a valid output state and/or legal output parameter value that make the post-condition true'

translates to:

$$\exists s_o, o \cdot post\text{-}op(i, s_i, o, s_o)$$

The logical assertion abstracts away 'to compute' and replaces it with the existential quantifier—there only needs to exist values for the output state and output parameter. Putting these together, the final assertion is:

$$\forall s_i, i \cdot (pre\text{-}op(i, s_i) \Rightarrow \exists s_o, o \cdot post\text{-}op(i, s_i, o, s_o)) \tag{3.10}$$

Note we are assuming that the quantifiers range across valid type values only: any data-type invariants that exist are implicitly included in the condition. A version of assertion (3.10) that makes the invariant of the state explicit is as follows:

$$\forall s_i, i \cdot (inv(s_i) \wedge pre\text{-}op(i, s_i) \Rightarrow \exists s_o, o \cdot (inv(s_o) \wedge post\text{-}op(i, s_i, o, s_o))) \tag{3.11}$$

This leads immediately to the formalization of assertions 1 and 2 of Sec. 3.5.4:

$$\forall s_i, i \cdot (inv(s_i) \wedge pre\text{-}op(i, s_i) \Rightarrow \exists s_o, o \cdot post\text{-}op(i, s_i, o, s_o)) \tag{3.12}$$

$$\forall s_i, i, s_o, o \cdot (inv(s_i) \wedge pre\text{-}op(i, s_i) \wedge post\text{-}op(i, s_i, o, s_o) \Rightarrow inv(s_o)) \tag{3.13}$$

These two assertions, interpreted as statements that must be proved true, are the formalized proof obligations. They generalize to operations that have zero or more than one input parameter, and possibly no output parameter. In Chapter 5 we will present the proof obligations for pure functions, an important special case of these assertions (in particular functions have no input or output state).

Running example As an example, we will formally prove assertion 2 for the *MAKE-OFFER* operator. Let f_i and u_i (f_o and u_o) be arbitrary instances of the input (output) state variables *forsale* and *underoffer* of *Db*.
  In this case, assertion (3.13) becomes (assuming all variables are universally quantified):

$$(f_i \cap u_i = \{ \ \}) \wedge (addr \in f_i) \wedge (f_o = f_i \backslash \{addr\}) \wedge (u_o = u_i \cup \{addr\}) \Rightarrow (f_o \cap u_o = \{ \ \})$$

To prove an assertion of the form $LHS \Rightarrow RHS$ is true, we need to prove that RHS is true whenever LHS is true, for arbitrary values of the universally quantified variables. Hence, what we need to show is that, if each of the four conditions preceding the '$\Rightarrow$' are met for arbitrary f_i, u_i, etc., then the condition after '$\Rightarrow$' is true. For the sake of the proof, we will number these conditions as follows:

$$f_i \cap u_i = \{ \ \} \tag{3.14}$$

$$addr \in f_i \tag{3.15}$$

$$f_o = f_i \setminus \{addr\} \tag{3.16}$$

$$u_o = u_i \cup \{addr\} \tag{3.17}$$

To show $f_o \cap u_o = \{ \ \}$ is true, it is sufficient to show that, given an arbitrary member of f_o, it is not a member of u_o (in the case of $f_o = \{ \ \}$, it is immediately true that $f_o \cap u_o = \{ \ \}$). We will let this be the starting point of the proof:

$$\text{let } x \in f_o \tag{3.18}$$

by (3.16) and (3.18):

$$x \in f_i \setminus \{addr\} \tag{3.19}$$

from (3.19) and the properties of sets:

$$x \in f_i \tag{3.20}$$

from conditions (3.14) and (3.20):

$$x \notin u_i \tag{3.21}$$

From (3.16) and (3.18), $x \notin \{addr\}$, so that $x \neq addr$. Hence, from (3.21):

$$x \notin u_i \cup \{addr\} \tag{3.22}$$

from (3.22) and (3.17):

$$x \notin u_o \tag{3.23}$$

and finally from (3.23) and (3.18), and the fact that x was chosen arbitrarily, we have the required result that:

$$f_o \cap u_o = \{ \ \}$$

3.7 SUMMARY

In this chapter we have introduced the idea of model-based specification. A specification is based around the creation of a system model using:

- A collection of operations defined by pre- and post-conditions

- A collection of data structures built from well-defined primitive types including the Set and the Composite
- A particular data model called the system state which operations are free to access

We also introduced a staged method of developing specifications by:

- Building abstract data structures (in particular a system state) from VDM's primitive data structures
- Constructing data type invariants, which embody constraints on a data type, restricting its set of values to precisely what is required
- Modelling the system's operations and discharging proof obligations on them

ADDITIONAL PROBLEMS

3.1 Using the model of Sec. 3.5, write the following estate agent database operations:
    (a) *PUT_UP_FORSALE*—inputs a new address and puts it in the database.
    (b) *UNDEROFFER?*—checks whether an address is under offer.
    Discharge the proof obligations for both operations.
3.2 Create a data type invariant for the lift composite that will rule out states that are not sensible, such as:

    mk-lift_status(THREE, THREE, UP)

3.3 Write an operation for the lift composite that outputs true if and only if its position is the same as its goal position.
3.4 Change the estate agent example, so that the database holds the price of each house. Write an operation that inputs a house price, and outputs the set of all houses that are at or below this price.
3.5 This problem involves further changes to the estate agent example. Assume the data type that represents a house, called *Address*, is given. The system should hold three sets of addresses:
    (a) 'on record'—all houses, including all those for sale and sold, that have been processed by the estate agent
    (b) 'for sale'—those houses on the market
    (c) 'sold'—those houses that the estate agent has sold, and are no longer on the market
    Note: The estate agent may sell the same house twice.
    (a) Create a suitable VDM data model called *Db* for the problem. Include a data type invariant to capture the constraints given above. Specify operations that:
        (i) put a house up for sale.
        (ii) take a house off the market that has not been sold.
        (iii) outputs the set of houses that were advertised but never sold.
    (b) Present an informal argument showing that the operations preserve the data-type invariant.
    (c) Suggest a change to your VDM data model that allows the system to record the resale of a previously sold house.

REFERENCES

Backhouse, R.C. (1986) *Program Construction and Verification*, Prentice-Hall, London.
Date, C.J. (1990) *An Introduction to Database Systems*, vol. 1, 5th ed., Addison-Wesley, Reading, MA.
Jones, C.B. (1979) *Software Development—A Rigorous Approach*, Prentice-Hall, London.
Jones, C.B. (1986) *Systematic Software Development using VDM*, 1st ed., Prentice-Hall, London.
Jones, C.B. (1990) *Systematic Software Development using VDM*, 2nd ed., Prentice-Hall, London.

4

THE SEQUENCE AND MAP TYPES

4.1 INTRODUCTION

This chapter introduces VDM's Sequence and Map data types, and shows their use in small specifications. When the ordering of instances of a data type matters, then the Sequence type is required to hold those instances; without the need for ordered data, then the Set type would be adequate. The Map type is used when there is a correspondence between two types of data: between people and their age, between bank accounts and account number, between cars and their engine type, between program variables and their data type, and so on. This correspondence must be functional, in the sense that people have only one age, bank accounts have a unique account number, cars have only one engine type, and program variables have a unique data type. As with the Set and Composite types, the Sequence and Map are actually polymorphic types, because they are built up from arbitrary base types.

The chapter ends with a small but useful example, that of formally specifying the standard operations required by a compiler on a symbol table. The symbol table is a data structure that holds the identifiers (and their associated attributes) that are declared within the program that a compiler is processing. This example is used to show the combination of all four data types.

As in the last chapter, we will use capital letters to refer to a type—hence 'Sequence' refers to the type, whereas 'sequence' refers to a particular or arbitrary instance of a sequence, that is an actual data structure.

4.2 THE SEQUENCE DATA TYPE

The Sequence data type is an abstraction of the List type found in many programming languages such as Prolog and Lisp. It has several features in common with the Set type that we met in the last chapter:

- A sequence value contains a collection of elements, all of the same type (called the *base type*). As with the Set, the Sequence type can take any type as its base type.
- A sequence can (theoretically) contain any number of elements.

On the other hand, there are two things that differentiate sequences from sets:

- The elements of a sequence are *totally ordered*. Ordering is determined by position in the sequence from left to right.
- Each element contained in a sequence is not necessarily unique, that is the same element may occur repeatedly.

When represented explicitly, sequence elements are written separated by commas, and the whole sequence is enclosed in square brackets. For example the following are sequences of base type $\mathbb{N}$:

$$[56, 34, 78, 56]$$
$$[34, 23, 12, 45, 56, 67]$$

The value '[ ]' is called the *empty sequence*, and is very similar to the empty set in many respects, as we shall see. Variables of type Sequence are declared by writing their base type followed by an asterisk. Hence, the type 'Sequence of Integers' would be declared $\mathbb{Z}*$. Sequences can be combined with other structures, for example

$$\{[true, true], [false, true, false], [true]\}$$

is a value of type Set whose base type is Sequence of Boolean. This type would be declared '$\mathbb{B}*$-set'. Similarly, the value

$$[\{3, 2, 1\}, \{42\}]$$

is of type Sequence of Sets of natural numbers, written '$(\mathbb{N}\text{-set})*$'.

The Sequence type comes equipped with its own collection of VDM functions and predicates. The main predicate is equality ('='), and two sequences are equal if and only if they have the same length and have identical elements in each position. Several examples of primitive operations are given below:

- $\frown$ this is the concatenate or join operation. It is binary infix, and has the effect of gluing its two arguments into one sequence, in the obvious fashion, as shown by the following examples.

$$[56, 34, 78, 56] \frown [34, 23, 12, 45, 56, 67] = [56, 34, 78, 56, 34, 23, 12, 45, 56, 67]$$
$$[34, 23, 12, 45, 56, 67] \frown [56, 34, 78, 56] = [34, 23, 12, 45, 56, 67, 56, 34, 78, 56]$$

Note that its two arguments must be of identical type—that is the base types of the sequences must be the same. Concatenating the empty sequence with any other sequence leaves that sequence unchanged:

$[34, 23, 12, 45, 56, 67] \frown [\ ] = [34, 23, 12, 45, 56, 67]$

$[\ ] \frown [true, false, true] = [true, false, true]$

$[\{3, 2, 1\}, \{42\}] \frown [\ ] = [\{3, 2, 1\}, \{42\}]$

- len   this is the operation that returns the length of a sequence, for example

    len $[34, 23, 12, 45, 56, 67] = 6$

    len $[56, 34, 78, 56] = 4$

    len $[\ ] = 0$

    len $[\{\ \}] = 1$

    len $[\{3, 2, 1\}, \{42\}] = 2$

    len $[true, false, true] = 3$

- hd   this is pronounced *head*. Its value when applied to a sequence is the first element, the head, of that sequence. For example

    hd $[34, 23, 12, 45, 56, 67] = 34$

    hd $[56, 34, 78, 56] = 56$

    hd $[\{\ \}] = \{\ \}$

    hd $[\{3, 2, 1\}, \{42\}] = \{3, 2, 1\}$

    hd $[true, false, true] = true$

    Note: hd is not defined on $[\ ]$.

- tl   this is pronounced *tail*. Its value when applied to a sequence is equal to the sequence with the first element (the head) removed, for example

    tl $[34, 23, 12, 45, 56, 67] = [23, 12, 45, 56, 67]$

    tl $[56, 34, 78, 56] = [34, 78, 56]$

    tl $[\{\ \}] = [\ ]$

    tl $[\{3, 2, 1\}, \{42\}] = [\{42\}]$

    tl $[true, false, true] = [false, true]$

    tl (tl $[34, 23, 12, 45, 56, 67]) = [12, 45, 56, 67]$

    hd (tl $[34, 23, 12, 45, 56, 67]) = 23$

    Note: tl is not defined on $[\ ]$.

- elems: this takes a sequence and returns the set of all its elements:

    elems $[34, 23, 12, 45, 56, 67] = \{34, 23, 12, 45, 56, 67\}$

    elems $[56, 34, 78, 56] = \{56, 34, 78\}$

elems $[\{\ \}] = \{\{\ \}\}$

elems $[\{3, 2, 1\}, \{42\}] = \{\{3, 2, 1\}, \{42\}\}$

elems $[true, false, true] = \{false, true\}$

elems $[\ ] = \{\ \}$

Sequences, just like sets, have a number of formally defined properties. For instance, given any nonempty sequence s, the following equality is true: concatenating the sequence consisting of one element, the head of s, with the tail of s, evaluates to s itself. This can be expressed more concisely as: for all non-empty sequences s,

$$[hd\ s] \frown (tl\ s) = s$$

Rather than providing a list of all such properties, we will introduce them as needed, but the reader is reminded that they are necessary so that we can *reason* with the data types. Since VDM data types are mathematically sound, any relevant property or theorem from mathematics can be used when reasoning about them.

Exercises 4.1

(a) Assume a sequence s is of length greater than 3. Then an expression that represents the second element of the sequence is:

hd (tl s)

Write down expressions which represent the third and fourth elements of s.

(b) Well-formed expressions consisting of the Sequence operators above may be evaluated. For example:

   (i) elems (hd (tl $[[1, 2], [5, 5, 1]]$)) = elems (hd $[[5, 5, 1]]$) = elems $[5, 5, 1] = \{5, 1\}$

   (ii) (tl $[true, true]) \frown [false] = [true] \frown [false] = [true, false]$

Evaluate the following in the same way:

   (iii) (hd (tl $[[1, 2], [5, 5, 1]]$)) $\frown [5, 5, 1]$

   (iv) tl $([\{1, 2\}, \{1, 2\}] \frown (tl\ [[\ ]]))$

   (v) elems ((tl (tl $[34, 23, 12, 45, 56, 67])) \frown [12, 45])$

(c) Substitute for s in the formula

$$[hd\ s] \frown tl\ s = s$$

some of the example sequences above, and evaluate the resulting expression to *true*.

(d) We stated that two sequences are equal if and only if they have the same length and have identical elements in each position. For any two sequence variables s and t, of base type T, and any elements a and b of type T, if we have:

$$[a] \frown s = [b] \frown t$$

show that $s = t$ and $a = b$.

4.3 A MODEL-BASED SPECIFICATION OF THE STACK

4.3.1 Requirement

Many computer-oriented data-structures can easily be specified in VDM: the queue and the stack are straightforward to write in VDM. As an example, we will choose a finite stack of numbers, and model it as the composite of a sequence and a size limit. (Although this is a well-worn example, the stack provides a simple introduction to the use of the Sequence, and also to algebraic specifications in Chapter 8.) The required operations are:

- *INIT* creates a new stack.
- *PUSH* puts a number onto the stack.
- *POP* returns the top element (number) of the stack *and* removes the top element (number) from the stack.
- *EMPTY* returns true if and only if the stack is empty.
- *FULL* returns true if and only if the stack is full.

Figures 4.1 and 4.2 give pictorial examples of the *PUSH* and *POP* operations on a stack of numbers.

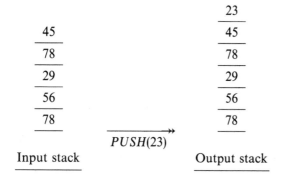

Figure 4.1 A *PUSH* operation on a stack.

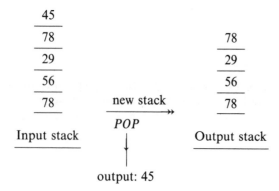

Figure 4.2 A *POP* operation on a stack.

4.3.2 Creation of the system state

It seems natural to model the stack with two components: a number, denoting the maximum stack size, and a sequence of numbers denoting the contents of the stack:

$Contents = \mathbb{N}^*$

$Max\_stack\_size = \mathbb{N}$

and our state becomes:

    state *Stack* of
      s: *Contents*
      n: *Max_stack_size*
    end

If we decide that the 'top' of the stack is going to be the left-hand end of the sequence, and the stack's maximum size is to be 100 numbers, then the input stack to the *PUSH* and *POP* operation in figs 4.1 and 4.2 is represented explicitly as

  mk-Stack([45, 78, 29, 56, 78], 100)

4.3.3 Construction of data type invariant

We need to relate the length of the stack to the maximum stack size in the following way: the length should always be less than or equal to the maximum size. The fact that stacks can never have 'negative' size is captured by the sequence, so we do not have to make this explicit in the invariant. Our completed state model is:

    state *Stack* of
      s: *Contents*
      n: *Max_stack_size*
      inv *mk-Stack*(s, n) $\triangle$ len $s \leqslant n$
    end

4.3.4 Modelling of the system's operations

By considering the pre- and post-conditions required for each of the operations, we can formalize them as follows. *INIT* will create a stack of potential length 'size' and initialize the sequence to be empty:

  INIT (*size*: $\mathbb{N}$)
  ext wr s: *Contents*
      wr n: *Max_stack_size*
  pre *true*
  post $s = [\ ] \wedge n = size$

EMPTY and *FULL* will monitor the size of the stack contents. Neither will change the stack's state, hence, the use of ext rd:

> *EMPTY( ) b: $\mathbb{B}$*
> ext rd *s: Contents*
> pre *true*
> post *b* ⇔ (*s* = [ ])

> *FULL( ) b: $\mathbb{B}$*
> ext rd *s: Contents*
>   rd *n: Max_stack_size*
> pre *true*
> post *b* ⇔ (len *s* = *n*)

Finally, we specify operations that change the stack, *PUSH* and *POP*. Informally, the conditions are (bearing in mind that the stack top is at the left-hand side of the sequence):

PUSH:
pre the stack should have enough room for another element
post the output stack is made up of the stack whose tail is the input stack and whose head (top) is the input value

POP:
pre the stack should contain at least one element
post the output stack is the tail of the input stack and the output value is the head (the top) of the input stack

The completed operations are:

> *PUSH (c: $\mathbb{N}$)*
> ext wr *s: Contents*
>   rd *n: Max_stack_size*
> pre len *s* < *n*
> post *s* = [*c*] ⌢ $\overleftarrow{s}$

> *POP ( ) c: $\mathbb{N}$*
> ext wr *s: Contents*
> pre len *s* > 0
> post $\overleftarrow{s}$ = [*c*] ⌢ *s*

Modelling the Stack introduces some of the subtleties of VDM:

- Concatenate ('⌢') is used in the post-condition of *PUSH* and *POP* to show the *relation* between the input and output states. The output state is often defined by an implicit relation between input and output states, as in the *POP* operation. It is left to the implementor to design an actual algorithm that changes the input sequence to obtain the output sequence. The value of output parameters, such as the Boolean b in the *EMPTY* and *FULL* operations, can also be defined implicitly.

- Details that are normally found in implementations—such as the 'stack pointer'—are not necessary here.
- Operations such as *INIT* create the first or initial value(s) in the data model that represents the state—in this case the empty stack.

4.3.5 Proof obligations for the Stack

Recall from Sec. 3.6 that for each operation we have to prove that the following are true:

$$\forall t_i, i \cdot (inv(t_i) \wedge pre\text{-}op(i, t_i) \Rightarrow \exists t_o, o \cdot post\text{-}op(i, t_i, o, t_o)) \tag{4.1}$$

$$\forall i, t_i, o, t_o \cdot (inv(t_i) \wedge pre\text{-}op(i, t_i) \wedge post\text{-}op(i, t_i, o, t_o) \Rightarrow inv(t_o)) \tag{4.2}$$

where i represents zero, one or more input parameters, o represents zero or one output parameter, and t_i, t_o represent (possibly lists of) input and output state variables. (We have changed the usual letter s to t so that it is not confused with the stack variable s.) For the stack, these proofs can be carried out relatively simply for each operation. In the case of *POP*, the assertions (4.1) and (4.2) turn out to be:

$$\forall n, s_i \cdot (\text{len } s_i \leqslant n \wedge \text{len } s_i > 0 \Rightarrow \exists s_o, c \cdot s_i = [c] \frown s_o) \tag{4.1'}$$

$$\forall n, s_i, c, s_o \cdot (\text{len } s_i \leqslant n \wedge \text{len } s_i > 0 \wedge s_i = [c] \frown s_o \Rightarrow \text{len } s_o \leqslant n) \tag{4.2'}$$

Note that we need only represent the maximum stack size by one variable n because that part of the state does not change under the action of *POP*. As in Sec 3.6, we prove an assertion of the form $\forall \ldots LHS \Rightarrow RHS$, by assuming the *LHS* is true, then showing that the *RHS* must also be true, for arbitrary, universally quantified variables.

To prove Condition (4.1'), assume the two predicates on the left-hand side of the '$\Rightarrow$' are true. The condition 'len $s_i > 0$' implies that '$s_i \neq [\ ]$'; now any nonempty sequence has a head and a tail, so we can take c to be 'hd s_i' and s_o to be 'tl s_i', and these values satisfy the existentially quantified condition on the right-hand side. Hence, Condition (4.1') is true, because we have shown that, assuming the left-hand side is true, the right-hand side must be true.

To prove Condition (4.2'), we use the fact that *POP* never invalidates the invariant since it decreases the size of the stack. From the assumption:

$$s_i = [c] \frown s_o$$

it follows that the input stack s_i is bigger than the output stack s_o, and from the assumption len $s_i \leqslant n$ it therefore follows that len $s_o < n$. In this case, the right-hand side, len $s_o \leqslant n$, must also be true.

Discharging the proof obligations for *PUSH* is left as an exercise. The other operations are easily dealt with: *EMPTY* and *FULL* do not affect the state, and so cannot invalidate the invariant, hence Condition (4.2') holds. Condition (4.1') holds since the predicate expressions in their post-conditions are trivially defined for all input values. Hence b will output *true* or *false* for any values of s and n. For *INIT*, Condition (4.1′) is immediately true, and Condition (4.2′) holds since the length of the output sequence is zero, which is less than or equal to any choice of maximum stack size.

4.3.6 Validation: a simple example

Working through these specification development phases, and the prototyping phase described in Chapter 7, eliminates many sources of error from a specification, but we still may not have captured the required system. To help in validating that the *Stack* operations are those we want, we can indulge in a little reasoning with their specification. Certain desirable properties of the required system may not be explicitly stated in the model, but we can reason with the model to predict whether these properties are in fact true.

For example, assuming the stack value in a state is $s1$, then the operations *PUSH* and *POP* executed in sequence should leave the stack as it was (regardless of the value of *PUSH*'s parameter). In other words, the input stack of *PUSH* should be identical to the output stack of *POP*. If we call the output stack value of *POP* $s3$ and the stack value between the operations $s2$, then

$$s1 \mapsto PUSH \mapsto s2 \mapsto POP \mapsto s3$$

represents the sequence of operator executions and the values of the stacks between them. We can formally derive $s1 = s3$ using our specification. From the post-condition of *PUSH* we have that:

$$s2 = [c] \frown s1$$

and from the post-condition of *POP*:

$$s2 = [c'] \frown s3$$

because $s2$ is the input stack of *POP*. Combining these we have:

$$[c] \frown s1 = [c'] \frown s3$$

and using Exercise 4.1(d) we deduce that:

$$s1 = s3$$

It also follows from this exercise that $c = c'$.

Exercises 4.2

(a) The proof obligations for *PUSH* are as follows:

    (i) $\forall n, s_i, c \cdot (\text{len } s_i \leqslant n \wedge \text{len } s_i < n \Rightarrow \exists s_o \cdot (s_o = [c] \frown s_i))$

    (ii) $\forall n, s_i, c, s_o \cdot (\text{len } s_i \leqslant n \wedge \text{len } s_i < n \wedge s_o = [c] \frown s_i \Rightarrow \text{len } s_o \leqslant n)$

Give a formal or informal proof of them. If the pre-condition of *PUSH* was changed to *true*, could the proof obligations still be discharged?

(b) Write an 'explicit' post-condition for *POP*, using the hd and tl sequence operations.

(c) The stack can effectively be defined without the use of an external state. Redefine it with the same operations, but only using input and output parameters.

(d) Specify a bounded 'Queue of Integers' data type in VDM notation (readers who are unfamiliar with this data type can consult Chapter 9 for an introduction).

4.4 A HORSE RACING INFORMATION SYSTEM

This worked example demonstrates further the uses of the Sequence type. It also develops the use of composites and sets, and in particular the *set comprehension* technique.

A horse racing trainer wants a system that maintains the horse and jockey information in her horse racing 'stable', including the sequence of races left in a season in which her horses might run. For the moment, assume only two operations are required:

1. Output the names of the most successful horses.
2. Update the horse information after race results.

This example will be extended in the exercises at the end of the section, and in the problems at the end of the chapter.

4.4.1 Creation of a system state

In horse racing the 'form' of a horse can be represented as a sequence of placings in the season's races in which it has competed. If we decide to store whether a horse was the winner, placed (second, third, or fourth) or unplaced (not in the first four), then we can define an appropriate type:

Position = WINNER | PLACED | UNPLACED

A horse's placings in the races it has completed in a season can be represented as a chronological sequence, with the most recent result at the front of the sequence:

Placings = *Position**

We also might want to record a horse's favourite racing surface ('going'), which corresponds to the condition of the ground on which it performs best:

Going = GOOD | GOOD_TO_SOFT | SOFT

and finally a horse's (or person's) name can be represented as a sequence of tokens:

Full_name = *Token**

For example, the name Northern Boy would be represented thus:

[NORTHERN, BOY]

Putting these definitions together, we get the following horse record type:

    Horse:: *name*: *Full_name*
           pos : *Placings*
           go   : *Going*

Assume that jockeys each have a horse that they normally ride, called a mount. As well as this, we store their name and sex. Again, relying on a composite structure, we have:

    Jockey:: *name* : *Full_name*
           mount: *Full_name*
           sex   : MALE | FEMALE

The Stable information system also needs to hold a chronologically ordered list of the race meetings still to run in the season. If a race meeting can be represented as a unique token:

    Race = *Token*

then the races left in the season will be represented by:

    Races_left = *Race**

The information about a stable forms our state: the horses owned by the stable, the jockeys riding for the stable, and the names of the race meetings left in the season (that is those that the stable's horses will run in).

    state *Stable* of
      hrs: *Horse*-set
      jks: *Jockey*-set
      rcl: *Races_left*
    end

The following expression (called *H*1) is a simple example of the state:

    mk-Stable({*mk-Horse*([RED, WINE], [WINNER, PLACED], GOOD),
    mk-Horse ([NORTHERN, BOY], [UNPLACED, PLACED], SOFT)},
    {*mk-Jockey*([LESTER, PLOD], [NORTHERN, BOY], MALE),
    mk-Jockey([FREDA, BLOGGS], [RED, WINE], FEMALE},
    [NEWMARKET, NEWCASTLE, AINTREE])

4.4.2 Construction of data type invariant

At this stage we include only the assertion 'Every jockey has a mount within the stable'. The state definition becomes:

    state *Stable* of
      hrs: *Horse*-set

    jks: *Jockey*-set
    rcl: *Races_left*
    `inv` *mk-Stable(hrs, jks, rcl)* $\triangle \forall j \in jks \cdot \exists h \in hrs \cdot j.mount = h.name$
  `end`

Exercise 4.3 Check that our state example *H*1 satisfies the state invariant.

4.4.3 Modelling of the system's operations

Let *WINNERS* be the operation that returns the set of all horses in the stable that have won a race. Then the operation only needs read permission on part of the system state:

  WINNERS ( ) *ws*: *Full_name*-set
  `ext rd` *hrs*: *Full_name*-set

The post-condition needs to form a *set* and in this case the use of *set comprehension* is advised. The output parameter should contain all those horses that:

1. Belong to the stable
2. Have been a winner in any of the season's races

(1) and (2) are the two predicates used in the set comprehension expression below. No pre-condition is necessary on this operation (it is defined on any state), hence we have:

  WINNERS ( ) *ws*: *Full_name*-set
  `ext rd` *hrs*: *Full_name*-set
  `pre` *true*
  `post` $ws = \{x.name \mid x \in Horse \cdot x \in hrs \land \text{WINNER} \in \text{elems } x.pos\}$

Applying the operation to *H*1 would give the result:

  $\{[\text{RED, WINE}]\}$

Let *UPDATE* be the operation that updates the state with the results of the (newly run) next race. Let us assume that the race results are a sequence of horse's names, such that the order in the sequence corresponds to their position in the race (thus the winner will be first in the sequence):

  Race_result = *Full_name**

The operation *UPDATE* will input the name of the meeting and the race results. The operation will change the horses' details and the sequence of race meetings left in the season. As a pre-condition to the operation, we insist that the input meeting has the same name as the head of the sequence of stored 'races left'. Also, in every race at least four horses must finish. The first part of *UPDATE* is therefore:

UPDATE (*meeting*: *Race*, *rr*: *Race_result*)
ext wr *hrs*: *Horse*-set
   wr *rcl*: *Races_left*
pre Len *rcl* > 0 ∧ *meeting* = hd *rcl* ∧ Len *rr* > 3

As an example input

meeting = NEWMARKET,
rr = [[MR, NOSY], [RED, WINE], [DICKENS], [PROOF, ASSISTANT], [NORTHERN, BOY]]

The post-condition is somewhat complex, so we start with an informal description of what is required, in terms of state components:

- *rcl* should have the name of the meeting that has taken place removed
- The new *hrs* component should be the union of the following sets:
  - All the horse records in the old state where the horse was not in the current race results
  - Updated horse records for the stable's horses that competed in the race

If state *H*1 was updated with the race results given above, then the new state, *H*2, would be:

mk-Stable({*mk-Horse*([RED, WINE],
[PLACED, WINNER, PLACED], GOOD),
mk-Horse([NORTHERN, BOY], [UNPLACED, UNPLACED, PLACED], SOFT)},
{*mk-Jockey*([LESTER, PLOD], [NORTHERN, BOY], MALE),
mk-Jockey([FREDA, BLOGGS], [RED, WINE, FEMALE)},
[NEWCASTLE, AINTREE])

The updated horse records are specified by stating that the relevant result must appear (in the output state) at the front of the corresponding sequence of race positions. Consider the problem of forming the set of new horse records for those horses that were second, third or fourth in the race. In the sequence *rr* of race results, which must be of length greater than three, we have (using the answer to Ex. 4.1(a)):

the horse that came second = second element of the list *rr* = hd (tl *rr*)

the horse that came third = third element of the list *rr* = hd (tl (tl *rr*))

the horse that came fourth = fourth element of the list *rr* = hd (tl (tl (tl *rr*)))

The new set of records for these three horses will be the same as the old, except that the value PLACED is put at the beginning of their *pos* component. To capture this set, we use the set comprehension facility in such a way that it specifies a collection of records. The set of the three updated horse records, for example, is given by:

$$\{mk\text{-}Horse(n, [\,placed\,] \frown s, g) \mid mk\text{-}Horse(n, s, g) \in \overleftarrow{hrs}$$
$$\cdot\, n \in \{\text{hd (tl } rr), \text{hd (tl (tl } rr)), \text{hd (tl (tl (tl } rr)))\}\}\}$$

Using the set comprehension technique, we can specify the other two sets, containing the winning horse and the unplaced horses respectively. The whole operation can be written:

UPDATE (*meeting*: *Race*, *rr*: *Race_result*)

ext wr *hrs*: *Horse*-set

    wr *rcl*: *Races_left*

pre len *rcl* $> 0 \land$ *meeting* $=$ hd *rcl* $\land$ len *rr* > 3

post *rcl* $=$ tl $\overleftarrow{rcl}$ $\land$

    hrs $= \{x \mid x \in \overleftarrow{hrs} \cdot x.name \notin$ elems *rr*$\} \cup$

    $\{mk\text{-}Horse(n, [\text{WINNER}] \frown s, g) \mid mk\text{-}Horse(n, s, g) \in \overleftarrow{hrs} \cdot n =$ hd *rr*$\} \cup$

    $\{mk\text{-}Horse(n, [\text{PLACED}] \frown s, g) \mid mk\text{-}Horse(n, s, g) \in \overleftarrow{hrs} \cdot$

        $n \in \{\text{hd (tl } rr), \text{hd (tl (tl } rr)), \text{hd (tl (tl (tl } rr)))\}\} \cup$

    $\{mk\text{-}Horse(n, [\text{UNPLACED}] \frown s, g) \mid mk\text{-}Horse(n, s, g) \in \overleftarrow{hrs} \cdot$

        $n \in ((\text{elems } rr) \backslash \{\text{hd } rr, \text{hd (tl } rr), \text{hd (tl (tl } rr)), \text{hd (tl (tl (tl } rr)))\})\}\}$

At this point we notice that the size of VDM post-conditions may start to be a problem. We will use two techniques to alleviate this: *user-defined functions*, introduced in the next chapter, and the *let* construct, introduced below. These methods can be used to factor out and decompose conditions in such a way that they not only look neater, but are also easier to understand.

Let *E* be an expression occurring within a larger expression (such as a large post-condition). The *let* construct allows us to evaluate *E* and bind that value to a variable name. Wherever *E* occurs in the larger expression, the variable name can be put in its place. Its full form in VDM is more general than this, possibly involving pattern matching, but the syntax that will be used here for the *let* clause is:

let *variable_name* $=$ *expression* in *large_expression*

The *let* construct can be nested, so that *large_expression* above could itself start with a *let* construct.

For example, the *UPDATE* operation can be restated thus:

UPDATE (*meeting*: *Race*, *rr*: *Race_result*)

ext wr *hrs*: *Horse*-set

    wr *rcl*: *Races_left*

pre len *rcl* $> 0 \land$ *meeting* $=$ hd *rcl* $\land$ len *rr* > 3

post let *stf_set* $= \{\text{hd (tl } rr), \text{hd (tl (tl } rr)), \text{hd (tl (tl (tl } rr)))\}$ in

let $last\_lot = (\text{elems } rr)\backslash(\{\text{hd } rr\} \cup stf\_set)$ in
$rcl = \text{tl } \overline{rcl} \wedge$
$hrs = \{x \mid x \in \overline{hrs} \cdot x.name \notin \text{elems } rr\} \cup$
$\{mk\text{-}Horse(n, [\text{WINNER}] \frown s, g) \mid mk\text{-}Horse(n, s, g) \in \overline{hrs} \cdot n = \text{hd } rr\} \cup$
$\{mk\text{-}Horse(n, [\text{PLACED}] \frown s, g) \mid mk\text{-}Horse(n, s, g) \in \overline{hrs} \cdot n \in stf\_set\} \cup$
$\{mk\text{-}Horse(n, [\text{UNPLACED}] \frown s, g) \mid mk\text{-}Horse(n, s, g) \in \overline{hrs} \cdot n \in last\_lot\}$

4.4.4 Proof obligations

The proof obligations for these operations turn out to be easy. Neither disturbs the relationship between jockey and horse, so the invariant is preserved. The existence of an output state in *UPDATE* is guaranteed, in essence, by the explicit nature of the post-condition—one can always evaluate the output state components given an input state.

Exercises 4.3

(a) Assuming the current state of the Stable is *H2*, use the definition of *UPDATE* to calculate a new state after the results of the next race are known:

$meeting = \text{NEWCASTLE}$
$rr = [[\text{PROOF, ASSISTANT}], [\text{MR, WHIPPY}], [\text{LEGINSKY}], [\text{SHERBAR}], [\text{RED, WINE}]]$

(b) Specify an operation *NUM_RACES_LEFT* which outputs the number of races left in the season.
(c) Extend the data type invariant to include the assertion 'No horse has the same name as a jockey'.
(d) When the stable acquires a new horse its favourite 'going' is determined, then its details are added to the system (initially it has no race record, so its '*pos*' value will be the empty sequence). Given the specification heading is:

ADD_NEW_HORSE(hname: Full_name, fgoing: Going)

complete the specification of this operation.

4.5 THE MAP DATA TYPE

4.5.1 Intuitive view of maps

VDM maps are data structures associating two sets of values, where each set is a subset of a predefined type. This association is a special kind of relation in that one set is called the *domain* of the map, the other the *range*, and every element in the domain is associated with exactly one element in the range. Maps were introduced as mathematical objects in Secs 2.4 and 2.5, but here we view them as a VDM built-in data type just like the Set or Sequence.

Assume *Person* and *Age* are predefined types. Declaring two state component variables (or operator parameters) *how_old* and *left_school* as maps associating values in *Person* with values in *Age* is written as follows:

$$how\_old: Person \xrightarrow{m} Age$$

$$left\_school: Person \xrightarrow{m} Age$$

Let us assume that these maps give someone's current age and the age someone left school respectively. The declarations tell us that the domain of maps *how_old* and *left_school* is a set of values from the type *Person*, their range is a set of values from the type *Age* and their map type is $Person \xrightarrow{m} Age$. An explicit representation for a map is allowed in VDM, the associated elements being simply listed together. Assuming *Person* and *Age* values are represented by tokens and numbers respectively, instances of our example maps could be:

$$how\_old = \{\text{BOB} \mapsto 18, \text{FREDA} \mapsto 20, \text{JIM} \mapsto 18\}$$

$$left\_school = \{\text{FREDA} \mapsto 16, \text{JIM} \mapsto 18\}$$

Each association in a map is called a *maplet*, so *how_old* contains three maplets and *left_school* contains two. The potential for using a mapping as a data structure can be seen by considering its major characteristic: every element in its domain is mapped to exactly one element in its range. Objects that display this property can be usefully modelled by maps—maps intrinsically hold the 'functional relationship' that is natural in some problems. Thus, in the examples above, the map tells us that the current age of a person is unique (no person can have two ages) and that the school leaving age of a person is unique. This is akin to the use of *keys* in databases—we want the data that a key allows a process to access to be functionally dependent on the key. We will see later that the use of maps tends to simplify data type invariants, since the functional relationship is held implicitly in the map.

A similar data structure to the Map is the familiar *array type*, used in most programming languages. There is a correspondence between them as follows:

- Array variable—*map name*
- Array index—*map domain*
- Array range—*map range*

For example, suppose that *Age* and *Person* had been suitably declared as types in a Pascal-like language. Declaring two Pascal array variables corresponding to our maps *how_old* and *left_school* would be written as:

$$how\_old: array[Person] \ of \ Age$$
$$left\_school: array[Person] \ of \ Age$$

In fact, the Map type is more abstract and general than the array. Arrays that feature in Pascal-like programming languages have at least the restriction that their index-type be ordinal; this condition may be stricter depending on the implementation language. The array concept was originally a machine-oriented idea, because it reflected the sequential storage arrangement in digital computers. Maps in VDM, on the other hand, have no restrictions on the types they are made up from and they reflect the mathematical notion of a map.

4.5.2 Map operations

In Sec. 4.5.1 we described how the user can declare and explicitly represent maps, given an explicit representation for their component types. As with the other VDM types, the Map has associated with it various well-defined primitive operations, some of which we list below:

- dom and rng dom takes a map and returns the set of domain values that the map is defined on, and rng returns the set of values that are mapped to in the range. For example:

    dom $how\_old = \{$BOB, FREDA, JIM$\}$
    dom $left\_school = \{$FREDA, JIM$\}$
    rng $how\_old = \{20, 18\}$
    rng $left\_school = \{16, 18\}$

- *Map application*   given a map f and a domain value v, map application returns the corresponding range value, written $f(v)$. For example:

    $how\_old($BOB$) = 18$
    $left\_school($FREDA$) = 16$

- †   this is termed 'overwrite' (recall it was introduced in Problem 2.17). It is an infix operator that manipulates two maps, say f and g, to produce a third map written $f \dagger g$. The map $f \dagger g$ is identical to g with one exception: on domain values where g is not defined, $f \dagger g$ is identical to f. Sometimes, $f \dagger g$ is described as the map f *overwritten* by g. The two arguments of † *must* be of the same Map type, meaning that f and g must have the same domain and range types. For example:

    $how\_old \dagger left\_school = \{$FREDA $\mapsto 16$, JIM $\mapsto 18$, BOB $\mapsto 18\}$
    $left\_school \dagger how\_old = \{$FREDA $\mapsto 20$, JIM $\mapsto 18$, BOB $\mapsto 18\}$

  Note that

    $left\_school \dagger how\_old = how\_old$

  because

    dom $left\_school \subseteq$ dom how_old

- *Map equality*   Two maps, f and g, are equal if and only if they have the same domain and their application on every domain element is identical. This can be expressed formally as:

    $f = g \Leftrightarrow$ dom $f =$ dom $g \land \forall x \in$ dom $g \cdot f(x) = g(x)$

The characteristic of any map f can be summed up by the logic condition:

$$\forall a, b \in \text{dom } f \cdot a = b \Rightarrow f(a) = f(b)$$

There are more operations associated with the Map type, notably *map comprehension* which is similar in operation to the set comprehension technique. Rather than introducing 'excess baggage' for the sake of it, we move on to some examples.

Example 4.1 Assume we are trying to model the state of execution of a program written in a simple language that has only a variable store and no explicit type declarations (as in some old dialects of the Basic programming language). Variable identifiers can be defined in VDM as tokens:

$Identifier = Token$

For variables' values we will use the natural numbers:

$Vals = \mathbb{N}$

Then, any program store, during program execution, can be represented as a mapping between the identifiers and their values:

state *Program_store* of
    $store: Identifier \xrightarrow{m} Vals$
end

At the start of any program, we could assume that each identifier is zero and model this with an operation *INIT*:

INIT( )
ext wr $store: Identifier \xrightarrow{m} Vals$
pre *true*
post $\forall i \in \text{dom } store \cdot store(i) = 0$

Now we can model a basic command in the programming language. Consider a simple assignment statement which is of the form:

$x := y$

where both x and y are identifiers. The operation for this could be written:

ASSIGNMENT(x, y: *Identifier*)
ext wr $store: Identifier \xrightarrow{m} Vals$
pre *true*
post $store = \overleftarrow{store} \dagger \{x \mapsto \overleftarrow{store}(y)\}$

Exercises 4.5

(a) Write an operation that specifies the assignment of a variable to a number.
(b) Write an operation for performing *multiple assignments* in the language. This would correspond to the action of the statement $x, y := u, w$ on the state, for identifiers x, y, u and w. You may assume that this has the same effect as the composition $x := u$; $y := w$.

4.6 THE SYMBOL TABLE

We will finish this chapter with a worked example that serves to show the use of the four main data structures in VDM: Sets, Sequences, Composites and Maps. Rather than showing the specification as a *fait accompli*, in which readers may be lost as to how the creators came to arrive at a particular representation, we will try to show a little of the mental process involved in specification construction.

4.6.1 Requirement

A common module required for a program compiler is a *symbol table*, a data structure that holds the attributes of all the identifiers in scope at a point in the text of a block structured program. Attributes of an identifier might denote whether it is a program variable, a constant or a function. If it is a variable, a further attribute would be its type. After reading the declaration:

   var x: integer;

in a Pascal program the compiler may update the symbol table with the information that identifier x has been declared as a variable, and is of type integer. During the execution of the compiler, the state of the symbol table will be affected by various operations as the focus of the compiler moves through the program text. In general, the following five operations are required (this example is inspired by Guttag's algebraic specification of a symbol table in Guttag (1977)):

1. *INIT*: set up a new symbol table.
2. *ENTER_BLOCK*: add a new scope to the program's block structure.
3. *ADD*: add an identifier and its attributes to the current block.
4. *LEAVE_BLOCK*: discard the current scoping block.
5. *RETRIEVE*: retrieve the attribute(s) of an identifier from the innermost declaration.

4.6.2 Creation of a system state: first attempt

Despite the order in our phased method of specification construction, it is always a good idea to keep in mind the operations required when deciding on a suitable data representation. We may still need several attempts before we arrive at the final one, however. The reader should not be deterred by this: the larger the application, the more trial and error is required to discover an appropriate representation. Considering the operations required, we might proceed along the following lines:

- A program's block structures can be nested to an arbitrary depth. Ordering of blocks is important (since the same identifier can be declared in more than one block) with the most recent declaration being the significant one. This suggests we use a Sequence type, with block declarations being added or removed from one end of the sequence, in a first-in-first-out manner, rather like a stack.
- In a particular block we can declare an arbitrary number of identifiers. The declarations do not have to be in any particular order, for example, in Pascal:

  var x: *real*; *y*: *integer*

  means the same as

  var y: *integer*; *x*: *real*

  Also we need to avoid repeated elements, so this suggests we use the Set type for each block.
- We require a structure to hold the identifier name and attributes, which will be retrieved by operation 5: since we need a fixed size structure with two components of different types, this suggests we use the Composite type.

VDM allows us to leave out the unnecessary details (at this stage) of what constitutes the types Identifier and Attribute. This is a useful form of abstraction, and helps to give specifications a more 'top-down' flavour. We need to give some concrete examples, however, so in the symbol tables given below, we have assumed:

Attribute = REAL | CHAR | INTEGER
Identifier = *Token*

A first attempt at the symbol table representation is then:

symbol_table = sequence of sets of identifier-attribute pairs

or in VDM syntax,

Pair:: *id*: *Identifier*
    att: *Attribute*

Block = *Pair*-set

Symbol_table = *Block**

state *Program_info* of
    s: *Symbol_table*
end

To summarize, each set in the sequence represents a group of identifiers declared in a block, the left-hand sets being the innermost and the last of the sequence being the outermost block. Any sequence of sets of pairs, where pairs are made up from a valid identifier and attribute, is then a state of this system model.

For example:

$$S1 = [\{mk\text{-}Pair(\text{X}, \text{INTEGER}), mk\text{-}Pair(\text{Y}, \text{CHAR})\}, \{mk\text{-}Pair(\text{X}, \text{REAL})\}]$$

is a valid instance of the symbol table. It represents the declarations of one *real* variable *x* within the outer block, and *integer* and *char* variables *x*, *y* within an inner block, of some notional program:

```
program exampleS1;
var x: real;
    . . . .

        procedure fred;
        var x: integer; y: char;
            . . . .
        †
        end;


    . . . .
    end;
```

S1 describes the scope of variables in the block at point †. But consider the following:

$$S2 = [\{mk\text{-}Pair(\text{X}, \text{INTEGER}), mk\text{-}Pair(\text{X}, \text{CHAR})\}, \{mk\text{-}Pair(\text{Z}, \text{REAL})\}]$$

This is a symbol table that is allowed by the model, but obviously violates the rules of a Pascal-like language, as can be seen by its program illustration:

```
program exampleS2;
var z: real;
    . . . .
        procedure fred;
        var x: integer; x: char;
            . . . .
        †
        end;
    . . . .
    end;
```

At this point we may move into the second phase of our systematic method and start to develop a data type invariant *inv* to restrict the type, so that *inv*(S1) would be true but *inv*(S2) would be false. Instead, we shall shift the representation to fit the problem more fully and leave this line of development to an exercise below.

4.6.3 Creation of the system state: a better attempt

As is often the case when creating VDM specifications, we may shorten or simplify *inv* by choosing a more apt representation. We noticed above that each declaration in the block consisted of two components: an identifier and its attribute. The symbol table model can be simplified by incorporating the constraint that the attribute of an identifier is *functionally dependent* on it (that is each identifier has a unique attribute). This can be done using a Map type to model the set of declarations in a block, and so we have:

symbol_table = sequence of (Identifier to Attribute maps)

or in VDM syntax

$Block = Identifier \xrightarrow{m} Attribute$

$Symbol\_table = Block*$

state *Program_info* of
   s: *Symbol_table*
end

$S2$ would not then be a valid data structure. $S1$ would be represented as a sequence of two maps:

$$S1 = [\{x \mapsto \text{INTEGER}, y \mapsto \text{CHAR}\}, \{x \mapsto \text{REAL}\}]$$

4.6.4 Construction of the data type invariant

The need for a data type invariant has been avoided by the map representation chosen above. Thus this representation is a good fit for the problem.

4.6.5 Modelling of the operations

Now we need to construct the operations with respect to the requirements outlined in the first section. The following operations are straightforward:

- *INIT*'s post-condition states that the new symbol table is modelled by the empty sequence.
- *ENTER_BLOCK* has the effect of adding a new, empty block, denoted by the *empty map* $\{\mapsto\}$, to the front of the block sequence. Its post-condition must state that this empty map is the head of the sequence of which the old symbol table is the tail.
- *LEAVE_BLOCK* is an operation that discards all the declarations in the current block. The output symbol table will therefore be the old table with its current block (that is the map at the hd of the sequence) removed.

   INIT( )
  ext wr *s*: *Symbol_table*
  pre *true*
  post *s* = [ ]

ENTER_BLOCK ( )
ext wr *s*: *Symbol_table*
pre *true*
post $s = [\{\mapsto\}] \frown \overleftarrow{s}$

LEAVE_BLOCK ( )
ext wr *s*: *Symbol_table*
pre $s \neq [\ ]$
post $s = \text{tl } \overleftarrow{s}$

The *ADD* operation has two pre-conditions: the symbol table must not be empty (otherwise there would be no block to *ADD* to) and the identifier to be added must not have already been declared in that block. In the post-condition the new state is the same as the old except that the new maplet $\{i \mapsto a\}$ is added to the map at the front of the sequence, representing the current block's symbols.

ADD (*i*: *Identifier, a*: *Attribute*)
ext wr *s*: *Symbol_table*
pre $s \neq [\ ] \wedge i \notin \text{dom (hd } s)$
post $s = [(\text{hd } \overleftarrow{s}) \dagger \{i \mapsto a\}] \frown \text{tl } \overleftarrow{s}$

The final operation, *RETRIEVE*, inputs an identifier value *i* and outputs an attribute value *a*. Note that:

- The pre-condition must check that *i* is actually declared somewhere in the block structure.
- The post-condition must specify that *a* is taken from the *innermost* block in which *i* is declared. To state this we use a function *get_from_table*, which searches through the sequence of blocks starting from the head of the sequence (we take the liberty of introducing a function before the next chapter, where they are discussed at length).
- Each element of the *Symbol_table* sequence *s* is a map. Applying the head of the sequence *s* to an identifier *i*, we obtain *i*'s corresponding attribute *a*. We use the notation (hd *s*)(*i*) for this form of map application below. For example, using the symbol table called *S*1 generated from the program example *S*1 above, (hd *S*1)(Y) would produce the result CHAR.

The function definition is thus:

get_from_table: *Symbol_table* × *Identifier* → *Attribute*
get_from_table(*s, i*) $\triangleq$
  if $i \in \text{dom (hd } s)$
  then (hd *s*)(*i*)
  else *get_from_table*(tl *s, i*)

and finally the operation *RETRIEVE* is defined using *get_from_table*:

RETRIEVE (*i*: *Identifier*) *a*: *Attribute*
ext rd *s*: *Symbol_table*

pre $\exists b \in$ elems $s \cdot i \in$ dom b
post $a = get\_from\_table(s, i)$

4.7 SUMMARY

This chapter introduced two more VDM data structures, the *Sequence* and the *Map*. We used the *Stack*, the *Stable*, and the *Symbol_table* examples to illustrate the steps involved in producing specifications.

- In the *Stack* example, we introduced the idea of reasoning with specifications.
- In the *Stable* example, we showed how data structures can be built up, and how the *let* clause could be used to structure post-conditions. The use of sequences and the set comprehension technique were also practised.
- In the *Symbol_table* example we specifically tried to show the kind of process that the reader might initially go through in creating specifications (after more practice, of course, one would probably make the correct choices first time!).

ADDITIONAL PROBLEMS

4.1 A particular symbol table consists of:
   (a) An outer block declaring two real variables x and y
   (b) An inner block declaring two integer variables z and y
   (c) An inner, inner block declaring two character variables x and z
   Represent this explicitly as a structure using both specification models discussed in Sec. 4.6.

4.2 Removing the need for a data type invariant alleviates the proof obligations to the extent of making assertion (3.13) redundant. Check that each symbol table operation that we have designed satisfies assertion (3.12).

4.3 Write the five operations on the symbol table given the initial representation. Create a data type invariant that will exclude blocks containing an identifier declared more than once.

4.4 Specify a stack without a size limit, called an *unbounded* stack, in VDM (the answer to this exercise is given in Chapter 9).

4.5 Write an operation called *UPDATE*3 for the Stable application which performs the same operation as the original *UPDATE*, except that its input is only allowed to contain a race result containing three or less horses.

4.6 Specify another two operations for the Stable application:
   (a) *FJOCKS* outputs a set of the names of all the female jockeys in the stable.
   (b) *SEASON_INIT* initializes the Stable information system at the beginning of the season. Actual jockeys and horses do not change, but the form of all the horses is empty, and a new sequence of races should be input.

REFERENCE

Guttag, J. (1977) Abstract Data Types and the Development of Data Structures, *Communications of the ACM*, **20**, 396–404.

5

BUILDING UP VDM SPECIFICATIONS

5.1 INTRODUCTION

In this chapter we discuss specifications of functions, which can be used as components for larger specifications in VDM. In the second half of this chapter one such component, a bounded, strong partial order, is constructed. It is then used as a building block for the case study in Chapter 6. The process of creating larger specifications requires intellectual and notational tools not unlike those used in programming. One must *decompose* the specification sensibly, and it is essential that the specification language itself has notational devices to support this. *Abstraction*, like decomposition, is another intellectual tool, where one concentrates on certain aspects of a specification while suppressing the details of other parts.

Of great importance in programming is the *module* concept, which helps in both decomposition and abstraction. A module construction (sometimes called a Package or a Class as well as a Module) provides an intermediate structuring device between the program and procedure levels. It is used best to encapsulate a bundle of procedures implementing operations on a data type. The advantage of this is that the module's well-defined interface can keep the data type it encapsulates secure and maintainable. A similar structuring device to the module can also be used at the specification level, to help in decomposition and abstraction, and such a device is at the heart of the *algebraic approach* described in Chapter 8 onwards. The VDM-SL standard also includes a module construct, allowing operations within a module to have their own local system state (for an introduction the interested reader can consult Chapter 9 in Jones (1990)). Although this gives the advantage of having a structuring device above the operation level, it also introduces problems of its own to do with extra notation and complexity.

Rather than using a module device which allows localized states, we will adopt a simpler approach, creating new data structures only with the use of functions. In other words, our building blocks will take the form of data structures which, while grounded in the VDM primitive data structures, are constructed and accessed by pure functions.

5.2 USER-DEFINED FUNCTIONS

It is often convenient to structure and simplify specifications with user-defined functions. For example, in the symbol table example of Chapter 4 we created a user-defined function *get_from_table* which searched through the symbol table for a particular identifier. The post-condition of *RETRIEVE* determined the value of its output parameter as the result of the function *get_from_table*.

In the two previous chapters we have seen the method of building up and accessing a data structure, representing a state, using operations on the state. Instances of the state are identified with the values of a composite data structure. In this chapter we will temporarily abandon the idea of a VDM state; the reader should see that, using only functions, one can build up *the whole specification of a data structure*. After all, the VDM state was only introduced as a convenience, and is best employed in an application where operations access part of a complex state, leaving the rest unchanged. To translate a specification into one consisting only of functions, one needs do little more than represent the external state with input and output state parameters (although there are some complications as we shall see later when we re-examine the definition of functions). The *Symbol_table*'s operations can all be re-expressed as functions, for instance the *ADD* operation would be:

> ADD (*i*: *Identifier*, *a*: *Attribute*, *s_in*: *Symbol_table*) *s_out*: *Symbol_table*
> pre $s\_in \neq [\ ] \land i \notin \text{dom (hd } s\_in)$
> post $s\_out = [(\text{hd } s\_in) \dagger \{i \mapsto a\}] \frown (\text{tl } s\_in)$

The input and output states are here represented as the input and output parameters *s_in* and *s_out*.

Within their pre- and post-conditions, VDM operations *cannot* have references to (or *call*) other operations that are not functions. The reason for this was explained in Section 3.5.3: conditions are logical formulae, which, given values for their parameters, are meant to evaluate to true or false. Operations which may as a side effect change the system state should not therefore appear in these logical formulae. Thus larger specifications should be structured using function calls within their pre- and post-conditions. In particular, if a structured data type is to be used as a building block for a specification, then functions must be used to construct, manipulate and access the type.

5.2.1 Function definitions in VDM

Mathematical functions were introduced in Chapter 2: here we remind the reader of their two defining characteristics, since functions in VDM must also conform to them. Given that a function has a number of typed arguments (represented by parameters) which are supplied with values, the following two properties are always true:

- A function evaluates to (or *returns*) a unique, single value of a predetermined type.
- The value a function returns depends *only* on the values of its arguments.

Functions can be thought of as operations that do not access an external state, and that have exactly one output parameter whose value is unique for any given set of input values.

In VDM there are two ways to define functions: *implicitly* or *explicitly*. Functions are implicitly defined in VDM in exactly the same way as operations, that is their output value is specified by stating a property or relationship that the value must satisfy. The definition must be restricted of course so that exactly one output parameter is used, and no external state is accessed. In this sense *functional* operations are simply a special case of the general operation idea.

The exponent example in Sec. 3.2.1 can be specified using an implicit function definition:

$EXPONENT\ (x:\mathbb{Z},\ n:\mathbb{N})\ y:\mathbb{Z}$
pre *true*
post $y = x^n$

$EXPONENT$ is a function because it returns one output value which is unique for a given set of inputs, and this output value is dependent solely on those inputs (that is *no external state is accessed*).

Now consider the definition of INT_SQR, another example from Chapter 3:

$INT\_SQR\,(x:\mathbb{N})\,z:\mathbb{N}$
pre $x \geqslant 1$
post $(z^2 \leqslant x) \wedge (x < (z+1)^2)$

Although INT_SQR has one output parameter and does not access an external state, it is not obvious that only one output value satisfies its post-condition for any given input parameter value. In fact, in Sec. 3.2.2 we provided just such a proof, one that showed z to be uniquely determined by the value of x, and the fact that INT_SQR specifies a function follows.

Exercises 5.1

(a) Exercise 4.2(c) asked you to re-specify the *Stack* type without the use of an external state. Are all the *Stack* operations converted into functions this way? In particular, how can the *POP* operation be translated to a functional equivalent? (This problem is discussed further in Chapter 8.)

(b) Compare the definition and use of functions as used in programming languages with the mathematical definition given above. In Pascal, for example, the value of a function may not depend solely on its parameter's values; it could depend on the value of a *global* variable, or on values read from an external file. Can you see any other differences?

(c) You may have noticed a similarity between map application in Sec. 4.5.2 and function evaluation. Investigate the general connection between the Map data structure and the function concept introduced above.

5.2.2 Proof obligations for implicitly-defined functions

Implicit function specifications incur proof obligations on the specifier as do general VDM operations. One should check that the function's post-condition can be satisfied—that is there exists a valid output value that makes the post-condition true for any set of valid inputs that make the pre-condition true (where *valid* means of the correct type). In particular, a function that *constructs* a new value of a user-defined data type should be checked to ensure that its output value always satisfies that data type's invariant, if one exists (for example, the explicit specification of *ADD* at the beginning of Sec. 5.2 creates new symbol tables). One should also make sure that the post-condition is satisfied by exactly one value, for any set of valid inputs.

Adapting condition (3.10) of Chapter 3, this idea is captured thus

$$\forall i_1, \ldots, i_n \in inputs \cdot pre\text{-}op(i_1, \ldots, i_n) \Rightarrow \exists! o \in output \cdot post\text{-}op(i_1, \ldots, i_n, o) \qquad (5.1)$$

where *inputs* is a list of the type names associated with each of the input parameters, and by $\exists! o$ we mean *there exists exactly one o*. Given a function defined by a post-condition that relates input to output in an implicit way (such as the *INT_SQR* post-condition), it may not be easy to show that the post-condition is satisfiable. Also, if the output type's invariant is non-trivial, it may be necessary to adopt a two-step argument to show that the output value satisfies its invariant (which is similar to verifying the truth of conditions (3.12) and (3.13) in Chapter 3).

5.2.3 Explicitly-defined functions

Explicitly-defined functions are those for which we can use the definition to calculate an output, given input values for the function's arguments. The explicit definition usually involves recursion, and is in a sense less abstract than an implicit definition. This is because there may be many ways of calculating an output value that satisfies the implicit definition's post-condition. Explicit definitions therefore involve a commitment to a particular algorithm, and as such are close to implementations themselves.

The explicit function definition is separated into a signature and a meaning (in common with the algebraic approach expounded later in this book, and with modern functional programming languages). The signature has the form:

function_name:*input_types*→*output_type*

If there is more than one type in the input then the type names will be separated by the '×' symbol. For example, the signature of *get_from_table* in Sec. 4.6 is

get_from_table:*Symbol_table* × *Identifier* → *Attribute*

The meaning of a function is expressed on the right-hand side of the '≙' sign, and the full form of a function definition is thus:

function_name:*input_types*→*output_type*
function_name(*input parameters*) ≙
    expression

The *expression* may contain parameters, constants, built-in functions, predicates and user-defined functions. It can also take the form of a selection statement as follows:

function_name:*input_types*→*output_type*
function_name(*input parameters*) ≙
    if *boolean_expression*
    then *expression*
    else *expression*

In particular, the selection statement may be nested, and may involve recursion. The function *get_from_table* of Chapter 4 is an example defined in this way:

get_from_table:*Symbol_table* × *Identifier* → *Attribute*

get_from_table(*s*, *i*) ≙
    if *i* ∈ dom (hd *s*)
    then (hd *s*) (*i*)
    else *get_from_table*(tl *s*, *i*)

As another example, consider a specification of the *factorial* function. An explicit definition is:

factorial:$\mathbb{N}$→$\mathbb{N}$
factorial(*n*) ≙
    if $n \geqslant 1$
    then $n \times factorial\,(n-1)$
    else 1

5.2.4 Proof obligations for explicitly-defined functions

For an explicitly-defined function f which constructs a new value of a type, we are obliged to demonstrate that the data type invariant holds on every output value.

We can derive this result by considering a version of condition (5.1) that makes the invariant on the output parameter o explicit:

$$\forall i_1, \ldots, i_n \in inputs \cdot pre\text{-}op(i_1, \ldots, i_n) \Rightarrow \exists! o \in output \cdot post\text{-}op(i_1, \ldots, i_n, o) \wedge inv(o)$$

An explicitly defined function f does not have pre- and post-conditions as such, and the value of o is given by function evaluation (applying the definition of f to the input values). The proof obligation in this case reduces to:

$$\forall i_1, \ldots, i_n \in inputs \cdot inv(f(i_1, \ldots, i_n)) \tag{5.2}$$

If the function f involves recursion and selection, this expression is not straightforward to prove true. In particular, if f involves recursion, we should, strictly speaking, provide a proof that the recursion is eventually going to terminate, given any legal input values.

5.2.5 The relationship between implicit and explicit functions

Explicit function definitions can be thought of as *implementations* for a corresponding implicit definition. In fact one path towards the proof of satisfiability of an implicitly defined function f_i is to create an *explicit* function f_x whose definition *satisfies* f_i. This means that f_x must output a unique value that makes the post-condition of f_i true for any values input that make f_i's pre-condition true (see Fig. 5.1).

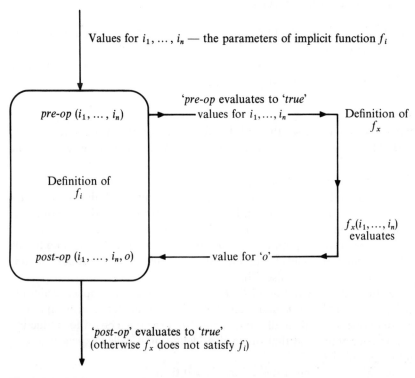

Figure 5.1 Explicit function f_x satisfies implicit function f_i.

The *EXPONENT* example of Sec. 3.2 çan be defined explicitly by function *exponent_x*:

$exponent\_x : \mathbb{Z} \times \mathbb{N} \to \mathbb{Z}$
$exponent\_x(x, n) \triangleq$
   if $n = 0$
   then 1
   else $x \times exponent\_x(x, n-1)$

In his most recent book on VDM (Jones 1990), Jones devotes several pages to proving formally that explicit definitions satisfy implicit ones. Constructing such proofs needs a high degree of mathematical maturity on the part of the specifier: an in-depth discussion is therefore beyond the scope of this book, but we do provide an example below.

5.2.6 An inductive proof

The general mathematical method for proving that an explicit function definition satisfies an implicit one is to use the *induction* technique on the input values of one of the parameters. The procedure is to:

- Prove that satisfaction holds for a *base* case.
- Prove that if the satisfaction property holds for some arbitrary input value, then it will hold when that input value is incremented.

Having proved these two cases, the law of induction says that the satisfaction property holds for all values of the input.

Understanding induction is easy if we relate it to the physical analogy of knocking down *dominoes*. Imagine a collection of dominoes standing up in a line, all close enough so that if one falls it will knock down its neighbour. If it was known that:

- Someone was going to knock down the end domino in the direction of its neighbour.
- If *any* one of the dominoes were to fall, it would knock down its neighbour in the direction of fall,

then we would believe correctly that all the dominoes were going to fall down, *no matter how many of them there were*. The base case in induction corresponds to the end domino; the assumption that 'the property we are trying to prove is true for an arbitrary value of the input type' corresponds to the hypothesis that an arbitrary domino N was going to fall. Finally, proving that the property holds for an incremented value of the input corresponds to showing that N's neighbour would also fall.

We will show that the explicit definition of $EXPONENT$ satisfies our implicit definition by induction on its first parameter n and keep the other parameter x arbitrary. If a function has more than one input, then all inputs apart from the one chosen for induction must be kept arbitrary. Keep in mind that the *explicit* definition is called *exponent_x*, and the *implicit* definition is called $EXPONENT$.

First the *base* case: from the explicit definition, if $n=0$ then

$$exponent\_x(x, 0) = 1$$

If we substitute this output value '1' for the parameter 'y' which represents the output in the post-condition of $EXPONENT$, the condition evaluates to true and so is satisfied. Hence we have proved the base case.

For $n \geqslant 1$, using the definition of *exponent_x*, its output is:

$$exponent\_x(x, n) = x \times exponent\_x(x, n-1) \tag{5.3}$$

Again, if we substitute this output value $x \times exponent\_x(x, n-1)$ for the parameter y in the post-condition of $EXPONENT$, and it evaluates to true, then we have proved satisfiability. With this substitution, the post-condition is:

$$x \times exponent\_x(x, n-1) = x^n$$

Assume for the purposes of the induction proof that the explicit definition satisfied the post-condition for value $n-1$, that is

$y = exponent\_x(x, n-1)$

satisfies the post-condition:

$y = x^{n-1}$

which implies:

$$x^{n-1} = exponent\_x(x, n-1) \tag{5.4}$$

We now have to show that the truth of the result for $(n-1)$ implies the truth of the result for n. Using Eq. (5.4) to substitute x^{n-1} for $exponent\_x(x, n-1)$ in Eq. (5.3), we have:

$x \times x^{n-1} = x^n$

which evaluates to true by the properties of exponentiation and the fact that we have assumed $n \geqslant 1$. It follows that, since the result is true for $n=0$ (the established base case), it is also true for $n=1$. Since it is true for $n=1$, it must be true for $n=2, \ldots$, and so on.

5.2.7 Induction and proof obligations

In the last section, if the data type of the input parameter was other than $\mathbb{N}$, induction can still be used in a generalized form called *structural induction*. We will return to this topic in Chapter 12, since the principle of mathematical induction is also used in discharging proof obligations for algebraic specifications.

The reader may also see the connection between induction and discharging the proof obligation of condition (3.13). Setting aside the problem of the *existence* of an implementation of an operator's specification, in discharging the proof obligations we are effectively performing a kind of inductive argument that a property is true for all instances of the state that can be generated. In this case, the property we are trying to prove for all instances is none other than the state invariant (i.e. the state's data type invariant).

The assumption that the pre-condition and the state invariant on the input state is true for an operator OP is similar to the inductive assumption that the 'property holds for $n-1$'. Proving it follows that the invariant is true on the output state generated by OP is therefore akin to the induction step of proving that 'the property holds for n'. The essential connection is that while '$+1$' generates the next value in type $\mathbb{N}$, OP generates the 'next' value of the VDM state.

Exercise 5.2 Write an explicit definition for INT_SQR. Show by induction on its input value that it satisfies the implicit definition (an answer to the first part of the question is given at the beginning of Chapter 6).

5.2.8 Partial functions

A total function is one that is defined for all argument values that satisfy its type definition; in other words, for every value in the domain type of the function, there is a corresponding (unique) range value. A *partial* function is one that is undefined for some values of its input type (see Sec. 2.5.4). If an implicit function has a pre-condition (other than '*true*') then it is a partial function, and the result of calling the function with parameter values that do not satisfy the pre-condition is undefined. The definition of *INT_SQR* is an example of a *partial function* since it is undefined for $n = 0$.

The problem with *partial* functions is that as functions, they are allowed to appear in expressions in other function definitions, and in pre- and post-conditions of operations. The question then arises, how do they evaluate in an expression if the binding of values to parameters makes their pre-condition false?

To avoid functions that can return 'undefined' values, one might conjecture that the types of the parameters could be designed and constrained so that the function is total. This solution relies on the designer to 'push the pre-conditions into the parameter type definitions'. We could easily make *INT_SQR* a total function in this way:

$positive\_nums = \mathbb{N}$

inv $positive\_nums(n) \triangleq n > 0$

$INT\_SQR(x : positive\_nums)\ z : \mathbb{N}$
pre *true*
post $(z^2 \leqslant x) \wedge (x < (z+1)^2)$

The flaw with this approach is that the 'undefined-ness' of the function may depend on two or more of its parameters rather than one as in this example. These two or more parameters would have to be merged into one by putting their types together in a composite, allowing a suitable data type invariant to be put on the composite. This data type invariant would effectively do the job of the pre-condition of the operation. In general though, this process proves messy and unnatural.

In fact VDM has associated with it a 'Logic of Partial Functions' (called LPF) which allows logical expressions three values: true, false and undefined. 'undefined' is the value returned if the function's pre-conditions are not met. This can be used to give expressions involving partial functions a sound semantics, but in the general field of formal specification it is not a standard solution. In this book our aim is to allow the reader to take a first step towards constructing sound specifications, hence we will sidestep this controversial issue by insisting that functions are defined total whenever possible. That said, we have already relied on the intuitive notion that 'false and undefined' evaluates to 'false'. For example, consider the pre-condition of the *UPDATE* operation in Chapter 4 in the case where there are no races left. Although the first predicate evaluates to false in this case, the next predicate is undefined.

5.3 THE SPECIFICATION OF A PARTIAL ORDER

5.3.1 Weak and strong partial orders

A sequence is sometimes called a total ordering because all its elements are in a strict linear order (although the use of *total* to describe orderings should not be confused with its use in describing functions, as in *total function*). A set with an ordering on its elements in which some but not necessarily all the elements are ordered is called a partially ordered set or a *poset*. As a motivating example for the application of posets (and as a grounding for our case study in Chapter 6), we will use a poset data structure to represent the necessary ordering of actions in a simple home decorating plan. Figure 5.2 shows a graphical representation of an example plan structure, a plan to paint a wall, a ceiling and a ladder. Nodes in this partial order represent the execution of actions, and arcs represent a temporal precedence between two actions. This example will be referred to as the 'Painting World'.

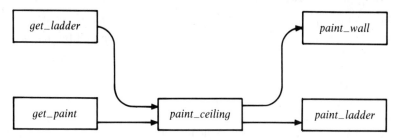

Figure 5.2 A partial ordering of actions in the Painting World.

The actions in the figure are constrained by the minimum ordering necessary to ensure that all the action's pre-conditions are achieved, and no goal achieved by one action is undone by the effects of another. For example, if we painted the ceiling *after* painting the ladder, we might well find ourselves having to repaint the ladder later. Programs that reason with actions to produce such plans are called *automatic planners*. In the next chapter we will specify an automatic planning program that relies on a partial order, such as this one, as one of its data structures. In fact, the 'Painting World' is formalized in Exercises 6.2.

In Sec. 2.6.3 the idea of a weak partial order was introduced and defined by the axioms of *transitivity*, *reflexivity* and *antisymmetry*. A *weak* poset is characterized by the reflexivity axiom, that is the statement 'x is ordered before x' is always true. A typical weak poset is the natural numbers with '$\leqslant$' as the ordering relation. Within this model, '$n \leqslant n$' is true for all $n \in \mathbb{N}$.

In the Painting World, the poset relation is one of time, and the things it relates are actions. We can call the relation informally 'is before': thus it is true in Fig. 5.2 that *get_paint* 'is before' *paint_ladder*, but it is not true that *paint_ceiling* 'is before' *get_paint*. Unfortunately, a collection of actions with the ordering relation 'is before' is not a model that fits the weak poset theory because of the reflexivity axiom: this would assert

'for all actions *x*, *x* is before *x*'

and as we know, actions are not executed before themselves! In fact, we want 'action x is before action x' to be *false* for all actions.

Instead this model fits what is called a *strong* partial order, which is defined by the axioms of *transitivity* and *irreflexivity*. If 't' stands for the strong poset relations on a set S then these axioms are:

$\forall x \in S \cdot \neg\, t(x, x)$ (*irreflexivity*)
$\forall x, y, z \in S \cdot t(x, y) \wedge t(y, z) \Rightarrow t(x, z)$ (*transitivity*)

As shown in Fig. 5.2, the partial order can be visualized as a special kind of directed graph consisting of nodes and directed arcs. In such a diagrammatic interpretation, the mathematical axioms make the graph 'acyclic', meaning that one cannot start at a node, follow the directed arcs, and end up back at the same node.

5.3.2 A plan as a strong partial order of actions

If we formalize the temporal ordering relation in the Painting World so that 'x is before y' is written $before(x, y)$, and let the set of possible nodes in the poset be denoted by *Actions*, then these axioms can be rewritten:

$\forall x \in Actions \cdot \neg\, before(x, x)$
$\forall x, y, z \in Actions \cdot before(x, y) \wedge before(y, z) \Rightarrow before(x, z)$

Then, for two nodes x and y, the relation $before(x, y)$ is true if and only if:

- There is a directed arc connecting x to y; or
- There is a sequence of two or more arcs connecting x and y

The action instances in the poset form a *base set* of nodes. Assuming that the base set is the following:

$\{get\_ladder,\ get\_paint,\ paint\_ceiling,\ paint\_ladder,\ paint\_wall\}$

then the relational instances asserted true by Fig. 5.2 are given in set R below:

$R = \{before(get\_ladder,\ paint\_ceiling),\ before(get\_paint,\ paint\_ceiling)$
$before(get\_ladder,\ paint\_wall),\ before(get\_paint,\ paint\_wall)$
$before(get\_ladder,\ paint\_ladder),\ before(get\_paint,\ paint\_ladder)$
$before(paint\_ceiling,\ paint\_ladder),\ before(paint\_ceiling,\ paint\_wall)\}$

In mathematics such objects as posets tend to be static, whereas in computing we need to build up and manipulate them dynamically during the course of program execution. Likely requirements for changing a poset might be the addition of an arc from some node x to some node y, or the addition of more elements into the base set. In the Painting World the addition of such an arc corresponds to putting a temporal constraint between actions, and can be read as 'x must occur before y'. Generally, the set of true relations R will change after arc addition, and the exercises below explore this in more detail.

Exercises 5.3

(a) As in Sec. 5.3.2 above, let the set of all relational instances asserted true in the Painting World be denoted by *R*. Would adding an arc from *get_ladder* to *paint_wall* change *R*? Under what conditions does adding an arc between nodes in a poset *not* change the set of relational instances such as *R*?

(b) (i) Add an arc from *paint_wall* to *paint_ladder* in Fig. 5.2, and write down the set of true relational instances *Q* that the new directed graph now asserts.

(ii) Verify that $R \subseteq Q$.

(iii) Now let *P* be the set of relational instances obtained by (legally) adding *any* arc to two nodes in the figure. Give reasons why the relation $R \subseteq P$ is necessarily true.

(c) This question follows on from Exercise 5.3(b). A strong poset *p* can be said to define a *set S(p)* whose elements are sequences of all the nodes within the poset, *and* every sequence conforms to the ordering constraints in *p*. That is:

$S(p) = \{s \,|\, s$ contains the same nodes as the base set of p and all the orderings in p are preserved by $s\}$

For example, all the orderings in Fig. 5.2 are preserved by the sequences:

[*get_ladder, get_paint, paint_ceiling, paint_ladder, paint_wall*]

[*get_paint, get_ladder, paint_ceiling, paint_wall, paint_ladder*]

and hence these two sequences are members of this set. The sequence:

[*get_paint, paint_ceiling, paint_ladder, get_ladder, paint_wall*]

is not a member of *S(p)* because it does not conform to all the relations imposed by the ordering, such as *before(get_ladder, paint_ceiling)*.

(i) Construct the whole set *S(p)* for the Painting World (you only need to find another two sequences as well as the two given above).

(ii) Construct an argument showing that if an arc is added to *p* to make it into another ordering *q* (without introducing a cycle), then:

$S(q) \subseteq S(p)$

(d) Prove that the *antisymmetry* property:

$\forall x, y \in S \cdot t(x, y) \Rightarrow \neg t(y, x)$

is a logical consequence of the *transitivity* and *irreflexivity* axioms. Now show that, given *transitivity* and *antisymmetry*, the *irreflexivity* property holds.

Exercise 5.3(d) shows that a strong partial order can be defined by the *transitivity* and *irreflexivity* axioms OR by *transitivity* and *antisymmetry*.

5.3.3 Developing the specification

Assume a module in a computer system is needed to create, store and update a strong partial order on a set of objects. To formally define the required poset we follow a modified method to the one in Chapter 3, as introduced at the beginning of this chapter. We specify operations (to create partial orders) that are pure functions, in particular, they do not access an external state.

In developing the specification we use the graphical nomenclature of nodes and arcs because it has a general but simple interpretation. The operations we require to build up the partial order are initialization, node addition and arc addition. Node addition is required because it is conceivable that a node can be in the partial order, but not related to any of the other existing nodes. In developing a plan for the Painting World, we might add an action to the plan that could be executed in any position with respect to the other actions (such as 'make a cup of tea').

The three functions that we require to construct partial orders are:

- *init_poset'* — creates the empty partial order
- *add_node'* — adds a new node to the base set of the partial order
- *make_before'* — adds an arc between two nodes x and y from the base set, to ensure x is before y.

Primes are used on the end of names to distinguish them from names used in an extension of this specification in Sec. 5.4.

5.3.4 Creation of the partial order data type

A token set will suffice to represent the possible nodes in the partial order although we will use lower case character strings to represent them. Consideration of the required operations *add_node'* and *make_before'* suggests that we represent nodes in the base set, and the arcs between them, in separate components. An arc between nodes is captured here using a composite type, whose first component is the node at the source of an arc, and whose second is the node at the destination. The component types of the poset are thus

$Node = Token$

$Arc :: source : Node$
$\qquad dest \quad : Node$

A poset is defined as a composite of arcs and nodes:

$Poset :: nodes : Node\text{-set}$
$\qquad arcs \quad : Arc\text{-set}$

Nodes that are not referenced in the *Arc*-set are assumed to be unordered.

5.3.5 The data type invariant

One obvious invariant of our representation of a poset p is that all the nodes contained in the *arcs* component are also present in the base set, *nodes*:

$$(\{a.source \,|\, a \in p.arcs\} \cup \{a.dest \,|\, a \in p.arcs\}) \subseteq p.nodes$$

We also need to exclude any orderings allowed by this definition that are not valid partial orders. The type definition will therefore be constrained with an invariant that incorporates the strong partial order axioms. Using the result of Exercise 5.3(d), we let these axioms be *transitivity* and *antisymmetry*.

In the graphical interpretation, the invariant will disallow *cycles*. Figure 5.3 shows an example of a relation which is not a partial order, as it contains a cycle and invalidates the *antisymmetry* axiom.

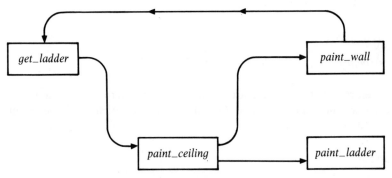

Figure 5.3   An ordering which contains a cycle.

To exclude orderings that contain cycles we phrase the invariant as follows:

'For any nodes x and y, it cannot be the case that following a sequence of directed arcs we can get from x to y *and* following another sequence of directed arcs we can also get from y to x.'

or more concisely:

'for any nodes x and y, it cannot be the case that x is ordered before y *and* y is ordered before x.'

The 'is ordered before' relation is defined via a function that, given two node identifiers x and y, and an arc set, returns true if x is constrained by the ordering to be before y, and false otherwise. This is identical to computing whether *before*(x, y) is in the set of relational instances asserted true by the poset's graph (as explained in Sec. 5.3.2).

The function's signature is as follows:

before$: Node \times Node \times Arc\text{-set} \rightarrow \mathbb{B}$

If there is an arc from node x to node z in arc set *as*, then *before*(x, z, as) is true:

mk-Arc$(x, z) \in as \Rightarrow before(x, z, as)$

The *transitivity* axiom gives us another way of finding out whether two nodes x and y satisfy *before*

$$(\exists y \in get\_nodes(as) \cdot before(x, y, as) \wedge before(y, z, as)) \Rightarrow before(x, z, as)$$

where *get_nodes* collects the set of nodes in an arc set:

> *get_nodes*: *Arc*-set → *Node*-set
> *get_nodes(as)* ≙
>   {*a.source* | *a* ∈ *as*} ∪ {*a.dest* | *a* ∈ *as*}

Putting the two components of *before* together, we arrive at a final definition:

> *before*: *Node* × *Node* × *Arc*-set → $\mathbb{B}$

> *before(x, z, as)* ≙
>   *mk-Arc(x, z)* ∈ *as* ∨
> $\exists y \in get\_nodes(as) \cdot before(x, y, as) \wedge before(y, z, as)$

In other words, x is before z if there is an arc from x to z or there is a sequence of arcs involving at least one intervening node y. Our data type complete with invariant follows:

> *Poset* :: *nodes*: *Node*-set
>   *arcs* : *Arc*-set

> inv *mk-Poset(nodes, arcs)* ≙
>   *get_nodes(arcs)* ⊆ *nodes* ∧
> $\forall x, y \in nodes \cdot \neg (before(x, y, arcs) \wedge before(y, x, arcs))$

Exercise 5.4

(a) Let p represent the poset in Fig. 5.2. Write down an explicit representation of p using the data type we have just constructed.

(b) Another useful function we could define is called *possibly_before*. Given two nodes x and y in the base set, and a set of arcs *as*, *possibly_before(x, y, as)* returns true if it is possible to add arc *mk-Arc(x, y)* to *as* without introducing a cycle into *as*, and false otherwise. For example:

> *possibly_before(get_ladder, get_paint, as)* is true
> *possibly_before(paint_ladder, get_paint, as)* is false

where *as* represents the arcs in the poset in Fig. 5.2. The signature for the required function is:

> *possibly_before*: *Node* × *Node* × *Arc*-set → $\mathbb{B}$

Complete the definition of *possibly_before*. (Hint: use the previously defined function *before*.) If *as* has no cycles, and *before*(*x*, *y*, *as*) is true, what can you say about the truth of *possibly_before*(*x*, *y*, *as*)?

5.3.6 Modelling the operations

The specification of the three constructors (that is, those functions that construct posets) is now quite straightforward and requires little explanation. The function *init_poset'* initializes the poset to be empty:

$init\_poset'$: $\rightarrow Poset$
$init\_poset'(\ )$ ≜
  $mk\text{-}Poset(\{\ \},\{\ \})$

The operation *add_node'* adds node *u* to the base set:

add_node' : $Node \times Poset \rightarrow Poset$
$add\_node'(u, p)$ ≜
  $mk\text{-}Poset(p.nodes \cup \{u\}, p.arcs)$

while *make_before'* adds an ordering of two nodes, *u* and *v*, to the current partial ordering. To ensure that the poset remains valid, we must check that *u* *can* be put before *v* without introducing a cycle. We do this using the *possibly_before* function of Exercise 5.4:

$make\_before'$: $Node \times Node \times Poset \rightarrow Poset$
$make\_before'(u, v, p)$ ≜
  if $possibly\_before(u, v, p.arcs)$
  then $mk\text{-}Poset(p.nodes \cup \{u, v\}, p.arcs \cup \{mk\text{-}Arc(u, v)\})$

5.3.7 Proof obligations

As we are dealing with explicitly defined functions, the proof obligation equation (5.2) will be employed.

Proof obligation for *init_poset'*
The output value of *init_poset'* is:

$mk\text{-}Poset(\{\ \},\{\ \})$

The invariant bound to this value of the poset is:

$\{\ \} \subseteq \{\ \} \wedge$
$\forall x, y \in \{\ \} \cdot \neg (before(x, y, \{\ \}) \wedge before(y, x, \{\ \}))$

which evaluates to true.

Proof obligation for *make_before'*
We need to show that

> *inv* (if *possibly_before(u, v, p.arcs)*
> then *mk-Poset(p.nodes* ∪ {*u, v*}, *p.arcs* ∪ {*mk-Arc(u, v)*}))

is true, assuming *inv*(*p*) holds. In other words, given *possibly_before(u, v, p.arcs)* is true, we need to prove:

> *inv* (*mk-Poset(p.nodes* ∪ {*u, v*}, *p.arcs* ∪ {*mk-Arc(u, v)*}))

The first condition in the invariant is:

> *get_nodes(arcs)* ⊆ *nodes*

where in this case:

> *nodes* = *p.nodes* ∪ {*u, v*}

and

> *arcs* = *p.arcs* ∪ {*mk-Arc(u, v)*}

The truth of the first condition follows, because:

> *inv*(*p*)
> ⇒ *get_nodes(p.arcs)* ⊆ *p.nodes*
> ⇒ *get_nodes(p.arcs* ∪ {*mk-Arc(u, v)*}) ⊆ (*p.nodes* ∪ {*u, v*})

It is not obvious or particularly easy to show formally that the second condition of the invariant is true:

> ∀*x, y* ∈ *nodes* · ¬ (*before(x, y, arcs)* ∧ *before(y, x, arcs)*)

but an informal argument will be used to show that it is the case. The second condition states that there is no sequence of connected arcs from one node to another in the partial order—we must show this is true of the poset output from *make_before'*. We first need to state the definition of *possibly_before* (and hence the answer to Exercise 5.4) which is:

> *possibly_before*: *Node* × *Node* × Arc-set → $\mathbb{B}$
> *possibly_before(x, y, p)* ≜
>   *x* ≠ *y* ∧ ¬ *before(y, x, p)*

From the definition of *possibly_before(u, v, p.arcs)* we have

> ¬ *before(v, u, p.arcs)*

which asserts that there is no sequence of connected arcs from v to u in the valid partial order p. Hence, introducing an arc from u to v will not introduce a cycle going through these two nodes. If it introduced a cycle between u and another node z, then that cycle would have to go through arc v (if not the input ordering would not have been a valid poset), which contradicts what we have already established. Hence the new poset satisfies the data type invariant.

Exercises 5.5

(a) Discharge the proof obligation for *add_node'*.
(b) We will define a poset p to be a completion of another poset q if p and q contain the same set of nodes *and* for any nodes x and y, if x is ordered before y in q, then x is also ordered before y in p. Formally specify this relation between posets in VDM, giving it the following signature:

$$is\_completion\_of : Poset \times Poset \rightarrow \mathbb{B}$$

(c) Inserting the arc *before(get_ladder, paint_wall)* into the poset represented in Fig. 5.2 is redundant as it does not change the poset. Modify the definition of *make_before'* so that it does not add superfluous arcs into the *Poset* data structure.

5.4 AN EXTENSION TO THE SPECIFICATION

5.4.1 New requirements

Let us now extend this specification by requiring a poset in which a special node is identified to act as the lower bound, and another node is identified to act as the upper bound of the ordering. In the Painting World plan, these special nodes could be two dummy actions *init* and *goal* which provide limits for the plan (see Fig. 5.4). We require that all nodes are ordered before *goal*, apart from *goal* itself; and likewise, that *init* is ordered before every node, apart from itself.

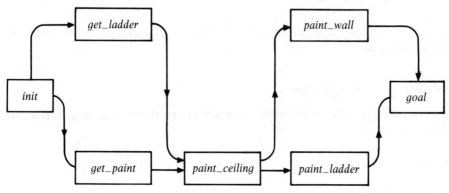

Figure 5.4   The Painting World plan: a partial order with bounds.

5.4.2 A new data model

There seem to be two main ways to create a VDM model that embeds this extension:

- Initialize the type by explicitly including the bound nodes in the base set and in the arc set. Every node subsequently added to the base set will have arcs from *init* and to *goal* added.
- Leave the bound nodes *init* and *goal* implicit in the type (in other words do *not* include them in the poset's representation), but change the functions on the poset to take them into account.

Choosing between such representations is not easy, and largely a matter of trial and error. As a rule, an explicit representation tends to be more maintainable and transparent, although less 'efficient', if considered from an implementation viewpoint. We will therefore choose to develop the former here, and leave the implicit form as an exercise.

Changing to a bounded poset means that all nodes in the poset will have to be ordered in some way, since every node must at least be ordered between the bounds. Thus the set inequality on the poset's components changes to an equality:

$$get\_nodes(arcs) = nodes$$

This simplifies the poset representation, because it means that representing the base set of nodes is superfluous. We define the bounded poset as simply:

$$Bounded\_Poset = Arc\text{-set}$$

The invariant on the new bounded poset is initially simplified, because there is now only one component in the data model. We must, however, assert the invariant properties of the bounds *init* and *goal*:

$$
\begin{aligned}
\text{inv } & mk\text{-}Bounded\_Poset(p) \triangleq \forall x, y \in get\_nodes(p) \cdot \\
& \neg (before(x, y, p) \wedge before(y, x, p)) \wedge \\
& x \neq init \Rightarrow before(init, x, p) \wedge \\
& x \neq goal \Rightarrow before(x, goal, p)
\end{aligned}
$$

Both the function definitions of *before* and *possibly_before* can be used in the new bounded version without change.

5.4.3 Modelling the new operations

The *init_poset* operation includes the initial arc which asserts that the *init* node is prior to the *goal* node.

$$
\begin{aligned}
& init\_poset: \rightarrow Bounded\_Poset \\
& init\_poset\ (\ ) \triangleq \\
& \quad \{mk\text{-}Arc(init, goal)\}
\end{aligned}
$$

Adding a new node to the order now involves placing the node between the two bounds:

$add\_node: Node \times Bounded\_Poset \rightarrow Bounded\_Poset$
$add\_node(u, p) \triangleq$
  $p \cup \{mk\text{-}Arc(init, u), mk\text{-}Arc(u, goal)\}$

The new *make_before* is virtually the same as the old operation, except it needs an extra pre-condition that checks that the nodes are already in the partial order. This is necessary because any nodes put in the partial order have to be put in between the bounds first:

$make\_before: Node \times Node \times Bounded\_Poset \rightarrow Bounded\_Poset$
$make\_before(u, v, p) \triangleq$
  if $possibly\_before(u, v, p) \wedge \{u, v\} \subseteq get\_nodes(p)$
  then $p \cup \{mk\text{-}Arc(u, v)\}$

5.5 SUMMARY

In this chapter we have presented a purely functional approach to creating new data structures which may then be used as building blocks in a larger specification. Functions are special kinds of operation which return a unique, single value, and do not access an external system state. They may be specified:

- *Implicitly,* using the pre- and post-condition form; or
- *Explicitly,* using an algorithm that one can use to calculate an output given a set of legal input values.

Finally, we built up a data structure representing a partial order, which will be used as a building block for the case study of the next chapter.

5.6 ADDITIONAL PROBLEMS

5.1 Change the definition of *make_before* in the same way as *make_before'* in Exercise 5.5(c) to make it more efficient.
5.2 Write down an explicit representation of the bounded partial order in Fig. 5.4.
5.3 Perform the proof obligations for the new bounded poset.
5.4 Exercise 5.3(d) asked you to argue that *transitivity* can be paired with either the *irreflexivity* axiom or the *antisymmetry* axiom to create the strong poset theory. Explain why this argument breaks down when the ordering is bounded.
5.5 Refer to the horse racing example of Chapter 4. Simplify *UPDATE*'s post-condition through the use of function definitions.

REFERENCE

Jones, C.B. (1990). *Systematic Software Development using VDM*, 2nd ed., Prentice-Hall, London.

6

SPECIFICATION CASE STUDY IN VDM

6.1 INTRODUCTION

One interesting application area in which formal specification can be used is that of *artificial intelligence* (AI). This involves the creation of computer systems that perform tasks normally associated with human intelligence, such as planning, reasoning, vision, natural language understanding and learning.

AI applications tend to be complex, leading to huge implementations. In some cases, scientists create theories and models of intelligence with which to guide or base their computational models. With such large engineering tasks, an interesting question arises: how do scientists know that their computer models have been implemented faithfully? One approach is to use a formal specification as a *bridge* that links the high-level model at one extreme, and the implementation at the other. That way, the model can be mapped to the specification, which can then itself be prototyped, or used as a contract with respect to which the correctness of the implementation is checked.

An easy mistake to make, especially in complex application areas such as those in AI, is to assume that, if the problem is ill defined, formal specification techniques are not applicable. 'Such and such an area is not capable of being fully captured, therefore formal specification is not appropriate' one might say. This misses the point: if a complex program is to be written to simulate an unfathomable application then the program itself can (and should) be formally specified, even though the area it is approximating cannot.

In this chapter we will develop a VDM specification of the main procedure in a *planning* program, that is a program that generates plans automatically. Specifically, our design level specification in Sec. 6.4 captures the goal achievement procedure in a 'constraint posting nonlinear conjunctive planner' (the reader is referred to Chapman (1987) and McCluskey (1988) for the background on this). As well as being an interesting and nontrivial specification, it involves the use of all of the techniques we have met so far.

In the next chapter we will prototype this specification using Prolog. As with any substantial case study, however, the reader must become familiar with the application area, and we devote several pages to giving a simple introduction to planning. Those who need more information on automatic planning could consult textbooks on artificial intelligence (refer to Rich and Knight (1991) for a good introduction to planning).

6.2 AUTOMATIC PLANNING

Planning is what we do when we assemble orderings of actions to achieve goals. These orderings are *temporal*—they involve the concept of time. In Chapter 5 we introduced the idea of using a partial ordering to represent temporal relations between actions. As well as actions, we must represent objects that are being acted on, and properties and relationships between these objects.

In the model developed in this chapter, we will often refer to the actions, objects and relationships that are relevant as the *planning world* or simply *the world* for short.

Going on holiday requires a simple form of planning—actions are packing suitcases, going to the travel agent, going to the airport, booking a hotel and so on. Orderings include 'obtain tickets before flying' and 'pack suitcases before going to the airport'. Objects related to the actions are travel tickets, passports, currency, people, planes, baggage and so on, and these objects may have a myriad of important properties and relationships.

Computer programming is another type of planning. Typical actions are programming commands such as assignment, procedure call and iteration; in most programming languages, commands are applied (or *executed*) sequentially, so here we have a *total ordering* of actions in time. For example, the code fragment:

$$z := 0;\ while\ (z + 1)^2 \leqslant x\ do\ z := z + 1$$

means apply action $z := 0$ *before* the iterative action *while* $(z + 1)^2 \leqslant x$ *do* $z := z + 1$. Objects are modelled by data types, and relations between objects are the relational operators of the data types used. Goals may be posed by stating conditions on output data. Here, the goals may be given by a program specification, and in VDM these would be the post-conditions of operations. The goal of our program example is:

$$(z^2 \leqslant x) \wedge (x < (z + 1)^2)$$

which was the post-condition of the *INT_SQR* example in Sec. 3.2.

The form of planning we will model in this chapter is called *generative* because the planner proceeds to work out a complete plan to achieve some given goals, assuming it has a fixed, correct representation of the planning world. Where the interaction of a plan execution mechanism with a largely unknown environment is the most important factor, a different kind of planning, called *reactive* planning, may be called for. Our model will be restricted by a number of other simplifying assumptions to make the case study small enough to fit into a chapter. As a working example we use a world often referred to in the planning literature as *the blocks world* (see Fig. 6.1(a)). Here a robot is given a goal in the form of an arrangement of stacked blocks, and has to work out a plan to achieve that goal. The plan must consist of actions to be applied by a robot arm (a *gripper*).

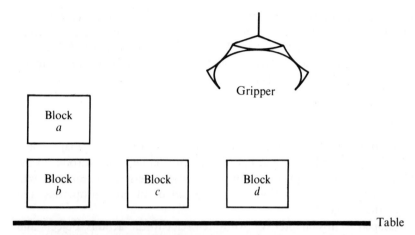

Figure 6.1 (a) The Blocks World (state $S1$).

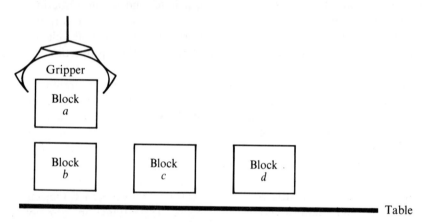

Figure 6.1 (b) The Blocks World (state $S2$).

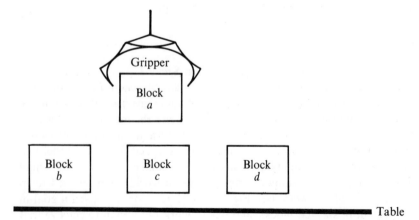

Figure 6.1 (c) The Blocks World (state $S3$).

6.2.1 Objects in the blocks world

Objects in the blocks world are the blocks, the table and the gripper. Typical goals involve block stacking, using the gripper. We express properties and relationships in planning worlds in the form of *literals*, such as 'block *a* is on *b*' and 'block *d* has a clear top'. The imaginary world given in Fig. 6.1(a) could be represented by asserting the following literals, which we will refer to as state *S*1:

> 'block *a* is on block *b*', 'block *c* is on the table', 'block *b* is on the table',
> 'block *d* is on the table', 'block *d* has a clear top', 'block *a* has a clear top',
> 'block *c* has a clear top', and 'the gripper is free'.

A set of literals that is assumed to capture a snapshot of the world adequately is called a *state*. To keep the representation of a state simple, we will insist that each literal making up a state asserts a single, positive fact about the world. Negative literals such as:

> 'block *b* has not got a clear top'

can be represented implicitly: we assume that whatever is *not* asserted is false: hence, if it is not asserted that 'block *b* has a clear top', then we assume it is not the case.
Certain facts such as:

> 'the table always has space for a block'

can be also be represented implicitly, within the actions that model block stacking. The assumed infinite size of the table, for example, can be represented by assuming that a block can always be put down onto it.
Note also that the choice of which literals to use depends totally on the user and the sort of tasks that the user has in mind for the planner. For instance, we have chosen not to record any shape information about the blocks, or the fact that they are all the same size.

6.2.2 Actions in the blocks world

We choose to model four types of action in the blocks world, all performed by the robot gripper: grasping a block, picking up a block, putting a block down onto another, and putting a block down onto the table. Our planner will embody the assumption that the effect of actions changing states can be stated by defining actions via pre-conditions and post-conditions, in a similar form to a VDM operation. An action that models the gripper grasping hold of block *a* is defined as follows:

> **pre-conditions**—literals that must be true before the action can be applied:
> 'block *a* has a clear top', 'the gripper is free'
> **post-conditions**—literals made true by the effect of the action:
> 'gripper grasps block *a*'
> literals made false by the effect of the action:
> 'block *a* has a clear top', 'the gripper is free'

The pre-conditions are assumed to be those facts needed to be true in a state for the action to be applicable. So before this action can be executed on a state, the literals 'block *a* has a clear top' and 'the gripper is free' must be asserted in the state description. The post-condition of an action is traditionally split into two separate structures: the *add-set*, holding those literals made true by the effect of the action, and the *delete-set*, holding only those literals made false by the effect of the action. Complete with a name, *grasp a*, a shortened form of this action is then (we assume *a*, *b*, *c* and *d* denote blocks from now on):

> name: *grasp a*
> pre-conditions: '*a* has a clear top', 'gripper is free';
> add-set: 'gripper grasps *a*';
> delete-set: '*a* has a clear top', 'gripper is free';

In the same way we can model lifting up block *a* from another block, lifting up block *a* from the table, putting *a* down onto another block, and putting *a* down onto the table:

> name: *liftup a from b*;
> pre-conditions: 'gripper grasps *a*', '*a* is on *b*';
> add-set: '*a* lifted up', '*b* has a clear top';
> delete-set: '*a* is on *b*';

> name: *liftup a from table*;
> pre-conditions: 'gripper grasps *a*', '*a* is on table';
> add-set: '*a* lifted up';
> delete-set: '*a* is on table';

> name: *putdown a onto c*
> pre-conditions: '*a* lifted up', '*c* has a clear top';
> add-set: '*a* is on *c*', 'gripper is free', '*a* has a clear top';
> delete-set: '*a* lifted up', 'gripper grasps *a*', '*c* has a clear top';

> name: *putdown a onto table*;
> pre-conditions: '*a* lifted up';
> add-set: '*a* is on table', 'gripper is free', '*a* has a clear top';
> delete-set: '*a* lifted up', 'gripper grasps *a*';

The actions moving the other blocks *b*, *c*, *d* can all be written in exactly the same form, giving a total of 36 action instances (4 *grasps*, 4 *liftups* from the table, 4 *putdowns* onto the table, 12 *putdowns* between blocks and 12 *liftups* between blocks). In fact, we could reduce the action set to just 5 actions if we used parameters for the block names *a*, *b*, *c*, *d* (see Exercise 6.2(b)) but this would overcomplicate the VDM specification we are about to develop.

6.2.3 Action application

Next, we define how actions change states. An action can be *applied* to a state if its pre-conditions are literals contained in that state. For example, *grasp a*'s pre-conditions are contained in state $S1$, so *grasp a* can be applied to it. The effect of applying an action to a state is that any literals in the action's *delete-set* are deleted from the old state, and all the literals in the action's *add-set* are 'unioned' to the result, generating a new state. In summary, applying action A to any state S, denoted *apply(A, S)*, is given by:

$$apply(A, S) = (S \setminus A\text{'s delete-set}) \cup A\text{'s add-set}$$

Important note: in the rest of the chapter the name of an action will often be identified with the full action representation that it stands for. This is a shorthand device, because when we refer to actions we do not want to keep repeating their full representation, including their pre- and post-conditions. For example, when we write 'apply action *grasp a*', we actually mean apply the action *named grasp a*.

Examples 6.1

(a) Applying *grasp a* to state $S1$ results in a new state, called state $S2$, as follows (see Fig. 6.1(b)):

> state $S2$
> $=$ apply *grasp a* to state $S1$,
> $=$ (state $S1 \setminus$ delete-set of *grasp a*) $\cup$ add-set of *grasp a*
> $=$ (state $S1 \setminus \{$'a has a clear top', 'gripper is free'$\}) \cup \{$'gripper grasps a'$\}$,
> $= \{$'a is on b', 'c is on the table', 'b is on the table',
> 'd is on the table', 'd has a clear top', 'gripper grasps a', 'c has a clear top'$\}$.

Note that *grasp a* is applicable to state $S1$ because its pre-conditions ('a has a clear top', 'gripper is free') are contained in $S1$.

(b) The pre-conditions of *liftup a from b* ('gripper grasps a', 'a is on b') are contained in state $S2$ so we may apply this action to it. Calling the new state $S3$ (see Fig. 6.1(c)), we have:

> state $S3$
> $=$ apply *liftup a from b* to state $S2$
> $=$ (state $S2 \setminus$ delete-set of *liftup a from b*) $\cup$ add-set of *liftup a from b*
> $=$ (state $S2 \setminus \{$'a is on b'$\}) \cup ($'a lifted up', 'b has a clear top'$\}$,
> $= \{$'a lifted up', 'b has a clear top', 'c is on the table', 'b is on the table',
> 'd is on the table', 'd has a clear top', 'gripper grasps a', 'c has a clear top'$\}$.

Exercise 6.1 Apply the action *putdown a onto c* to state $S3$ to obtain a new state, $S4$.

6.2.4 Plans

A solution plan to a planning problem is an ordering of actions that achieves a set of goals, and the ordering may be total or partial. A plan is executed by applying each of its individual actions in turn. Planning problems can be posed by describing:

- An initial state: that is the state from which the solution must start execution.

- A set of goal literals: these are the literals that must be *achieved*. A goal literal is said to be achieved by an action sequence if it is contained in the final state after the actions have all been applied (a more general definition of goal achievement is given in Sec. 6.4).

To be able to solve a planning problem, a planner must have access to a set of actions. A subset of these actions will be used to form the solution. A solution to a planning problem is simply a correct plan, defined as follows:

- *A correct plan is a complete plan which when applied sequentially to the initial state produces a state that contains all the goal literals.*
- *A complete plan is a total order of actions which can be applied sequentially to an initial state to produce a final state.*

Note that the correctness of a plan can only be checked if we have a set of goals in mind. These definitions generalize easily to partially ordered plans, since a partially ordered plan can be thought of as specifying a set of totally ordered plans (see Exercise 5.3(c)). Hence we have:

- *A partially ordered plan is complete (correct) if all the totally ordered plans it specifies are complete (correct).*

This model of planning sidesteps many considerations such as the use of resources and the passage of time intervals. For example, in Exercise 6.2(a) we model the Painting World of Fig. 5.2 in Chapter 5. With our restricted model, it is impossible to consider such questions as 'have we enough paint to cover the wall?' and 'has the first coat of paint dried?'. It would be interesting to extend the model to cope with this kind of reasoning, but to keep the case study to a reasonable size we have to limit the planner's application.

Examples 6.2

(a) Consider 'going on a foreign holiday' as a planning scenario. A plan with the goal 'Holiday in Spain' which got us to an airport without bringing our passport would be an incomplete plan. The pre-condition of one of the actions, going through passport control, would not be met. Similarly, a plan which was complete, but landed us in Bermuda rather than Torremolinos would be an incorrect (although perhaps more desirable) plan.
(b) Consider the sequence of actions:

  grasp a, liftup a from b, putdown a on c

Examples 6.1 and Exercise 6.1 show that each of these three actions can be applied in sequence starting from state $S1$, hence it is a complete plan. If the goal was {'a is on c', 'b has a clear top'}, then the plan is correct with respect to this goal. This sequence is *not* correct with respect to goals {'c is on d', 'b has a clear top'}, because it does not achieve one of the literals in the goal set.

(c) The sequence:

> *grasp a, putdown a onto c, liftup b from table*

is not a complete plan starting at state *S*1, because *putdown a onto c* cannot be applied after *grasp a*, according to our definition of action application. After *grasp a* has been applied, the pre-condition '*a* lifted up' of *putdown a onto c* is not in the resulting state *S*2.

Exercises 6.2

(a) Referring to Fig. 5.2 in Chapter 5, we can capture the Painting World in our planning model. As a start, we model the operator *paint_ceiling* as follows:

> name: *paint_ceiling*
> pre-conditions: 'have ladder', 'ladder functional', 'have paint'
> add-set: 'ceiling painted'
> delete-set: empty

Within our simplification of reality, *paint_ceiling* does not delete any facts, and we state this as 'empty'. The other four actions are:

> name: *paint_wall*
> pre-conditions: 'have paint', 'ceiling painted'
> add-set: 'wall painted'
> delete-set: empty

> name: *paint_ladder*
> pre-conditions: 'have ladder', 'have paint'
> add-set: 'ladder painted'
> delete-set: 'ladder functional'

> name: *get_paint*
> pre-conditions: 'have credit card'
> add-set: 'have paint'
> delete-set: empty

> name: *get_ladder*
> pre-conditions: 'have credit card', 'own large car'
> add-set: 'have ladder', 'ladder functional'
> delete-set: empty

From initial state:

> {'have credit card', 'own large car'}

show that the plan illustrated in Fig. 5.2 is correct with respect to the goal set:

> {'ladder painted', 'ceiling painted', 'wall painted'}.

Note: To show correctness of the plan, you should show that every totally ordered plan conforming to the partial order, of which there are four, is correct (see Exercise 5.3(c)).

(b) Generalize the Blocks World action definitions so that you may use parameters, and express actions such as *putdown X onto Y* and *liftup Z from the table*. Are there any special problems arising when parameters are introduced? (For example, consider the case where $X = Y$ in the definition of *putdown X onto Y*.)

6.3 AN ABSTRACT SPECIFICATION OF THE PLANNER

The overall requirement of our planning program is to input a problem posed correctly in its input language, and output a correct plan. How are we to specify such a program? We will choose two levels on which to pose the specification. The first specification, given in Sec. 6.3, is more abstract, implicit and a good deal shorter than the more concrete specification developed in Sec. 6.4. It relies on a formalization of the input and captures the idea that the output must be an ordering of actions that is correct with respect to the input goal set. The second level of specification incorporates a *goal-directed solution method*, and is concrete enough for us to prototype in the next chapter.

We start, however, by creating a model of the input language to the planning program, which will be used for both levels. This input will contain the actions, the initial state, and the goal.

6.3.1 A VDM representation of planning problems

All components of our simplified planning system have as their basis the literal, so we shall start by modelling it. Order is important in a literal (for example 'block a is on block b' is not the same as 'block b is on block a'), and it can be of variable length, hence, we will use a sequence of tokens (identifiers) to represent it.

Literal = *Token**

Furthermore, if the literal contains a relation name or property name, it is customary to let it be the head element in the sequence, and the objects related by it, the tail. For example, in state *S1*, 'on' is a relation name and 'clear' a property name.

Both a state and a goal can be modelled as sets of Literals. In both cases, ordering of Literals is not assumed to be important, and there is no limit to the size of goals and states. The Set type is therefore chosen:[1]

State = *Literal*-set

Goal = *Literal*-set

[1]Note that our interpretations of *Goal* and *State* are different. A state is interpreted with the implicit assumption that anything not asserted in it is assumed to be false. A goal, on the other hand, specifies a set of states—exactly all those that contain all the goal's literals.

Actions have a fixed number of different components (a name, a pre-condition and so on) which leads us to choose a model using a composite:

Action :: *name*: *Literal*
        pre : *Literal*-set
        add : *Literal*-set
        del : *Literal*-set

Finally, we put the three components together in a composite type

Planning_Problem :: *AS* : *Action*-set
                I : *State*
                G : *Goal*

Here the component variables represent:

- The set of actions
- The initial state
- The goal literals

Examples 6.3

(a) State $S1$ is now explicitly represented in VDM as:

    {[on, a, b], [on, c, table], [on, b, table], [on, d, table],
    [clear, d], [clear, a], [clear, c], [free, gripper]}

(b) The goal set in Exercise 6.2(a) is represented in VDM as:

    {[painted, ladder], [painted, ceiling], [painted, wall]}.

(c) Action *grasp a* is represented in VDM by the expression:

    mk-Action([*grasp*, *a*],
    {[*clear*, *a*], [*free*, *gripper*]},
    {[*grasp*, *a*]},
    {[*clear*, *a*], [*free*, *gripper*]})

(d) In the Painting World, as in the Blocks World, when we translate the literals into VDM, we use the convention that the properties of objects head the literal sequence. Action *paint_ceiling* is represented by

    mk-Action([*paint*, *ceiling*],
    {[*have*, *ladder*], [*functional*, *ladder*], [*have*, *paint*]},
    {[*painted*, *ceiling*]},
    { })

Exercises 6.3 Using the explicit VDM representations of sequences, sets, and composites, write down the following:

(a) States *S2* and *S3*
(b) All the Blocks World actions
(c) The planning problem consisting of the actions in (b), the initial state *S1* and the goal expression:

$$\{[on, a, c], [clear, a]\}$$

6.3.2 Invariants for the planning problem

Many invariants can be captured to promote the validity of the planning problem. We will state several here, in terms of problem components *I*, *G*, and *AS*. The reader is invited to develop the model further in Exercise 6.4.

1. 'Every literal in the goal set appears in either the initial state or in some action's add-set.' This is required because the only way that literals can be added to the initial state in our model is through the application of actions. If it were not satisfied, then the goal set would not be achievable. The condition formalizes to:

$$\forall l \in G \cdot (l \in I \lor \exists A \in AS \cdot l \in A.add)$$

2. An invariant that invalidates trivial problems is: 'The goal set is not a subset of the initial state', captured by:

$$\neg (G \subseteq I)$$

3. Actions need to be restricted to disallow futile ones: 'No action can both add and delete the same literal'. This formalizes to:

$$\forall A \in AS \cdot \neg (\exists p \cdot p \in A.add \land p \in A.del)$$

Putting these together we obtain the data type:

$$Planning\_Problem :: AS : Action\text{-set}$$
$$I \ : State$$
$$G \ : Goal$$
$$\text{inv } mk\text{-}Planning\_Problem(G, I, AS) \triangleq$$
$$\forall l \in G \cdot (l \in I \lor \exists A \in AS \cdot l \in A.add) \land$$
$$\neg (G \subseteq I) \land$$
$$\forall A \in AS \cdot \neg (\exists p \cdot p \in A.add \land p \in A.del)$$

Exercises 6.4

(a) Check that your answer to Exercise 6.3(c) satisfies the data type invariant.
(b) Formalize the condition: 'every action has at least one literal in its add-set'.

(c) Formalize the condition: 'every pre-condition literal is either in the initial state or in some action's add-set'.

The conditions in Exercises 6.4(b) and (c) may well be worthy of inclusion in the invariant. If Exercise 6.4(b) were not satisfied by an action then one might ask why that action were included (because it could not help in achieving a goal). If Exercise 6.4(c) were not satisfied by an action, that action would not be able to be used in a plan, as its pre-conditions could never be achieved in (or added to) a state. On the other hand we may not want to be too strict, because we may pose different problems by changing the initial state and the goal, while keeping the action set fixed.

6.3.3 A first specification of the planner

In this section we build up an abstract specification using functions as building blocks. The planner itself is *implicitly* defined via an operation that inputs a *Planning Problem* and outputs a solution in the form of an ordering of actions. No notion of a VDM state is required, because of the very abstract nature of the specification.

We start by formalizing the application of actions in VDM with the following function, which applies an action to a state:

$apply: Action \times State \rightarrow State$

The definition of *apply* immediately follows from the definition given in Sec. 6.2.3. To make the function total, however, we introduce the idea of an 'error' state, and regard this as the empty set of literals. Applying an action to an error state should also result in an error state:

$apply: Action \times State \rightarrow State$
$apply\ (a, s) \triangleq$
   if $a.pre \subseteq s$
   then $(s \backslash a.del) \cup a.add$
   else $\{\ \}$

A planning problem is solved by the application of a *sequence* of action applications, and so we need to formalize the idea of the application of an action sequence to a state. This is done in terms of *apply*: the function *apply_seq* applies the head of an action sequence to obtain an advanced state, and recursively calls itself with the advanced state and with the tail of the action sequence:

$apply\_seq : Action^* \times State \rightarrow State$
$apply\_seq\ (as, s) \triangleq$
   if $as = [\ ]$
   then s
   else $apply\_seq(tl\ as, apply(hd\ as, s))$

Note:

- If the action sequence is empty, the state is returned unchanged.

- If *as* is an incomplete plan, then the definition of *apply* ensures that the function evaluates to the empty set, signifying an error state.

Next the notion of completeness of a plan is formalized, again using *apply* within a recursive function. The function *complete(as, s)* returns true if and only if every action in the sequence *as* is applicable, starting with state *s*. The function is Boolean valued:

$$complete: Action^* \times State \rightarrow \mathbb{B}$$

If the action sequence is empty it is considered complete, otherwise it is complete if

1. The pre-conditions of the head action of the sequence are contained in the current state, *and*
2. The tail of the sequence is complete when applied to the advanced state obtained by applying the head of the sequence to the current state.

This is summed up by the VDM function:

```
complete: Action* × State→𝔹
complete (as, s) ≜
    if as=[ ]
    then true
    else (hd as).pre⊆s ∧ complete(tl as, apply(hd as, s))
```

Using the functions *complete* and *apply_seq*, an implicit specification of a planner can be written. Essentially, the specification states that, for an input *Planning_Problem*, a correct plan in the shape of a sequence of actions is output:

```
PLANNER(pp: Planning_Problem) soln : Action*
pre true
post elems soln ⊆ pp.AS ∧
     complete(soln, pp.I) ∧
     pp.G ⊆ apply_seq(soln, pp.I)
```

The post-condition asserts that

- Only actions defined in the *Planning_Problem* are allowed in the action sequence.
- The plan is complete.
- Execution of the plan outputs a state that contains the goal.

Hence, the final two conjunctions formalize the correctness criterion given in Sec. 6.2. Note that *PLANNER* is not a function as there may be many plans that satisfy this specification, given a particular planning problem. Even if we added an extra constraint to the post-condition which insists on a minimum length solution, there may still be more than one correct plan.

Exercises 6.5 In the first three exercises, let $A1$ be the action called $[grasp, a]$, $A2$ the action called $[liftup, a, b]$, and $A3$ the action called $[putdown, a, c]$.

(a) Check that the expression:

$complete([A1, A2, A3], S1)$

evaluates to true.

(b) Evaluate the expression:

$apply\_seq([A1, A2, A3], S1)$

using the formal definition of *apply_seq*, verifying that it coincides with our informal notion of Sec. 6.2.

(c) Assume *PLANNER* has been input with the planning problem of Exercise 6.3(c). Using the results of Exercises 6.5(a) and (b) above, deduce that

$soln = [A1, A2, A3]$

makes the post-condition of *PLANNER* true.

(d) Generalize the specification of *PLANNER* to one that outputs a partially-ordered set of actions as a solution. *Hint*: *apply* must be redefined to apply a *set* of action sequences and return a *set* of states.

(e) Consider the following planning problem, where p and q are literals (this example is due to a personal communication from Yogesh Naik):

mk-$Planning\_Problem($
$\{mk$-$Action([bill], \{p\}, \{q\}, \{p\}), mk$-$Action([ben], \{q\}, \{p\}, \{q\})\},$
$\{p\},$
$\{p, q\})$

It has two actions, called *bill* and *ben*; its initial state is simply the set of one literal, p, and its goal is the set of two literals, p and q. Verify that this problem satisfies *Planning_Problem*'s invariant. With this problem as input, can you find an action sequence that satisfies *PLANNER*'s post-condition? What conclusions can you draw about the satisfiability of *PLANNER*? In fact, this exercise shows that we can pose problems in the planning language for which there are no solutions—planning is hard!

6.4 A DESIGN LEVEL SPECIFICATION

In this section we construct a more concrete specification for the planner, which incorporates a goal-directed procedure for solving planning problems. Most nontrivial problems can be usefully specified at one or more 'design levels', in which commitments to particular solution techniques and data structures are progressively made. After having completed a more detailed design level, it is up to the designer to check it is adequate with respect to the more abstract level. VDM encompasses a well-developed process called *reification*, in which operators and data types are re-expressed at a more detailed level after their initial specification, and the detailed level is checked for adequacy using a *retrieve function*. Showing how the design level of the planner described in this section conforms to the abstract level given above is not too difficult, and is left as a project for the interested reader.

The specification, certainly towards the end of this chapter, becomes rather complicated and may be difficult for some readers. In this case, the reader is encouraged to move on to the next chapter, where the prototyping of the planner may shed more light on its specification, or to consult Appendix 1, where sample inputs and outputs of the planner are given, as well as its implementation.

6.4.1 A technique for solving planning problems

The more concrete specification commits our planner to a particular solution method in which the planning program generates plans in a systematic manner and then terminates when it finds a plan that is correct. The solution method runs as follows:

- Start with an initial plan that only contains the initial state and goal set, viewed as special actions
- Incrementally achieve goal literals by:
  - identifying an action already in the plan that achieves the goal literal; or
  - adding a new action to the plan to achieve the goal literal (in which case the new action's pre-conditions themselves must be achieved).

When an action is added to the plan, rather than storing it in a sequence, it is stored within a partially-ordered set of actions, as we have seen in the Painting World example.

The planner's job is to find a plan in which all literals in the goal set and in every action's pre-conditions are achieved, in the sense that the final solution is complete (the pre-conditions of each action are met as they are applied) and correct (the final state produced contains the goal set). This means that an action's pre-conditions must be achieved at an earlier time than the goal set, and we will identify this time with the position of an action in the plan. The combination of a goal literal with a position in the temporal ordering at which it must be achieved we call a *goal instance*.

In Fig. 6.2 we present a top-level algorithm of a planning program. If we assume that the choices in steps 1 and 2 are made randomly, then the heart of this algorithm is step 3—generating new plans which achieve previously unachieved goal instances. The specification developed here will consist of the initialization operation carried out before the loop, and two operations that perform goal achievement necessary for step 3. The

```
START: Initialize the Planning Problem by generating
the initial plan, and put the initial plan in a Store;
LOOP:
    1. —Choose and remove a plan pp from the Store;
    2. —Choose an unachieved goal instance Gi from pp;
    3. —Generate plans to achieve Gi in pp in all ways possible;
    4. —Add all new plans generated by step 3 to the Store
UNTIL there exists a plan in Store that has no unachieved goal instances.
```

Figure 6.2 The top-level loop of a naive planning algorithm.

terminating condition of the loop is dependent on a plan being found in Store that has no unachieved goal instances. In fact, the specification of the goal achievement operations ensures that once a plan is found with an empty set of unsolved goal instances, that plan will contain a set of linear solutions, each conforming to our abstract specification in Sec. 6.3.

6.4.2 An introduction to goal achievement in planning

A goal instance is any pre-condition literal and action pairing in a plan. To use a concrete example, consider Fig. 5.4. We know 'have ladder' is a pre-condition of action *paint_ceiling*, hence the pair ('have ladder', *paint_ceiling*) is a goal instance in the plan represented by Fig. 5.4. One of the goal literals of the Painting World is 'ladder painted', so the pair ('ladder painted', *goal*) is another goal instance. In this example, *goal* is considered a special kind of action, whose pre-conditions are the literals in the goal set. The same can be done for the initial state—it can be considered to be an action that has an add-set containing all the literals in the initial state.

For a more abstract example, refer to Fig. 6.3. It is a bounded poset representing an abstract plan containing some imaginary actions which we call $C1$, $C2$, $C3$, $C4$, A and O. Assume p in the diagram is a literal contained in the pre-conditions of O; then the pair (p, O) is an example of a goal instance.

Now we can give a full definition of **goal achievement**:

- *A goal instance (p, O) is achieved in a plan if some action X is constrained to be necessarily before O, X contains p in its add-set, and no action that could possibly occur between X and O contains p in its delete-set. In this case, X is said to be the achiever of p at O.*

We can define a *complete plan* in terms of goal achievement: a complete plan is a bounded ordering of actions in which every goal instance is achieved by some action (compare this definition with our earlier definition of completeness for sequential plans in Sec. 6.3). A complete plan in this sense is also correct because a subset of these goal instances are those taken from the goal set and combined with dummy action *goal*. We will finish this section with several examples and exercises, so that the reader may get an intuitive feel for our goal achievement definition.

Examples 6.6

(a) The goal instance ('ladder functional', *paint_ceiling*) is achieved in the Painting World plan of Fig. 5.4 by action *get_ladder*. We can check the conditions are true by our definition of goal achievement:
   (i) *get_ladder* is necessarily before *paint_ceiling*, as there is a path of directed arcs (in this case just one) from the former to the latter.
   (ii) *get_ladder* contains 'ladder functional' in its add-set (see Exercise 6.2).
   (iii) The only action that can possibly occur between *get_ladder* and *paint_ceiling* is *get_paint*. It does not contain 'ladder functional' in its delete-set and so this condition is met.

Note that if *paint_ladder* was *not* ordered to be after *paint_ceiling*, then goal achievement would not necessarily be true, because *paint_ladder* contains 'ladder functional' is its delete-set.

(b) The goal instance ('have paint', *paint_wall*) is achieved by action *get_paint*. The conditions are true as follows: *get_paint* is necessarily before *paint_wall*; *get_paint* contains 'have paint' in its add-set (see Exercise 6.2); none of the three actions that could be between *get_paint* and *paint_wall* contain 'have paint' in their delete-set.

(c) In Fig. 6.3, action instance *A could* be the achiever of goal instance (p, O) if
   (i) *A* contains *p* in its add-set
   (ii) *C1* does not contain *p* in its delete-set
   (iii) Either *C4* does not contain *p* in its delete-set OR an arc is added from *C4* to *A* to constrain *C4* to be before the achiever, *A*.

(d) *C4* could be the achiever of goal instances (p, O) if all the following conditions are made true:
   (i) An arc is added from *C4* to *O* to ensure *C4* is executed before *O* in an application of the completed plan.
   (ii) *C4* contains *p* in its add-set.
   (iii) Either *C1* does not contain *p* in its delete-set OR an arc is added from *C1* to *C4* to constrain *C1* to be before the achiever, *C4*.
   (iv) Either *A* does not contain *p* in its delete-set OR an arc is added from *A* to *C4* to constrain *A* to be before the achiever, *C4*.

Actions that could not possibly be used to achieve *p* are those that do not contain *p* in their add-sets, those that are necessarily after *O* (for example, *C2*), and those that have an action, in between them and the goal instance, that deletes *p*.

Of course, another way to achieve a pre-condition literal *p* is to add another action to the plan to achieve it. In this case we must go through the same procedure to make sure *p* is not 'undone'. Note that, although any further temporal constraints on the plan (that is additional arcs) will not invalidate the achievement of *p*, the addition of an action to achieve some other goal instance may well undo its achievement (we return to this point later).

Exercises 6.6

(a) Using the example plan in Fig. 6.3, state the conditions under which the following operators achieve (p, O):
   (i) *C1*
   (ii) *C3*
   (iii) *init*

(b) Assume another action *Y* is added to the plan in Fig. 6.3 and constrained to be before *O* in the new plan (see Fig. 6.4). State the conditions under which *Y* achieves (p, O).

(c) Assume the conditions of *Y* being an achiever for *p* in Exercise 6.6(b) are true. Now add extra temporal constraints to Fig. 6.4, for example, an arc from *Y* to *C1*, and another from *C4* to *O*. Is *Y* still an achiever for *p*? Form an argument showing that for any *X* that is an achiever for a literal *p* at action instance *O*, no legal additions of temporal constraints (that is arcs) will affect *X*'s achievement of *p*.

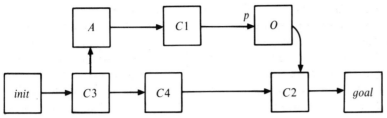

Figure 6.3 A plan (*C1, C2, C3, C4, O, A* are arbitrary action identifiers, *init* and *goal* identify the initial state and goal conditions as special actions).

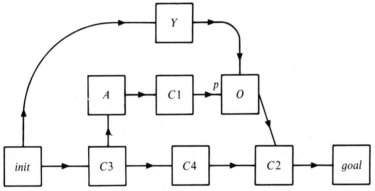

Figure 6.4 A new plan.

(d) List all the goal instances in the Painting World plan of Fig. 5.4. Convince yourself, using our definition of goal achievement, that the plan contains an achiever for each one.

6.4.3 Modelling the VDM state

The VDM state will represent a developing plan, as discussed above. The developing plan consists of some actions, a temporal ordering on those actions, some outstanding goal instances to be achieved, and some goal instances already achieved. The 'achieve' operations defined later will change the state by achieving one of the unachieved goal instances either through the addition of an action to the plan or through an existing action in the plan.

Although it will also contain the planning problem itself, we will call the whole system state a *Partial_Plan*, and give it five state components named *pp, Os, Ts, Ps, As* as follows:

state *Partial_Plan* of
   pp: *Planning_Problem*
   Os: *Action_instances*
   Ts: *Bounded_Poset*
   Ps: *Goal_instances*
   As: *Goal_instances*
end

Actions, states, and the structure of *Planning_Problem* were all defined in Sec. 6.3.

The *Action_instances* data structure   This component holds the actions occurring in a plan—called the *action instances*. It is necessary to allocate each action instance a unique identifier as it is added to the developing plan because the same action may occur more than once in the plan. In this case *Os* needs to be represented using a mapping from identifiers to actions, and an invariant is used to constrain the range of *Os* to be members of *pp.AS* (recall from Sec. 6.3 that *AS* represents the component of *Planning_Problem* in which the action definitions are held). This map captures the constraint that no identifier can point to more than one action but allows one action to be pointed to by more than one identifier.

For the sake of uniformity, the initial state and the goal set will be modelled as special actions, occurring in every plan. More importantly, they will become the lower and upper bounds, respectively, of the bounded poset in *Ts* below. These special actions are formed explicitly as:

$$mk\text{-}Action([init],\{\ \},pp.I,\{\ \})$$
$$mk\text{-}Action([goal],pp.G,\{\ \},\{\ \})$$

and will be identified by *init* and *goal* respectively. The translation of these two literal sets into the actions above is intuitively sound: the initial state needs no pre-conditions, does not delete any literals but has the effect of 'adding' all its literals; the goal does not have any post-condition effects, but to achieve its pre-conditions a plan must have asserted all the literals in the goal.

The type of *Os* is *Action_instances*, and is defined as follows:

$$Action\_id\ =\ Token$$

$$Action\_instances\ =\ Action\_id\ \xrightarrow{m}\ Action$$

The *Bounded_Poset* data structure   *Ts* holds a strong partial-order relation on the action identifiers in *Os*, bounded by *init* and *goal* which identify the special initial and goal actions. The poset specification developed in the last chapter is adapted and used below to provide the temporal structure for the plan:

$$Arc\ ::\ source:\ Action\_id$$
$$\qquad dest\quad :\ Action\_id$$

$$Bounded\_Poset\ =\ Arc\text{-set}$$

$$\text{inv }mk\text{-}Bounded\_Poset(p) \triangleq \forall x,\ y \in get\_nodes(p)\ \cdot$$
$$\quad \neg\,(before(x,\ y,\ p) \wedge before(y,\ x,\ p)) \wedge$$
$$\quad x\ \neq\ init \Rightarrow before(init,\ x,\ p) \wedge$$
$$\quad x\ \neq\ goal \Rightarrow before(x,\ goal,\ p)$$

The associated functions change little from Chapter 5:

$$get\_nodes\ :\ Arc\text{-set}\ \rightarrow Action\_id\_set$$
$$get\_nodes(p) \triangleq$$
$$\quad \{a.source\,|\,a \in p\} \cup \{a.dest\ |\ a \in p\}$$

$before : Action\_id \times Action\_id \times Arc\text{-set} \rightarrow \mathbb{B}$
$before(x, z, p) \triangleq$
  $mk\text{-}Arc(x, z) \in p \lor$
  $\exists y \in get\_nodes(p) \cdot before(x, y, p) \land before(y, z, p)$

$possibly\_before : Action\_id \times Action\_id \times Arc\text{-set} \rightarrow \mathbb{B}$
$possibly\_before(x, y, p) \triangleq$
  $x \neq y \land \neg before(y, x, p)$

Likewise, the three operations *init_poset*, *add_node*, and *make_node* are easily adapted to fit this application:

$init\_poset : \rightarrow Bounded\_Poset$
$init\_poset(\ ) \triangleq$
  $\{mk\text{-}before(init, goal)\}$

$add\_node : Action\_id \times Bounded\_Poset \rightarrow Bounded\_Poset$
$add\_node(u, p) \triangleq$
  $p \cup \{mk\text{-}Arc(init, u), mk\text{-}Arc(u, goal)\}$

$make\_before : Action\_id \times Action\_id \times Bounded\_Poset \rightarrow Bounded\_Poset$
$make\_before(u, v, p) \triangleq$
  if $possibly\_before(u, v, p) \land \{u, v\} \subseteq get\_nodes(p)$
  then $p \cup \{mk\text{-}Arc(u, v)\}$

The *Goal_instances* data structure   *Ps* represents a collection of unachieved goal instances, those that are still to be achieved by some action. A goal instance is a relation between goal literals and action identifiers, therefore we represent *Ps* as a set of ordered pairs as follows:

$Goal\_instance :: gl : Literal$
$\qquad\qquad\qquad ai : Action\_id$

$Goal\_instances = Goal\_instance\text{-set}$

Action instances that are added to the plan to *achieve* the goal instances in *Ps* may themselves have pre-condition literals: these will then be added to *Ps* as goal instances. At initialization, *Ps* will record the goal set *pp.G*, and will take the form:

$\{mk\text{-}Goal\_instance(g1, goal), \ldots , mk\text{-}Goal\_instance(gn, goal)\}$

where $pp.G = \{g1, \ldots , gn\}$. This can be written more concisely using set comprehension:

$\{mk\text{-}Goal\_instance(g, goal) \mid g \in pp.G\}$

Likewise, *As* holds a collection of achieved goal instances. This set will be initially empty, but each execution of the 'achieve' operations defined below will result in a literal being achieved at some point in the plan, and so this goal instance will be added to *As*.

6.4.4 The state invariant

Some possible states of the *Partial_Plan* structure that we have defined are clearly not valid, and our discussion has already thrown up some useful invariants. We start by listing the easier ones:

1. *Os* always contains the two special actions formed from the initial state and goal literals.
2. The range of the map *Os* (the *Action*-set) is a subset of actions posed in the *Planning_Problem* augmented with the *init* and *goal* actions.
3. The nodes in *Ts* and the identifiers from *Os* are the same: this ensures that *Ts* is a partial order on all (and only) those action instances in *Os*.
4. *Ps* and *As* are disjoint: no goal instance can be both achieved and not achieved.
5. All the pre-conditions of the action instances in *Os* are recorded as goal instances in either *As* or *Ps* (which means they have been achieved or are not achieved).

Finally we express the most important invariant of a plan:

6. Every goal instance *mk-Goal_instance*(p, O) (for a goal literal p and an action identifier O) in *As* is *achieved* using the definition in Sec. 6.4.2:
   (a) There is an action identified by A in the plan which is necessarily before O and contains p in its add-set; AND
   (b) no action in the plan that could possibly occur between A and O contains p in its delete-set.

Notice that O could itself be *goal*, in which case p would be one of the goal literals, or again, A could be the *init* action, in which case p would have to be contained in the initial state. Invariant (6) corresponds to the informal definition of goal achievement described at the beginning of Sec. 6.4.

The first five conditions are expressed in VDM as follows. Readers are encouraged to try to formalize the conditions themselves before reading on.

1. $Os(init) = mk\text{-}Action([init], \{\ \}, pp.I, \{\ \}) \land Os(goal) = mk\text{-}Action([goal], pp.G, \{\ \}, \{\ \})$
2. $\text{rng } Os \subseteq pp.AS \cup \{Os(init), Os(goal)\}$
3. $\text{dom } Os = get\_nodes(Ts)$
4. $As \cap Ps = \{\ \}$
5. $\forall A \in \text{dom } Os \cdot (p \in Os(A).pre \Rightarrow mk\text{-}Goal\_instance(p, A) \in (Ps \cup As))$

The first part of (6):
'there is an action identified by A in the plan which is necessarily before O and contains p in its add-set ... '
formalizes to

$$\exists A \in \text{dom } Os \cdot$$
$$before(A, O, Ts) \land$$
$$p \in Os(A).add$$

To formalize the second part, we make use of the partial order's *possibly_before* function. The expression:

$$possibly\_before(A, C, Ts) \wedge possibly\_before(C, O, Ts)$$

means that A could be ordered to be before C, and C could be ordered to be before O, with respect to the partial order Ts. This captures the idea that C could be ordered to be *between* A and O in partial order Ts. In Fig. 6.3, for example, this expression is true for $C = C4$, and for A and O as they actually appear in the figure. Hence the second part:

'no action in the plan that could possibly occur between A and O contains p in its delete-set'.

formalizes to:

$$\neg(\exists C \in \text{dom } Os \cdot$$
$$possibly\_before(C, O, Ts) \wedge$$
$$possibly\_before(A, C, Ts) \wedge$$
$$p \in Os(C).del)$$

We put these conditions together into a function definition that defines what it means for A to be an achiever of p at O in Ts:

$$achieve: Action\_instances \times Bounded\_Poset \times Action\_id \times Goal\_instance \to \mathbb{B}$$
$$achieve(Os, Ts, A, mk\text{-}Goal\_instance(p, O)) \triangleq$$
$$before(A, O, Ts) \wedge$$
$$p \in Os(A).add \wedge$$
$$\neg(\exists C \in \text{dom } Os \cdot$$
$$possibly\_before(C, O, Ts) \wedge$$
$$possibly\_before(A, C, Ts) \wedge$$
$$p \in Os(C).del)$$

and finally we can write condition (6) as:

$$\forall gi \in As \cdot \exists A \in \text{dom } Os \cdot achieve(Os, Ts, A, gi)$$

Hence, the final VDM state definition is:

```
state Partial_Plan of
       pp: Planning_Problem
       Os: Action_instances
       Ts: Bounded_Poset
       Ps: Goal_instances
       As: Goal_instances
inv mk-Partial_Plan( pp, Os, Ts, Ps, As) ≜
     Os(init) = mk-Action([init], { }, pp.I, { }) ∧
     Os(goal) = mk-Action([goal], pp.G, { }, { }) ∧
```

rng $Os \subseteq pp.AS \cup \{Os(init), Os(goal)\} \wedge$
dom $Os = get\_nodes(Ts) \wedge$
$As \cap Ps = \{\ \} \wedge$
$\forall A \in$ dom $Os \cdot (p \in Os(A).pre \Rightarrow mk\text{-}Goal\_instance(p, A) \in (Ps \cup As)) \wedge$
$\forall gi \in As \cdot \exists A \in$ dom $Os \cdot achieve(Os, Ts, A, gi)$
end

Exercise 6.7

(a) Check that the Painting World examples in Examples 6.6(a)/(b) satisfy the formal definition of goal achievement.
(b) The definition of *achieve* may be logically transformed to make prototyping more straightforward in the next chapter. Using the definitions of *possibly_before* and *before* already supplied, show that:

$\neg (\exists C \in$ dom $Os \cdot$
possibly_before$(C, O, Ts) \wedge$
possibly_before$(A, C, Ts) \wedge$
$p \in Os(C).del)$

transforms to:

$\forall C \in$ dom $Os \cdot$
$C = O \vee$
$C = A \vee$
before$(O, C, Ts) \vee$
before$(C, A, Ts) \vee$
$\neg (p \in Os(C).del)$

6.4.5 VDM operations

Operation *INIT* As usual we will construct the initialization operation first. This inputs a *Planning_Problem* and outputs the first plan. In the output plan, the only action instances in Os are *init* and *goal*, there are no achieved goal instances, and the only goal instances to be achieved are those from the goal set itself, *pp.G*.

INIT(*ppi*: *Planning_Problem*)
ext wr *pp*: *Planning_Problem*
    wr *Os*: *Action_instances*
    wr *Ts*: *Bounded_Poset*
    wr *Ps*: *Goal_instances*
    wr *As*: *Goal_instances*
pre *true*
post *pp* = *ppi* $\wedge$
    $Os = \{init \mapsto mk\text{-}Action([init], \{\ \}, ppi.I, \{\ \}), goal \mapsto mk\text{-}Action([goal], ppi.G, \{\ \}, \{\ \})\} \wedge$

$$Ts = init\_poset(\ ) \land$$
$$Ps = \{mk\text{-}Goal\_instance(g, goal) \mid g \in ppi.G\} \land$$
$$As = \{\ \}$$

Operation *ACHIEVE_1* The first operation we shall specify to achieve a goal instance uses an action instance already present in *Os* to be the achiever. Labelled ext rd below, *Os* is for access only and does not change. The first post-condition predicate we need is therefore:

$$\exists A \in \text{dom } Os \cdot achieve(Os, Ts, A, gi)$$

It is not just a question of verifying that the *achieve* function is true for this instance, however; it may be necessary to change the bounded poset *Ts* to make sure that the *achieve* predicate is true. The variable *Ts* is therefore labelled ext wr below.

Exercise 5.5(b) required the reader formally to specify

$$is\_completion\_of\,(Ts, \overleftarrow{Ts})$$

which defines a relation between two posets. The relation is true if the two posets contain the same set of nodes, and any nodes that are ordered in $\overleftarrow{Ts}$ are also ordered in *Ts*. This relation will be used to provide the constraint on the change to the input partial order that we require: *Ts* must be a completion of $\overleftarrow{Ts}$.

Finally, the goal instance being achieved is essentially passed from *Ps* to *As*:

$$Ps = \overleftarrow{Ps} \setminus \{gi\} \land$$
$$As = \overleftarrow{As} \cup \{gi\}$$

Putting these predicates together, we get:

$$ACHIEVE\_1(gi: Goal\_instance)$$
$$\text{ext rd } Os: Action\_instances$$
$$\qquad \text{wr } Ts: Bounded\_Poset$$
$$\qquad \text{wr } Ps: Goal\_instances$$
$$\qquad \text{wr } As: Goal\_instances$$
$$\text{pre } gi \in Ps$$
$$\text{post } \exists A \in \text{dom } Os \cdot achieve(Os, Ts, A, gi) \land$$
$$\qquad is\_completion\_of\,(Ts, \overleftarrow{Ts}) \land$$
$$\qquad Ps = \overleftarrow{Ps} \setminus \{gi\} \land$$
$$\qquad As = \overleftarrow{As} \cup \{gi\}$$

Operation *ACHIEVE_2* The second achieve operator achieves a goal instance by the introduction of a new action instance into *Os* (recall Exercise 6.6(b)). This is necessary if no action already in the plan can be found to achieve the goal.

The new action will need a new identifier and to create a *unique* one for the action instance we assume the existence of a function that inputs a set of *Action_id* and outputs one not in the set:

> *newid(is : Action_id*-set) *i : Action_id*
> pre *true*
> post *i ∉ is*

The introduction of a new action instance can be written using the let construct as follows:

> let *NewA = newid*(dom $\overleftarrow{Os}$) in
> $\exists A \in pp.AS \cdot Os = \overleftarrow{Os} \dagger \{NewA \mapsto A\}$

and in fact we will use the let construct to bind *NewA* to the new identifier throughout the whole post-condition.

Now that there is a new action in the developing plan, we have the added problem that certain goal instances in *As* may be rendered unachieved (the technical term in planning for the plight of such unfortunate goal instances is that they have been *clobbered*). Consider Fig. 6.4 in Sec. 6.4.2. Assume that a goal instance $(q, C1)$ had been achieved by action *A*, and that *q* was a member of *Y*'s delete-set. Then, the addition of *Y* to achieve goal instance (p, O) would clobber *q*, as in this case the 'achieve' predicate

> *achieve(Os, Ts, A, mk-Goal_instance(q, C1))*

would evaluate to false, because the following expression is true:

> *possibly_before(Y, C1, Ts)* ∧
> *possibly_before(A, Y, Ts)* ∧
> *q ∈ Os(Y).del*

The preceding argument necessitates the 'declobber' condition in the post-condition of *ACHIEVE_2* (we will define it fully later).

The relationship between the old and new temporal orders ($\overleftarrow{Ts}$ and *Ts*) is a little more subtle in this second achieve operation. Here, *Ts* must be a completion of *add_node(NewA, $\overleftarrow{Ts}$)*, which is the ordering with the new node added. The constraint we need on the output temporal order is therefore:

> *is_completion_of(Ts, add_node(NewA, $\overleftarrow{Ts}$))*

Finally, $\overleftarrow{Ps}$ is augmented with the pre-conditions of the new action, and the achieved goal instance *gi* is passed to *As*:

> $Ps = (\overleftarrow{Ps} \setminus \{gi\}) \cup \{mk\text{-}Goal\_instance(p, NewA) \mid p \in A.pre\}$ ∧
> $As = \overleftarrow{As} \cup \{gi\}$

Putting these conditions together gives us the following operation:

$ACHIEVE\_2(gi: Goal\_instance)$
ext rd pp: $Planning\_Problem$
  wr Os: $Action\_instances$
  wr Ts: $Bounded\_Poset$
  wr Ps: $Goal\_instances$
  wr As: $Goal\_instances$
pre $gi \in Ps$
post let $NewA = newid(\text{dom } \overleftarrow{Os})$ in
  $\exists A \in pp.AS \cdot Os = \overleftarrow{Os} \dagger \{NewA \mapsto A\} \wedge$
  $achieve(Os, Ts, NewA, gi) \wedge$
  $\forall gj \in \overleftarrow{As} \cdot declobber(Os, Ts, NewA, gj) \wedge$
  $is\_completion\_of(Ts, add\_node(NewA, \overleftarrow{Ts})) \wedge$
  $Ps = (\overleftarrow{Ps} \setminus \{gi\}) \cup \{mk\text{-}Goal\_instance(p, NewA) \mid p \in A.pre\} \wedge$
  $As = \overleftarrow{As} \cup \{gi\}$

The *declobber* condition effectively insists that each *gi* in *As* remains achieved after the addition of $\{NewA \mapsto A\}$ to *Os*. If we let $gi = mk\text{-}Goal\_instance(q, C)$ then this is so if one of the following conditions is met:

1. *C* is necessarily before *NewA* in *Ts*:

   $before(C, NewA, Ts)$

2. *NewA* does not contain *q* in its delete-set:

   $\neg(q \in Os(NewA).del)$

3. There is an achiever for *gi* called *W* which is constrained to be between *NewA* and *C*:

   $\exists W \in Os \cdot$
   $(before(NewA, W, Ts) \wedge$
   $before(W, C, Ts) \wedge$
   $q \in Os(W).add)$

Let us return to the example in Fig. 6.4 in Sec. 6.4.2. We had assumed above that a goal instance $(q, C1)$ had been achieved by action *A*, and that q was a member of *Y*'s delete-set. After the addition of *Y* to the plan (to achieve goal instance (p, O)), the goal instance $(q, C1)$ therefore had been clobbered by *Y*. Consideration of condition (1) above leads us to one way of declobbering: the temporal order can have an arc added from *C1* to *Y*, to make sure that the clobbering action would be applied *after* *C1*.
Putting the disjunction of conditions together, the definition of function *declobber* is formed:

$declobber$: $Action\_instances \times Bounded\_Poset \times Action\_id \times Goal\_instance \rightarrow \mathbb{B}$
$declobber(Os, Ts, NewA, mk\text{-}Goal\_instance(q, C)) \triangleq$

$before(C, NewA, Ts) \lor$
$\neg (q \in Os(NewA).del) \lor$
$\exists W \in Os \cdot$
$(before(NewA, W, Ts) \land$
$before(W, C, Ts) \land$
$q \in Os(W).add)$

Exercise 6.8   Consider our running example using Fig. 6.4 of Exercise 6.6(b). Under what other conditions (apart from the one we have given above) could goal instance $(q, C1)$ be declobbered?

6.4.6 Proof obligations

We discharge the proof obligation for $ACHIEVE\_1$, while leaving the proof obligations for $INIT$ and $ACHIEVE\_2$ as an exercise.

Firstly, we make the observation that $ACHIEVE\_1$ as it stands is *not* satisfiable! In other words, there is a binding of inputs that will result in no output state. This is demonstrated by considering the VDM state output from $INIT$ and input to $ACHIEVE\_1$: the only 'action' in the plan before *goal* is *init*, and if *gi* cannot be achieved by *init*, then $ACHIEVE\_1$ will fail. Exercise 6.5(e) asks you to find a pre-condition that renders this operation satisfiable.

We can show, however, that if $ACHIEVE\_1$ outputs a state (and it is nondeterministic in that there may be many states satisfying the post-condition) then the state is valid with respect to the invariant. In the informal proof below, we refer to the state invariant's components (1) through to (6):

- (1) and (2) remain true because Os is unchanged.
- The truth of (3) is preserved over the state change because the nodes in Ts remain constant, and Os is unchanged.
- The final two conditions in the post-condition take a *gi* from Ps and put it in As. By a similar argument to that used to show $MAKEOFFER$'s satisfiability in Chapter 3, these two sets stay disjoint, and so (4) is true.
- The specification preserves the sets $Ps \cup As$ and Os, hence (5) is preserved.

To finish, we must show (6) is true in the output state. $ACHIEVE\_1$'s post-condition asserts that the new goal instance is achieved, and in the old state we have (asserted by the invariant) that all the other *gi*'s were achieved. It remains, therefore, to show that these *gi*'s are still achieved in the new state. By Exercise 6.6(c), the addition of extra temporal constraints into Ts does not invalidate any achieved goal instances, and so, also using the fact that Os is unchanged, we argue that the final part of the invariant remains intact.

6.5 SUMMARY

In this chapter we have introduced the interesting and nontrivial application of automatic plan generation. Making assumptions about the nature of actions and plans, we created a model of a general planner in VDM.

In Sec. 6.3 we produced an abstract specification of a plan operation, which contained no commitment to any planning algorithm. In Sec. 6.4 we went on to introduce a design level solution to planning in the form of a goal-directed algorithm whose basic operation was to achieve goals within a developing partially-ordered plan. We then progressed to modelling the plan as a VDM state and finally we specified the 'achieve' operations on this state.

ADDITIONAL PROBLEMS

Some of the problems below are quite hard. The reader who wants to get a better feel for the specification is encouraged to proceed to the next chapter, where it is prototyped.

6.1 Specify a function that reads a *Partial_Plan* and returns true if the problem it contains has been solved. (*Hint*: the problem is solved if all the goal instances in the plan have been achieved.)

6.2 Perform the proof obligations for *INIT* and *ACHIEVE_2*.

6.3 (Project.) The four Blocks World *grasp* actions may be written as one parameterized action (refer to Exercise 6.2(b)):

name: *grasp X*
pre-conditions: '*X* is a block', '*X* has a clear top', 'gripper is free';
add-set: 'gripper grasps *X*';
delete-set: '*X* has a clear top', 'gripper is free';

and in general it is much more expedient to pose actions as parameterized structures. Respecify both design levels of the planner with the extension that actions can be posed with parameters.

6.4 (Hard.) Show that a *Partial_Plan* that has an empty *Ps* necessarily contains a plan that satisfies the post-condition of *PLANNER*. Hence, demonstrate the connection between the abstract planning specification of *PLANNER* and the design level planner of Sec. 6.4.

6.5 Add a pre-condition to *ACHIEVE_1* to make it satisfiable.

REFERENCES

Chapman, D. (1987) Planning for Conjunctive Goals, *Artificial Intelligence*, **32**, July, 333–377.

McCluskey, T.L. (1988) Deriving a Correct Logic Program from the Formal Specification of a Non-Linear Planner, *Methodologies for Intelligent Systems*, **3**, 466–475, North-Holland, New York.

Rich, E., and Knight, K. (1991) *Artificial Intelligence*, 2nd ed. McGraw-Hill, New York.

7

PROTOTYPING VDM SPECIFICATIONS

7.1 INTRODUCTION

In this chapter we will describe some of the principles of prototyping model-based specifications and illustrate the idea by constructing prototypes in the Prolog programming language. Our main example will be prototyping the case study of the last chapter, resulting in a full implementation of the design level specification of the nonlinear planner, which is supplied in Appendix 1.

Prototyping a model based specification S means translating S into a program P which, though not necessarily satisfying efficiency or other nonfunctional constraints, is correct with respect to S. This allows the specification to be *animated*, which enables developers and end users to check early in the development stage that the specification is a valid representation of their requirements. Other advantages include:

- The promise of a working prototype lessens the risk factor involved for a software purchaser: instead of waiting until a full implementation is available, the prototype is a working model that gives a good indication of what the final product will be like.
- Constructing a prototype helps in debugging the specification: even after proof obligations have been successfully discharged, there may remain errors in the logic.
- It is pleasing, after expending much effort on a static, mathematical specification, to be able to get something working!

If the programming language in which P is created (call it PL) is well chosen, then prototyping P can be a semiautomatic process with a very high degree of certainty that P will be correct with respect to S. To be a good prototyping language, PL should contain constructs that are similar to the specification language (say SL) in which S is written. In effect, this means that the *semantic gap* between *SL* and *PL* should be small with respect to:

- Operations—it should be straightforward to translate operations and functions written in *SL* into *PL*.
- Data types—*PL* should either support the same data types as SL , or it should be easy to implement them.

The main difference between an *SL* and a *PL* is that a *PL* has a *procedural semantics*. This means that a program *P* written in *PL* is executable in the sense that it (together with an interpreter for *PL*) can accept input data and should output data. If *P* is a correct implementation this input–output relationship will always conform to specification *S*. For example, with *SL* = VDM and *PL* = Prolog, our prototype planning program in Appendix 1 should input planning problems and output solutions conforming to the specification in Sec. 6.4. The relationship between implicit and explicit function definitions is analogous to the relationship between a specification and its prototype. Recall from Sec. 5.2.6 that, given arbitrary input values for *exponent_x*, the result that this explicit definition produced was proved to satisfy the post-condition of the implicit operation *EXPONENT*, given the same inputs.

The main deficiency of prototyped specifications is that they tend to be *inefficient* in time and space. This is due to two factors:

- A naive implementation—if *P* is written following the same structure as *S*, the program itself may be grossly inefficient (some examples of this are given in Sec. 7.3.5).
- Compilers producing slow code—good candidates for *PL* (such as Prolog) have compilers that tend to produce less efficient code than imperative languages (such as Ada or Modula-2). This is not surprising, as imperative languages reflect the prevailing computer architecture.

Another problem faced when prototyping many specifications that concern the functional aspects of software is that an interface must be constructed to handle input and output. In the simplest terms, procedures for efficiently allowing the input of data, and presenting the output in an intelligible form, need to be written.

7.2 PROLOG AS A PROTOTYPING LANGUAGE FOR VDM

7.2.1 Prolog

Prolog is a general purpose logic programming language that was developed in the 1970s for use in artificial intelligence, especially in the area of natural language processing. Although many interpreters, compilers, and software development environments exist for it, most dialects conform to a standardized version called Edinburgh Prolog. We will assume that the reader is familiar with Edinburgh Prolog and use it as our prototyping language (in what follows by *Prolog* we mean *Edinburgh Prolog*). Interested readers will find a good introduction to Prolog in Clocksin and Mellish (1984).

There are many advantages in the use of Prolog, including its:

- Simple form—a Prolog program is a list of clauses, each clause being a *fact* or a *rule*. Facts are predicate structures of the form *fact_name*$(t_1, ..., t_n)$, where $n \geqslant 0$, and each t_i is a *term* defined as:
  - A constant or
  - A variable or
  - A function symbol containing zero or more terms as arguments.

  Rules are of the form $a \text{ :- } b, c, ..., d.$ where:
  - '$a, b, c, ..., d$' are predicate structures.
  - 'a' is called the *head* of the rule.
  - '$b, c, ..., d.$' is called the *tail* of the rule.
  - ' :- ' is read as 'follows from'.

  A group of clauses that share the same head predicate is called a procedure.
- 'Dual' semantics—Prolog programs can be interpreted in two ways:
  - *declaratively*—each clause can be interpreted as a logic formula, generally a fact or a rule. Our typical rule $a \text{ :- } b, c, ..., d$, corresponds to the logical formula $(b \wedge c \wedge ... \wedge d) \Rightarrow a$ where all variables in the rule are universally quantified.
  - *procedurally*—each clause can be read as a goal-oriented procedure that asserts 'to solve the head, solve all the predicates in the tail'. The head predicate is akin to a procedure's heading, whereas the predicates in the tail can be interpreted as procedure calls. One consequence of the goal-oriented interpretation of Prolog's clauses is that a VDM post-condition can be modelled as a set of Prolog goals to be achieved.
- High-level data structures—Prolog's term and list data structures can be easily adapted to implement VDM data structures.
- Backtracking—Prolog's backtracking mechanism is a form of control that resembles naive search. The search is for instances of a goal predicate's variables that make a goal succeed. Later, we will see how backtracking can be used to prototype existentially quantified conditions in VDM operations.

The first two advantages pointed out above just apply to *Pure Prolog*, a subset of Prolog which does not contain any side effects. Of course, as a programming language Prolog contains expressions that cannot readily be given a logical interpretation, such as *read* and *write* procedures. The language has various other disadvantages of which the user should be aware:

- Prolog is not a strongly-typed language, and in fact variables in predicates are not type-restricted in any way. This means that there is a danger of procedures being called with unsuitable parameter values. With a strongly-typed language (Pascal, for example), if a procedure is called with too many or the wrong type of argument values, the implementation would automatically flag a type mismatch at or before run time, and the user would be aware of and could pin-point the error. In Prolog, the run time behaviour in this case would be unpredictable and the error would be difficult to detect and fix.
- Prolog has no (standard) module mechanism. This means data type encapsulation and information hiding are not supported.

- Prolog does not support functional evaluation, except in some special circumstances such as numerical evaluations. This means that every functional expression in a VDM condition must be translated into a Prolog procedure that has an extra slot for an output value. This extra slot contains a dummy parameter that carries the function value to the next evaluation. For example, consider the following VDM expression:

$$S \cap \mathrm{dom}\ M$$

where S is a set, and M a map. Both functions 'dom' and '$\cap$' must be implemented as Prolog procedures. If we let these procedures be called 'dom_map' and 'intersect_set', then this expression translates to the Prolog predicates:

```
dom_map(M,   DomM), intersect_set(S,DomM,   Result)
/* post-condition: Result = S intersect dom(M) */
```

DomM is the dummy parameter carrying the result of the first function evaluation to the next evaluation.
- Prolog is case sensitive in that all variables have to start with a capital letter, and all predicate, function and constant names start with a lower-case letter.

7.3 VDM TO PROLOG TRANSLATION

The prototyping process needs to be supported with a set of tools and techniques specific to Prolog. Firstly, we will show how a set of tools can be created to support VDM data types; then we will devise a method to translate systematically VDM operations into Prolog clauses. The fact that the logic of pre- and post-conditions can be reflected within the declarative semantics of Prolog makes the translation relatively straightforward, although one must also be aware of certain pitfalls.

VDM has been successfully prototyped using other programming languages, and various support kits have been written. For example, 'me too' (Henderson and Minkowitz, 1986) was an early system for prototyping VDM, using LISP as the target language. As a preliminary to our implementation fragments below, we set out some conventions for Prolog:

- Code will be put in a typewriter face (unlike *pseudocode* which appears in the text face italics).
- Procedures in the toolkits implementing the Set, Sequence, Map, and Composite will have 'set', 'seq', 'map', and 'comp' tagged on to the end of their names accordingly.
- Primitive recursive procedures will be headed with pre- and post-conditions, relating input and output parameters.
- Output parameters will be placed to the right in a procedure heading, separated from the input parameters by three spaces where this improves clarity (there may be occasional exceptions to this, as some parameters may be used for input *or* output).
- Where we represent VDM states as parameters below, the input state parameters will be tagged with the letter 'I' and output state parameters with the letter 'O'.

7.3.1 Data type implementation

VDM's Set, Sequence, Map and Composite types can all be implemented quite easily. In this section we show the reader how to implement the Set type only, although implementations of all the four types are given in Appendix 1. First it is necessary to represent the Set with a Prolog structure, and to do this we will use Prolog's List. The examples of sets in Chapter 3:

$\{1, 4, 9, 16, 25, 36, 49, 64, 81\}$
$\{1, 3, 5, 7, 9, 11\}$
$\{\ \}$

can be written as Prolog lists as follows

$[1, 4, 9, 16, 25, 36, 49, 64, 81]$
$[1, 3, 5, 7, 9, 11]$
$[\ ]$

Recall that whereas in a set representation the left to right ordering of elements is irrelevant, in a list (which is similar to a sequence) different orderings of the same elements denote different lists. Hence a special set equality predicate must be defined, and we do this in terms of the subset ($\subseteq$) relation, which in turn will be defined using the 'element of' ($\in$) relation (refer to Sec. 2.2.3):

$X = Y$ if and only if $X \subseteq Y \wedge Y \subseteq X$
$X \subseteq Y$ if and only if $\forall e \in X \cdot e \in Y$

To implement set equality, we first implement the '$\in$' relation using a simple list processing procedure:

```
/* element_of_set(E,Y)                        */
/* pre: Y is a set                            */
/* post: E is an element of Y                 */
/*       iff element_of_set(E,Y) succeeds     */
/*(1)*/ element_of_set(E,[E|Y]).
/*(2)*/ element_of_set(E,[_|Y]) :-
           element_of_set(E,Y).
```

(1) reads as: 'element_of_set succeeds if the element to be tested is at the head of the list'. The rule in (2) reads as: 'if (1) is not the case, then apply element_of_set to the tail of the list'. The empty slot '_' in element_of_set(E,[_|Y]) represents a variable that we do not need to give a name to (as it is not used elsewhere in the rule). Next we can define subset and finally the equality predicate (which we call eq_set):

```
/* sub_set(X,Y)                        */
/* pre: X,Y sets                       */
/* post: X is a subset of Y            */
/*       iff sub_set(X,Y) succeeds     */
sub_set([First_Element|Rest],Y) :-
    element_of_set(First_Element,Y),
    sub_set(Rest,Y),!.
sub_set([],Y).
```

```
/* eq_set(X,Y)                              */
/* pre: X,Y sets                            */



/* post: X=Y iff eq_set(X,Y) succeeds       */
eq_set(X,Y) :-
    sub_set(X,Y),
    sub_set(Y,X),!.
```

Note the use of Prolog's 'cut' (!) in the last two procedures. The 'cut' is a device to stop Prolog's backtracking mechanism: procedures that are implementing *functions* have only one output value that satisfies their inputs, therefore backtracking within their procedural definition is worthless. Using the 'cut' in the manner above stops backtracking *within* the function definition.

The subset procedure shows the disadvantage of Prolog not being a strongly-typed language: the second clause asserts that the empty list (or empty set in our interpretation) is a subset of *anything*. We have to rely on the commented pre-conditions being followed for the integrity of this procedure. An alternative suggested in Exercise 7.2 would be to create the procedure *is_a_set*(X) which checks variables, returning true only if its argument is a set. This way a type mechanism can be implemented on top of Prolog.

The other Set functions introduced in Sec. 3.3.2 are implemented in terms of the element_of_set procedure:

- The union operator '∪':

```
/* union_set(X,Y,Z)                         */
/* pre: X,Y sets                            */
/* post: Z = X union Y                      */

union_set([E|X],Y,[E|Z]) :-
    not(element_of_set(E,Y)),
    union_set(X,Y,Z),!.
union_set([E|X],Y,Z) :-
    element_of_set(E,Y),
    union_set(X,Y,Z),!.
union_set([],Y,Y).
```

- The intersection operator '∩':

```
/* intersect_set(X,Y,Z)                     */
/* pre: X,Y sets                            */
/* post: Z = X intersect Y                  */

intersect_set([E|X],Y,[E|Z]) :-
    element_of_set(E,Y),

    intersect_set(X,Y,Z),!.
intersect_set([E|X],Y,Z) :-
    not(element_of_set(E,Y)),
    intersect_set(X,Y,Z),!.
intersect_set([],Y,[]).
```

- The set difference operator '\':

```
/* minus_set(X,Y,Z)                          */
/* pre: X,Y sets                             */
/* post: Z = X minus Y                       */

minus_set([E|X],Y,Z) :-
    element_of_set(E,Y),
    minus_set(X,Y,Z),!.
minus_set([E|X],Y,[E|Z]) :-
    not(element_of_set(E,Y)),
    minus_set(X,Y,Z),!.
minus_set([],Y,[]).
```

Exercise 7.1 These exercises are for those keen on developing their Prolog skills only. Other readers may immediately consult the answers to these exercises in Appendix 1.

(a) The VDM primitive function tl can be implemented with just one Prolog fact:

```
/* tl_seq(List_in, List_out):               */
/* post:  List_out = tl(List_in)            */
tl_seq([H|T], T).
```

Implement the rest of the Sequence data structure's functions in Prolog.

(b) Implement the Composite and Map types in Prolog, ensuring that the representations of these structures is insulated from the rest of the program. To do this you need to provide the implementations for the procedures specified below, which initialize, add, and retrieve values to and from these structures.

```
/* init_comp(Name, List_of_slot_names, List_of_slot_values,  Comp ):   */
/* post: Comp is a composite structure with name Name, and a list      */
/* of component names given in List_of_slot_names, with corresponding  */
/* values in List_of_slot_values                                       */

/* put_comp(Comp, Slot_name, Value,   NewComp):                        */
/* post: NewComp = Comp except Slot_name(NewComp) = Value              */


/* get_comp(Comp, Slot_name,   Value):                                 */
/* post: Value = Slot_name(Comp)                                       */

/* init_map(  Map)                                                     */
/* post: Map is an empty map                                           */

/* overwrite_map(Map, Dom, Value,   NewMap):                           */
/* post: NewMap = Map + [Dom -> Value]                                 */

/* apply_map(Map, Dom,   Value):                                       */
/* post: Value = Map(Dom)                                              */
```

```
/* dom_map(Map,    Dom_Map):                                    */
/* post: Dom_Map = dom(Map)                                     */


/* ran_map(Map,    Ran_Map):                                    */
/* post: Ran_Map = ran(Map)                                     */
```

7.3.2 Operator translation

Some basic rules for the translation of VDM operators into Prolog are given below. We start with the assumption that a VDM operator has the following form (similar to the general form used in Sec. 3.5.3):

$OP\_NAME(i_1:ti_1,\ldots,i_n:ti_n)\,o:to$
ext wr $s:state\_type$
pre $pre(i_1,\ldots,i_n,s)$
post $post(i_1,\ldots,i_n,\overleftarrow{s},o,s)$

where $i_1,\ldots,i_n$ is a list of input parameters, o an output parameter, and $ti_1,\ldots,ti_n$, to their respective types.

The head of the Prolog procedure that is created from this will have the following form:

$op(i_1,\ldots,i_n,\overleftarrow{s},o,s)$

Input and output states are represented with explicit parameters, to avoid the problem of managing global data. Otherwise, the VDM state can be represented in Prolog as a collection of facts, or as a single fact, and state changes performed by Prolog's *assert* and *retract* predicates. The ad hoc use of global data effected by *assert* and *retract* tends to make Prolog programs unmaintainable.

The *op* procedure can have a number of clauses, depending on the logical form of the pre- and post-conditions. Disjunction or implication in an operator's conditions leads to a definition with several clauses. We will assume for the moment that the conditions are conjunctions of predicates without any quantified variables, that is:

$pre(i_1,\ldots,i_n,s)=p_1\wedge p_2\wedge\ldots\wedge p_k$
$post(i_1,\ldots,i_n,\overleftarrow{s},o,s)=q_1\wedge q_2\wedge\ldots\wedge q_l$

Now each of the p_i and q_j could be one of the following:

- Primitive predicates, predefined in VDM
- User-defined predicates, such as *achieve* and *before* of Chapter 6

We let each of these predicates be implemented by a corresponding Prolog procedure: $proc\_p_1$ for p_1, $proc\_q_1$ for q_1, and so on. The names $proc\_p_1$, $proc\_p_2,\ldots$, represent procedures that may contain input parameters (including the input state parameter). The names $proc\_q_1$, $proc\_q_2,\ldots$, each represent procedures, but they may contain references to any input or output parameters or states. A simple monolithic translation, combining pre-condition procedures with those in the post-condition into one clause, gives:

$$op(i_1, \ldots, i_n, o_1, \ldots, o_m, \overleftarrow{s}, s) :-$$
$$proc\_p_1,$$
$$proc\_p_2,$$
$$\ldots,$$
$$proc\_p_k,$$
$$proc\_q_1,$$
$$proc\_q_2,$$
$$\ldots,$$
$$proc\_q_l.$$

The specification of each $proc\_p_i$ is given essentially by treating p_i as its post-condition. The specification of each $proc\_q_i$ is a little more complicated since these procedures effectively have to achieve the post-condition of op. In achieving a predicate, there is always the possibility that an already achieved predicate may be unachieved! The reader should see the parallel with *clobbering* in the planning application of Chapter 6, where the effect of one action could undo the achievement of one goal. The similarity is not surprising since programming to achieve a specification is a form of planning.

In fact, the post-condition of $proc\_q_j$ is $q_1 \wedge q_2 \wedge \ldots \wedge q_j$, since we require $proc\_q_j$ to achieve condition q_j while preserving conditions $q_1 \wedge q_2 \wedge \ldots \wedge q_{j-1}$. Although strictly speaking this is the case, it is more expedient to consider q_j as the post-condition of $proc\_q_j$ and keep a watchful eye that previous predicates are not undone.

A more elaborate way to translate operators into Prolog procedures is first to create a procedure that executes the post-condition procedures only if the pre-condition is met:

$$op(i_1, \ldots, i_n, o_1, \ldots, o_m, \overleftarrow{s}, s) : -$$
$$proc\_p_1,$$
$$proc\_p_2,$$
$$\ldots,$$
$$proc\_p_k,$$
$$execute\_op\_name(i_1, \ldots, i_n, o_1, \ldots, o_m, \overleftarrow{s}, s).$$
$$op(i_1, \ldots, i_n, o_1, \ldots, o_m, \overleftarrow{s}, s) : -$$
$$write(\text{`operator pre-condition failure'}).$$

If the pre-condition procedures succeed, the first clause calls $execute\_op\_name$ which 'executes' the operator. The second clause outputs an error message if the pre-condition procedures fail, which means the operator cannot be executed. $execute\_op\_name$ is defined as:

$$execute\_op\_name(i_1, \ldots, i_n, o_1, \ldots, o_m, \overleftarrow{s}, s) : -$$
$$proc\_q_1,$$
$$proc\_q_2,$$
$$\ldots,$$
$$proc\_q_l.$$

This second form, although longer, is more secure, since errors in the implementation of the post-condition will not be confused with failing pre-conditions. To keep the length of the code fragments in this chapter to a minimum, however, we adopt the first form.

Examples 7.1

(a) The estate agent database operator *MAKEOFFER* introduced in Sec. 3.5 was defined thus:

> *MAKEOFFER*(*addr*: *Address*)
> ext wr *forsale, underoffer*: *Address*-set
> pre *addr* ∈ *forsale*
> post *forsale* = $\overline{forsale}$ \ {*addr*} ∧ *underoffer* = $\overline{underoffer}$ ∪ {*addr*}

Prototyping *MAKEOFER* is straightforward, because its pre- and post-conditions are conjunctions of predicates. It translates into one clause consisting of primitive procedures:

```
makeoffer(Addr, ForsaleI, UnderofferI, Forsale0,    Underoffer0) :-
      element_of_set(Addr,    ForsaleI),
      minus_set(ForsaleI, [Addr],    Forsale0),
      union_set(UnderofferI, [Addr],    Underoffer0).
```

(b) Consider the *ADD* operator of the *Symbol_table* of Chapter 4:

> *ADD*(*i*: *Identifier*, *a*: *Attribute*)
> ext wr *s*: *Symbol_table*
> pre *s* ≠ [ ] ∧ *i* ∉ dom(hd *s*)
> post *s* = [(hd $\overline{s}$)†{*i*↦*a*}]⌢tl $\overline{s}$

Again, the implementation is made up completely from data structure primitives:

```
add(I, A, SI,    SO) :-
      not(SI = [ ]),                        /* pre-conditions:  */
      hd_seq(SI,    SIhd),
      dom_map(SIhd,    DomSIhd),
      not(element_of_set(I,    DomSIhd)),
      overwrite_map(SIhd,I,A,    SIhd1),     /* post-conditions: */
      tl_seq(SI,    SItl),
      append_seq([SIhd1],SItl,    SO).
```

Notice how the dummy variables (SIhd, DomSIhd, SIhd1) are required to store the results of operator evaluation.

Exercise 7.2

(a) Prototype the *DELETE_HOUSE, PUSH* and *POP* operations of Chapters 3 and 4.
(b) Create a general translation method for VDM operations that includes conditions containing '∨', the logical 'or' operator.

(c) Implement the type checking predicate $is\_a\_set(X)$ and hence create a type checking mechanism for the Prolog implementation of VDM data structures.

7.3.3 The existential quantifiers

The quantifier '∃' invariably occurs in a VDM condition in the following type of expression:

$$\exists X \in some\_set \cdot p \dots$$

where X occurs as a free variable in p. This can be simulated in Prolog using a free variable for X in the 'element_of_set' procedure. Assuming procedure 'proc' achieves predicate p (that is 'proc' is the prototyped version of p), the expression above can be translated to the piece of code:

```
element_of_set(X, Some_set), proc, ...
```

X will become instantiated with the first element of 'Some_set' by the execution of 'element_of_set'. If 'proc' fails with that instantiation, Prolog's backtracking mechanism will recall 'element_of_set' which will succeed with another instance for X. This will continue systematically (because 'Some_set' is implemented as a list) until 'proc' eventually succeeds. Hence Prolog's backtracking mechanism persists in backtracking to 'element_of_set' until the correct element is picked. If all the elements are exhausted and 'element_of_set' eventually fails, the condition cannot be satisfied.

Example 7.2 The *RETRIEVE* operation in Chapter 4 relied on an existentially quantified variable b in its pre-condition:

> *RETRIEVE*(i: *Identifier*) a: *Attribute*
> ext rd s: *Symbol_table*
> pre $\exists b \in$ elems $s \cdot i \in$ dom b
> post $a = get\_from\_table(s, i)$

This translates into:

```
retrieve(I,S,   A) :-
    elems_seq(S,    SetS),
    element_of_set(B,    SetS),
    dom_map(B,   domB),
    element_of_set(I,    domB),
    get_from_table(I,S,   A).
```

In this example, backtracking actually occurs across the middle procedure dom_map. Whatever instance of B the procedure element_of_set produces, dom_map, being a total function, succeeds. The fourth procedure call in the clause fails until the correct choice of B has been picked.

7.3.4 The universal quantifier

The universal quantifier appears in a VDM condition in the same context as the existential quantifier above:

$$\forall X \in some\_set \cdot p \dots$$

where X occurs as a free variable in p. To implement this expression in Prolog, the procedure (call it 'Proc') corresponding to the predicate p has to be called repeatedly for all instances of X in *some_set*. This contrasts with the case of the existentially quantified variable, where only one successful procedure call needs to be made. Also, if the scope of X is more than one predicate, then we let 'Proc' correspond to all these predicates.

For this implementation we need two special Prolog predicates (the reader who is not too concerned about low-level implementation may simply examine the post-condition of the implementing procedure below and move to the next section):

- The metapredicate call(X), which executes its argument X as a normal Prolog goal.
- The infix operator =.., which succeeds if its right-hand argument is a list of terms making up the structure of its left-hand argument. For example, the Prolog goal f(x)=..X would succeed with X bound to [f, x].

Using call(X) we can create an iterative procedure with the name for_all_els which repeatedly calls the procedure Proc. This procedure call will have a different value from *some_set* on each invocation:

```
/* post: for_all_els( Some_set, Proc) is true
         iff for all X in Some_set : p is true */
for_all_els( [ ], Proc).
for_all_els( [E|L], Proc) :-
      Proc =.. OL,
      append(OL,[E], OL1),
      ProcE = ..OL1,
      call(ProcE),
      for_all_els( L, Proc).
```

For this to succeed, the procedure Proc must be defined so that its last argument expects a value from the set Some_set; for_all_els is then supplied with the Proc procedure instance without its last argument. Then, the three procedure calls

```
Proc =.. OL,
append(OL,[E], OL1),
ProcE =.. OL1,
```

succeed in gluing on an element of Some_set to the end of the procedure Proc, which is then called with the correct number of arguments.

Example 7.3 The specification for *MAX_IN* in Chapter 3 contained a universal quantifier:

> MAX_IN (s: $\mathbb{N}$-set) m: $\mathbb{N}$
> pre $s \neq \{\ \}$
> post $m \in s \wedge \forall i \in s \cdot i \leqslant m$

It translates as follows:

```
max_in(S,    M) :-
    not( S = [ ]),
    element_of_set(M, S),
    for_all_els(S, less_eq(M)).
less_eq(M, E) :- M =< E.
```

The output parameter M here is systematically instantiated with elements of S, until eventually one is found that satisfies the universally quantified condition. Procedures like for_all_els that invoke metapredicates act in a similar fashion to *higher-order functions* in functional programming languages.

Exercise 7.3 A complication arises if the universal quantifier occurs in the post-condition and the predicate *p* relates input and output (state) parameters. Each time Proc is invoked, its output parameters need to be supplied as input to the next call of Proc with a new set element. In this case, the procedure implementing 'for all' must keep track of the changing input parameter as each version of Proc is called.

Implement a new version of for_all_els called for_all_elsIO along these lines. It should include two extra arguments for the input and output parameters, as follows:

```
/* post: for_all_elsIO(S, Proc, In, Out) is true iff
         forall X in S: p(In, Out, X) is true        */
```

The answer to this exercise also appears in Appendix 1.

7.3.5 Prototyping pitfalls

The main problem in producing naive prototypes along the lines given above is the threat of producing grossly inefficient code. The implementation of *MAX_IN* was such an example. A more extreme case arises from the specification of a sort function given below, which inputs an arbitrary sequence of integers and outputs the ordered sequence:

> $SORT$ (in: $\mathbb{N}^*$) out: $\mathbb{N}^*$
> pre *true*
> post *permutation*(in, out) $\wedge$ *ordered*(out)

Assuming *permutation* and *ordered* are defined elsewhere, the naive translation to the top-level procedures would be:

```
sort(In,    Out) :-
    permutation(In,Out),
    ordered(Out).
```

The implementation that this leads to is very inefficient: the first procedure *permutation* will blindly generate permutations of the initial sequence, until one is eventually found that is ordered. Though the specification of *sort* seems to be a natural one, an implementation that follows its structure is inadequate.

Output state variables and the output parameter in implicitly defined operations can cause related problems. In theory, they are dealt with in a similar way to existentially quantified variables: Prolog's backtracking mechanism iterates until values are found for them that satisfy the post-condition. Unfortunately, in very abstract definitions, this is impractical. An example, which we met in Chapter 6, was the top-level specification of the Planner:

$PLANNER(pp: Planning\_Problem)$ *soln*: *Action**
pre *true*
post elems $soln \subseteq pp.AS \wedge$
    $complete(soln, pp.I) \wedge$
    $pp.G \subseteq$ apply$\_seq(soln, pp.I)$

Taking the predicates in the order they are written, to produce a prototype we might construct a procedure to generate action sequences from the set of all actions in the planning problem, but this would lead to a hopeless implementation!

One general way of improving efficiency in prototypes is by judicious reordering of its procedures, although any ordering of the procedures produced from *SORT* and *PLANNER* would result in at least a very inefficient implementation. Specifications such as these would have to be transformed or refined before the kind of method we are advocating would be worth while. In fact, systematically generating instances of *soln* from *complete(soln, I(pp))* in a planner corresponds to very inefficient search strategies such as 'breadth-first search'.

We end the section on a more optimistic note: this final example will show how a computationally 'explosive' prototype can be rescued and made efficient with a correctness-preserving transformation. The *before* function in Chapter 5 was defined with the use of an existential quantifier:

$before: Node \times Node \times Arc\text{-set} \rightarrow \mathbb{B}$
$before(x, z, p) \triangleq$
    $mk\text{-}Arc(x, z) \in p \vee$
    $\exists y \in get\_nodes(p) \cdot before(x, y, p) \wedge before(y, z, p)$

Disjunction in the function definition means that the Prolog procedure will have to be split into a list of clauses, one for each formula connected by the disjunction. In this case we will have two clauses: the first constructs the arc composite and checks whether it already occurs in the poset (see Exercise 7.1(b) for the definition of init_comp):

```
before(X, Z, P) :-
        init_comp(arc, [source, dest], [X, Y],     ARC),
        element_of_set(ARC,      P), !.
```

The second clause contains the recursive calls to find arc paths:

```
before(X, Z, P) :-
        get_nodes(P,     Nodes),
        element_of_set(Y, Nodes),
        before(X, Y, P),
        before(Y, Z, P).
```

The problem is that the double call to procedure before does not lead to a systematic algorithm. A logically equivalent definition is as follows:

$before$: $Node \times Node \times Arc$-set $\rightarrow \mathbb{B}$
$before(x, z, p) \triangleq$
$mk\text{-}Arc(x, z) \in p \vee$
$\exists y \in get\_nodes(p) \cdot mk\text{-}Arc(x, y) \in p \wedge before(y, z, p)$

This version leads to a workable prototype because the search for a path is defined in a systematic manner:

```
before(X, Z, P) :-
        get_nodes(P,     Nodes),
        element_of_set(Y, Nodes),
        init_comp(arc, [source, dest], [X, Y],     ARC),
        element_of_set(ARC,    P),
        before(Y, Z, P).
```

Exercises 7.4

(a) Prototype the rest of the poset specification in Chapter 5 in Prolog (note that the solution can be found in Appendix 1).
(b) Using either a formal or diagrammatic argument, prove that the two versions of *before* given above are equivalent.

7.4 THE PLANNER PROTOTYPE

The method described above is used now to prototype the Planner specified in Sec. 6.4. Although the implementation of some of the functions is left as an exercise for the reader, the answers can be found in a full listing of the whole prototype in Appendix 1. We develop the prototype in a top-down fashion, rooting the procedures eventually in the primitive data structure functions of Sec. 7.3.1.

Each of the three operations *INIT, ACHIEVE_*1, and *ACHIEVE_*2 will be translated to a top-level Prolog procedure, using the methods outlined above. The efficiency problem is not so acute in this application, because of the fairly concrete and goal directed nature of the specification. Nevertheless, reordering the goals in some of the resulting Prolog clauses certainly makes the prototype more efficient, while preserving the correctness of the code.

7.4.1 The *INIT* operator

The initialization operator can be translated using the notation introduced in Exercise 7.1(b) for the Composite and Map types. One problem remains—that of set comprehension. Rather than producing a general procedure to deal with set comprehension, we present a specialized solution for the expression:

$$\{mk\text{-}Goal\_instance(g, goal) \mid g \in pp.G\}$$

This translates into Prolog using a recursive procedure that builds up a set of goal instances as follows:

```
/* make_goal_instances(A, Gs,    Gi)                        */
/* pre: Gs is a literal set, A is an action identifier      */
/* post: Gi = {mk-Goal_instances(g,A) : g is in Gs}         */
make_goal_instances(Action_Id, [G|G_rest],   [Gi|Gi_rest]) :-
    init_comp(goal_instance, [gl, ai], [Action_Id, G],   Gi),
    make_goal_instances(Action_Id, G_rest,   Gi_rest).
make_goal_instances(_, [],   []).
```

Making use of this predicate, the translation of the *INIT* operator is then:

```
init(PPI,   PPO) :-
    get_comp(PPI, planning_problem, i,   IPP),
    get_comp(PPI, planning_problem, g,   GPP),
    init_comp(action, [name,pre,add,del], [ init ,[], IPP, [] ],   INIT),
    init_comp(action, [name,pre,add,del], [ goal , GPP, [], [] ],   GOAL),
    init_map( OS),
    overwrite_map(OS, init, INIT,   OS1),
    overwrite_map(OS1, goal, GOAL,   OS2),
    make_goal_instances(goal, GPP,   GIs),
    initPO(Ts),
    init_comp(partial_plan, [pp,os,ts,ps,as], [PPI,OS2,Ts,GIs,[]],   PPO).
```

The proliferation in variable names (OS1, OS2, for example) is not only due to the lack of functional evaluation in Prolog, but also the price of abstraction: whereas we chose to make the representation of sequences and maps visible (as lists), the representation of maps and composites has been hidden within the definition of these structures' primitive functions.

*ACHIEVE_*1 can now be implemented by a procedure called achieve1, in which all the procedures are primitive data functions (which were covered in Sec. 7.2) except for the 'achieve' predicate itself. As an external state is not accessed, the operation must use an access function (get_comp) to break up the input plan:

```
achievel(PlanI, Gi,   PlanO) :-
    get_comp(PlanI, partial_plan, os,   Os),
    get_comp(PlanI, partial_plan, ts,   Ts),
    get_comp(PlanI, partial_plan, ps,   Ps),
    get_comp(PlanI, partial_plan, as,   As),

    element_of_set(Gi, Ps),     /* pre-condition */

    dom_map(Os,    DomOs),      /* post-condition: */
    element_of_set(A, DomOs),
    achieve(Os,Ts,A,Gi,   Ts_new),
    minus_set(Ps, [Gi],   Ps_new),
    union_set(As, [Gi],   As_new),

    put_comp(PlanI, partial_plan, ts, Ts_new,   Plan1),
    put_comp(Plan1, partial_plan, ps, Ps_new,   Plan2),
    put_comp(Plan2, partial_plan, as, As_new,   PlanO).
```

Notice how these implementations follow the specification virtually line by line, except that Prolog is more longwinded because of its need for procedures to return function values explicitly. Our 'predicate to procedure' correspondence is broken in that the implementation of the 'achieve' procedure has as its post-condition two predicates:

$$achieve(Os, Ts, A, gi) \land$$
$$is\_completion\_of(Ts, \overleftarrow{Ts})$$

The last conjunction is in effect met if we constrain the implementation of *achieve* so that it only adds constraints to *Ts*, and adds no new nodes (that is actions). The definition of *achieve* in Chapter 6 is:

$achieve : Action\_instances \times Bounded\_Poset \times Action\_id \times Goal\_instance \rightarrow \mathbb{B}$
$achieve(Os, Ts, A, mk\text{-}Goal\_instance(p, O)) \triangleq$
$before(A, O, Ts) \land$
$p \in Os(A).add \land$
$\neg(\exists C \in \text{dom } Os\cdot$
$possibly\_before(C, O, Ts) \land$
$possibly\_before(A, C, Ts) \land$
$p \in Os(C).del)$

It will need to be transformed somewhat, to give a simpler implementation. We move the negation '¬' inwards, using the result of Exercise 6.7, and introduce an auxiliary predicate *declobber_achieve* to produce the new form:

$achieve : Action\_instances \times Bounded\_Poset \times Action\_id \times Goal\_instance \rightarrow \mathbb{B}$
$achieve(Os, Ts, A, mk\text{-}Goal\_instance(p, O)) \triangleq$
$before(A, O, Ts) \land$
$p \in Os(A).add \land$
$\forall C \in \text{dom } Os\cdot declobber\_achieve(p, A, O, Os, C, Ts)$

where:

> *declobber_achieve(p, A, O, Os, C, Ts)* $\triangleq$
> $C = O$ $\vee$
> $C = A$ $\vee$
> *before(O, C, Ts)* $\vee$
> *before(C, A, Ts)* $\vee$
> $\neg(p \in Os(C).del)$

Now we have two distinct cases to consider: one in which `achieve` succeeds without changing the input state's temporal order *Ts* at all; and another in which constraints have to be added to *Ts*. Thus we have the following cases:

- An achieving action '*A*' is found for *p*, and no actions present in *Os* clobber (that is undo) this achievement. Therefore, no constraint need be added to the temporal order (in other words *Ts* would remain unchanged).
- An achieving action '*A*' is found for *p*, but there is at least one action that clobbers *p*, and there is at least one way of declobbering it (that is putting constraints into *Ts* that avoid the goal literal *p* being clobbered).

It is desirable to make the Planner take a *least commitment* approach to forming plans, so that if the first case is true then the second case need not be explored. On the other hand, if the first case is false then we want *ACHIEVE_1* to be able to make a nondeterministic choice among the set of possible declobbering constraints (potentially, therefore, a backtracking mechanism could generate every possible choice). The first part of the achieve implementation is (in the code below we put, in comments next to a procedure, its corresponding predicate post-condition, where possible):

```
achieve(Os,Ts,A,GI,    New_Ts) :-
    get_comp(GI,goal_instance, ai,   O),
    get_comp(GI,goal_instance, gi,   P),
    apply_map(Os,A,    ActionA),
    get_comp(ActionA,action,add,    AddA),
    element_of_set(P,    AddA),                /* P is in Os(A).add */
    make_before(A,O,Ts,    Ts1),              /* before(A,O,Ts1)    */
    dom_map(Os,    DomOs),
    for_all_elsIO(DomOs, declobber_achieve(P,A,O,Os), Ts1,    New_Ts).
```

Again, the reader should notice how the code mirrors the specification. One change in ordering we have made is in switching around the `apply_map` and `make_before` procedures—this improves the efficiency of the Planner.

The 'declobber_achieve' procedure has two parts: in the first, the partial order *Ts* remains unchanged, while in the second it is necessary to add a constraint to *Ts*. If the first part succeeds we do not require any other alternatives involving temporal constraint additions, therefore Prolog's 'cut' will be used to cut down the alternatives in that case:

```
declobber_achieve(P,A,O,Os,O,Ts,    Ts) :- !. /* C = O V */
declobber_achieve(P,A,O,Os,A,Ts,    Ts) :- !. /* C = A V */
declobber_achieve(P,A,O,Os,C,Ts,    Ts) :-
    before(O,C,Ts),!.                         /* before(O,C,Ts) V */
```

```
declobber_achieve(P, A, O, Os, C, Ts,    Ts) :-
    before(C, A, Ts), !.                          /* before(C, A, Ts) V */
declobber_achieve(P, A, O, Os, C, Ts,    Ts) :-
    apply_map(Os, C,    CA),
    get_comp(CA, action, del,    CAD),
    not(element_of_set(P, CAD)), !.               /* not( p in Os(C).del) */

declobber_achieve(P, A, O, Os, C, Ts,    New_Ts) :-
    make_before(O, C, Ts,    New_Ts).             /* make  before(O, C, Ts) */
declobber_achieve(P, A, O, Os, C, Ts,    New_Ts) :-
    make_before(C, A, Ts,    New_Ts).             /* make  before(C, A, Ts) */
```

Finally, the *ACHIEVE_2* operation is prototyped in a similar manner:

```
achieve2(PlanI, Gi, PlanO) :-
    get_comp(PlanI, partial_plan, pp,    PP),
    get_comp(PlanI, partial_plan, os,    Os),
    get_comp(PlanI, partial_plan, ts,    Ts),
    get_comp(PlanI, partial_plan, ps,    Ps),
    get_comp(PlanI, partial_plan, as,    As),
    element_of_set(Gi, Ps),                       /* pre-condition */

    dom_map(Os,    DomOs),                         /* post-condition: */
    newid(DomOs,    NewA),
    add_node(NewA, Ts,    Ts2),
    get_comp(PP, planning_problem, as,    ASpp),
    element_of_set(Action, ASpp),
    overwrite_map(Os, NewA, Action,    Os_new),

    achieve(Os_new, Ts2, NewA, Gi,    Ts3),
    for_all_elsIO(As, declobber(Os_new, NewA), Ts3,    Ts_new),

    get_comp(Action, action, pre,    PreA),
    make_goal_instances(NewA, PreA,    GIs),
    minus_set(Ps, [Gi],    Ps_new1),
    union_set(Ps_new1, GIs,    Ps_new2),
    union_set(As, [Gi],    As_new),
    put_comp(PlanI, partial_plan, os, Os_new,    Plan1),
    put_comp(Plan1, partial_plan, ts, Ts_new,    Plan2),
    put_comp(Plan2, partial_plan, ps, Ps_new2,    Plan3),
    put_comp(Plan3, partial_plan, as, As_new,    PlanO).
```

Exercise 7.4 Continue the prototyping exercise. You will need to implement procedures corresponding to the predicates *declobber* and *newid*, using the specifications in the last chapter, and also a top-level procedure conforming to the algorithm in Fig. 6.2. Compare your answers with the implementation in Appendix 1.

7.5 SUMMARY

Prototyping VDM specifications using Prolog involves, firstly, building a set of tools in Prolog to support the Set, Sequence, Map, and Composite data structures. VDM operators are then translated into Prolog clauses, roughly by considering each predicate in an operator's pre- and post-condition as the post-condition of its corresponding Prolog procedure.

The advantages in using Prolog are that there is a correspondence between Prolog's declarative semantics and the logic of an operator's conditions, and that Prolog's backtracking mechanism can be used to find the correct choice of existentially quantified variables.

The chief disadvantages are in the insecurities of Prolog (it is not strongly typed and has no data encapsulation mechanisms), and in its lack of functional evaluation, causing long winded implementations.

ADDITIONAL PROBLEMS: IMPROVEMENTS TO THE PLANNER AND THE PROTOTYPE

We offer some suggestions for improving and expanding both the specification and the prototype, which the reader may like to take up as a project (these suggestions range from 'extended coursework' upwards).

7.1 After extending the planner so that it accepts parameterized actions (see the additional problems at the end of Chapter 6), prototype your new specification.

7.2 A hierarchical planner is one whose domain must be specified at several levels of abstraction. The planner we have presented is 'flat', but it can be extended to plan within a hierarchy with the addition of a *refine* operation, which can be specified in much the same way as the *achieve* operations. By consulting the AI planning literature, try to extend the design level specification to that of a hierarchical planner (for some help in this consult Fox (1990)).

7.3 The planning algorithm involves three types of choice: which partial plan to choose from Store, which goal instance to achieve in that plan, and which way to achieve the goal instance. Letting these choices be random is very inefficient. Try to construct *heuristic* rules that influence these choices.

7.4 Rearrange the procedures in the achieve procedures to increase the planner's efficiency. For example, try to cut down the amount of backtracking Prolog has to perform to find an action to achieve a goal.

REFERENCES

Clocksin, W., and Mellish, C. (1984). *Programming in Prolog*, 2nd ed., Springer Verlag, New York.

Fox, M. (1990). A Constructive Paradigm of Hierarchical Planning, *PhD Thesis*, The University of Hertfordshire.

Henderson, P., and Minkowitz, C.J., (1986). Me too Methods of Software Design, *ICL Technical Journal*, 5(4).

8

ALGEBRAIC SPECIFICATION OF ABSTRACT DATA TYPES

8.1 INTRODUCTION

In this chapter we introduce the *algebraic* approach to specification by looking at its application to the specification of abstract data types. In particular, we start by considering one of the classical abstract data types, namely the stack. Although the algebraic approach to specification encompasses a wider class of applications than abstract data types, this particular use captures the spirit of the algebraic approach and so provides a natural and intuitive way of introducing it.

Informally, an *abstract data type* consists of a collection of values and operations where the values derive their meaning solely through the operations that can be performed upon them. For some time now it has been realized that distinct advantages can result from breaking down the data of a problem into smaller components such as abstract data types, not the least of which is the fact that due consideration of the attributes of the data for a particular problem often reveals an appropriate modularization of the software itself.

Abstract data types are also important in the context of *object-oriented programming languages* (OOPLs). The artefacts or *objects* that are manipulated by a program written in such a language are instances of abstract data types, that is an encapsulated data structure that can only be accessed by a well-defined collection of operations *specified* in an external interface.

Both the model-based approach (as typified by VDM) and the algebraic approach are classed as so-called 'formal methods' for specification, design and refinement. The vital feature of all formal methods is that they are built upon a mathematical framework, so that the powerful proof techniques afforded by mathematics can be brought to bear on the process of verification. In the case of algebraic specifications, the underlying mathematical theory that underpins the approach is *equational logic*. The mathematical *models* or *interpretations* that satisfy the theory are known as *algebras* of the theory.

Basically, an *algebra* consists of a set of values called the *carrier set* of the algebra together with a collection of operations (mathematical functions) that act upon these values. It was Zilles, back in 1974 (Zilles 1974) who first realized that a data type can be considered as an algebra, with the resulting implication that algebras can be used as a means of formally specifying abstract data types. With this approach, an *algebraic theory* defines types of values in terms of:

1. A *signature* which defines the syntax of the operations of the data type. The signature consists of a collection of *sorts* (data type identifiers) and operation names. Each operation has an associated sequence of sorts that denotes the domain and range sorts of the operation.
2. A set of *axioms* that relate the operations and that are to be satisfied by the values and operations of the data type using some *interpretation* or *model* of the theory.

One advantage of the algebraic approach is that specifications can be derived and tested using automated tools such as the *executable* algebraic specification language *OBJ*. This means that the specifications can be interpreted algorithmically and corresponds to the 'explicitly defined functions' introduced in Chapter 5.

It is important to realize that not all algebraic specification languages are procedurally executable. A nonexecutable specification language can be thought of as existing at a more abstract level than an executable specification. As such, it can provide a first iteration in the specification process from which an executable version may subsequently be derived.

Although we introduced VDM through both explicit and implicit specifications (corresponding to executable and nonexecutable specifications respectively), our aim is to concentrate on executable specification languages since we feel that these provide a natural introduction to the subject of algebraic specification. Furthermore, we focus on the application of the algebraic approach to the formal specification of abstract data types. We explain how algebraic specifications are used to describe and clarify the syntax and semantics of an abstract data type and it is this particular aspect of the algebraic approach which is developed here.

8.2 SPECIFICATION OF ABSTRACT DATA TYPES

In the early days, the computer scientist was very much preoccupied with machine-oriented problems of storage and data representation—that is *concrete* details. The realization that data types are not simply a set of values but consist also of a collection of operations that act upon the values led to an awareness of the importance of *data abstraction* for both programming language design and the specification of software systems. In particular, the importance of separating the specification of an abstract data type from its representation has long been recognized with the resulting benefits for the modularization of software, software reusability and data integrity. This concept is supported by a number of programming languages including Ada and Modula-2. In the case of Modula-2, a *definition module* provides information about the syntax of an abstract data type while the representation of the data type and the implementation of its associated operations are provided by a corresponding *implementation module*. The corresponding structures in Ada are provided by the *package header* (*specification*) and *package body* respectively.

As an illustration, consider the specification of an unbounded stack. The stack is an example of a LIFO (last-in-first-out) structure which has many applications in computer science. Yet, it is important to realize that the characteristic behaviour of a stack is quite independent of the data it manipulates or the representation of the stack itself. It is the collection of operations that can be performed upon a stack that defines its behaviour. In particular, data values can be *pushed* onto the top of a stack or *popped* and retrieved from the *top* of a nonempty stack so that the behaviour of a stack can be described in terms of the following operations:

- `init` an operation that creates an initial empty stack.
- `push` an operation that adds a data element to the top of an existing stack to produce a new stack.
- `pop` an operation that takes a stack as input and produces a new stack with the topmost element removed.
- `top` an operation that takes a stack as input and returns the element at the top of the stack.
- `isempty` an operation that takes a stack as input and returns *true* if the stack is empty, *false* otherwise.

As a prelude to the development of an algebraic specification for the stack, it will be instructive to look briefly at how such an abstract data type might be specified in a high-level imperative language such as Modula-2. This will serve not only to introduce some basic terminology and notation which will be used in the subsequent discussion on algebraic specifications, but will also help to put the algebraic approach into sharper perspective. Those not familiar with Modula-2, but with a working knowledge of any procedural language such as Fortran, Pascal, or C, will find no difficulty in understanding the specification.

With Modula-2, the user of an abstract data type is presented with a *signature* in the form of a DEFINITION MODULE which specifies the syntax of the components of an abstract data type by means of formal Modula-2 declarations (such as TYPE and PROCEDURE statements). The DEFINITION MODULE presents an external interface to users of the abstract data type and so must provide a clear and precise description of the resources available. In other words, the DEFINITION MODULE must adequately describe 'what the abstract data type does'. For a stack of natural numbers (nonnegative integers corresponding to the predefined data type CARDINAL in Modula-2) with the operations described above, the DEFINITION MODULE is given in Fig. 8.1. The following points should be noted:

- The representation of the abstract data type Stacks and the implementation of the operations are contained in a corresponding IMPLEMENTATION MODULE, the details of which are hidden from the *user*, and this module is the exclusive responsibility of the *implementor* of the abstract data type. Users can only access and manipulate the data items by means of the operations provided in the DEFINITION MODULE.
- The data type and its operations can be exported which means that other modules can declare variables of that type and modify them using the exported operations.
- The operations are expressed in terms of *function* procedures, which are subprograms that return a *single* result. The type identifier following the final semicolon states the type of the

```
DEFINITION MODULE Stacks;

    TYPE  Stack;    (* opaque type *)

    PROCEDURE init() : Stack;
    (* operation which creates an initial empty stack *)

    PROCEDURE push(s : Stack; n : CARDINAL) : Stack;
    (* operation which takes a stack 's' and a natural
        number 'n' and returns the stack with 'n' added
        to the top of the input stack 's'           *)

    PROCEDURE pop(s : Stack) : Stack;
    (* operation which takes a stack 's' and returns
        the stack with the top-most element removed   *)

    PROCEDURE top(s : Stack) : CARDINAL;
    (* operation which takes a stack 's' and returns
        the natural number on the top of the stack 's' *)

    PROCEDURE isempty(s : Stack) : BOOLEAN;
    (* operation which takes a stack 's' and returns
        TRUE if the stack is empty, FALSE otherwise   *)

END Stacks.
```

Figure 8.1   Modula-2 signature for an unbounded stack.

result returned for each function. The reason for using *functions* to provide all the operations of the abstract data type will be explained shortly.

- Note that the function init( ):Stack must be used to create an initially empty stack for each required instance of a stack. Here, it is a function without arguments and so essentially represents a constant value of type Stack. Such 'constant' operations (functions) are known as *nullary* operations.
- One implication of using functions to provide all the operations is that the traditional 'pop' operation which removes the topmost element from a stack *and* returns the value of that topmost element has been separated into *two* distinct operations. The function pop simply returns the truncated stack while top returns the value of the topmost element of the stack.
- The identifier Stack, following the reserved word TYPE, declares that the data type Stack is *opaque*. The implementation of such types is hidden from its users and resides in the corresponding IMPLEMENTATION MODULE where the full details of its representation and implementation are given.
- The *package specification* and *package body* of Ada are similar to the DEFINITION MODULE and IMPLEMENTATION MODULE of Modula-2 with the *access private type* of Ada being equivalent to the *opaque* type of Modula-2.

8.2.1 Sorts and types of interest

From the specification presented in Fig. 8.1 we see that the specification of the abstract data type Stacks involves three distinct sets of data values:

- Stack—the set of stacks

- CARDINAL—the set of non-negative integers 0, 1, 2, 3, ...
- BOOLEAN—the set of Boolean values *true* and *false*

The sets of values CARDINAL and BOOLEAN are built-in data types of Modula-2 and are therefore available for use in the specification of any abstract data type, while the set of values introduced by an abstract data type (Stack for this example) is of fundamental importance and is called the *type of interest*.

These sets of values, which correspond to the familiar data types in programming languages such as Pascal, relate to the *sorts* of an algebraic specification, a term that will be used frequently in the discussion of the algebraic approach.

8.2.2 The syntax of the operations

The syntax of an operation can be conveniently described in terms of a *signature*, which is the style adopted in the algebraic approach. Referring to the operation init above, we see that it has no input but returns a value of type Stack as its result. We can express this result concisely in terms of a signature and write.

    init : → Stack

where the type of the returned result appears after the arrow.

The operation push takes a value of type Stack together with a natural number and returns a value of type Stack as its result. This is expressed by the signature

    push : Stack CARDINAL → Stack

(This signature can also be written in mathematical style as

    push : Stack × CARDINAL → Stack

where $A \times B$ denotes the Cartesian product of the sets A and B and is the set of all ordered pairs of the form (a, b) where $a \in A$ and $b \in B$—see Sec. 2.3.)

Similarly, the operation pop which takes a value of type Stack and returns as its result a value of type Stack has a signature given by

    pop : Stack → Stack

Exercise 8.1   Write down the signature for each of the operations top and isempty.

8.2.3 Constructors and Accessors

Returning to the collection of operations that characterizes the stack, we observe that three of the operations, init, push, and pop, return results of type Stack, while top and isempty return values of type CARDINAL and BOOLEAN respectively. Operations such as init, push, and pop which return a result of type Stack are known as *constructor operations* or simply *constructors*, while operations such as top and isempty are known as *accessor operations* or *accessors*.

Exercise 8.2 Observe that the task of 'popping' a stack has been separated into two distinct operations pop and top. How would the DEFINITION MODULE of Fig. 8.1 need to be amended if a *single* operation pop_stack is to be provided which retrieves the topmost element of a stack *and* produces a new stack with the topmost element removed? Suppose an application requires the entire contents of a nonempty stack to be removed and displayed. This could be achieved as follows:

```
WHILE NOT isempty(s) DO
  pop_stack(s,value);
  Write(value)
END;
```

What is the corresponding Pascal-like code fragment using the specification of Fig. 8.1?

Exercise 8.3 Another widely used data structure is the *queue* which is a FIFO (first-in-first-out) structure. The behaviour of a queue can be described in terms of the following set of operations:

- new   an operation that creates an initial empty queue.
- add   an operation that adds a data element to the end of an existing queue to produce a new queue.
- remove   an operation that takes a queue as input and produces a new queue with the frontmost (least-recently added) element removed.
- front   an operation that takes a queue as input and returns the element at the front of the queue.
- isempty   an operation that takes a queue as input and returns *true* if the queue is empty, *false* otherwise.

If the data elements of the queue are natural numbers, produce a Modula-2 DEFINITION MODULE Queues for the abstract data type. For example, the procedure remove will have the header

```
PROCEDURE remove(q : Queue): Queue;
```

Demonstrate, by appropriate renaming of the operations (PROCEDURE names) and TYPE identifiers, that the abstract data types Stacks and Queues have the *same syntax* up to renaming.

8.3 SEMANTIC SPECIFICATION IN MODULA-2 AND ADA

When we talk about the *semantics* of an abstract data type, we are referring to the 'meaning', that is the behaviour of its operations. Before embarking on our discussion of the algebraic approach to specification, let us return to the Modula-2 'specification' of a stack presented in the DEFINITION MODULE of Fig. 8.1 and examine the nature of the information it conveys to a user. The first point to note is that the information available in the specification is rather restricted.

While it is true that the specification supplies precise *syntactic* information about each operation of the abstract data type in that the type of each input parameter and the type of the result returned are clearly stated, the use of comments to describe the behaviour of the operations (that is 'what the operations do!') poses problems. At best, use of natural language is an informal tool and, at worst, can often lead to an ambiguous and hazy description of the semantics of an abstract data type.

Another feature of the specification of Fig. 8.1 is that it provides a template that many implementations can fit. For example, in one implementation, the operation top might return the *first* natural number that was pushed onto the stack (and not the *most recent* value). Although this is at variance with the accepted behaviour of a stack, nevertheless the *syntax* of such an abstract data type is still specified by Fig. 8.1. A second implementation that fits the syntactic specification of Fig. 8.1 is the queue where, now, push and pop are interpreted as operations that insert and remove a natural number from different ends of a queue. (This example featured in Exercise 8.3 above.) Yet a third implementation that fits the specification is one whereby the operation push(s, n) now *replaces* the topmost element of the stack with the data value n.

On one level the DEFINITION MODULE of Fig. 8.1 consists of nothing more than a collection of identifiers (names) for the data types and operations (Stack, BOOLEAN, CARDINAL and init, push, pop, top, isempty respectively). Any consistent renaming of these identifiers would still specify a stack and, while using obscure names for the types and operations of Fig. 8.1 might appear to result in a less meaningful specification, the comparative clarity of the specification of Fig. 8.1 stems entirely from our familiarity with names such as push and pop. The use of such descriptive names does not endow the specification with a formal semantics.

Identifiers that appear in a DEFINITION MODULE (or package specification) therefore play a purely *symbolic* role (apart from BOOLEAN and CARDINAL which have an externally defined meaning) in the sense that they show us, for example, whether the values returned by the different operations are the same or not.

The following features emerge from this discussion:

- It is essential that the external interface provided to users of an abstract data type should provide a lucid and unambiguous specification of both the *syntax* and the *semantics* of an abstract data type.
- The DEFINITION MODULE (specification package) provides a formal statement of the *syntactic* component of the specification of an abstract data type, with the semantics of the abstract data type often provided informally by means of comment statements.
- The DEFINITION MODULE defines a template that many different implementations can be engineered to fit.

This last point reinforces the need to provide a *semantic* specification that formally describes the behaviour of the operations of an abstract data type.

It is observations such as these that lead naturally to the use of algebras for specifying an abstract data type. Algebraic specifications are similar in structure to abstract data types. They consist of a set (or sets) of values called *sorts* (which are symbolic set names) together with a collection of operations, each of which is a mathematical *function* defined over the sorts. This is one reason for the choice of *function* procedures in Fig. 8.1 for our Modula-2 specification of a stack. A further reason for confining the operations of an algebraic specification to functions is that *procedures*, which are often used to implement the operations of an abstract data type, have no obvious mathematical counterpart.

Another desirable feature of an algebraic specification is that it too has a number of possible *interpretations* or *models* which are mathematical 'implementations' of the specification. These ideas will be developed more fully later when we examine the role of algebras in the specification of abstract data types.

8.4 ALGEBRAIC SPECIFICATION OF ABSTRACT DATA TYPES

We have seen that the role of the DEFINITION MODULE in Modula-2 is to provide users with information on the type(s) and operations available to them. The operations specified in the DEFINITION MODULE are available to users of the abstract data type and allow them to manipulate values of the data type in any application program. However, it is these *and only* these operations, as stated in the DEFINITION MODULE, that are available to the user. The *representation* of the abstract data type and the *implementation* of the operations are *explicitly* programmed in the corresponding IMPLE-MENTATION MODULE by the implementor of the abstract data type which is hidden from the user.

In contrast, for an algebraic specification of an abstract data type, *there is no implementation*—the algebraic specification provides a complete mathematical description of both the syntax and semantics of an abstract data type. Hence, in a sense, the implementation is now shielded not only from the user but from everyone!

The virtue of the algebraic approach to specification is that, unlike its Modula-2 and Ada analogues, it also provides a means of specifying the *semantics* of an abstract data type in a formal manner. This is achieved by the use of *equations* or *axioms* which express relations between the operations in terms of compositions (applications) of two (or more) corresponding functions. Let us now examine the structure of an algebraic specification. An algebraic specification of an abstract data type provides a user with:

- The name of the abstract data type
- A collection of sorts, corresponding to the sets of objects (abstract data values) that are manipulated by the operations of the abstract data type
- A collection of operations together with their signatures which provides the syntactic component of the specification of the abstract data type
- A set of equations or axioms which relate the operations and which provide a formal description of their behaviour (the *semantics* of the abstract data type)

In the algebraic approach, the operations of an abstract data type are implicitly defined in terms of a set of *axioms* or *equations*, each of which relates two or more of the operations. The operations are therefore defined *implicitly* by relating their meanings to each other and there is no concept of a 'state' or 'model' as in VDM. These ideas will be explored shortly when we develop an algebraic specification for an unbounded stack of natural numbers.

8.4.1 An algebraic specification language

Throughout this text, we will write algebraic specifications in a *pseudocode* that is similar in style to the algebraic specification language *Axis* (© Hewlett-Packard 1988 (Coleman *et al.* 1988)). This specification language provides *clarity* and *conciseness*, two crucially important features for the presentation of any algebraic specification.

The following features of the specification language Axis are supported by most algebraic specification languages:

1. Although, in the algebraic approach to specification, all abstract data types are specified algebraically, we will assume the availability of three fundamental built-in ('predefined') data types and their associated operations. These basic abstract data types will be denoted by:
   (a) Natural with sort nat
   (b) Boolean with sort bool
   (c) Identifier with sort id
   We will make use of the data type Natural with associated sort nat which corresponds to the set of nonnegative integers (the sort CARDINAL of Modula-2) and operations:
   (d) < (*less than*)
   (e) > (*greater than*)
   (f) <= (*less than or equal to*)
   (g) >= (*greater than or equal to*)
   Remember that the specification Natural includes both a set (sort) of values (nat) and a collection of operations.

   For the stack example developed in this chapter, the model of Boolean merely requires a set containing the two distinguished values that represent the values true and false. The corresponding sort bool is therefore the set {true, false}. The abstract data type Boolean also includes the boolean operations not, and and or.

   Also, the data type Identifier with sort id is assumed to be available which supplies a finite set of distinct constants, written as arbitrary strings of characters enclosed between double quotation marks.

   It should be realized at the outset that these basic data types can themselves be specified algebraically. We will return to the issue of specifications of 'basic' abstract data types shortly.

2. We use the convention that operations declared with no operand positions are taken as prefix operations, with the operands enclosed in parentheses and separated by commas. This follows the conventional notation used for mathematical functions. For example, the application of a binary operation op with declared syntax op:nat nat → nat with operands 2 and 3 is written op(2, 3). If we specify explicitly that the signature of op is given by

   ```
   op _ _ : nat nat → nat
   ```

   then the same application is written as op 2 3. In this way, operations can be customized to suit individual applications. The underscore character '_' is used as a *place-holder* to denote the position of the arguments for an operation.

3. We use the hyphen for composite identifier names, a convention that will be used throughout this text. The underscore character '_' is used to denote operand positions in function and operation definitions.

4. It should be noted that every sort s is supplied with an equality operation $= =$ with signature

```
_ = = _ : s s → bool
```

which returns true when the two arguments of the operation are terms that the set of axioms force to be equivalent.

5. Each sort is also assumed to be supplied with the conditional operation

```
IF _ THEN _ ELSE _ ENDIF
```

defined by

```
IF true THEN s1 ELSE s2 ENDIF = s1
IF false THEN s1 ELSE s2 ENDIF = s2
```

where s1 and s2 are universally quantified variables or expressions belonging to sort s.

6. We will also assume the availabilty of the multiway selection operation

```
IF _ THEN _ ELSEIF _ THEN _ ELSE _ ENDIF
```

7. Each axiom will be numbered for ease of reference.

8.4.2 Predefined types

Whereas high-level programming languages have 'pre-defined' data types, it is important to understand that algebraic specifications have no equivalent structures. If an algebraic specification needs to use a 'simpler' abstract data type (such as a Boolean type), then that simpler type itself will have been created as an algebraic specification. The additional complexity in notation involved, were we to adopt this principle right from the outset, might confuse rather than enlighten our discussion of the algebraic approach. For this reason, we will use the familiar set of values {0,1,2,3, ...} to denote the sort nat of natural numbers, although algebraic specifications for these abstract data types will be introduced later.

We assume that the predefined specifications are available for use in any specification. To use ('import') the built-in specifications Natural and Boolean, we will write

```
USING Natural + Boolean.
```

8.5 ALGEBRAIC SPECIFICATION OF AN UNBOUNDED STACK

We are now ready to develop an algebraic specification Stack for an unbounded stack of natural numbers.

8.5.1 The operations and their syntax

The operations for the data type Stack are:

- init   an operation that requires no input data and produces a new empty stack as the result

- push   an operation that adds a new natural number to the top of the stack
- pop   an operation that removes the topmost element from a stack to produce a new stack
- top   an operation that returns the value of the top of the stack (without removing it)
- is–empty?   an operation that returns true if the stack is empty (contains no values) or false if the stack contains data values

with syntax (signature)

```
OPS
    init       : → stack

    push       : stack nat → stack

    pop        : stack → stack

    top        : stack → nat

    is-empty?: stack → bool
```

where the reserved word OPS introduces the list of operations (functions) of an abstract data type and the introduced sort of stack values is denoted by stack. Note that all operations are denoted by functions that return only a single value.

8.5.2 Sorts

The *sorts* in an algebraic specification are identifiers (symbolic names) for the 'abstract data elements' that can be constructed using the operations (functions) defined in the specification. The sorts therefore correspond to the names of data types that would appear in a Modula-2 DEFINITION MODULE that implements that abstract data type. Referring to the functions listed in the OPS declaration above, the sort stack contains items such as init and push(init, 6) which are syntactically legal *terms* or *expressions*, constructed from the functions (that is they conform to the stated signatures of the operations). It is important to understand that these expressions, which result from *functional composition* of the operations, are the *data elements* of the specification. When the specification is implemented, each of these data elements (which belong to the sort stack) must map onto some object that implements stack values of the abstract data type.

8.5.3 Axioms for the unbounded stack

Two axioms that relate the operations of the abstract data type Stack can be derived immediately by noting that the Boolean operation is–empty? applied to an empty stack (denoted by the operation init) will return true. This statement translates into the axiom

$$\text{is-empty?(init)} = \text{true} \tag{A8.1}$$

Consider now the stack produced by pushing the element n (a natural number) onto an existing stack s. The resulting stack is an instance of the set of stack values and corresponds to the application

```
push(s,n)
```

Clearly this stack will be nonempty, so that the operation is–empty? applied to the stack value push(s,n) will return the value false. This leads to the second axiom

```
is-empty?(push(s,n)) = false
```
(A8.2)

which holds for all stack values s and natural numbers n.

The remaining four axioms are obtained by considering the outcomes of applying the operations pop and top to an empty and nonempty stack, that is to init and push(s,n) respectively.

One problem that must now be addressed concerns the outcome of applying pop and top to an empty stack. It is necessary for the developer of the specification to be alert to the need for some decision on handling these *exceptions*. One approach to this problem is to introduce special or distinguished values of the appropriate type (as specified by the syntax of the relevant operation) which are treated as constant (nullary) operations and declared as such.

Since the signature of the operation pop is given by

```
pop : stack → stack
```

we introduce the nullary operation stack–error of sort stack such that

```
stack-error : → stack
```

The result of applying the operation pop to an empty stack then returns stack–error. This is expressed by the axiom

```
pop(init) = stack-error
```
(A8.3)

The outcome of applying pop to the nonempty stack push(s,n) will result in the stack s since, if we push a value n onto a stack s and then pop the resulting stack, we recover the original stack s. This result is expressed by the axiom

```
pop(push(s,n)) = s
```
(A8.4)

which holds for all stack values s of sort stack (that is s:stack) and natural numbers n of sort nat (that is n:nat). We will use the more 'formal' notation $\forall s \in$ stack and $\forall n \in$ nat here, and throughout this section on the algebraic approach, to denote such qualifications. It is worth recalling that in the VDM specification of a stack (Chapter 4) we had to *prove* this property.

In the case of the operation top which returns a value of sort nat, we introduce the nullary operation

```
nat-error : → nat
```

so that the outcome of applying top to an empty stack is given by the axiom

$$\text{top(init)} = \text{nat-error} \qquad\qquad (A8.5)$$

This is not the only way of dealing with error and exception conditions and a fuller discussion is deferred to the next chapter.

Finally, the operation top applied to the stack push(s, n) will return the most recently added value to the stack, which is the natural number n. This produces the final axiom

$$\text{top(push(s, n))} = \text{n} \qquad\qquad (A8.6)$$

$\forall s \in$ stack and $\forall n \in$ nat.

The complete algebraic specification for the abstract data type Stack can now be presented and is shown in Fig. 8.2. The following should be noted:

- The specification is enclosed between the SPEC and ENDSPEC delimiters of lines 1 and 24 respectively with the name Stack of the specification following immediately after SPEC.
- Line 2 states that Stack will use two existing specifications: Natural which denotes the natural numbers characterized by the sort nat, and Boolean with associated sort bool. Remember, a sort or more correctly a sort name is an identifier used to denote a set of values (just as the identifier INTEGER is used in Pascal to denote the set of allowable integer values). The specification Stack, therefore, essentially imports the two specifications Natural and Boolean. Not only are the associated sorts nat and bool imported,

```
SPEC    Stack                                          1
USING   Natural +  Boolean                             2
SORT    stack                                          3
OPS                                                     4
        init       :   -> stack                        5
        push       :   stack   nat  ->  stack          6
        pop        :   stack  ->  stack                7
        top        :   stack  ->  nat                  8
        is-empty?  :   stack  ->  bool                 9
        stack-error :  ->  stack                      10
        nat-error  :   ->  nat                         11
FORALL                                                12
    s   :   stack                                     13
    n   :   nat                                       14
AXIOMS for is-empty?:                                 15
(1)  is-empty?(init)  =   true                        16
(2)  is-empty?(push(s,n))   =   false                 17
AXIOMS for pop:                                       18
(3)  pop(init)  =  stack-error                        19
(4)  pop(push(s,n))  =   s                            20
AXIOMS for top:                                       21
(5)  top(init)  =  nat-error                          22
(6)  top(push(s,n))   =   n                           23
ENDSPEC                                               24
```

Figure 8.2 Algebraic specification for an unbounded stack.

but also any operations associated with these abstract data types are available for use in the enlarged specification.

- Line 3 states that Stack introduces a new sort, stack.
- The operation declaration section is presented in lines 4 to 11. The specification Stack introduces seven operations. An operation can be viewed as denoting a function on the values associated with the sorts of the operations. Each introduced operation has four associated components:
  - The *name* of the operation (to the left of the colon).
  - The *domain* of the operation, which is the sequence of sort names immediately following the colon and preceding the arrow →. In any application of an operation, only operands of the appropriate sort can appear in the *arguments* (*slots*) of the operation. An operation that has no domain sorts, such as init in line 5 is a *constant* or *nullary* operation.
  - The *range* of an operation is the sort corresponding to the result of that operation and appears to the right of the arrow.
  - The *attributes* of an operation, if appropriate, are stated within parentheses. Two attributes possessed by many operations are *associativity* and *commutativity* and these properties will be discussed later.
- The universally-quantified typed (that is 'sorted') variables to be used in the axioms are specified in lines 13 and 14 following the FORALL header in line 12.
- The axioms themselves are presented in lines 16, 17, 19, 20, 22, and 23. Each axiom is an equation relating two *terms* that are composed from the operations and/or some variables listed in the FORALL component of the module and is introduced using the keyword AXIOM or AXIOMS.

8.5.4 Interpretations of a signature

Lines 3 to 11 of Fig. 8.2 form the *algebraic signature* for the abstract data type Stack and correspond exactly to the syntactic information provided by the Modula-2 DEFINITION MODULE of Fig. 8.1. For this reason, we can think of the algebraic signature above (lines 3 to 11) as a 'trimmed down' version of a public interface that is language independent. This algebraic signature provides a template or pattern with many possible interpretations. The semantics of the operations is provided by the axioms of the specification and it is these axioms that 'narrow the choice' of interpretations to one that has the properties desired by the specifier.

8.5.5 Comparison with VDM

Comparison of the algebraic specification for a stack with the VDM counterpart for a similar structure in Chapter 4 illustrates their different styles. In the algebraic approach, no discrete mathematical structures are used to model the abstract data type and the semantics of the operations are expressed as a set of axioms that relate two or more of the operations. In the case of the VDM specification, the stack is modelled as a sequence (list) and *each* operation is specified implicitly in terms of pre- and post-conditions which state the properties that must be true before the operation can be applied and must be true after application of the operation (in Chapter 15 this comparison is explored in more detail).

Exercise 8.4 Although we have not yet discussed the algebraic specification of a queue, consider the abstract data type Queue of Exercise 8.3 with the operations as given. The corresponding algebraic specification will be of the form

    SPEC Queue

    USING Natural + Boolean

    SORT queue

    ....

Write down the syntax of the operations for Queue that corresponds to lines 4 to 11 of Fig. 8.2. Produce also the statements and axioms for Queue that correspond to lines 12 to 17 of Fig. 8.2.

8.6 Completeness

On first meeting algebraic specifications, an immediate question arises: how do we know that the given axioms provide a precise definition of the behaviour of the operations for the data type? Loosely speaking, *completeness* is concerned with the problem of whether there are enough independent axioms to describe adequately the behaviour of the operations of the abstract data type. The set of axioms that defines the semantics of an abstract data type should be complete in the sense that:

1. Operations must be defined that allow the construction of all possible legal instances (all the values we want) of the abstract data type.
2. The results for all legal applications and compositions of the operations must be defined.

As a simple illustration, consider the specification of Fig. 8.2 but with axiom (1) absent. Consider now the outcome of a composition of operations denoted by t (such compositions will also be referred to as a stack *expression* or just simply as an *expression* or *term*), where

    t = is-empty?(pop(push(init, 3)))

Intuitively, the expression push(init,3) corresponds to a stack containing the single value 3 so that popping this stack will produce the empty stack (init). Hence, the outcome of applying the operation is-empty? should recover the result true.

Looking at the formal specification of the stack, we observe from the syntax component of the specification that t is a legal composition of operations and that the outcome of t is Boolean. Application of axiom (4) reduces the expression t to give

    t = is-empty?(init)

With axiom (1) absent, no further reduction of t can be achieved and we are unable to determine the truth value of t (except to say that the value maps to a new Boolean value that is neither true nor false). This specification is therefore not complete, since the outcome of this legal expression t is undefined.

Heuristics have been developed to assist with the axiomatization for abstract data types and this is discussed in more detail in the next chapter.

Exercise 8.5 Determine which of the following are syntactically legal expressions with respect to the signature of Stack given in Fig. 8.2.

1. push(pop(push(init, 3)), 5)
2. pop(top(push(init, 1)))
3. top(pop(push(init, 1)))
4. push(push(init, 2), top(push(init, 2)))
5. is-empty?(push(pop(push(init, 3)), 5))

8.7 EXAMPLES OF EVALUATIONS

On one level, we can consider the axioms of an algebraic specification as equations and treat the operator '=' in a mathematical sense. In this manner, we can evaluate an expression. In other words, given some syntactically legal expression involving a composition of the operations of the abstract data type, we can use the axioms to transform the given expression into an equivalent form. The principal reason for producing *formal* specifications is that we can reason about them formally using the particular logic or inferencing system that underpins that specification method. Reasoning with the formal algebraic specification will then assist us in validating whether the introduced operations do indeed have the properties we require. This concept will be illustrated with two examples.

Example 8.1 As a first example, if the values 2 and 3 are successively pushed onto an initially empty stack and we then recover the topmost element of the resulting stack, we expect to recover the value 3. Expressed formally, given the expression

$$top(push(push(init, 2), 3)) \qquad\qquad (8.1a)$$

we should be able to use the axioms of the specification to show formally that the expression reduces to the value 3.

Firstly, observe that the subterm push(init, 2) is a stack value so that if we denote this *subterm* by s, then expression (8.1a) becomes

$$top(push(s, 3)) \qquad\qquad (8.1b)$$

Study of the axioms of Stack show that this expression is identical in structure with the left-hand side of axiom (6) if n has the value 3. It follows from axiom (6) that (8.1b) evaluates to 3. Hence, we have the result

$$top(push(push(init, 2), 3)) = 3$$

as expected.

Example 8.2 If we push the value 1 onto an empty stack, pop the stack and then push the value 4 onto the stack, the resulting stack will contain the single value 4. Application of the operation is-empty? to this stack should therefore return false. Consider

$$\texttt{is-empty?(push(pop(push(init, 1)), 4))} \qquad (8.2a)$$

which formally expresses this statement. Although the expression appears alarming at first sight with its composition of four operations, it can be evaluated directly as follows. The first thing to observe is that the subterm pop(push(init,1)) is a stack value (this follows from inspecting the signature of the operation pop), so denoting this value by s, expression (8.2a) is given by

$$\texttt{is-empty?(push(s, 4))} \qquad (8.2b)$$

Inspection of the set of axioms for Stack shows that (8.2b) is exactly of the form given by the left-hand side of axiom (2). We can therefore replace (8.2b) by the right-hand side of axiom (2), that is by the value false. Hence

$$\texttt{is-empty?(push(pop(push(init, 1)), 4))} = \texttt{false} \qquad (8.2c)$$

This result can be derived another way by looking firstly at the subterm pop(push(init,1)) and this is explored in the following exercise.

Exercise 8.6 Starting with the subterm pop(push(init,1)) of the expression (8.2a), use the axioms of Stack to show that

$$\texttt{is-empty?(push(pop(push(init, 1)), 4))} = \texttt{is-empty?(push(init, 4))}$$

and hence deduce the result (8.2c).

Exercise 8.7 Use the axioms of Stack to reduce all the syntactically legal expressions of Exercise 8.5.

Exercise 8.8 Show, using an argument similar to that used in Example 8.2 above, that pushing two values onto an empty stack and then popping the resulting stack twice will result in the empty stack.

Exercise 8.9 Evaluate the expressions:

(a) pop(push(pop(push(init, 5)), 4))
(b) pop(push(push(init, top(push(init, 2))), 1))

8.8 AXIOMS AND TERM REWRITING

The two evaluations above illustrate how we can 'check' an algebraic specification and so determine whether the appropriate inferences can be deduced from it. The technique used is called *term rewriting* whereby each axiom is interpreted as a left-to-right *rewrite rule*.

The operator '=' of each axiom is now treated as a *one-way* relation that states how the left-hand side of an axiom can be rewritten (transformed) to its corresponding right-hand side. This mechanism of treating axioms as rewrite rules is a key concept in the algebraic approach to specification and merits further discussion.

Consider the problem of reducing a general expression of the form

$$t = opa(opb(opc(...opn(...), ...), ...), ...)$$

using a set of axioms where opa, opb, opc, ..., opn denote operations whose domain arguments can themselves contain operations. The first task is to examine the left-hand sides of the axioms looking for those that have opa as the leftmost operation name. In order to explain the process, we consider a concrete example which should help to convey the mechanics of term rewriting.

To focus our ideas, consider an abstract data type that has four operations defined over the sorts s1, s2, s3 with syntax

$$opa : s1\, s2 \rightarrow s1$$

$$opb : s1\, s2 \rightarrow s2$$

$$opc : s1\, s2\, s3 \rightarrow s1$$

$$opd : s1 \rightarrow s1$$

and consider the reduction of the term t where

$$t = opd(opa(opc(k1, k2, k3), opb(m1, m2)))$$

where $k1, m1 \in s1$; $k2, m2 \in s2$ and $k3, m3 \in s3$. (Any variable identifier ending with 1 (2 or 3) will be taken to belong to sort s1 (s2 or s3) respectively).

We now look systematically down the set of axioms and look for those whose left-hand sides have opd as the leftmost operation. (Remember, we are choosing always to work from the left-hand side of a rule to the right.) For the purpose of this discussion, suppose two such axioms are found

```
FORALL
    u1 : s1
    u2 : s2
    u3 : s3

AXIOMS:

  (A1) opd(opc(u1, u2, u3)) = opa(u1,u2)

  (A2) opd(opa(u1, u2)) = u1
```

The next stage in the reduction process is to look at the immediate subterm inside opd of the term t which is opa(...) and see whether either of the two axioms (A1) and (A2) has opa(...) as an immediate subterm. We observe immediately that axiom (A2) has the required structural form and it is the left-hand side of this rule which we will use to reduce t.

This stratagem of looking for axioms that are structurally similar to an expression for the purpose of reducing or simplifying that expression is known as *pattern matching* and this idea should be familiar to those with a knowledge of Prolog or functional programming languages. The left-hand side of the axiom is treated as a pattern to be matched with the expression (or a subterm of the expression) we are trying to reduce.

8.8.1 Pattern matching and unification

Pattern matching and *unification* are topics that often present initial difficulties to students who have not met them before, so it is worth spending a little time discussing them. The term *unification* is used extensively in AI and logic programming. It means nothing more than finding a common form for two (or more) terms through the use of a suitable *instantiation* (substitution) by which they can be made identical. In other words, suppose t_1 and t_2 are two terms, then they are said to be *unified* if a substitution or sequence of substitutions S can be found that makes the two terms identical.

A set of terms unify if and only if each term of the set is identical or a step-by-step application of a sequence of legal substitutions makes them identical. *Identical* in this sense means that:

- They have the same operation name.
- They have the same number of slots (that is to say the same arity).
- They all have identical terms in corresponding slots.

Some worked examples should help to clarify these ideas. It is important to realize that variables can match any subterm or expression (in other words, variables do not have to match only with other variables). This is demonstrated in Examples 8.7 and 8.8 below.

Example 8.3

$$t_1 = g(x, y, z) \quad \text{and} \quad t_2 = h(x, y, 3)$$

These two terms do not unify since they have different operation names (g and h respectively)

Example 8.4

$$t_1 = f(s, t, u) \quad \text{and} \quad t_2 = f(3, t)$$

These two terms do not unify since they have different arities (3 and 2 respectively)

Example 8.5

$$t_1 = h(x, y, z) \quad \text{and} \quad t_2 = h(x, y, 3)$$

We see at once that t_1 and t_2 can be made identical if we substitute 3 for z in t_1. Hence, we have unification under the substitution sequence $z \leftarrow 3$.

Example 8.6

$$t_1 = g(t, u, v, w) \quad \text{and} \quad t_2 = g(2, u, a, 4)$$

In this case, t_1 and t_2 can be made identical with the sequence of substitutions 2 for t, a for v, and 4 for w. The *unifier* in this example is therefore

$$t \leftarrow 2; \quad v \leftarrow a; \quad w \leftarrow 4$$

Example 8.7

$$t_1 = f(x, y) \quad \text{and} \quad t_2 = f(6, p(u))$$

Here, t_1 and t_2 can be made identical if we substitute 6 for x and $p(u)$ for y. Hence, the unifier in this case is

$$x \leftarrow 6; \quad y \leftarrow p(u)$$

Example 8.8

$$t_1 = opa(u1, u2) \quad \text{and} \quad t_2 = opa(opb(m1, m2), opd(r1))$$

The appropriate unifier in this example is

$$u1 \leftarrow opb(m1, m2); \quad u2 \leftarrow opd(r1)$$

We are now in a position to return to our discussion of the reduction of the term

$$t = opd(opa(opc(k1, k2, k3), opb(m1, m2)))$$

8.2.2 Term rewriting example

Thus far we have our original expression

$$t = opd(opa(opc(k1, k2, k3), opb(m1, m2)))$$

and an axiom whose left-hand side is structurally of the form opd(opa(...)), that is

$$(A2) \quad opd(opa(u1, u2)) = u1$$

In order to apply (A2) to reduce t, we now need to find a unifier. From the discussion above, we observe immediately that the relevant unifier is

$$u1 \leftarrow opc(k1, k2, k3); \quad u2 \leftarrow opb(m1, m2)$$

and this result is demonstrated below

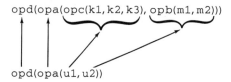

Having found an axiom whose left-hand side can be pattern matched with a subterm of t, that subterm is rewritten using the corresponding right-hand side of the relevant axiom. For this example, the right-hand side of axiom (A2) is u1 and since u1 ← opc(k1, k2, k3), the expression t rewrites to the value

    t = opc(k1, k2, k3)

In general, this process will continue until there are no more axioms that can be pattern matched. A sequence of terms $t, t_1, t_2, ..., t_N$ is thus obtained by repeatedly replacing instances of the left-hand sides of axioms with the corresponding right-hand sides. When the point is reached where no more axioms can be applied, the expression is in a *normal* or *reduced* form and such a normal form will be denoted by t ↓.

The discussion thus far has assumed that an axiom can be found at the outset that unifies with t. Suppose now that we wish to reduce the two separate expressions t1 and t2 where

    t1 = opa(opa(k1, k2), m2)

    t2 = opa(opc(opd(k1), k2, k3), m2)

and that there are no axioms with opa as the outermost leftmost operation on the left-hand side of an axiom. In the case of t1, since the immediate subterm of t1 also involves the operation opa, no axioms can be found to reduce t1 and it follows that the expression t1 is already in a normal (reduced) form.

With regards to t2, we start with the subterm opc(opd(k1), k2, k3) and then seek to pattern match this subterm with the left-hand side of an axiom that has opc as its outermost operation. The procedure then carries through as before. One important point must be emphasized—it is only the *variables* that appear in axioms that can be substituted for.

These ideas will now be explored further with the help of some examples using the specification Stack.

Exercise 8.10 Use the axioms (A1) and (A2) to reduce each of the terms:

(a) opd(opc(p1, p2, p3))
(b) opd(opc(opa(m1, m2), r2, r3))

Exercise 8.11 Given the additional axiom opa((u1, u2), v2) = opa(u1, v2) show that (b) of the previous exercise rewrites to the term opa(m1, r2).

8.8.3 Term rewriting for Stack

These ideas are explored further with the help of some examples for the stack. With reference to the specification Stack of Fig. 8.2 consider the term

```
t = push(pop(push(init, 3)), 1)
```

which has the subterm u = pop(push(init, 3)).

The first thing to note for this example is that there are no axioms that have push as the leftmost operation on the left-hand side of an axiom. Therefore, for the first reduction, looking down the list of axioms, we look for any axioms that have pop as the first operation on their left-hand side. The first such axiom, pop(init) = stack-error, cannot be used since init is not a variable, but the second axiom pop(push(s,n)) = s can be applied, with the left-hand side L as pop(push(s,n)), and the right-hand side R as s. The appropriate unifier is

```
s ← init;  n ← 3
```

or equivalently replace s by init and n by 3.

The subterm u of t is now replaced by the right-hand side of the rewrite rule R, with all variables in the substitutions replaced by their corresponding terms. Hence the subterm u of t rewrites to the value init and the term t becomes

```
t = push(init, 1)
```

This term, which corresponds to a stack containing the single value 1, is now in reduced form since there are no axioms that have push as the outermost operation on the left-hand side of a rule. In general, however, the process will continue until no further reductions are possible.

8.9 SUMMARY

- An algebraic specification language is introduced and used to derive a specification (Stack) for an unbounded stack of natural numbers.
- In the algebraic approach to the specification of abstract data types, operations are modelled using functions.
- The operations of an abstract data type can be classified as either *constructors* or *accessors*. Constructors are operations whose range sort is the same as the sort introduced by the specification. Accessors are operations with ranges of other introduced (imported) sorts.
- An algebraic specification consists of two major components:
    - a syntactic component which provides information on the sort(s) and the domain and range sorts of the operations.
    - a semantic component which defines the meaning (that is describes the behaviour) of the operations in terms of a collection of axioms that relate two or more of the operations.
- Examples of the evaluation of syntactically legal expressions for the specification Stack are presented whereby the axioms are used to transform the given expression into an equivalent one.

- Each axiom of an algebraic specification can be treated as a one-way *rewrite rule* which specifies how its left-hand side may be rewritten as its right-hand side. This technique is known as *term rewriting*.
- Term rewriting provides a means of 'testing' a specification to determine whether the intended properties follow from the stated axioms.

ADDITIONAL PROBLEMS

8.1 Show, using the axioms of Stack, that pushing three values onto an empty stack and then popping the resulting stack three times results in an empty stack.

8.2 Suppose a nonempty stack contains the values 3 and 8, with 8 on the top of the stack.
   (a) Express this stack, S, in terms of the constructor operations push and init.
   (b) If S is now popped and we then retrieve the topmost element of the resulting stack, we should recover the value 3. Demonstrate this result formally, using the axioms of Stack.

8.3 Suppose we wish to extend Stack by including an additional operation is-in? which takes a stack together with a natural number and returns true if that number is present in the stack, false otherwise.
   (a) State the signature of is-in?.
   (b) Construct axioms for is-in? by considering how the operation acts on init and push(s, n) where s ∈ stack and n ∈ nat.

8.4 In this extended example, we develop a specification of an ordered two-tuple ⟨f ; s⟩ whose first and second slots (f, s respectively) are both natural numbers. In a more generalized form, a tuple is a useful abstract data type since, for example, it provides an abstract model for *record* data types in languages such as Pascal, Modula-2 and Ada. In this example we will also explore some simple variations on a theme. These include ordered tuples whose elements are composed from different simple data types and ordered *triples*.

The following three mixfix operations are required:
   (a) ⟨ _ ; _ ⟩   an operation that takes two values f and s, where f, s ∈ nat, and forms the ordered tupe ⟨ f ; s ⟩.
   (b) 1-st   an operation that takes an ordered tuple and returns the value in the first slot. For example 1-st ⟨ 3 ; 5 ⟩ = 3.
   (c) 2-nd   an operation that takes an ordered tuple and returns the value in the second slot. For example 2-nd ⟨ 3 ; 5 ⟩ = 5.

The corresponding algebraic specification Ordered-tuple is shown in Fig. 8.3 where the identifier tuple denotes the *sort* of ordered tuples.
   (a) Identify the constructor and accessor operations.
   (b) Consider extending the specification by adding the Boolean operation equals? which takes two ordered tuples ⟨ f1 ; s1 ⟩, ⟨ f2 ; s2 ⟩ and returns true if both values in corresponding slots denote identical values (that is if f1 == f2 and s1 == s2) and false otherwise. We can express the signature of this operation in mixfix form as:

   _ equals? _ : tuple tuple → bool

   (i) is the operation equals? an accessor or constructor operation?

```
SPEC   Ordered-tuple
USING  Natural
SORT   tuple
OPS
     < _ ; _ >  :   nat  nat   ->  tuple
           1-st  :   tuple  ->  nat
           2-nd  :   tuple  ->  nat
FORALL
        f , s  :  nat
AXIOMS:
   (1)       1-st < f ; s >  =  f
   (2)       2-nd < f ; s >  =  s
ENDSPEC
```

Figure 8.3 Algebraic specification of a tuple.

(ii) complete the right-hand side of the axiom satisfied by equals?

$$\langle\, f1\,;s1\,\rangle \text{ equals? } \langle\, f2\,;s2\,\rangle = (f1 == f2) \text{ and } ??$$

(Note that the Boolean operation and is imported from the specification module Boolean).

(c) In order to specify an ordered tuple composed of identifier values, for example,

$$\langle\, \text{``John''}\,;\text{``Pascal''}\,\rangle$$

the specification would simply import the built-in specification module Identifier with sort id instead of Natural. Amend the specification Ordered-tuple to accommodate this change.

(d) Suppose now we want to specify an ordered tuple whose first slot is an identifier and whose second slot is a natural number. Adapt the specification Ordered-tuple appropriately.

(e) Adapt Ordered-tuple to specify an ordered *triple* $\langle\, f\,;s\,;t\,\rangle$ of natural numbers with f, s, $t \in$ nat.

REFERENCES

Coleman, D., Dollin, C., Gallimore, R., Arnold, P., and Rush, T. (1988) An Introduction to the Axis Specification Language, *Hewlett-Packard Information Laboratory Report HPL-ISC-TR-88-031*, Software Engineering Department, Hewlett-Packard, Bristol.

Zilles, S. N. (1974). Algebraic Specification of Data Types, *MIT, Laboratory for Computer Science, Progress Report XI*, Cambridge, MA (1974).

FURTHER READING

Of the many articles and collections of papers on the algebraic approach to specification, one of the most rigorous yet accessible is to be found in:

Goguen, J. A., Thatcher, J. W., and Wagner, E.G. (1978) An Initial Algebra Approach to the Specification, Correctness and Implementation of Abstract Data Types. In R. T. Yeh (Ed.) *Current Trends in Programming Methodology*, vol. 3, pp. 80–149, Prentice-Hall, Englewood Cliffs, N.J.

Of recent books on the algebraic approach to specification, a comprehensive account of the underlying concepts is given in:

van Horebeek, I., and Lewi, J. (1989) *Algebraic Specifications in Software Engineering*, Springer-Verlag, Berlin.

A brief yet lucid and informative account of the algebraic approach, which is well worth reading, is given in Chapter 9 of:

Ellis, R. (1991) *Data Abstraction and Program Design*, Pitman, London.

One other book which explores various formal approaches to specification, including the algebraic approach and concentrates, in particular, on explaining the mathematical foundations of such formal methods of software engineering is:

Woodcock, J., and Loomes, M. (1988) *Software Engineering Mathematics*, Pitman, London.

9

THE QUEUE AND BINARY TREE

9.1 INTRODUCTION

In this chapter, we develop algebraic specifications for two further classical abstract data types, namely the *queue* and the *binary tree*. The aim of these examples is twofold:

1. To enable the reader to gain further insight into the algebraic approach by means of specifications of standard data structures
2. To provide a foundation for the subsequent discussion on aspects of the theoretical background of the algebraic approach to specification

One area that we need to explore concerns the task of deriving a set of axioms for an abstract data type. There are a number of fundamentally important issues that arise from this *axiomatization* process, for example: 'how many axioms need to be provided?'; 'is the set of axioms *consistent*?'

An algebraic specification is *inconsistent* if the axiomatization has undesired consequences such as 'subverting' an existing imported specification (for example, by identifying terms as equivalent that were meant to be different). Heuristics, in the form of an informal set of rules, have been devised that assist with the process of axiomatization. (Heuristics are simply rules of thumb that usually succeed but are not guaranteed to do so.) These ideas are explored at the beginning of this chapter where they are used to develop algebraic specifications for the *queue* and *binary-tree*. The use of *hidden* or *private* operations is also discussed with an application to the specification of a binary search tree.

We also look briefly at the relation between algebraic specification languages and functional programming languages and we conclude the chapter by looking in more detail at the treatment of *exceptions* (errors), that is operations defined over only a subset of their domain values.

9.2 ATOMIC CONSTRUCTORS

As we saw in the last chapter, the operations of an abstract data type can be separated into *constructors* and *accessors*. Operations with ranges (results) of the sort (data type) being defined are called *constructors* whereas operations with ranges of other (imported) sorts are called *accessors*. This separation of operations into two disjoint classes is therefore based upon a syntactic distinction.

We can further divide the constructor operations into two distinct groups, namely *atomic constructors* (our terminology) and *nonatomic constructors*. For many abstract data types, including the standard ones such as the stack, queue, list and binary tree, a subset of the constructors can be found such that every syntactically legal term of the *principal* sort (type of interest) can be represented using a combination of these operations. In the case of Stack, the principal sort is stack and the atomic constructors are init and push. The operation pop is a nonatomic constructor for Stack in the sense that pop merely produces values of the data type (or, to be more precise, values of the sort stack) that could have been produced using applications of just the operations init and push.

It must be stressed that stacks have this property *not* on account of some formal mathematical requirement but because this is the property we *require* of stacks. More generally, it is important to note that there is no systematic procedure for determining the atomic constructors for an abstract data type. Identification of a collection of appropriate atomic constructors for a new data type results from our understanding and perceptions of the properties of that data type. They are a conceptualization of our ideas about the values of the abstract data type.

This subdivision of constructor operations into atomic and nonatomic constructors is therefore based upon a semantic distinction. This separation then implies that atomic constructors have the intuitively satisfying property that all instances of the data type can be represented using these atomic constructors. This classification scheme is summarized in Fig. 9.1.

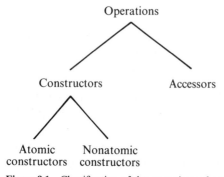

Figure 9.1 Classification of the operations of an abstract data type.

Hence, in the case of the abstract data type Stack, an arbitrary stack containing items e1, e2, ... , en (n ⩾ 1), with e1 on the bottom of the stack, e2 next to bottom, ... , en on the top of the stack, is given by the expression

```
push(... push(push(init, e1), e2)... , en)
```

In the case of our example Stack, the accessor operation top is also an example of what is called a *selector*. Basically, selectors allow access to individual components of a composite object. In the example of the stack, the operation selects the topmost value from the stack.

Readers should be aware that the terminology associated with the classification of operations is by no means standard and we summarize some of the alternative definitions in use. Some authors partition the operations into three distinct groups, namely *primitive constructors*, *combinatorial constructors*, and *accessors*. The term *primitive constructor* describes those nullary operations that yield results of the defined type (principal sort). For example, the operation init for our abstract data type Stack is a *primitive constructor* while *combinatorial constructors* are operations like push and pop which have some of their operands (arguments) in and yield results of the introduced sort (data type). This classification is used by Liskov and Zilles (1975).

9.3 HEURISTICS FOR AXIOMATIZATION

Heuristics have been devised to assist in the writing of an appropriate set of axioms for the specification. One such rule entails writing axioms to show how each accessor and nonatomic constructor operation acts upon each of the atomic constructor operations and this approach is exemplified in the specification Stack. In that example, we constructed all axioms with left-hand sides of the form $op_{na}(op_{atom})$ where op_{na} denotes a member of the set of accessor and nonatomic constructor operations {is-empty?, pop, top}, and op_{atom} denotes a member of the set of atomic constructors {init, push}.

This partitioning of the constructors into those that generate new values of the type (atomic constructors) and those (nonatomic constructors) that just produce values that can also be generated using only the atomic constructors is comparatively straightforward for the classical abstract data types. However, for the beginner, it may not always be easy to separate the constructors into these two groups. The outcome of an incorrect partitioning would be an axiom whose left-hand side would not be supplied with a corresponding 'simpler' right-hand side. Such a situation would indicate the need to re-examine the partitioning.

9.4 ALGEBRAIC SPECIFICATION OF A QUEUE OF NATURAL NUMBERS

Whereas the stack operates on a last-in-first-out basis (LIFO), the simple *queue* is a first-in-first-out storage device (FIFO). The data type is composed of a sequence of data elements together with a collection of operations:

- new   nullary (constant) operation that returns an empty queue as its result.
- add   operation that adds an element to the end of a queue and produces another queue as its result.
- remove   operation that removes the element at the head (front) of the queue to produce another queue as its result.
- front   operation that returns the value of the element at the front of the queue.
- is-empty?   operation that tests whether a queue is empty, returning the value true if the queue is empty or false if the queue is not empty.

The signature of these operations is given by

```
new        : → queue

add        : queue nat → queue

remove     : queue → queue

front      : queue → nat

is-empty?  : queue → bool
```

where the introduced sort of the abstract data type is denoted by queue.

Having completed the syntactic component of the specification, we are now faced with the task of providing a set of axioms that relate the five operations.

Exercise 9.1 Suppose we require an additional operation length which returns the length of a given queue (that is the number of elements in the queue). State the signature of length and whether it is a constructor or accessor operation.

9.4.1 Axiomatization for the specification Queue

The first thing to note is that the operations new, add, and remove are constructors, while front and is-empty? are accessors. We can also identify the *atomic constructors* for this abstract data type, namely new and add, since an arbitrary queue containing the elements e1, e2, ..., en ($n \geqslant 1$) in that order is given by

```
add( ...add(add(new, e1), e2) ..., en)
```

Hence the axiomatization will consist of six axioms with left-hand sides given by:

1. front(new)

2. front(add(q,n))

3. is-empty?(new)

4. is-empty?(add(q,n))

5. remove(new)

6. remove(add(q,n))

where $q \in$ queue and $n \in$ nat (that is q belongs to the sort queue and n is a natural number).

To start, we observe immediately that is–empty?(q) should return true if q is the empty queue, so the corresponding axiom is

```
is-empty?(new) = true
```

Also, the operation is–empty? acting on any queue to which an element has been added will return the value false, so that

```
is-empty?(add(q,n)) = false
```

Consider now the operation front. An attempt to access the frontmost element of an empty queue will result in an error, so introducing the error value nat-error : → nat we have

```
front(new) = nat-error
```

If a natural number n is added to a queue q, where q is nonempty, the frontmost element of the resulting queue (that is the one at the head of the resulting queue) is just the frontmost element of the original queue q. On the other hand, if q is the empty queue and a natural number n is added to q, then the frontmost element of the resulting queue is simply the value n. The corresponding axiom that states these results is

```
front(add(q,n)) = IF is-empty?(q) THEN n ELSE front(q) ENDIF
```

Consider now the effect of the operation remove acting on a queue. If the queue is empty, the effect of attempting to remove the element at the head of the empty queue will result in an error. Introducing the error value queue–error with signature

```
queue-error : → queue
```

this result is expressed by the axiom

```
remove(new) = queue-error
```

If the queue contains a *single* value n, corresponding to the expression add(new,n), then application of the operation remove to add(new,n) will result in the empty queue new. If, on the other hand, a number n is added to the end of a nonempty queue q, then the effect of removing the element at the head of the resulting queue, that is remove(add(q,n)), is equivalent to first removing the element at the head of the original queue q and then appending the number n to the end of that queue, that is add(remove(q),n). We thus have the axiom

```
remove(add(q,n)) = IF is-empty?(q) THEN new ELSE add(remove(q),n) ENDIF
```

The previous natural language description certainly demonstrates the superiority of mathematical notation over natural language for stating the semantic properties of the operations of an abstract data type! The complete specification is shown in Fig. 9.2. Four points are worth noting about the specification Queue of Fig. 9.2

```
SPEC    Queue
USING   Natural + Boolean
SORT    queue
OPS

        new   :   -> queue
        add   :   queue   nat  ->  queue
     remove   :   queue  ->  queue
      front   :   queue  ->  nat
  is-empty?   :   queue  ->  bool
queue-error   :   -> queue
  nat-error   :   -> nat
  FORALL
          q   :   queue
          n   :   nat

AXIOMS:
   (1)   front(new)  =  nat-error
   (2)   front(add(q,n))  =  IF  is-empty?(q)  THEN  n
                                ELSE  front(q)  ENDIF
   (3)   is-empty?(new)  =  true
   (4)   is-empty?(add(q,n))  =  false
   (5)   remove(new)  =  queue-error
   (6)   remove(add(q,n))  =  IF  is-empty?(q)  THEN  new
                                ELSE  add(remove(q),n)  ENDIF

ENDSPEC
```

Figure 9.2 Algebraic specification for an unbounded queue.

- The Boolean condition IF is-empty?(q) THEN ... which appears on the right-hand sides of axioms (2) and (6) could also be written IF q = = new THEN ....
- Note that axioms (2) and (6) are recursive in form, and the use of recursion in the statement of axioms is a feature of many algebraic specifications.
- At first sight, the right-hand side of axiom (6) does not look any simpler than its left-hand side, yet this axiom does indeed effect a reduction as the second example below demonstrates. On a more general point, when constructing the right hand side of an axiom, care should be taken to avoid rejecting an acceptable expression because it seems at first sight no simpler than the left-hand side.
- With appropriate renamings of the sort and operations of Queue, in particular queue → stack, new → init, add → push, remove → pop, front → top and queue-error → stack-error, the abstract data types Stack (Fig. 8.2) and Queue (Fig. 9.2) have the same syntax (signature). The difference in their semantics is conveyed by the different forms that the axioms for top and front, and pop and remove take.

This last point is important in that it reinforces the observation made in the previous chapter that a signature provides a pattern that *many* different implementations can fit.

9.4.2 Examples of evaluating terms

First consider reduction of the term t1 where

    t1 = front(add(add(new, 3), 5))

The first thing to note is that the type of the resulting expression is nat since front has signature queue → nat. The term t1 is of the form op(subterm) where op is the accessor front and the subterm is add(add(new, 3), 5), so that we look down the set of axioms looking for those whose left-hand side is of the form front(add ...). We need go no further than axiom (2) which provides the appropriate rewrite rule to apply.

Applying axiom (2) with the instantiation

    q ← add(new, 3) ; n ← 5

the right-hand side of axiom (2) produces

    IF is-empty?(add(new, 3)) THEN 5 ELSE front(add(new, 3)) ENDIF

From axiom (4), we observe that is-empty?(add(new, 3)) is false so that t1 rewrites to the term

    front(add(new, 3))

This term can be further reduced by noting that axiom (2) can be applied once again with the instantiation

    q ← new ; n ← 3

The right-hand side of axiom (2) now gives

    IF is-empty?(new) THEN 3 ELSE front(new) ENDIF

and from axiom (3), since is-empty?(new) is true, we recover the normal form of t1 which is the natural number 3, so that

    t1 = 3

As a second example, consider the reduction of the term t2 given by

    t2 = remove(add(add(new, 4), 2))

The type of the resulting operation in this case is queue and looking down the list of axioms for those that have remove as the leftmost operation on their left-hand side, we see that axiom (6) can be applied with the instantiation

    q ← add(new, 4) ; n ← 2

so that t2 rewrites to

    IF is-empty?(add(new, 4)) THEN new ELSE add(remove(add(new, 4)), 2) ENDIF

From axiom (4) is-empty?(add(new, 4)) is false, so that t2 rewrites to

    t2 = add(remove(add(new, 4)), 2)

There are no axioms that have add as the first operation on their left-hand side. However, note that the subterm u of the outermost add operation is remove(add(new, 4)) so that axiom (6) can be applied to the subterm u with the instantiation

    q ← new ; n ← 4

to give

    IF is-empty?(new) THEN new ELSE add(remove(new), 4) ENDIF

and since is-empty?(new) is true by axiom (3), the subterm u rewrites to the term new, that is

    remove(add(new, 4)) = new

It follows that the expression t2 rewrites to the term

    add(new, 2)

9.4.3 Exercises

The following four exercises are based on the specification Queue of Fig. 9.2.

Exercise 9.2 A queue Q consists of a single element e1 so that Q = add(new, e1).

(a) Use axiom (2) to show that front(Q) = e1.
(b) Use axiom (6) to show that remove(Q) = new.

Exercise 9.3 A queue Q consists of two elements e1 and e2 and is given by the expression Q = add(add(new, e1), e2).

(a) Apply axiom (6) once to show that

    remove(Q) = add(remove(add(new, e1)), e2)

(b) Apply axiom (6) once more to show that the subterm remove(add(new, e1)) rewrites to the value new. Hence, show that

    remove(Q) = add(new, e2)

and interpret this result.

Exercise 9.4 The abstract data type Queue can be enlarged by including a further operation join which takes two queues and appends the second to the first so that the head of one queue follows immediately after the tail of the other queue. The signature of join is

```
join : queue queue → queue
```

and the axioms satisfied by join are

```
join(q,new) = q
join(q1, add(q,n)) = add(join(q1,q), n)
```

$\forall q, q1 \in$ queue and $\forall n \in$ nat. The first axiom states that joining an empty queue to a queue q results in q, while the second axiom states that joining a queue, to which an element n has been added, to a queue q1 is equivalent to joining q to q1 and adding n to the resulting queue.

If Q consists of the two elements n1 and n2, use the above axioms to express join(Q, Q) in terms of the atomic constructors new and add.

Exercise 9.5 Construct axioms for the operation length introduced in Exercise 9.1 using the fact that the length of an empty queue is zero while the length of a queue to which an element has been added is the length of the original queue incremented by one.

9.4.4 Specification of Stack and Queue using VDM

This observation that the syntax of Stack and Queue are identical (with appropriate renamings) yet their axioms are quite different is worth exploring further by comparing the corresponding VDM specifications. To enable direct comparison with the algebraic specifications developed here and in the previous chapter, we model our stack and queue as unbounded sequences of natural numbers. The VDM specifications for Stack and Queue which correspond to the algebraic specifications of Figs 8.2 and 9.2 are shown in Fig. 9.3.

Immediately we are struck by the similarity between the VDM specifications for Queue and Stack. In fact, the corresponding operations are identical apart from the operations *PUSH* and *ADD*. This contrasts with the behaviour of the algebraic specifications. The reason why the VDM specifications are so similar stems from the fact that both have been modelled using an unbounded sequence. The only difference in behaviour between the stack and the queue is that with the stack, elements are pushed and popped from the same end of the sequence while for the queue, elements are added and retrieved from different ends.

9.5 ALGEBRAIC SPECIFICATION OF A BINARY TREE

Our next example features the algebraic specification of a familiar data structure, the *binary tree*. Trees are one of the most important nonlinear structures in computer science. In part, this is due to the fact that they provide natural representations for many kinds of hierarchical and nested data that arise in computer applications. File index schemes and hierarchical data base management systems, for example, often make use of tree structures.

$Stack = \mathbb{N}*$	$Queue = \mathbb{N}*$

$INIT(\ )$	$NEW(\ )$
ext wr s : $Stack$	ext wr q : $Queue$
pre $true$	pre $true$
post $s = [\ ]$	post $q = [\ ]$

$IS\_EMPTY?(\ )\ b : \mathbb{B}$	$IS\_EMPTY?(\ )\ b : \mathbb{B}$
ext rd s : $Stack$	ext rd q : $Queue$
pre $true$	pre $true$
post $b \Leftrightarrow (s = [\ ])$	post $b \Leftrightarrow (q = [\ ])$

$PUSH(n : \mathbb{N})$	$ADD(n : \mathbb{N})$
ext wr s : $Stack$	ext wr q : $Queue$
pre $true$	pre $true$
post $s = [n] ^\frown \overleftarrow{s}$	post $q = \overleftarrow{q} ^\frown [n]$

$POP(\ )$	$REMOVE(\ )$
ext wr s : $Stack$	ext wr q : $Queue$
pre len $s > 0$	pre len $q > 0$
post $s = $ tl $\overleftarrow{s}$	post $q = $ tl $\overleftarrow{q}$

$TOP(\ )\ n : \mathbb{N}$	$FRONT(\ )\ n : \mathbb{N}$
ext rd s : $Stack$	ext rd q : $Queue$
pre len $s > 0$	pre len $q > 0$
post $n = $ hd s	post $n = $ hd q

Figure 9.3 VDM specifications for the unbounded Stack and Queue using sequences.

This example of the specification of a *binary* tree (a tree where each node has no more than two child nodes) will be further explored later when we discuss *hidden* or *private* operations. For the binary tree, the operations normally required are:

- empty allocates and initializes the binary tree.
- make takes a data element and two binary trees and constructs a tree with the data element as the root and the two binary trees as left and right subtrees.
- left takes a binary tree and returns the left subtree.
- right takes a binary tree and returns the right subtree.
- node takes a binary tree and returns the value of the data element corresponding to the root of the tree.
- is-empty? returns true if the binary tree is empty and false if the tree is not empty.
- is-in? returns true if a specified data element is present in the tree and returns false if the data element is not present.

As with the previous examples, we assume for the sake of expediency, that the data elements are natural numbers. The individual signatures of the operations are then given by

```
empty     : → binary-tree

make      : binary-tree nat binary-tree → binary-tree

left      : binary-tree → binary-tree

right     : binary-tree → binary-tree

node      : binary-tree → nat

is-empty? : binary-tree → bool

is-in?    : binary-tree nat → bool
```

where binary-tree is the sort introduced by the abstract data type Binary-tree.

The atomic constructors for this abstract data are empty and make since any binary tree can be constructed using a composition of these two constructors (the operations left and right are nonatomic constructors for this example and such operations are sometimes referred to as 'destructors'). The complete specification is shown in Fig. 9.4. We

```
SPEC  Binary-tree
USING  Natural  +  Boolean
SORT binary-tree
OPS
   empty  :   ->  binary-tree
    make  :  binary-tree  nat  binary-tree  ->  binary-tree
    left  :  binary-tree  ->  binary-tree
   right  :  binary-tree  ->  binary-tree
    node  :  binary-tree  ->  nat
is-empty? :  binary-tree  ->  bool
   is-in? :  binary-tree   nat  ->  bool
nat-error :  -> nat
  FORALL
      l,r  :  binary-tree
      n,nl :  nat
  AXIOMS:
  (1)  left(empty)  =  empty
  (2)  left(make(l,n,r))  =  l
  (3)  right(empty)  =  empty
  (4)  right(make(l,n,r))  =  r
  (5)  node(empty)  =  nat-error
  (6)  node(make(l,n,r))  =  n
  (7)  is-empty?(empty)  =  true
  (8)  is-empty?(make(l,n,r))  =  false
  (9)  is-in?(empty,n)  =  false
  (10) is-in?(make(l,n,r),nl)  =  IF  n == nl  THEN  true
                                  ELSE  is-in?(l,nl)
                                  or is-in?(r,nl) ENDIF

ENDSPEC
```

Figure 9.4 Algebraic specification for a binary tree.

have introduced the nullary operation nat–error : → nat to deal with the result of trying to access the value corresponding to the root of an empty tree.

9.5.1 Simple examples of binary trees

The following examples should help the reader to relate the formal algebraic specification of a binary tree presented in Fig. 9.4 with the structures it describes.

For example, the binary tree given by

corresponds to the expression

```
make(make(empty, 1 , empty), 6 , make(empty, 2 , empty))
```

while the tree

corresponds to the expression (term)

```
make(make(make(empty, 3, empty), 1, make(empty, 5, empty)) , 6 ,

        make(make(empty, 2, make(empty, 4, empty))))
```

It is important to note that there is no implicit ordering among the nodes of the binary tree. In other words, we are *not* assuming, for example, that all data values in the left subtree of any given node are less than the value of that node and all data values in its right subtree are greater than the values at the node.

Exercise 9.6 Use the axioms of Binary–tree presented in Fig. 9.4 to show that the data element 5 is present in the tree

```
      9
     / \
    4   3
   / \   \
  8  2    5
```

9.5.2 Tree traversal

There are three further operations that could have been included in our specification for the binary tree, corresponding to the usual *pre-order*, *in-order* and *post-order* traversal of a binary tree. A *traversal* of a binary tree is an operation that accesses each node in the tree exactly once. As each node is encountered, it might be simply printed out or subject to some sort of processing. Each mode of traversal imposes an order in which the nodes are accessed.

For our example, the resulting sequence of values produced can be represented as a queue of natural numbers so that the range of such operations will be of sort queue. The enlarged data type for Binary-tree would thus import Queue and contain the three extra operations:

```
pre-order  : binary-tree → queue
in-order   : binary-tree → queue
post-order : binary-tree → queue
```

together with the two extra axioms for each of the three new operations

$$in\text{-}order(empty) = new$$

$$in\text{-}order(make(l,n,r)) = join(add(in\text{-}order(l),n)\,,\,in\text{-}order(r))$$

$$post\text{-}order(empty) = new$$

$$post\text{-}order(make(l,n,r)) = join(post\text{-}order(l)\,,\,add(post\text{-}order(r),n))$$

$$pre\text{-}order(empty) = new$$

$$pre\text{-}order(make(l,n,r)) = join(join(add(new,n),\,pre\text{-}order(l)),\,pre\text{-}order(r))$$

The use of recursion produces very elegant axioms for these operations. Their form is easily understood with reference to the mode of traversal:

in-order   : *left → data element → right*

post-order : *left → right → data element*

pre-order : *data element → left → right*

For in-order traversal, start at the root and first traverse the root's left branch, then the root, and finally the root's right branch. This is a recursive process since each left and right branch is a tree in its own right. For example, with the tree of Exercise 9.6 above, in-order traversal produces the sequence of values 8 4 2 9 3 5.

For post-order traversal, start at the root and first access the root's left branch, then the root's right branch, and finally the root itself. For the tree of Exercise 9.6, the corresponding sequence is 8 2 4 5 3 9.

In the case of pre-order traversal, start at the root and access the root itself, its left branch and finally its right branch. This leads to the sequence 9 4 8 2 3 5 for the tree of Exercise 9.6.

Note the more cumbersome form of the pre-order operation—this stems from the fact that the add operation for Queue places the element at the end of the queue, which means we can simply use the add operation to append the element to the left/right component for in-order/post-order traversal. However, for the case of pre-order traversal, in order to place the element at the front, we need first to create a queue containing the single element n, that is add(new, n).

Within the context for programming language execution, compilers utilize tree structures to obtain forms of an arithmetic expression that can be evaluated efficiently. The in-order traversal of the binary tree for an arithmetic expression produces the infix form of the expression, while the pre-order and post-order traversal lead to the prefix and postfix (reverse Polish) forms of the expression respectively. The advantage of reverse Polish notation is that arithmetic expressions can be represented in a way that can be simply read from left to right without the need for parentheses. For example, consider the expression a * (b + c). This expression can be represented by the binary tree

If we perform a post-order traversal in which we traverse the left branch of the tree, then the right branch, followed by the node, we immediately recover the reverse Polish form of the expression, namely abc+*. This expression can then be evaluated using a stack. Starting from the left of the expression, each time an operand (one of the numerical values a, b or c in this example) is found, it is placed on the top of the stack. When an operator (* or +) is read, the top two elements are removed from the stack, the appropriate operator is applied to them, and the result placed on the stack. When the complete expression has been evaluated, the stack will contain a single item which is the result of evaluating the expression.

9.6 HIDDEN OPERATIONS

In the examples considered so far, we have seen the fundamental role played by the atomic constructors and in particular how every instance of the specified abstract data type can be constructed using just these operations. In the case of the specification Binary-tree of Fig. 9.4, the data values at a node of the tree can be *any* natural number. Any arbitrary binary tree is a legal value of the sort binary-tree since it can be constructed from the atomic constructors make and empty.

However, in many applications of binary trees such as sorting and searching, the data elements in the tree are required to have a precise ordering and so we now turn our attention to the specification of an *ordered* binary tree.

The basic problem is that, unlike the VDM approach, algebraic specifications do not allow *pre-* and *post-conditions* to be expressed directly, so that the necessary pre-condition that the binary search tree is ordered cannot be stated. One way that algebraic specifications handle this problem is to make use of so-called *hidden* or *private* operations.

In the case of the ordered binary tree, the first thing to note is that the constructor make is too general, in that it allows for the construction of any binary tree, ordered or not. Therefore, we introduce a new constructor operation, called build, which strictly preserves the ordering relation between the data elements of the tree and relate it to the general constructor make.

The operation build thus provides the 'proper' means for inserting values into an ordered tree. We require the operation build to provide the *only* means for creating an ordered tree and so insist that the original operation make, present in the specification of the abstract data type Binary-tree must be *inaccessible* to any specification that imports Binary-tree. (Were the operation make to be available, we would be unable to ensure the integrity of the data type.)

To ensure that make is inaccessible we treat the operation as a *private* operation and declare it thus by prefixing an *exclamation mark* (!) to its name in the specification. *Private* operations cannot be used outside the specification module in which they are declared, but may be freely used within it. The result is that !make cannot be exported, so that a user views build as the atomic constructor. In other words, any other specification module that uses (imports) the specification Ordered-tree cannot access !make and will view build and empty as the atomic constructors for the data type Ordered-tree. All other operations of Ordered-tree would be available for use by any importing module.

Denoting the sort of ordered binary trees by ordered-tree, the signature of build is:

```
build : ordered-tree nat → ordered-tree
```

The operation build is required to take an ordered binary tree and a natural number n1, and insert n1 into its appropriate location to produce a new ordered tree (provided that n1 is not already present in the tree). Starting at the root of the tree, if n1 is less than the value at the root, go left to the next node; otherwise go right and repeat the process with the new node as the root. The value is inserted into its correct position by making a tree with n1 at the node and empty left and right subtrees.

The corresponding axioms that relate build and !make are therefore:

```
build(empty,n) = !make(empty,n,empty)

build(!make(l,n,r),n1) = IF n = = n1 THEN !make(l,n,r)
                         ELSEIF n1 < n THEN
                         !make(build(l,n1),n,r)
                         ELSE !make(l,n,build(r,n1))
                         ENDIF
```

The new constructor build takes on the role of an *atomic* constructor for the ordered binary tree, as seen from the 'outside' and any instance of an ordered tree is then constructed from a composition of build and empty operations. The complete specifications Ordered-tree is shown in Fig. 9.5.

Note how axiom (10) for is-in?(!make(l,n,r),n1) above differs from the corresponding axiom (10) in the abstract data type Binary-tree given in Fig. 9.4.

9.7 VDM SPECIFICATION OF AN ORDERED BINARY TREE

It will be of interest to compare the algebraic specification Ordered-tree with its VDM counterpart. A binary tree is a *recursive* data structure in the sense that the structure

```
SPEC   Ordered-tree
USING  Natural + Boolean
SORT   ordered-tree
OPS
      empty  :  -> ordered-tree
      build  :  ordered-tree  nat  -> ordered-tree
      !make  :  ordered-tree  nat  ordered-tree  -> ordered-tree
       left  :  ordered-tree  ->  ordered-tree
      right  :  ordered-tree  ->  ordered-tree
       node  :  ordered-tree  ->  nat
  is-empty?  :  ordered-tree  ->  bool
      is-in?  :  ordered-tree  nat  ->  bool
  nat-error  :  -> nat
FORALL
       l,r  :  ordered-tree
       n,nl :  nat
AXIOMS:
   (1)   left(empty)  =  empty
   (2)   left(!make(l,n,r))  =  l
   (3)   right(empty)  =  empty
   (4)   right(!make(l,n,r))  =  r
   (5)   node(empty)  =  nat-error
   (6)   node(!make(l,n,r))  =  n
   (7)   is-empty?(empty)  =  true
   (8)   is-empty?(!make(l,n,r))  =  false
   (9)   is-in?(empty,n)  =  false
   (10)  is-in?(!make(l,n,r),nl)  =  IF n == nl THEN true
                                     ELSEIF  nl < n THEN
                                        is-in?(l,nl)
                                     ELSE is-in?(r,nl) ENDIF
   (11)  build(empty,n)  =  !make(empty,n,empty)
   (12)  build(!make(l,n,r),nl) =  IF n == nl THEN !make(l,n,r)
                                    ELSEIF nl < n THEN
                                       !make(build(l,nl),n,r)
                                    ELSE !make(l,n,build(r,nl)) ENDIF
ENDSPEC
```

Figure 9.5 Algebraic specification for an ordered binary tree.

consists of *either* an 'empty' root node *or* a root node that has a value together with two 'branches' (*left* and *right*) which are themselves further instances of the same data structure. In VDM, we can specify such a data structure using a composite that is recursively defined, with an extension of a type definition method introduced in Chapter 3. Recall that a type can be defined using the bar '|', meaning 'or', for example:

type_name = CONSTANT1 | CONSTANT2 | CONSTANT3 | CONSTANT4

These constants, however, can be generalized to be *type names* and this gives us a way of 'unioning' types. For example, if we wanted to create a type natural numbers with an error value, we would write:

Nat_error = $\mathbb{N}$ | ERROR

This allows types to be recursively defined and, but for syntax, is the same as the signature of a constructor operation in an algebraic specification. The VDM binary tree is defined thus:

$Ordered\_tree = Ord\_bin\_tree \mid \text{EMPTY}$

$Ord\_bin\_tree :: l \quad : Ordered\_tree$
$\qquad\qquad\qquad val : \mathbb{N}$
$\qquad\qquad\qquad r \quad : Ordered\_tree$
$\quad \text{inv } mk\_Ord\_bin\_tree(l, val, r) \triangleq$
$\forall n \in node\_values(l) \cdot n < val \land \forall n \in node\_values(r) \cdot n > val$

In this definition, we have introduced the function

$node\_values : Ordered\_tree \rightarrow \mathbb{N}\text{-set}$

that retrieves all the node values from an ordered tree and places them in a set. The invariant then states that all natural numbers n that belong to the set of node values returned from the *left* subtree of the tree with '*val*' as the root must be less than *val*, and all the numbers returned from the *right* subtree must be greater than *val*.

The introduced function *node_values* is itself defined recursively by observing that we can construct the set of all node values of a given tree by applying *node_values* to the left subtree and the right subtree and taking the union of these two sets with the set $\{val\}$ where *val* is the natural number at the root node. The recursion is terminated by noting that applying *node_values* to an empty tree will produce the empty set $\{\ \}$. This leads immediately to the definition

$node\_values : Ordered\_tree \rightarrow \mathbb{N}\text{-set}$
$node\_values (t) \triangleq$
$\quad \text{if } t = \text{EMPTY}$
$\quad \text{then } \{\ \}$
$\quad \text{elseif } t = mk\text{-}Ord\_bin\_tree(l, val, r)$
$\quad \text{then } node\_values(l) \cup \{val\} \cup node\_values(r)$

We are now ready to model the operations (recall from Chapter 5 that operations that are explicitly defined functions have their names written in lower case).

9.7.1 The VDM operation *build*

The first operation is *build* which inserts a number into an ordered tree. This operation must preserve the data type invariant and can be specified thus:

$build : Ordered\_tree \times \mathbb{N} \rightarrow Ordered\_tree$
$build(t, n) \triangleq$
$\quad \text{if } t = \text{EMPTY}$
$\quad \text{then } mk\text{-}Ord\_bin\_tree(\text{EMPTY}, n, \text{EMPTY})$
$\quad \text{elseif } t = mk\text{-}Ord\_bin\_tree(leftsub, value, rightsub) \land n < value$

```
then build(leftsub, n)
elseif t = mk-Ord_bin_tree(leftsub, value, rightsub) ∧ n > value
then build(rightsub, n)
else t
```

This algorithm for build will ensure that the data type invariant is satisfied. It is left as an exercise for the reader to show that the invariant is preserved each time a value is inserted into an ordered tree.

9.7.2 The VDM operations *left* and *right*

The operations *left* and *right* are rather more straightforward.

```
left : Ordered_tree → Ordered_tree
left (t) ≙
  if t = EMPTY
  then EMPTY
  elseif t = mk-Ord_bin_tree(l, val, r)
  then l
```

Similarly

```
right : Ordered_tree → Ordered_tree
right (t) ≙
  if t = EMPTY
  then EMPTY
  elseif t = mk-Ord_bin_tree(l, val, r)
  then r
```

9.7.3 The VDM operation *node*

This operation returns the value of the data element corresponding to the root of the tree

```
node : Ordered_tree → ℕ
node (t) ≙
  if t = mk-Ord_bin_tree(leftsub, value, rightsub)
  then value
```

9.7.4 The VDM operation *is_empty?*

The operation *is_empty?* returns true if and only if the tree is equal to the constant EMPTY

```
is_empty? : Ordered_tree → 𝔹
is_empty? (t) ≙
  if t = EMPTY
  then true
  else false
```

9.7.5 The VDM operation *is_in?*

The operation *is_in?* checks whether a specified data value is present in the tree. It makes use of our auxiliary function *node_values*

$$is\_in? : Ordered\_tree \rightarrow \mathbb{B}$$
$$is\_in? \ (t) \ \triangle$$
  if $n \in node\_values(t)$
  then *true*
  else *false*

9.8 FUNCTIONAL PROGRAMMING LANGUAGES AND DATA TYPES

It may seem strange at first sight that an abstract data type can be specified completely with just a collection of operations together with a set of axioms that relate these operations. However, if we think of the operations as functions, then this is similar to the approach adopted in *functional* programming.

Functional programming languages and *executable* algebraic specification languages do have a number of features in common. A functional program consists essentially of a collection of equations that define various functions. Functions are not restricted to 'normal' data types, they can take functions as inputs and return a function as a result. Therefore, loosely speaking, functional programs consist of a number of equations whose left- and right-hand sides can contain compositions (combinations) of functions. Similarly, the semantics of the *operations* of an abstract data type are expressed in terms of a collection of axioms or equations that involve compositions (applications) of two or more operations.

The similarity in style between algebraic specifications and functional languages is illustrated in Fig. 9.6 which is a *Miranda script* (program) that implements the data type queue

```
||    Miranda implementation of the adt "queue"
queue ::= New | Add queue num
||    the 'operations' of the adt "queue" are
remove :: queue  -> queue
front :: queue   -> num
isempty :: queue  -> bool
||    the 'axioms' for the adt "queue" :
front New = error "invalid application of 'front' to an empty queue"
front (Add q n)
          = n         , if isempty q
          = front q   , otherwise
isempty New = True
isempty (Add q n) = False
remove New = error "invalid application of 'remove' to an empty queue"
remove (Add q n)
          = New             , if isempty q
          = Add (remove q) n , otherwise
```

Figure 9.6 Miranda definition of the abstract data type Queue.

(© Miranda is a trademark of Research Software Ltd). In common with most modern programming languages, Miranda has facilities that support data types and one such feature is the so-called 'algebraic type'. Such types are characterized by a set of constructors (that are precisely the *atomic constructor* operations of algebraic specifications).

Referring to the Miranda script of Fig. 9.6, the statement

```
queue ::= New | Add queue num
```

introduces the data type queue where, following BNF notation, the symbol ::= means 'comprises' and the symbol | denotes alternate constructors. (In Miranda, constructors must start with an upper-case letter.) The constructor Add takes two parameters, a queue and a number.

The following three statements state the signature of the three operations remove, front, and isempty, while the six function definitions provide the semantics of the data type queue and correspond to the *axioms* of our algebraic specification. Note that Miranda employs postfix notation. Any conditions placed on the definition of a function (known as *guards* in Miranda) appear on the far right following the comma and the reserved word if. These guards must be predicate expressions that can be interpreted as either True or False.

For the queue q1 defined by

```
q1 = Add (Add (Add New 3) 4) 5
```

the applications

1. front q1
2. remove q1
3. isempty q1

result in the evaluations

1. 3
2. Add (Add New 4) 5
3. False

respectively.

This similarity in style between executable algebraic specification languages and *declarative* or *functional* programming languages explains, in part, why such languages (for example, *Miranda* and *SML*) provide natural vehicles for *rapid prototyping*. In rapid prototyping, the aim is to develop a trial model of a system quickly that exhibits all the important features of the intended system, but without the expenditure of excessive resources. Such prototyping provides a means for the production of a correct, although often inefficient, implementation. This feature was introduced in Chapter 7 and will be developed further in Chapter 13 where we discuss prototyping algebraic specifications.

Often, however, at the end of the day, implementations are required that use some *target* high-level *procedural* language. In this case, proofs that the implementation meets the specification should be carried out using the semantics of that target language. The onus on the implementor of the data type is to *prove* that every axiom *and* theorem of the algebraic specification is *satisfied* by the corresponding implementation. In practice, it usually suffices to prove that the axioms for each operation are satisfied by that operation's implementation. This *proof obligation* of verifying that an implementation satisfies its corresponding algebraic specification is an area of study that has still not been satisfactorily addressed in computer science. We will look briefly at some of the issues involved with respect to proof obligations for algebraic specifications later in Chapter 12.

Exercise 9.7 Implement the algebraic specifications Binary-tree and Ordered-tree (Figs 9.4 and 9.5 respectively) in Miranda.

9.9 ERRORS AND ALGEBRAIC SPECIFICATIONS

For an abstract data type there will often be situations in which it is not meaningful to apply certain operations. For the stack, attempting to pop an empty stack or attempting to remove the topmost element from an empty stack are two such abnormal situations. The basic problem is that these operations possess domain values with no corresponding range value and they are *partial* in the sense described in Secs 5.2.8 and 2.5.4. It is vital that an algebraic specification should not only formally describe the behaviour of the operations of an abstract data type in *normal* situations but also in these *abnormal* or *exceptional* ones.

The problem of dealing with *errors* in algebraic specifications is not as straightforward as might be supposed. Some of the methods described in the early literature for treating error values were not mathematically sound and in an attempt to put error handling onto a rigorous footing, techniques were developed that turned 'a little local difficulty' into 'major mathematical mayhem'. This particular aspect of algebraic specification is, however, not as awkward as some critics of the approach would have us believe.

To date, we have handled errors by the seemingly simple expedient of introducing an additional constant *error value* of the appropriate sort. In the case of Stack, as given, for example, in Fig. 8.2, we introduced the nullary operations

```
stack-error : → stack ; nat-error : → nat
```

to accommodate the outcomes of applying pop and top to an empty stack. This approach was adopted initially at the outset to allow the reader to gain an *immediate* foothold onto algebraic specification without getting bogged down with the subtleties of error handling. It is now time to appraise the implications of the use of error values.

9.10 USE OF ERROR VALUES

This approach to error handling is similar to that deployed in some of the early literature on algebraic specification, by authors such as Guttag (1977). However, the technique does have its problems. To see the difficulties that arise, consider the reduction of the term

```
top(push(pop(init), 3))
```

(E1)

for the unbounded stack of Fig. 8.2. Using *normal-order evaluation* in which expressions are evaluated from the 'outside in', we can apply axiom (6), and (E1) rewrites directly to the value 3.

On the other hand, using *applicative-order evaluation* in which the innermost arguments of expressions are evaluated first, we can apply axiom (3) first to replace pop(init) by stack-error so that (E1) rewrites to

```
top(push(stack-error,3))
```

which is undefined since the outcome of push(stack-error,3) has not been specified by the axioms.

This example highlights two deficiencies of our approach for dealing with errors, namely *nonunique termination* and an *incomplete semantics*. On the first point, we see that the two strategies for reducing (E1) result in two different outcomes. The resulting reduced form is not unique and depends on the order in which the axioms are applied. Hence, even with small specifications, the 'simple' expedient of introducing special or *distinguished* values (constants) to denote error values produces a specification with a set of axioms that does not produce unique rewrites for *all* syntactically legal expressions.

On the second point, we recall that a set of axioms is semantically complete if the outcomes of *all* syntactically legal compositions of operations are defined by the axioms. With reference to the specification of Fig. 8.2, although the outcomes of terms such as pop(init) and top(init) are defined by the axioms, the outcomes of syntactically legal terms such as pop(pop(init)) and top(pop(init)) are not. Also, what are we to make of stack expressions such as

```
push(s,top(init))
```

where $s \in$ stack? This rewrites to the expression push(s, nat-error) which is from sort stack. We can envisage applying additional push operations to this stack using 'safe' data values n (that is $n \in$ nat and $n \neq$ nat-error). The result of such a sequence of applications would be a stack value with a concealed error lurking somewhere inside. This level of 'uncertainty' is totally inappropriate for a *formal* specification.

9.10.1 Strictness and implicit axioms

We have seen that the basic problem with using error values is nonunique termination and an incomplete semantics. A sensible and natural way of dealing with these is to include an additional set of *implicit* axioms. A plausible set of such axioms for the stack is

```
push(stack-error,n) = stack-error
```

```
push(s, nat-error) = stack-error
```

```
pop(stack-error) = stack-error
```

```
top(stack-error) = nat-error
```

where $n \in$ nat (which includes the value nat–error) and $s \in$ stack (which includes the value stack–error).

We can achieve unique reductions for a given expression by constraining the order in which axioms are applied. For example, axioms whose right-hand sides are error values should be applied *first* to reduce any term or subterm that evaluates to an error value. Such axioms should be applied, wherever appropriate, *before* any 'normal' (nonerror) axioms. In other words, any stack with an error value lurking inside it is considered to be a totally erroneous stack value, denoted by the single value stack–error. The use of such implicit axioms then ensures unique *termination* (that is a unique result when evaluating and reducing any given expression) and such an axiomatization is said to have *strictness*.

However, problems still arise with the completeness of such a specification. Since all erroneous stack values reduce to stack–error, which is a member of the sort stack, we need to consider the outcome of the syntactically legal term is–empty?(stack–error). Clearly neither true nor false is apt so we need to include an additional error value in the sort bool resulting in a three-valued Boolean type which, at the very least, is counter to our perceived notions of the nature of a Boolean type. Fortunately exceptions can be handled much more simply using *subsorts*.

9.11 SUBSORTS AND SUBTYPES

We take the view that exceptions (errors) in algebraic specification languages are treated most simply using *subsorts* and *overloaded operations*. This approach provides a satisfyingly simple yet natural way of dealing with errors. In the case of the stack, for example, the idea is to introduce a subsort of *nonempty* stack values ne–stack and declare that the operations pop and top are *defined only* on this subsort. The fact that operations are defined over a subsort, and therefore undefined over part of a domain, implicitly defines erroneous applications and so provides a means of *error detection*. (This is very much in keeping with our adopted stance to formal specification.) This is a similar but simpler idea to that of restricting a type in VDM with a data type invariant. Alternatively, a *supersort* which includes the sort stack (and so itself contains both init and 'nonempty' stack values) can be introduced which allows the inclusion of error messages and other exception handling mechanisms. The inclusion of 'distinguished' error values into a specification can be accomplished by introducing supersorts that contain appropriate error messages and that are used to handle exceptions. Our reservations about this approach have been explained above; however, for those interested, the approach is outlined in the Additional Problems at the end of this chapter.

The concept of subsorts is intimately tied up with the idea of *subtypes* provided in languages such as Pascal, Modula-2, and latterly by Ada. Programmers are used to the idea of one set of data values being contained in or containing another. In Pascal and Modula-2, the *subrange* type supports this application where, for example, the Pascal code fragment

```
TYPE exam_marks = 0 .. 100;
```

declares that the data type exam_marks is the set of integers that lies in the range 0 to 100. Here, the data type exam_marks is a subtype of the predefined data type INTEGER. Another example of a subtype is the predefined data type CARDINAL of Modula-2 which is a subtype of another predefined type INTEGER. (Equivalently, we might say that INTEGER is a 'supertype' of CARDINAL.)

9.11.1 Operation overloading

Overloading is the technique of using the same symbol name to represent more than one operation and it is present, to a certain extent, in many programming languages. With the example above, we can *overload* the Boolean-valued operation '<' so that it can be used to compare integer or examination mark operands, despite the fact that the underlying operations are different. Similarly, in Modula-2, the addition operation + defined by

```
_+_ : CARDINAL CARDINAL → CARDINAL
```

is a restricted form of the operation

```
_+_ : INTEGER INTEGER → INTEGER
```

Here, the operation '+' is overloaded and the meaning of an overloaded operation is determined from the context provided by the types of its parameters (operands). Overloading is an essential feature for algebraic specifications based on subsorts. We do not want to have to devise new operation names,

```
push1 : stack nat → ne-stack

push2 : ne-stack nat → ne-stack
```

for what are essentially similar operations, simply because they have different domain sorts. Without the facility to overload operations, the resulting proliferation of operation names will add to the complexity of a specification and obscure its meaning. A more detailed discussion of subsorts and operation overloading is presented in Chapter 13.

9.12 ERROR DETECTION AND ERROR HANDLING

There are other ways of handling exceptions (errors) and we present a brief overview of some of them. This section is included for completeness only and can be omitted on a first reading.

One method used to treat errors in algebraic specifications involves constructing a specification in two stages. Initially, a specification is derived that deals exclusively with normal situations (which provides a partial semantics for the operations). Subsequently, all abnormal situations are included. Roughly speaking, we can think of the first stage of the specification as providing *error detection*, while the second stage of the specification deals with *error handling*.

There are a number of variations on this theme, but common to all is the need to include *additional* axioms *and* Boolean-valued operations or functions (sometimes referred to as *safety-markers*). These extra operations indicate whether an object is safe ('ok') or unsafe, returning the value true for the safe object and false for the latter. For example, with the stack, the constructor init denotes a safe object while push(s, n) is safe if and only if s and n denote safe objects. On the other hand, the values stack-error and nat-error denote unsafe objects. The safety-markers appear on the right-hand sides of an axiom. We can give a flavour of their use by showing an application to our old friend, the stack, and consider how the axioms for the operation pop are affected. Introducing the safety-marker (operation) okstack : stack → bool with the axioms

```
not okstack(s) = (s = = stack-error)

not okstack(push(s, n)) =
        (s = = stack-error) or (n = = nat-error) or (not okstack(s))
```

the axiom for pop takes the form

```
pop(s) = IF okstack(s) THEN
            IF s = = init THEN
               stack-error
            ELSE s1 WHERE s = push(s1, n)
            ENDIF
         ELSE stack-error
         ENDIF
```

with similar *guarded* axioms for the operations top and is-empty?.

It is interesting to note that some of the early algebraic specification languages, including the executable language *OBJ0*, used a similar construction. The operations of an algebraic specification were separated into *three* kinds, *normal* or 'ok' operations, *abnormal* or 'error' operations and finally *recovery* or 'fix' operations. The axioms, referred to as *equations* in OBJ, were then separated into 'ok-equations' and 'error-equations'.

The fundamental criticism of this general approach is that although it provides specifications with a complete semantics, unique term rewriting, and error handling and recovery capabilities, it also leads to a proliferation of error values and error axioms for even the simplest abstract data type. The added complexity for larger specifications results in cumbersome and often unreadable specifications. There is no doubt that this treatment of errors obscures the intrinsic simplicity and elegance of the algebraic approach. Indeed, this may have been one of the reasons that led to the abandonment of this approach for error handling in the later version of the language *OBJ2*.

The approach we have adopted, based upon the idea of *subsorts*, was developed by Goguen (1978) and has a number of advantages, not the least of which is that it avoids the questionable concept of linking sorts with error values, which, at this formal level, are nothing more than symbolic objects anyway. Another advantage of the approach is that it preserves the clarity and conciseness of the algebraic technique. No implicit axioms or hidden Boolean operations have to be introduced and the technique preserves the preciseness and readability that is the essence of the algebraic approach. It is for these reasons that we have adopted the subsort approach to handle exceptions.

9.13 SPECIFICATION OF A STACK

We apply the technique of domain subsorts to the specification of an unbounded stack of natural numbers and the corresponding specification Stack-nat is shown in Fig. 9.7. The

```
SPEC   Stack-nat
USING  Natural + Boolean
SORTS  stack  ne-stack
SUBSORT  ne-stack  <  stack
OPS
    init      :   -> stack
    push      :   stack  nat  ->  ne-stack
    pop       :   ne-stack  ->  stack
    top       :   ne-stack  ->  nat
    is-empty? :   stack  ->  bool
FORALL
    s  :  stack
    n  :  nat
AXIOMS:
(1)  is-empty?(init)  =  true
(2)  is-empty?(push(s,n))  =  false
(3)  pop(push(s,n))  =  s
(4)  top(push(s,n))  =  n
ENDSPEC
```

Figure 9.7 Algebraic specification of a stack using domain subsorts.

essence of this approach to exceptions is to observe that pop and top are *total* on the subsort ne-stack of nonempty stacks and then declare that these operations are *only defined* on this subsort. Observe first that the specification Stack-nat of Fig. 9.7 introduces *two* sorts, namely stack and ne-stack. The statement

```
SUBSORT ne-stack < stack
```

will be used to express the fact that ne-stack is a subsort of stack. Note also that since the outcome of pushing a value onto any stack will result in a nonempty stack, the signature of push is given by push : stack nat → ne-stack.

Exercise 9.8   Recast the specification Queue using this approach by introducing a subsort ne-queue of nonempty queues. You will need to redefine the domain sorts of the operations front and remove and produce four axioms.

9.14 SUMMARY

- Algebraic specifications for two classical abstract data types, namely the *queue* and the *binary tree*, are derived.
- *Atomic constructors* are a subset of the constructors that have the property that every value of the principal sort (type of interest) can be represented using a composition (combination) of constructors drawn from this subset.
- The remaining constructors which are not atomic are called *nonatomic constructors*.
- Heuristics have been devised to guide the specifier in writing an appropriate collection of axioms. One such rule involves writing axioms to show how each accessor and nonatomic constructor operation acts upon each of the atomic constructors.
- *Hidden* operations, also called *private* operations, are introduced into a specification when some kind of *pre-condition* needs to be stated. Hidden operations are introduced

in situations where the required values of a sort need to be 'restricted' to conform to some 'well-definedness' predicate. The specification Ordered-tree for an ordered binary tree is an example where the well-definedness predicate is 'that the data elements of the tree are required to have a precise ordering'.

- The treatment of errors is discussed and the implications of using error values are explored. Problems of an incomplete semantics can arise with this approach.
- The use of subsorts to handle errors is explained and the advantages of adopting this approach are discussed.

ADDITIONAL PROBLEMS

9.1 A queue Q contains the three data values 5, 7, and 9, with 5 at the front of the queue and 9 at the end.
(a) Express Q in terms of the *atomic* constructors add and new.
(b) Use the axioms of Queue to reduce the term remove(Q).

9.2 Use the axioms of Queue to show that

    front(remove(add(add(new, 2), 4))) = 4

9.3 Suppose we wish to extend Queue by including an additional operation is-in? which takes a queue together with a natural number and returns true if that number is present in the queue, false otherwise.
(a) State the signature of is-in?.
(b) Construct axioms for is-in? by considering how the operation acts on new and add(q,n) where q ∈ queue and n ∈ nat.

9.4 (a) Express the following binary tree in terms of the atomic constructors make and empty.

(b) Use the axioms of Binary-tree, to show that the data element 2 is present in the tree.
(c) Use the axioms of Binary-tree, to show that the data element 7 is not present in the tree.

9.5 The ordered binary tree shown below

is constructed from the data values 4, 6, and 3, with 4 at the root of the tree, and corresponds to the term

    build(build(build(empty, 4), 6), 3)

Use the axioms of Ordered-tree to show that this expression rewrites to the term

```
!make(!make(empty, 3, empty), 4, !make(empty, 6, empty))
```

To start, you should demonstrate that

```
build(build(empty, 4), 6) = !make(empty, 4, !make(empty, 6, empty))
```

9.6 In this extended problem, a specification for a simple *directory* that stores a table of user-names with their corresponding user-number will be developed. We can take the set of user-names to come from the sort id supplied by the pre-defined abstract data type Identifier and the user-numbers to come from the sort nat.

This problem will explore the use of hidden operations for the specification and show their use for constraining the values of an abstract data type.

We will assume that all user-names that have no user-numbers yet allocated are given the default user-number 0. This has the effect of ensuring that the mapping is *total*. We require that user-names with corresponding user-number pairs can be inserted into a directory and also removed from a directory. The specification of the abstract data type Directory-Map with introduced sort dir will therefore need the operations:

```
⟨ _ ⟩ : nat → dir
_[_ to _] : dir id nat → dir
```

The first operation creates an initial directory in which no user-numbers have been allocated. The domain value specifies an appropriate default user-number (which we have already chosen to be 0).

The second operation adds a *user-name*, *user-number* pair to a directory to produce a new directory, regardless of whether the user-name or user-number is already present in the existing directory.

These two operations provide the *atomic* constructors for Directory-Map from which all values of the directory can be built. For example, the directory containing the three *user-name*, *user-number* pairs ("John", 23), ("Ann", 9), and ("Lee", 16) will correspond to the expression:

```
⟨ 0 ⟩ ["John" to 23] ["Ann" to 9] ["Lee" to 16]
```
(D9.1)

Three further operations to be included are:

```
_ remove _ : dir id → dir
_ number _ : dir id → nat
_ is-in? _ : dir id → bool
```

The operation remove takes a directory together with a user-name and removes the corresponding *user-name*, *user-number* pair from the directory. For example:

```
(⟨ 0 ⟩ ["John" to 23] ["Ann" to 9] ["Lee" to 16]) remove "Ann"
```

produces the directory

⟨ 0 ⟩ ["John" to 23] ["Lee" to 16]

The operation number takes a directory together with a user-name as input and returns the corresponding user-number. For example:

(⟨ 0 ⟩ ["John" to 23] ["Ann" to 9] ["Lee" to 16]) number "Ann"

returns the user-number 9.

The operation is-in? takes a directory together with a user-name as input and returns true if the user-name is present in the directory, false otherwise. For example:

(⟨ 0 ⟩ ["John" to 23] ["Ann" to 9] ["Lee" to 16]) is-in? "John"

returns the value true.

The role of the accessor operations is to permit interrogation of the directory.
(a) Identify the accessors.
(b) Identify the nonatomic constructors.
(c) How many axioms are needed for the specification?
(d) Write down the syntactic component of the specification, that is the SPEC, USING, SORT and OPS components.
(e) The axioms are presented below. Complete the axioms by inserting the appropriate expressions in the places marked ??.

```
FORALL

        d  : dir

     n1,  n2 : nat

  un , un1, un2 : id

AXIOMS for is-in?:

(1) ⟨ 0 ⟩ is-in? name = false

(2) (d [un1 to n1] ) is-in? un2 = IF un1 = = un2 THEN ??

                              ELSE d is-in? un2 ENDIF

AXIOMS for number:

(3) ⟨ 0 ⟩ number un = 0

(4) (d [un1 to n1] ) number un2 = IF un1 = = un2 THEN ??

                           ELSE ?? ENDIF
```

```
AXIOMS for remove:
```

(5) ⟨ 0 ⟩ remove un = ⟨ 0 ⟩

(6) (d [un1 to n1]) remove un2 = IF un1 = = un2 THEN ??

ELSE (d remove un2) [un1 to n1]

ENDIF

Note that this specification will permit a user to be allocated more than one user-number, since the operation _[_ to _] permits *user-name, user-number* pairs to be added to an existing directory regardless of whether the user has already been allocated a number.

The question now arises: how is the specification affected if we want the facility of updating a user-number. In other words, suppose the state of the directory is as given in (D9.1) above and it is now required to change John's user-number from 23 to 12. This idea corresponds to the familiar concept of *map* or *function overwrite*.

We have already noted that the existing operation _[_to_] does not incorporate this feature. However, we can achieve this updating property by first removing the existing *user-name, user-number* pair from the directory (if one exists) and then adding the updated entry. We therefore make the existing operation _[_to_] *hidden* and introduce a new operation _[_is_] which provides the required updating facility. The OPS component of the specification is then amended to:

_[_ !to _]: dir id nat → dir

_[_ is _]: dir id nat → dir

with corresponding amendments to the axioms (that is all instances of _[_ to _] are replaced by _[_!to_]). We need a seventh axiom which relates these two operations (just as we had an axiom that related !make and build for the ordered tree). The corresponding axiom is:

(7) d ([un is n1]) = (d remove un) [un !to n1]

The operation _[_is_] therefore provides the 'proper' way of inserting *user-name, user-number* pairs into a directory. The operation _[_!to_] is flagged as hidden and so cannot be exported to any module that may subsequently want to use it.

(f) Suppose further that we wish to ensure that no two users can have the same user-number. If the result of attempting to add a new entry to the directory with an existing user-number is to be treated as an error, show how axiom (7) is amended to deal with this new constraint. (You will need to use a conditional on the right-hand side of the axiom).

9.7 Attempting to access the root of an empty tree is an erroneous application. Introduce a subsort of nonempty tree values and so recast the specifications Binary-tree and Ordered-tree by redefining the domain and range sorts of the appropriate operations.

```
SPEC   Stack-nat
USING  Natural + Boolean
SORTS  stack  super-stack  super-nat
SUBSORT  stack  <  super-stack
SUBSORT  nat  <  super-nat
OPS
    init         :   -> stack
    push         :   stack  nat  ->   stack
    push         :   super-stack  nat  ->  super-stack
    pop          :   stack  ->  super-stack
    top          :   stack  ->  super-nat
    is-empty?    :   stack  ->  bool
    stack-error  :   ->  super-stack
    nat-error    :   ->  super-nat
FORALL
    s  :   stack
    n  :   nat

AXIOMS:
(1)  is-empty?(init)  =  true
(2)  is-empty?(push(s,n))  =  false
(3)  pop(push(s,n))  =  s
(4)  top(push(s,n))  =  n
(5)  pop(init)  =  stack-error
(6)  top(init)  =  nat-error
ENDSPEC
```

Figure 9.8 Algebraic specification of a stack using error supersorts.

9.8 In this example, we introduce supersorts that contain distinguished values (for example, 'error messages') to handle exceptions.

For the stack, we introduce super-stack which is a supersort of stack to cater for applying pop to an empty stack. We also introduce super-nat, a supersort of nat to accommodate the outcome of top applied to an empty stack.

In other words, super-stack is a subsort of stack and super-nat is a subsort of nat. The syntax of pop and top now becomes

    pop : stack → super-stack

    top : stack → super-nat

and the exceptional values (error messages) stack-error and nat-error (which correspond to the original error values of Stack in Fig. 8.2) have signature

    stack-error : → super-stack

    nat-error   : → super-nat

The operation push cannot produce exceptions when acting on any stack value from the sort stack and we can overload push by defining a corresponding operation over the supersort super-stack. The corresponding specification Stack-nat is given in Fig. 9.8.

(a) Transform the specification `Queue` of Fig. 8.2 into an equivalent one that uses error supersorts.

(b) Introduce appropriate supersorts into the directory example of Exercise 8.6 and produce the corresponding revised specification.

REFERENCES

Goguen, J. (1978) Order Sorted Algebra, *Technical Report 14—Semantics and Theory of Computation Series*, UCLA Computer Science Department, Los Angeles. For a more detailed exposition see Goguen *et al.* (1985) below.

Guttag, J. (1977) Abstract Data Types and the Development of Data Structures, *Communications of the ACM*, **20**, 396–404.

Liskov, B., and Zilles, S. (1975) Specification Techniques for Data Abstractions, *IEEE Transactions on Software Engineering*, **SE-1**, 7–19.

FURTHER READING

Goguen, J.A., Jouannaud, J.-P., and Meseguer, J. (1985) Operational Semantics of Order-sorted Algebra. In *Proceedings of the 12th. International Conference on Automata, Languages and Programming*, published in *Lecture Notes in Computer Science*, vol. 194, Springer-Verlag, Berlin, pp. 221–231.

ALGEBRAS AND ABSTRACT DATA TYPES

10.1 INTRODUCTION

We now look at some of the background theory that lies at the heart of the algebraic approach to specification. The aim of this discussion is not to explore these theoretical aspects in great depth but to provide an overview of some of the important concepts upon which the approach is based.

Some of the ideas introduced here are not always immediately accessible and sometimes present difficulties when first encountered. If readers do find problems with some of the material in this chapter they can proceed, without penalty, to the next chapter, which looks at building larger specifications and develops a number of small case studies. Study of these examples of algebraic specifications and how they are constructed should provide further insight into the algebraic approach and serve to reinforce the fundamental concepts discussed here. The reader can subsequently return to this chapter and gain a better understanding of these more formal ideas.

In this chapter we explain what is meant by an *algebra* and discuss the role of *initial* algebras for the specification of abstract data types. We look more formally at the notions of a *signature* and the relationship between a signature and an algebra. We shall see that algebras provide *models* of our specifications in the sense that they provide abstract *implementations* of a specification. These ideas are developed and explained with the aid of a number of examples.

We discuss the idea of structure-preserving transformations between algebras (so-called *homomorphisms*) and the implications for the specification of data types. With no axioms, the class of algebras that interprets a given signature is very broad, often too broad to be of use for specifying the required behaviour of an abstract data type. Extending a signature with axioms allows specifications to be 'tightened' in the sense that the specification can be tailored to capture the required properties of an abstract data type. A signature together with a set of axioms that relate terms constructed from the signature constitutes a *presentation*. Use of the axioms together with the inference rules of *equational logic* allows equivalences between terms (*theorems*) to be established and the resulting formal system is known as a *theory presentation*. We consider algebras that provide models of theory presentations and look at one model in particular, the *quotient term algebra*. This algebra, whose existence is guaranteed for a given theory presentation, provides a unique semantics for that presentation. The importance of this algebra lies in the fact that it contains exactly what the specification requires and nothing more. These concepts will be explained in this chapter.

We look also at the implications of treating the axioms of an algebraic specification as a set of *rewrite rules* and explore further the reduction and evaluation of terms. We should emphasize that the aim is not to provide an in-depth account of this particular aspect of the algebraic approach, but to furnish the reader with an intuitive idea of the principles involved. The chapter concludes with a summary of the principal results.

10.2 ALGEBRAS

Algebras or *algebraic systems* have long been a fertile area of study in mathematics and their relevance in relation to the theory of abstract data types was first pointed out in the mid-1970s by Zilles (1974). Basically, an algebra consists of a set of values (the *carrier* set) together with a collection of operations (functions) with domain and range values defined over the carrier set. If we pause for a moment and examine this definition, we realize that it also provides an informal description of an abstract data type.

It is, therefore, hardly surprising that algebras play a fundamental role in the theory of abstract data types. The importance of algebras lies in the fact that they provide mathematical models of specifications. Different types of algebraic models can be chosen for the underlying mathematical framework although we will concentrate on the so-called *initial algebra* approach in which *initial* models are used. To start, let us explore what is meant by an *algebra*.

10.2.1 Homogeneous or single-sorted algebras

A *homogeneous* (or *single-sorted*) algebra $\mathscr{A}$ is

$$\mathscr{A} = [A, \Omega]$$

where

- A is a nonempty set that contains values of the type and is known as the *carrier* set
- Ω is a set of operations defined over the carrier set which may include *nullary* operations (constants)

and the square brackets simply signify that an algebra consists of a pair of items, namely a set of values and a collection of operations. These homogeneous algebras describe small 'self-contained' data types like the natural numbers or Boolean values. As an example, an algebra, $\mathscr{A}_{Natl}$, describing the data type Natural with the familiar operations of addition ($+$) and multiplication ($\times$) is $\mathscr{A}_{Natl} = [\mathbb{N}, \{0, +, \times\}]$ where $\mathbb{N} = \{0, 1, 2, 3, ...\}$. (Note that we have included the value '0' (zero) as a nullary operation.) Addition and multiplication are both binary operations that take two natural numbers and return a natural number as a result.

10.2.2 Heterogeneous or many-sorted algebras

The definition above is readily extended to *heterogeneous* or *many-sorted* algebras. In this case, $A = \{A_i\}$ is a family of nonempty carrier sets A_i. Such algebras describe more interesting abstract data types such as stacks and queues. For example, the structure of the algebra describing stacks of natural numbers consists of the set of stack values, the set of natural numbers, the set of Boolean values, and the operations that manipulate these values. The operations of a heterogeneous algebra have domain and range values drawn from the sets of carriers A_i.

10.2.3 Models

The fundamental importance of algebras is that they provide *models* of algebraic specifications. As we shall see, a given specification has many algebras as a model so we therefore need to examine how such algebras might be related and whether there is one particular algebra (or algebras) that provides a standard representational model in the sense that it (or they) capture the essential properties of the whole class of models.

It is very important to realize that the term 'model' in this context is very different from its meaning in VDM. In VDM, a specification is based upon creating a *system model* using a collection of operations defined by pre- and post-conditions together with a collection of data structures that are built up from well-defined simple types (such as sets and composites) and a particular data structure (the *system state*) that the operations can access. Hence, the system model in VDM is essentially an implementation based on discrete mathematical primitives. The operations are then defined *individually* in terms of their effect upon the system state.

With the algebraic approach, the behaviour of the operations is always described in terms of how two or more of them interact—they are never defined individually. The underlying 'structure' associated with an algebraic specification is an algebra. Such an algebra is a *model* or *interpretation* of the specification and is defined without reference to any 'better described' or 'more concrete' entities. We will return to this point later in Sec. 10.9.4.

10.3 SIGNATURES AND HETEROGENEOUS ALGEBRAS

We need to stand back for a moment and formalize some of the ideas and concepts that have been used to date in our study of algebraic specifications. To start, we recall some basic definitions from our earlier discussion.

- **Signature**—a signature, Σ, is a set of sorts together with a finite set of formal function symbols. Each function symbol has an associated *arity* which embodies the number of domain arguments and their sorts together with a range sort which represents the sort of the result.

The signature thus defines the syntax of operations using functions defined over the sorts and from which *terms* (or *expressions*) can be constructed that denote specific values. With reference to our specifications, Σ corresponds to the information contained in the SORTS and OPS components of a specification.

Suppose we have a many-sorted signature Σ and a heterogeneous algebra $\mathscr{A}$. The algebra $\mathscr{A}$ is said to be a *model* of the signature if:

- $\mathscr{A}$ possesses a set of values (a carrier set) for each sort of Σ.
- $\mathscr{A}$ has an operation for each operation symbol of Σ, whose domain and range sets correspond exactly with those imposed by the pattern given in the signature.

The signature thus lays out a pattern or template that must be conformed to by any algebra that is to be a model of the signature (and therefore of the specification). Hence, an algebra, $\mathscr{A}$, is a model of a signature, Σ, if we can 'assign' the sort identifiers and operation symbols of Σ to corresponding carrier sets and operation names, respectively, in $\mathscr{A}$. We then say that $\mathscr{A}$ is a model of Σ with this *interpretation* or *denotation*.

An analogy with programming in a language such as Modula-2 or Ada might be helpful here. In this context, we can think of a *signature* as a Modula-2 DEFINITION MODULE (or Ada package specification), which defines an interface and describes the syntax of an abstract data type. Any *algebra* that is a model of that signature then corresponds to an *implementation* of that abstract data type in which the carrier set of the algebra contains the values of the abstract data type.

Such algebras which are models of a signature, Σ, are commonly referred to as Σ-*algebras*. Let us examine these ideas with some examples.

10.4 INTERPRETATIONS OF A SIGNATURE

What should be realized at the outset is that there is *not* a one-to-one correspondence between signatures and algebras. One signature can denote (can be interpreted by) many algebras. Consider, for example, the signature of Fig. 10.1. An algebra that interprets this signature and provides a simple model of the natural numbers is

$$\mathscr{A}_{Nat} = [\mathbb{N}, \{0, Succ\}]$$

where the carrier $\mathbb{N} = \{0, 1, 2, ...\}$ and $Succ : \mathbb{N} \rightarrow \mathbb{N}$ is a unary operation defined by $Succ(n) = n + 1$ with $n \in \mathbb{N}$. This algebra represents the 'familiar' (in the sense of the expected) interpretation of the function symbols in Σ over the natural numbers with $Succ$ as the *successor* operation '+1'. For this signature, we have used the set $\mathbb{N}$ as our interpretation of the sort nat, interpreted succ as $Succ$ and used the denotation (that is correspondence)

$$\{\text{zero} \longrightarrow 0, \text{succ(zero)} \longrightarrow 1, \text{succ(succ(zero))} \longrightarrow 2, ...\}$$

```
SORT   nat
OPS
    zero :  ->  nat
    succ :  nat  ->  nat
```

Figure 10.1 A signature for the natural numbers.

so that every syntactically legal term of the signature is given as its interpretation a member of the set $\{0, 1, 2,...\}$.

Another model of the signature is the algebra

$$\mathcal{A}_{NatEven} = [\mathbb{N}_{Even}, \{0, Succ_{Ev}\}]$$

where the carrier $\mathbb{N}_{Even} = \{0, 2, 4,...\}$ is the set of *even* natural numbers and $Succ_{Ev}: \mathbb{N}_{Even} \to \mathbb{N}_{Even}$ is defined by $Succ_{Ev}(n) = n + 2$. In this case, $\mathbb{N}_{Even}$ interprets the sort nat, the function $Succ_{Ev}$ has been assigned to the symbol succ, and we have used the denotation

$$\{\texttt{zero} \longrightarrow 0, \texttt{ succ(zero)} \longrightarrow 2, \texttt{ succ(succ(zero))} \longrightarrow 4, ...\}$$

One final example worth noting is that the signature of Fig. 10.1 also has as a model the algebra $\mathcal{A}_1$, where $\mathcal{A}_1 = [\{e\}, \{e, Ide\}]$, which consists of a carrier set with a single value e and the identity function Ide which maps the element e onto itself, that is $Ide(e) = e$. In this example, nat $- \to \{e\}$, succ $- \to Ide$, and

$$\{\texttt{zero} \longrightarrow e, \texttt{ succ(zero)} \longrightarrow e, \texttt{ succ(succ(zero))} \longrightarrow e, ...\}$$

so that $\mathcal{A}_1$ provides yet another model of the signature of Fig. 10.1.

10.5 TERM ALGEBRA

One model, which mathematicians tend to ignore, is that in which the values of the carrier set are the *terms themselves* constructed from the function symbols (operations) in the signature Σ. Such a model always exists and this interpretation is called the *term algebra* or *term structure*. Hence, for the signature of Fig. 10.1, one model is given by the *term algebra*

$$\mathcal{A}_{NatTerm} = [\{\texttt{zero, succ(zero), succ(succ(zero))}...\}, \{\texttt{zero, succ}\}]$$

For the term algebra, each member of the carrier set is denoted by a variable-free or *ground term*. All the ground terms make up the 'language' generated by the signature, in much the same way as BNF (Backus–Naur Form—see Chapter 1).

The term algebra is based upon the *signature* Σ of a specification and the carrier set corresponding to each sort consists of all the syntactically legal terms (with results of that sort) that can be constructed using Σ. In the case of the specification Stack, for example, the carrier set corresponding to the sort stack will contain not only terms involving the atomic constructors init and push, but also terms involving pop. The carrier set of the term algebra will therefore include terms such as

```
pop(push(init, 2))  and   push(init, top(push(init, 3)))
```

The important property of a term algebra is that it provides a symbolic representation of a specification that can be manipulated and treated as a model *in its own right*.

10.6 TRANSFORMATIONS BETWEEN ALGEBRAS

At this point, the bewildering number of different models of a single given signature leads us to wonder:

- Is there is some kind of 'equivalence' or 'resemblance' between the members of the *class* (*family*) of algebras that are models of a given signature?
- Is there one member (or group of members) of this class that somehow captures the intrinsic properties of that entire class?

Before we can address these issues, we need to examine how an algebra can be transformed into another using a mapping between the carrier sets of the algebras. In the following discussion, we will confine ourselves to homogeneous algebras. The ideas developed here extend quite naturally to heterogeneous algebras but the added complexity of notation needed would only serve to obscure the fundamental concepts.

Two algebras, $\mathscr{A} = [A, \Omega_A]$ and $\mathscr{B} = [B, \Omega_B]$, that are denoted by a common signature can certainly be said to be *similar* in the sense that they will have the same number of operations of matching arities which allows the sets of operations Ω_A and Ω_B to be put into a one-to-one correspondence. This is a weak form of equivalence and is based purely on a syntactic classification. Nothing is stated about any connection between the semantic properties of the algebras that are prescribed by equations satisfied by the operations. We might expect, for example, to be able to map one algebra onto another while preserving the inherent structure and behaviour of the operations.

10.6.1 Homomorphism

A stronger form of relationship (than equivalence) between algebras that does assert such a structure-preserving property is *homomorphism*. Suppose two algebras $\mathscr{A}$ and $\mathscr{B}$, as defined above, are denoted by the same signature. The operations $\omega_{A_k} \in \Omega_A$ from algebra $\mathscr{A}$ and $\omega_{B_k} \in \Omega_B$ from algebra $\mathscr{B}$ of arity k can therefore be put into a one-to-one correspondence as noted above.

Consider a mapping $h: A \rightarrow B$ between the carrier sets A and B. Then h is a *homomorphism* from algebra $\mathscr{A}$ to algebra $\mathscr{B}$ if for *every* operation $\omega_A \in \Omega_A$ of arity k with corresponding operation $\omega_B \in \Omega_B$

$$h(\omega_A(a_1, a_2, ..., a_k)) = \omega_B(h(a_1), h(a_2), ..., h(a_k)) \tag{10.1}$$

where $a_i \in A$ and $1 \leqslant i \leqslant k$. To be a homomorphism, this result must hold for all operations of every arity.

This rather formidable equation states the following. The outcome of applying an operation ω_A from $\mathscr{A}$ to values of the carrier of A and then finding the result when the mapping h is applied is the same as finding the transform of the values of A using h first and then applying the corresponding operation ω_B of $\mathscr{B}$.

(Note that the existence of a homomorphism from $\mathscr{A}$ to $\mathscr{B}$ does not imply that a homomorphism exists from $\mathscr{B}$ to $\mathscr{A}$ and that although, by convention, we talk about a homomorphism h from one algebra $\mathscr{A}$ to another algebra $\mathscr{B}$, and write $h: \mathscr{A} \rightarrow \mathscr{B}$, the mapping h is strictly a mapping between the carrier sets. Also $h: A \rightarrow B$ is only well defined if the operations $\omega_A \in \Omega_A$ and $\omega_B \in \Omega_B$ are in one-to-one correspondence.)

We can get a feel for the nature of homomorphisms and the meaning of Eq. (10.1) by looking at one particular homomorphism that has been used over the years to ease the effort involved in multiplying real numbers.

Consider the (homogeneous) algebras $\mathscr{A}$ and $\mathscr{B}$

$$\mathscr{A} = [\mathbb{R}^+, \{\times\}] \ ; \ \mathscr{B} = [\mathbb{R}, \{+\}]$$

where $\mathbb{R}$ is the set of real numbers, $\mathbb{R}^+$ is the set of positive real numbers, and $\times$ and $+$ denote the familiar arithmetic operations of multiplication and addition respectively.

The mapping $h: \mathbb{R}^+ \to \mathbb{R}$ given by $h(x) = log(x)$ where $x \in \mathbb{R}^+$ is a *homomorphism* between $\mathscr{A}$ and $\mathscr{B}$ and we can formally prove this result by demonstrating that Eq. (10.1) holds. To start, we note that the two operations $\times$ and $+$ have arity 2, so that the arity constraint of Eq. (10.1) is satisfied. Furthermore, since each algebra has only the one operation, the correspondence between the operations of $\mathscr{A}$ and $\mathscr{B}$ is immediate and we can therefore take ω_A as $\times$ and ω_B as $+$ respectively.

Using the familiar infix form for the operations $\times$ and $+$, the left-hand side of Eq. (10.1) is $h(a_1 \times a_2)$, that is

$$log(a_1 \times a_2)$$

where $a_1, a_2 \in \mathbb{R}^+$. The expression that corresponds to the right-hand side of Eq. (10.1) is

$$log(a_1) + log(a_2)$$

These two expressions are equal since $\forall a_1, a_2 \in \mathbb{R}^+$, $log(a_1 \times a_2) = log(a_1) + log(a_2)$. It follows that the function $h: \mathbb{R}^+ \to \mathbb{R}$ given by $h(x) = log(x)$ is a homomorphism. This result is illustrated in Fig. 10.2 which demonstrates that a mapping h is a homomorphism if, starting from the top-left-hand corner of the diagram, you end up with the same result (bottom-right-hand corner), irrespective of which 'path' you choose. In other words, the elements of the algebra $\mathscr{B}$ can be generated *either* by first applying the operation $\times$ to elements of $\mathscr{A}$ and then converting the result using h (dotted path) *or* by first converting elements of $\mathscr{A}$ using h and then applying the operation $+$ of $\mathscr{B}$ (dashed path).

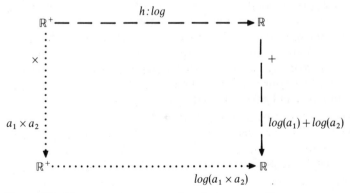

Figure 10.2 Diagrammatic representation of a homomorphism.

This particular homomorphism has been used for many years and forms the basis of the application of logarithms to multiply two numbers. Prior to the early 1970s, when cheap pocket calculators became available, the result of *multiplying* two numbers was evaluated by first finding their individual logarithm (usually to base 10) using tables or a slide rule, then *adding* the two logarithms together, and finally inverting the resultant sum.

10.6.2 Isomorphism

Homomorphisms can be classified according to the type of mapping h between the algebras. A homomorphism is an *isomorphism* if $h: A \rightarrow B$ is *bijective*. In other words, the elements of A and B can be put into one-to-one correspondence. This means that not only every value in B is mapped to, but there is also an *inverse* function that will map each value in B to a value in A. If two Σ-algebras, denoted by the same signature Σ are *isomorphic*, they are 'equivalent' in all respects apart from the names of their sets and operations. Any statement expressed in terms of the function symbols of Σ that is true in $\mathscr{A}$ will also be true of $\mathscr{B}$ and vice versa. Although the algebras may appear quite different, in that the elements of the carriers are different, structurally the algebras are identical.

If an isomorphism exists between two algebras, those algebras possess the strongest type of similarity and are equivalent in all respects apart from the symbols that name the elements of their respective carrier sets. The concept of an isomorphism between algebras is a fundamental one in relation to the specification of abstract data types because it expresses *formally* the *independence of representation* inherently necessary for values of abstract data types.

10.6.3 Some examples and a counter example

The ideas presented so far in the whole of this section on transformations are not readily accessible at first, so we now present some examples which should help to clarify them.

Example 10.1 Consider the two algebras $\mathscr{A}_{Nat} = [\{\mathbb{N}, \{0, Succ\}]$ and $\mathscr{A}_{NatEven} = [\{\mathbb{N}_{Even}, \{0, Succ_{Ev}\}]$ introduced in Sec. 10.4. The mapping $h: \mathbb{N} \rightarrow \mathbb{N}_{Even}$ from the natural numbers to the even natural numbers defined by $h(n) = 2n$ for every $n \in \mathbb{N}$ is a *homomorphism*.

To show that h is a homomorphism, we simply need to demonstrate that Eq. (10.1) holds for every operation in $\mathscr{A}_{Nat}$, including all nullary operations (constant values). Observe that if the operation ω_A of $\mathscr{A}$ is a nullary operation with corresponding nullary operation ω_B in $\mathscr{B}$, then Eq. (10.1) asserts that h will be a homomorphism if $h(\omega_A) = \omega_B$.

In this example, for the nullary operation 0 of $\mathscr{A}_{Nat}$, the left-hand side of Eq. (10.1) becomes $h(0)$, which is equal to $2 \times 0 = 0$. Hence, the left-hand side of Eq. (10.1) produces the result 0, which is equal to the corresponding nullary operation of $\mathscr{A}_{NatEven}$. Hence, Eq. (10.1) is satisfied for the nullary operations of the algebras.

For the operation $Succ$, the left-hand side of Eq. (10.1) is

$$h(Succ(n)) = h(n+1) = 2(n+1) = 2n+2$$

and the corresponding right-hand side of Eq. (10.1) is

$$Succ_{Ev}(h(n)) = Succ_{Ev}(2n) = 2n+2$$

The values are the same, so that the function $h: \mathbb{N} \rightarrow \mathbb{N}_{Even}$ where $h(n) = 2n$ is a homomorphism and the algebras $\mathscr{A}_{Nat}$ and $\mathscr{A}_{NatEven}$ are *homomorphic*. This mapping is bijective so that these algebras are also *isomorphic*. The function h is bijective because any given natural number n will map to the unique value $2n$ and, conversely, any even natural number m will map to the corresponding unique natural number $m/2$. The inverse function $h_{inv}: \mathbb{N}_{Even} \rightarrow \mathbb{N}$ in this example is given by $h_{inv}(m) = m/2$.

Example 10.2 Consider the algebra $\mathscr{A}_{Nat}$ of Example 1 and the algebra $\mathscr{A}_1 = [\{e\}, \{e, Ide\}]$ of Sec. 10.4 whose carrier is the singleton set $\{e\}$. Consider the mapping $h: \mathbb{N} \rightarrow \{e\}$ defined by $h(n) = e$ for every $n \in \mathbb{N}$. This mapping is also a homomorphism from $\mathscr{A}_{Nat}$ to $\mathscr{A}_1 = [\{e\}, \{e, Ide\}]$, since, for the nullary operation e, the left-hand side of Eq. (10.1) is $h(0)$ which, using the definition of h, produces the value e and the right-hand side of Eq. (10.1) reduces immediately to the corresponding nullary operation of $\mathscr{A}_1$, which is e. Equation (10.1) is therefore true for the nullary operation 0 since both sides of the equation produce the same result e.

For the function *Succ*, the left-hand side of Eq. (10.1) is

$$h(Succ(n)) = h(n+1) = e$$

and the corresponding right-hand side is

$$Ide(h(n)) = Ide(e) = e$$

so that again Eq. (10.1) holds. Hence h is a homomorphism. In this case, the mapping $h: \mathbb{N} \rightarrow \{e\}$ is many-to-one and not bijective, so that the algebras are not isomorphic.

Example 10.3 Consider the set T of tuples (ordered pairs) $\langle n, n \rangle$ of natural numbers with $n \in \mathbb{N}$ whose first and second slots are equal so that $T = \{\langle 0,0 \rangle, \langle 1,1 \rangle, \langle 2,2 \rangle, \langle 3,3 \rangle, ...\}$. Then the algebra $\mathscr{A}_{Tuple} = [T, \{\langle 0,0 \rangle, Succ_T\}]$, where $Succ_T: T \rightarrow T$ is defined by $Succ_T(\langle n, n \rangle) = \langle n+1, n+1 \rangle$, is also an interpretation of the signature of Fig. 10.1. For this algebra, T interprets the sort nat, $Succ_T$ interprets succ, and we have used the denotation

```
{zero ⟶⟨ 0,0 ⟩, succ(zero) ⟶ ⟨ 1,1 ⟩, succ(succ(zero)) ⟶ ⟨ 2,2 ⟩,

        succ(succ(succ(zero))) ⟶ ⟨ 3,3 ⟩, ... }
```

Consider the mapping $h: T \rightarrow \mathbb{N}$ defined by $h(\langle n, n \rangle) = n$ which maps a tuple $\langle n, n \rangle$ to its common slot value n. We can show that h is a homomorphism from $\mathscr{A}_{Tuple}$ to $\mathscr{A}_{Nat}$ as follows.

Consider first the nullary operation $\langle 0, 0 \rangle$ of $\mathscr{A}_{Tuple}$. For this operation, the left-hand side of Eq. (10.1) is $h(\langle 0, 0 \rangle)$ which results in the value 0. This in turn is equal to the value of the corresponding nullary operation 0 of $\mathscr{A}_{Nat}$, so we have

$$h(\langle 0, 0 \rangle) = 0$$

and Eq. (10.1) is therefore satisfied by the corresponding nullary operations of the two algebras.

For the operation $Succ_T$, the left-hand side of Eq. (10.1) is

$$h(Succ_T(\langle n, n \rangle)) = h(\langle n+1, n+1 \rangle) = n+1$$

while the corresponding right-hand side is

$$Succ(h(\langle n, n \rangle)) = Succ(n) = n+1$$

The two sides are equal, so that h is a homomorphism from $\mathscr{A}_{Tuple}$ to $\mathscr{A}_{Nat}$. This mapping is bijective so that the two algebras are isomorphic.

The discussion so far has centred on algebras that are models of a *signature*. Our specifications have also included a collection of *axioms* so we now need to extend the discussion and examine algebras as models of these 'enlarged' signatures.

Exercise 10.1 Show that the mapping $h': T \to \mathbb{N}$ defined by $h'(\langle n, n \rangle) = 2n$ is *not* a homomorphism from $\mathscr{A}_{Tuple}$ to $\mathscr{A}_{Nat}$, and determine whether the mapping $h'': T \to \mathbb{N}$ defined by $h''(\langle n, n \rangle) = 0$ is a homomorphism from $\mathscr{A}_{Tuple}$ to $\mathscr{A}_{Nat}$.

Exercise 10.2 Show that the algebras $\mathscr{A}_{Nat}$ and $\mathscr{A}_{Tuple}$ are isomorphic.

10.7 AXIOMS AND THEORY PRESENTATIONS

Consider a signature Σ with v function symbols (operations) and *no* axioms. The algebras denoted by such a signature with no axioms form a very broad class of algebras in the sense that the *only* restriction on these algebras is the existence of v operations with the appropriate domain and range carriers. These algebras can be thought of as providing very general models—often too general for modelling abstract data types, in the sense that no 'restrictions' are placed on the properties of the operations. The fundamental importance of axioms in a specification is that they impose constraints to be satisfied by the values and operations in any interpretation (model). The inclusion of axioms allows us to tailor specifications to meet the behavioural requirements of our abstract data type.

Such specifications, which consist of a signature Σ, extended by a collection of axioms E, where the axioms relate terms constructed from the signature, are known as *presentations*. A presentation is therefore given by a tuple $\langle \Sigma, E \rangle$. The set of *all* identities $t = t'$ that can be derived from the given set of axioms E using equational logic, where t and t' are terms constructed from Σ, is called the *closure* of E. The closure defines all the theorems provable within the presentation and so we can think of the closure as a *theory*. The presentation $\langle \Sigma, E \rangle$ together with the closure of E then defines what is called a *theory presentation* or *theory* for short. The reader should be aware that some authors use the word 'presentation' as a synonym for what we call a 'theory presentation', although the context in which the word is used usually makes it clear as to which meaning is intended.

An example of a presentation is shown in Fig. 10.3 where we have appended the operation add to the signature of Fig. 10.1 together with two axioms satisfied by add. This example will be used to illustrate and help explain a number of important features of theory presentations and their models. Observe that the atomic constructors for Natural are zero and succ, while add is a nonatomic constructor. (The reader may wonder if a

```
SPEC   Natural
SORT   nat
OPS
    zero  :   ->  nat
    succ  :   nat  ->  nat
    add   :   nat nat  ->  nat
  FORALL
    m, n  :  nat
  AXIOMS:
  (1)  add(zero, n)  =  n
  (2)  add(succ(m), n)  =  succ(add(m, n))
  ENDSPEC
```

Figure 10.3 Specification (presentation) for natural numbers.

third axiom add(n, zero) = n is also required, but, as we shall show in Chapter 12, this result can be derived formally from the two given axioms of Natural using equational inference and structural induction).

We say that an algebra is *denoted* by a presentation if the algebra is denoted by the signature of that presentation and the *variety* over the presentation is the set (class) of all algebras denoted by the presentation that satisfy the axioms. An algebra that is denoted by a signature Σ is said to *satisfy* the axioms E of the presentation $\langle \Sigma, E \rangle$ if, for each axiom, evaluation of each side of the axiom produces identical results for *all* possible assignments of values of the carrier set to the variable of the corresponding sort. We will expand upon these ideas shortly but first we need to look briefly at *equational logic* and its role in theory presentations.

10.7.1 Axioms and equational logic

For algebraic specifications, each axiom is an equation of the form $L = R$ which relates two terms constructed from the signature. Each axiom states that the two terms L and R are to denote the same value. We can use the axioms together with the inference rules of *equational logic* to generate new theorems. For example, we can use the axioms of Stack to deduce the theorem

pop(push(push(init, 3), 5)) = push(init, 3)

Implicit as part of the semantics of the data type, therefore, is not only the axioms themselves, but all their consequences under equational logic, and it is this particular logic system (also known as *equational inference*) that lies at the heart of the algebraic approach to specification. Equational logic makes use of axioms with universally quantified variables, with equality as the only predicate. The axioms may be *unconditional* ones of the form $L = R$ or conditional axioms predicated by a Boolean expression that determines the context in which the axiom holds. Conditional axioms take the form $L = R$ IF b where b is a Boolean expression. In fact, a conditional axiom can always be transformed to an unconditional one since $L = R$ IF b is equivalent to

$L = $ IF b THEN R ELSE L ENDIF

In the equational approach, we treat the axioms that relate operations as substitution rules, so that the substitution of one term (or subterm) by an equal term (using an axiom) permits the original term to be *rewritten* into an *equivalent* one.

Under equational inference, given a set of axioms E, two *well-formed* terms t_1 and t_2 denote the same value if and only if they can be proved equal from the axioms. (Well-formed in this context means that t_1 and t_2 are syntactically-legal terms generated from the signature.) In other words, they denote the same value if and only if the axiom $t_1 = t_2$ can be proved as a consequence of using the axioms. In more detail, an axiom $t_1 = t_2$ is provable from a set of axioms if either:

1. $t_1 = t_2$ is a member of E (in other words, $t_1 = t_2$ is one of the stated axioms)

or:

2. $t_1 = t_2$ can be derived from E using a finite sequence of
   (a) $t = t$ (*reflexive property*)
   (b) If $u = t$ then $t = u$ (*symmetric* property)
   (c) If $s = u$ and $u = t$, then $s = t$ (*transitive* property)
   (d) If $x_1 = y_1, x_2 = y_2, \ldots, x_n = y_n$ and *op* is an operation with *arity* n (that is it has n argument slots), then

$$op(x_1, x_2, \ldots, x_n) = op(y_1, y_2, \ldots, y_n)$$

   (e) If $s = t$ where s and t both contain the same universally-quantified variables, and well-formed terms are substituted for all or some of the variables, resulting in corresponding terms s' and t', then $s' = t'$.

Unlike the model-based approach to specification in which explicit system models in the form of discrete mathematical structures are used to build an abstract mathematical model of the state of a system, an algebraic specification of an abstract data type defines the data type, its operations and their meaning without any knowledge of the representation. Algebraic specifications use *only* the underlying logical system (*equational inference*) to formally specify a system. These ideas are developed later in this chapter where we discuss the difference between VDM *models* and algebras as *models* of algebraic specifications.

Exercise 10.3 Given a set of axioms E and that $t = t1$ and $t = t2$ are equations provable from E, use the inference rules listed above to show that the equation $t1 = t2$ is provable from E.

Use the above result together with the inference rules and the set of axioms of Stack to show that the equation

```
push(pop(push(init, n1)), n2) = pop(push(push(init, n2), n3))
```

where $n1, n2, n3 \in$ nat is provable from the axioms of Stack.

10.8 ALGEBRAS AS MODELS OF A THEORY

We now explain more precisely what is meant when we say that *an algebra is a model of a theory presentation*. Consider, for simplicity, a single-sorted theory presentation characterized by a sort S, signature Σ, and a collection of m axioms, $L_i = R_i$ $(1 \leqslant i \leqslant m)$. A homogeneous algebra $\mathscr{A} = [A, \Omega]$ is a *model* of the theory presentation if:

- $\mathscr{A}$ is denoted by the signature of the presentation.
- All the axioms of the presentation are *satisfied* by $\mathscr{A}$, that is to say, for all axioms $L_i = R_i$ of the presentation, both terms (L_i and R_i) evaluate to the same value (denote the same object of the algebra) for all assignments of values in the carrier set A to the variables in S.

This result readily extends to heterogeneous algebras which provide models for many-sorted theory presentations.

As an illustration, consider the presentation Natural of Fig. 10.3. We will consider two possible models that are isomorphic to each other.

10.8.1 Model 1

One model, is provided by the algebra

$$\mathscr{A}_{Nat} = [\{0, 1, 2, \ldots\}, \{0, Succ, +\}]$$

with the interpretation:

$$\text{succ}: \text{nat} \longrightarrow \text{nat} \longrightarrow Succ: \mathbb{N} \to \mathbb{N} \quad \text{where} \quad Succ(n) = n + 1$$
$$\text{add}: \text{nat nat} \longrightarrow \text{nat} \longrightarrow +: \mathbb{N}^2 \to \mathbb{N} \quad \text{where} \quad +(m, n) = m + n$$

where the double length arrow $\longrightarrow$ signifies 'is denoted by', '$+$' denotes the usual arithmetic addition operator, together with the denotation

$$\{\text{zero} \longrightarrow 0, \text{succ(zero)} \longrightarrow 1, \text{succ(succ(zero))} \longrightarrow 2, \ldots, \text{add(zero, zero)} \longrightarrow 0,$$

$$\text{add(succ(zero), zero)} \longrightarrow 1, \text{add(succ(zero), succ(zero))} \longrightarrow 2, \ldots\}$$

To show that this algebra is indeed a model of our presentation, we must show that axioms (1) and (2) of the presentation are true with this interpretation.

With our interpretation, the natural number $n \in \mathbb{N}$ is denoted by n applications of the operation succ to zero and will be written $\text{succ}^n(\text{zero})$ as a convenient shorthand. Consider the left-hand side of axiom (1)

$$\text{add(zero, succ}^n\text{(zero))} \longrightarrow +(0, n) = 0 + n = n$$

The right-hand side of axiom (1) is

$$\text{succ}^n(\text{zero})$$

which also interprets to n, so that axiom (1) is satisfied by the algebra.

Consider now the left-hand side of axiom (2), that is

$$\texttt{add(succ(succ}^m\texttt{(zero)), succ}^n\texttt{(zero))} \longrightarrow +((m+1), n) = (m+1) + n = (m+n) + 1$$

The right-hand side of axiom (2) is

$$\texttt{succ(add(succ}^m\texttt{(zero),succ}^n\texttt{(zero)))} \longrightarrow Succ(+(m, n)) = Succ(m+n) = (m+n) + 1$$

so that axiom (2) is also satisfied by the algebra. Since both axioms are satisfied by the interpretation, it follows that $\mathscr{A}_{Nat}$ is a model of the presentation.

10.8.2 Model 2

Another model of the same presentation is given by the algebra $\mathscr{A}_{NatEven}$ where

$$\mathscr{A}_{NatEven} = [\{0, 2, 4, \dots\}, \{0, Succ_{Ev}, +_{Ev}\}]$$

where the carrier set is now the set of even natural numbers, $\mathbb{N}_{Even}$ and we use the denotation

$$\texttt{succ : nat} \rightarrow \texttt{nat} \longrightarrow Succ_{Ev} : \mathbb{N}_{Even} \rightarrow \mathbb{N}_{Even} \quad \text{where} \quad Succ_{Ev}(n) = n + 2$$

$$\texttt{add : nat nat} \rightarrow \texttt{nat} \longrightarrow +_{Ev} : \mathbb{N}^2_{Even} \rightarrow \mathbb{N}_{Even} \quad \text{where} \quad +_{Ev}(m, n) = m + n$$

so that $+_{Ev}$ is again the conventional arithmetic addition operator together with

$$\{\texttt{zero} \longrightarrow 0, \texttt{succ(zero)} \longrightarrow 2, \texttt{succ(succ(zero))} \longrightarrow 4, \dots, \texttt{add(zero, zero)} \longrightarrow 0,$$

$$\texttt{add(succ(zero), zero)} \longrightarrow 2, \texttt{add(succ(zero), succ(zero))} \longrightarrow 4, \dots\}$$

With this interpretation, the even natural number $2n$ is denoted by n consecutive applications of the operation succ to zero and will be written $\texttt{succ}^n\texttt{(zero)}$ for convenience. Consider the left-hand side of axiom (1)

$$\texttt{add(zero, succ}^n\texttt{(zero))} \longrightarrow +_{Ev}(0, 2n) = 0 + 2n = 2n$$

The right-hand side of axiom (1) is

$$\texttt{succ}^n\texttt{(zero)}$$

which interprets to $2n$ also so that axiom (1) is satisfied by the algebra.
    Consider now the left-hand side of axiom (2)

$$\texttt{add(succ(succ}^m\texttt{(zero)), succ}^n\texttt{(zero))} \longrightarrow +_{Ev}(2(m+1), 2n) = (2m+2) + 2n = (2m+2n) + 2$$

The right-hand side of axiom (2) is

$$\text{succ}(\text{add}(\text{succ}^m(\text{zero}), \text{succ}^n(\text{zero})))$$

$$\rightarrow Succ_{Ev}(+_{Ev}(2m, 2n)) = Succ_{Ev}(2m + 2n) = (2m + 2n) + 2$$

so that axiom (2) is also satisfied by the algebra. Since both axioms are satisfied by the interpretation, it follows that $\mathscr{A}_{NatEven}$ is also a model of the presentation (specification).

10.9 INITIAL ALGEBRAS

We can now return to the conjectures posed earlier concerning the class of algebras which are models of a given specification:

- How are the algebras that interpret a theory related?
- Is there one particular member (or subclass) of the class of algebras that captures the essential properties of that entire class?

It is important to remember that our specification provides a theory which describes the required properties and behaviour of a data type yet to be implemented. When an algebraic specification of an abstract data type is *implemented*, an appropriate *representation* for each value of the data type is chosen from the various models of the theory, with each operation being interpreted by a 'function' or algorithm over that chosen representation. The *design* of the data type entails determining which of the various models of the presentation is the most appropriate.

The connection or 'family resemblance' between the various algebras which make up the class (family) of algebras that models a given specification is provided by a special subset of that class. These special algebras are known as *initial* algebras. An initial algebra has the fundamental property that a unique homomorphism exists between that initial algebra and each member of the class. This means that every algebra that belongs to the class of models can be reached by application of a unique mapping (transformation) from an initial algebra.[1] Furthermore, it can be shown that all initial algebras (which interpret a theory) are isomorphic to each other and so are 'indistinguishable'. This formal statement simply expresses the fact that there is more than way of implementing a given data type, all of which are valid with respect to the theory. We can therefore talk about a *single* initial algebra which is *unique* up to isomorphism.

Another way of looking at this result is to think of the initial algebra(s) as the hub or centre of a wheel with all the other algebras of the class that interpret a signature placed radially around the wheel's circumference. Each of these perimeter algebras is connected to the hub by a single 'spoke' which is the unique homomorphism from the 'focal' initial algebra(s) to that perimeter algebra. Every algebra of the class can therefore be 'reached' or 'derived' from an initial algebra.

---

[1] For completeness, and for the mathematically curious, we append a formal definition of *initiality*. An algebra $\mathscr{I}$ is initial in a category $\mathscr{C}$ of algebras over a presentation if and only if $\mathscr{I}$ is a member of $\mathscr{C}$ and for every algebra $\mathscr{A}$ which belongs to $\mathscr{C}$, a unique homomorphism from $\mathscr{I}$ to $\mathscr{A}$ exists. (A *category* of algebras with respect to a given presentation is a set of algebras denoted by the presentation together with a number of homomorphisms between these algebras. For our purposes, the category $\mathscr{C}$ is the *variety* over a presentation together with *all* possible homomorphisms between the algebras of the variety.)

It is this observation which provides the answers to the two questions posed earlier and explains why the *initial* algebra is often used as the 'standard' in the sense of being the 'most representative' model of a theory presentation, This is the approach adopted in this text. One advantage of using initial models is that they do not have some of the undesirable properties that characterize many of the models. For example, models that have either *junk* or *confusion* (evocative terms!) are often discarded – initial algebras do not have these undesirable properties. These ideas will be examined shortly with the aid of an illustrative example using a simple theory for Boolean values.

10.9.1 Initial models—junk and confusion

For the specification of abstract data types, we usually focus upon initial algebras as models of the theory presentation. We now examine some of the (desirable) properties of such initial models. It can be proved that an algebra is *initial* if and only if it possesses the following properties

- **No junk**—the model should not have unnecessary elements. Models in which the carrier set has an element or elements which do not correspond to any term in the theory presentation are said to have 'junk'. The property of having 'no junk' therefore asserts that all values of the carrier are denoted by terms which can be constructed from the signature, so that *every* element of the carrier can be named using the operation symbols of the signature.
- **No confusion**—terms should not be equal unless they are forced to be so by the axioms. Interpretations with 'no confusion' have the property that two terms denote the same value if and only if they can be proved equal from the given axioms (using equational inference). The only equalities between values of the carrier are those which can be deduced from the axioms of the presentation.

We need to emphasize one crucially important point that the reader needs to grasp. The property of *initiality* is a characteristic of the *interpretation* of a theory and *not* a property of the theory itself. Theory presentations can be given various forms of semantics: in our case we concentrate on their *initial semantics*.

10.9.2 Models of a Boolean theory

The idea of algebras as models of a theory and the concept of an initial model which has the *no junk, no confusion* property are not always immediately accessible at first, so it will be worth exploring these features with the aid of an example. Our starting point will be a simple theory of Boolean values. We can specify a small Boolean theory Boolean with the two nullary operations true and false together with the unary operation not and the binary operation and. The complete specification is given in Fig. 10.4.

This theory has many algebras as its models and we will look at three different models, *Model A*, *Model B*, *Model C* and discuss their properties. The labels A, B, C are used to differentiate the three cases.

Algebra A In the first model, suppose the carrier set contains the single value 2, that is $A = \{2\}$ and $\Omega = \{2, not_A, and_A\}$. This means that every term of the data type Boolean must

```
SPEC   Boolean
SORT   bool
OPS
    true   :   -> bool
   false   :   -> bool
     not   :   bool  ->  bool
     and   :   bool  bool  ->  bool
FORALL
        b  :   bool
AXIOMS:
   (1)    not(true)   =   false
   (2)    not(false)  =   true
   (3)    and(true,b)   =   b
   (4)    and(b,true)   =   b
   (5)    and(false,b)  =   false
   (6)    and(b,false)  =   false
ENDSPEC
```

Figure 10.4   Algebraic specification of a Boolean data type.

be given as its interpretation a member of the set $\{2\}$. We therefore use the denotation

$$\{\texttt{true} \longrightarrow 2, \texttt{false} \longrightarrow 2\}$$

together with

$$not_A(2)=2 \; ; \quad and_A(2, 2)=2$$

First, consider the left- and right-hand sides of axiom (1). We have used the symbol '$\longrightarrow$' to signify 'is denoted by' (as in Sec. 10.4), so for the left-hand side of axiom (1)

$$\texttt{not(true)} \longrightarrow not_A(2)$$

while for the right-hand side

$$\texttt{false} \longrightarrow 2$$

and $not_A(2)=2$, so that axiom (1) is satisfied in this model.

Consider now the left-hand side of axiom (2)

$$\texttt{not(false)} \longrightarrow not_A(2)$$

while for the right-hand side

$$\texttt{true} \longrightarrow 2$$

and $not_A(2)=2$, so that axiom (2) is also satisfied in this model.

In the case of axiom (3), if b has the value true, we have for the left-hand side of that axiom

$$\text{and}(\text{true}, \text{true}) \longrightarrow and_A(2, 2)$$

while for the right-hand side of axiom (3) when b has the value true

$$\text{true} \longrightarrow 2$$

and, from our model, $and_A(2, 2) = 2$, so that axiom (3) is satisfied. Turning to the case when b has the value false, we have for the left-hand side of axiom (3)

$$\text{and}(\text{true}, \text{false}) \longrightarrow and_A(2, 2)$$

while for the right-hand side of axiom (3) when b has the value false

$$\text{false} \longrightarrow 2$$

and, from our model, $and_A(2, 2) = 2$, so that axiom (3) is again satisfied.

We can repeat this process for the remaining three axioms. It can be seen immediately that the left-hand sides of axioms (4), (5) and (6) will all be denoted by $and_A(2, 2)$ while all the right-hand sides will be denoted by 2. Since $and_A(2, 2) = 2$ in our model, it follows that axioms (4), (5) and (6) are also satisfied. *All* the axioms are therefore satisfied by this model.

Hence, this algebra

$$\mathsf{A} = [\{2\}, \{2, not_A, and_A\}]$$

is a model of Boolean. In this model, every term in the theory maps onto the single value 2. The Boolean values true and false are therefore indistinguishable, so that clearly this model would be of no practical use in computer science! Nevertheless it is a valid model of the theory Boolean.

Since the carrier set contains only the single value 2, the *interpretation* is enforcing the equality true=false, which does not follow from the given axioms. This model has the 'confusion' property and is therefore not an initial one.

Algebra B This model will be familiar to all computer scientists where

$$A = \{0, 1\}, \quad \Omega = \{0, 1, not_B, and_B\}$$

In this case we use the set $\{0, 1\}$ to model the sort bool using the denotation

$$\{\text{false} \longrightarrow 0, \text{true} \longrightarrow 1\}$$

together with

$$not_B(0) = 1 ; \quad not_B(1) = 0$$
$$and_B(0, 0) = 0 ; \quad and_B(0, 1) = 0$$
$$and_B(1, 0) = 0 ; \quad and_B(1, 1) = 1$$

Consider first the left- and right-hand sides of axiom (1). As before, using the symbol '$\longrightarrow$' to signify 'is denoted by', we have for the left-hand side

    not(true) $\longrightarrow$ $not_B(1)$

while for the right-hand side

    false $\longrightarrow$ 0

and $not_B(1) = 0$ so that axiom (1) is satisfied in this model.

    Consider now the left-hand side of axiom (2)

    not(false) $\longrightarrow$ $not_B(0)$

while for the right-hand side

    true $\longrightarrow$ 1

and $not_B(0) = 1$ so that axiom (2) is satisfied in this model.

    For the remaining axioms, we need to study each of the four axioms for *all* values of the Boolean variable b. On the face of it this appears to involve eight further analyses. However only four further cases need be considered since there is some duplication. In particular, axioms (3) and (4) are identical when b has the value true as are axioms (3) and (6) when b has the value false in (3) and the value true in (6). Likewise, axioms (5) and (6) are identical when b has the value false as are (4) and (5) when b has the value false in (4) and true in (5).

    For axiom (3), we therefore need only consider the case when b has the value true. For the left-hand side

    and(true, true) $\longrightarrow$ $and_B(1, 1)$

while for the right-hand side

    true $\longrightarrow$ 1

and $and_B(1, 1) = 1$, so axiom (3) is satisfied in this model.

    For axiom (4), we consider the situation when b has the value false, in which case for the left-hand side, we have

    and(false, true) $\longrightarrow$ $and_B(0, 1)$

while for the right-hand side

    false $\longrightarrow$ 0

and $and_B(0, 1) = 0$, so axiom (4) is satisfied in this model.

Coming on to axiom (5), we need only analyse the case when b has the value false, so for the left-hand side

and(false, false) $\longrightarrow$ $and_B(0, 0)$

while for the right-hand side

false $\longrightarrow$ 0

and $and_B(0, 0) = 0$, so axiom (5) is also satisfied in this model.

Finally, with axiom (6), when b has the value true, we have for the left-hand side

and(true, false) $\longrightarrow$ $and_B(1, 0)$

while for the corresponding right-hand side

false $\longrightarrow$ 0

and $and_B(1, 0) = 0$, so axiom (6) is satisfied in this model.

All the axioms are therefore satisfied by this model. Hence, this algebra is also a model of Boolean and is likely to have been the one intended! This model has the required 'no junk, no confusion' property and so is an example of an initial model.

Algebra C For the last model, we take the algebra A $= [A, \Omega]$ where the carrier set A consists of the three values 0, 1, 2 so that

$$A = \{0, 1, 2\}$$

and $\Omega = \{0, 1, not_C, and_C\}$. In this case we use the set $\{0, 1, 2\}$ to model the sort bool using the denotation

$\{$false $\longrightarrow$ 0, true $\longrightarrow$ 1$\}$

together with

$$
\begin{array}{lll}
not_C(0) = 1 ; & not_C(1) = 0 ; & not_C(2) = 2 \\
and_C(0, 0) = 0 ; & and_C(0, 1) = 0 ; & and_C(0, 2) = 0 \\
and_C(1, 0) = 0 ; & and_C(1, 1) = 1 ; & and_C(1, 2) = 2 \\
and_C(2, 0) = 0 ; & and_C(2, 1) = 2 ; & and_C(2, 2) = 2
\end{array}
$$

This algebra can also be shown to be a model of Boolean. However, it has the superfluous element 2 which does not correspond to any term in the signature and so does not contradict any axiom of the theory. This extra value is known as 'junk' and the model is again not initial.

Exercise 10.4 Show that Algebra C is a model of Boolean. Show also that the axioms of the theory are not violated if either of the following interpretations are used

$and_C(2, 2) = 0$ or $and_C(2, 2) = 1$

10.9.3 The importance of initial models

We have seen that there are many models of an equational theory presentation, some of which have undesirable properties. There are benefits in confining our attention to *initial* models. The initial algebra approach has proved to be an appropriate framework for defining specification correctness criteria such as consistency and sufficient completeness. With the initial algebra approach, the *unique* initial algebra (up to isomorphism) is used as the 'standard' model of a set of axioms and many (but not all) algebraic specification languages have an initial algebra semantics.

The reason why initial models are very important and hence widely used in algebraic specification is worth emphasizing. The fundamental property possessed by initial models is that they provide precisely what the specification requires and nothing extra. They have no superfluous elements (*no junk*) and do not force two values of the data type to be equal that were meant to be distinct (*no confusion*). They therefore provide faithful interpretations of a specification which explains why they are often used as the standard representational model of a specification. This is the principal reason why we have concentrated on the initial approach in this text.

Indeed, for *executable* algebraic specification languages, the semantics must be initial (an issue we take up later in Chapter 13). A further illustration of models with junk and confusion is given at the end of this chapter in the Additional Problems (Problem 10.7).

Exercise 10.5 Show that the algebra $A = [A, \Omega]$ where $A = \{0, 1\}$, $\Omega = \{0, 1, not, and\}$ with false $\longrightarrow 0$; true $\longrightarrow 1$; $not(0) = 1$; $not(1) = 0$; $and(1, 0) = 0$; $and(1, 1) = 1$; $and(0, 1) = 0$; $and(0, 0) = 1$ is *not* a model of Boolean.

10.9.4 Models in VDM

Before looking at how an initial algebra can be derived for a given specification, it is important that we understand the fundamental difference between algebras as *models* of an algebraic specification and *abstract models* in the context of VDM. In VDM, discrete mathematical structures such as sets, sequences, and mappings are used as models for an abstract data type which essentially provide abstract implementations of that data type. The meanings of the operations of an abstract data type are then defined, in isolation, in terms of their effect on the mathematical model. The semantics of the abstract data type is therefore defined in terms of another 'better understood' object, which is an implementation, albeit a very abstract one. This is not altogether satisfactory. One problem with using an explicit mathematical model is that although the model may provide all the desired properties of an abstract data type, it may also have additional properties which are not appropriate to or may even be undesirable for that abstract data type.

You may think similar comments apply to algebraic specifications where the underlying object is now the *initial algebra*. However, this is not the case: algebraic specifications do not specify the semantics of an abstract data type in terms of some 'better understood' and slightly more concrete object. The semantics of the operations of an abstract data type are defined not in terms of some other object but in terms of the set of operations themselves. Their semantics is expressed as a collection of axioms, each of which shows how two or more operations are related.

Algebraic specifications are theory presentations which use only the underlying logical system (equational inference) to specify an abstract data type. No general mathematical models are introduced to provide an explicit abstract implementation. The algebras are simply interpretations that satisfy the theory and contain precisely what the corresponding specification requires and nothing more.

10.10 Deriving an Initial Algebra

The importance of *initial* algebra semantics in the specification of abstract data types cannot be overstated. The initial algebra for a specification captures the essential properties of a specification in the sense that it contains exactly what the specification requires and nothing more. It is the 'best' model for a given specification because it contains no superfluous terms (no *junk*) and does not make two terms indistinguishable which were intended to be distinct (no *confusion*). The presence of junk or confusion in a model excludes it from consideration as a faithful interpretation of the corresponding specification.

Although we have discussed at length the important properties possessed by initial algebras and the key role that initial algebras play in the specification of abstract data types, we have not yet addressed how a suitable initial algebra can be derived for a given specification. The answer lies in the *quotient term algebra*.

10.10.1 Quotient term algebra

Under equational inference, with *no* axioms, each term of a theory presentation would denote a *distinct* value for any *initial* interpretation. The axioms identify those terms that are to have *equivalent* meanings in the intended semantic domain (model), that is those that are to denote the same value. Pairs of terms not equivalent under the axioms are treated as denoting distinct values. Identifying equivalent terms in the *term algebra* generates what is called the *quotient term algebra* or *quotient term structure*, and this aspect is worth developing in a little more detail.

The axioms of a specification define a collection of equality relations between the variable-free (ground) terms for each sort. These equality relations are *equivalence relations* in that they are reflexive, symmetric and transitive. For example, for the specification Stack of Fig. 8.2, the following ground terms are all equal

```
init, pop(push(init, 3)), pop(pop(push(push(init, 1), 2))),
pop(push(init, top(push(init, 1))))
```

and this property stems directly from the inference rules of equational logic. If we use the notation $\langle t \rangle$ to denote the set of all terms equivalent to a given term t, the above terms are members of the equivalence class $\langle \text{init} \rangle$ where we have selected the 'simplest' term init (simplest in the sense of being the shortest string) to represent the class, although any member of the equivalence class could have been chosen.

For each sort, the axioms (equality relations) therefore partition the ground terms of the term algebra into a number of equivalence classes. If we imagine partitioning *all* the ground terms of the *term algebra* into the appropriate collection of equivalence classes, the resulting algebra whose carrier set(s) consist of this collection of equivalence classes is called the *quotient term algebra*. For the quotient term algebra, each member of the carrier(s) is an equivalence class of terms and we are at liberty to choose *any* member of an equivalence class to represent that class. An important property of the quotient term algebra is that this algebra is *initial*. A distinct advantage of using term algebras is that term rewriting can be performed directly upon the theory presentation itself.

10.10.2 Canonical term algebra and reduced expressions

While the basic idea of generating all the terms of the *term algebra* and then placing each term in an appropriate equivalence class may seem attractive, the approach does not provide a *practical* method for deriving an initial algebra. However, the use of *canonical terms*, also referred to as *canonical forms* provides us with a pragmatic solution to this problem. It is often possible to identify a *subset* of the terms such that each term in the subset is a member of a *different* equivalence class and every term of the term algebra is equivalent to exactly one member of this subset. The individual terms that comprise such a subset are called *canonical terms* and algebras whose carrier sets consist of such a collection of canonical terms are referred to as *canonical term algebras*. It is not hard to see that the resulting algebra whose carrier set consists of these canonical terms will be isomorphic to the quotient term algebra and hence will itself be initial.

Moreover, if an appropriate set of *atomic* constructors can be identified, it can be shown that each *reduced* expression (that is any ground term consisting of a composition of atomic constructors) is also a *canonical* term. This result is proved in Chapter 12. Canonical terms can therefore be systematically generated using the atomic constructors and a canonical term algebra derived. Identification of a set of atomic constructors for an abstract data type therefore provides a valuable link between the (initial) canonical term algebra and our intuitive conception of the properties of that abstract data type.

In the case of the presentation of Fig. 10.3, the initial algebra $A_{CanonicalNat}$ of canonical terms can be derived using the corresponding atomic constructors zero and succ

$$A_{CanonicalNat} = [A_{CanonicalNat}, \{\text{zero, succ, add}\}]$$

where the carrier set of the algebra is

$$A_{CanonicalNat} = \{\text{zero, succ(zero), succ(succ(zero)), \ldots}\}$$

Note that each member of the carrier set of a canonical term algebra is an individual *term* drawn from the term algebra. Compare this with the quotient term algebra where the individual members of the carrier set are sets of values (equivalence classes).

10.10.3 Canonical term algebras and implementations

When an algebraic specification is refined into an implementation (no easy task for reasons we will explain later), a suitable representation for the values of the abstract data type is chosen from among the different models of the theory. More precisely, elements of the carrier set of the chosen model provide the representations for the values of the abstract data type. Each operation of the specification is then defined by a function (algorithm) whose domain and range data values are drawn from the terms of the carrier set of the implementation algebra. The derivation of a canonical term algebra often provides a useful starting point for refining the specification into an implementation. The fundamental property that characterizes a collection of canonical terms, namely that every term is equivalent to *one* canonical term, is used as an intrinsic property of the implementation in the sense that the implemented operations only act upon or return values that are the representations of canonical terms. Such an implementation reaps the benefit that the *equality* predicate $==$, which must be supplied in any implementation of an abstract data type, simply reduces to comparing canonical terms (normal forms). This leads naturally to the question of term-rewriting and the reduction of terms to canonical form. These ideas are now briefly explored.

10.11 AXIOMS AS EQUATIONS

We have already seen that at one level, the axioms of an algebraic specification can be treated as *equations* in the mathematical sense. These equations can be used as rules of substitution that permit syntactically legal terms to be expressed in an equivalent form. In this situation, the equality relation '=' is reflexive, symmetric, and transitive.

10.12 AXIOMS AS REWRITE RULES

We know also that the axioms of an algebraic specification can be treated as a collection of *rewrite rules* in which we use a restrictive form of equational logic. It is important to understand the difference between axioms (in the strict equational sense) and rewrite rules. We can represent a typical rewrite rule by

$$L \rightarrow R$$

where L, R denote the left and right components of the rule.

The fundamental difference between an axiom and a rewrite rule is that while equality for axioms is symmetric, that is $L=R$ implies $R=L$ and $R=L$ implies $L=R$, term rewriting schema treat axioms *unidirectionally*, for example, as one way replacements from L to R say. Hence, when axioms are treated as *rewrite rules*, the operator '$\rightarrow$' is *transitive*, but **not** *symmetric* or *reflexive*. A computation that uses rewrite rules will produce a sequence of expressions $E_1, E_2, \ldots, E_i$ by repeatedly replacing instances of the left-hand side of rules within an expression by their corresponding right-hand sides. This process will continue until an expression is obtained that contains no instances of any left-hand rule, in which case the process terminates. The resulting expression is said to be in a *normal* or *reduced form*. One restriction for such rewriting systems is that any free variable that occurs in the right-hand side R must also occur in the left-hand side L.

10.13 OPERATIONAL SEMANTICS

The operational semantics of a programming language shows how computations are done in that language and, in the case of algebraic specification languages, the operational semantics is based on term rewriting. For our language, the semantics of a SPEC module is prescribed by its axioms which are interpreted operationally as left-to-right rewrite rules in which instances of left-hand sides of axioms are replaced by their corresponding right-hand sides until a value is obtained that contains no instance of any left-hand side.

The axioms of an algebraic specification can therefore be given an *operational semantics* by treating them as *left-to-right* rewrite rules and term rewriting provides the *operational semantics* used by executable algebraic specification languages such as OBJ and Axis to execute equationally defined specifications. It results in efficient computations without any need for backtracking.

If a set of rewrite rules has the following properties:

1. *Finite termination*—every sequence of rewrites from a given term t terminates after a finite number of steps (that is there are no infinite sequences of reductions from any term). (The *Noetherian* property.)
2. *Unique termination*—every terminating sequence of rewrites from a given term t stops at a unique minimal form. This is the *normal* or *reduced form*, which will be denoted by $t \downarrow$. (The *Church–Rosser* property.)

it is said to be (*finitely*) *convergent*.

For these finitely convergent systems, term rewriting provides a feasible decision procedure for determining whether $s = t$ can be proved as a consequence of a set of axioms, where s and t are syntactically legal terms that contain no variables (that is s and t are *ground terms*). In order to ascertain whether $s = t$, first generate a sequence of rewrites for s until s is in normal form and then repeat the process for t. If the normal forms $s \downarrow$ and $t \downarrow$ are identical, then the terms s and t are equal in the sense that they both belong to the same equivalence class.

Exercise 10.6 Given a set of axioms E, suppose that repeated term rewriting applied to the terms s and t produces the sequence of rewrites $s, s1, s2, s3, s \downarrow$ and $t, t1, t2, t \downarrow$ respectively where $s \downarrow$ and $t \downarrow$ denote the corresponding normal forms.

(a) Express these rewrites as a collection of individual rewrites.
(b) If $s \downarrow = t \downarrow$ use the inference rules of equational theory to show that the theorem $s = t$ belongs to the equational theory of E.

Exercise 10.7 Use the axioms of `Stack` to reduce each of the following terms to a normal form:

(a) `pop(push(init, 4))`
(b) `top(push(init, 4))`
(c) `is-empty?(push(init, 3))`
(d) `push(pop(push(init, 2)), 3)`
(e) `push(push(init, 2), 3)`
(f) `top(pop(push(push(init, 2), 3)))`

10.14 INITIAL VERSUS FINAL SEMANTICS

To conclude this chapter, we include, for completeness, a brief introduction to *final* semantics. We have seen that the feature of initial models that makes them so significant for algebraic specification is that they contain 'no junk, no confusion' and so capture the vital qualities ('nothing more, nothing less') of their specifications. There is an alternative way of handling the semantics of algebraic specifications, namely the *final* (also called the *terminal*) approach. This approach, as promoted by Guttag, considers the *entire* class or family of algebras defined by a specification. Whereas with *initial* semantics, two ground (variable-free) terms of the type of interest denote *different* (distinct) values unless they can be proved to be equivalent from the given axioms, with *final* semantics, two ground terms of the same sort denote the *same* value unless it can be proved from the axioms that they denote a different value. The meaning of this statement may not be immediately clear at first, so we will explain the concept with a small example!

We can illustrate the difference between the two approaches by considering the specification Dual of Fig. 10.5. The *initial* algebra of this specification describes the *bag* of natural numbers with the operations empty (corresponding to the empty bag), add and is-in?. Under an initial interpretation, the axioms cannot be used to show, for example, that

add(add(add(empty, 1), 1), 2) = add(add(empty, 1), 2)

so that these two terms denote *distinct* values. Axiom (1) is necessary since it states a fundamental property of bags, namely that the order in which elements are added to a bag is irrelevant.

```
SPEC   Dual
USING  Boolean  +  Natural
SORT   dual
OPS
   empty  :                -> dual
   add    : dual  nat  ->  dual
   is-in? : dual         -> bool
FORALL
   n, n1, n2  :  nat
           d  :  dual
AXIOMS:
  (1)  add(add(d, n1), n2)       =  add(add(d, n2), n1)
  (2)  is-in?(empty, n)          =  false
  (3)  is-in?(add(d, n1), n2)    =  IF  n1 == n2  THEN  true
                                    ELSE  is-in?(d, n2)  ENDIF

ENDSPEC
```

Figure 10.5 Algebraic specification Dual.

The *final* algebra of this specification has as a model the *set* of natural numbers with the operations empty (corresponding to the empty set, ∅), add, and is-in?. With final semantics, to show that two expressions are not equal, we have to demonstrate that application of accessor operations to the expressions produces different results. For this example, with final semantics, two set values will be equal unless the application of is-in? to them results in different outcomes. For example, under a final interpretation, the terms s1 and s2 where

s1 = add(add(add(empty, 1), 1), 2) ; s2 = add(add(empty, 1), 2)

now denote the same value since the expression is–in?(s, n) will return true for both
s = s1 and s = s2 when n=1 or n=2 and will return false when s = s1 and s = s2 for
all other values of n. In fact, it can be seen that we can remove the first axiom without
altering the *final* semantics.

Exercise 10.8 With reference to the specification Dual given in Fig. 10.5, show that the
terms add(add(empty, 3), 4) and add(add(empty, 4), 3) are equivalent under an *initial*
interpretation and that they are equivalent under a final interpretation with or without
axiom (1). Observe that the corresponding set of rewrite rules for Dual is not finitely
convergent since axiom (1) would supply a nonterminating sequence of rewrites.

With final value semantics, the quotient term algebra for any given specification will
contain *fewer* equivalence classes compared with the corresponding quotient term algebra
for an initial interpretation. (This follows because more of the ground terms are equivalent
under a final interpretation than with an initial one.) It follows that the number of distinct
values in the carrier set of a final model is less than for the corresponding initial model.

Both the initial and final approaches to semantics have their advantages and disadvantages and the ultimate reason for choosing one or the other is often a methodological one.
In this respect, specification reusability and modularity considerations may well have an
influence on the semantics chosen for a formal specification language. A more detailed
discussion of these issues is beyond the scope of this book.

As a postscript, we present a mathematical definition of *final* algebras that can be
compared with a corresponding definition for *initial* algebras:

- An algebra $\mathscr{F}$ is final in a category $\mathscr{C}$ of algebras over a presentation if and only if
  $\mathscr{F} \in \mathscr{C}$ and, for each algebra $\mathscr{A} \in \mathscr{C}$, a unique homomorphism in $\mathscr{C}$ from $\mathscr{A}$ to $\mathscr{F}$ does
  exist.

10.15 SUMMARY

The principal results are presented in the summaries below.

10.15.1 Signatures and algebras

- A many-sorted *signature* Σ consists of a collection of sorts and function symbols
  (operation names). Each function symbol has an associated domain and range which
  are taken from the collection of sorts.
- The function symbols of a signature are high-level abstractions of the operations of an
  abstract data type.
- There is no one-to-one correspondence between algebras and signatures.
- Signatures determine the set of all *well-formed terms* for each sort.
- A *term* (*expression*) of an algebraic specification is well-formed if it is a constant (nullary
  operation), a variable or an operation applied to the correct number of arguments, with
  each argument itself a well-formed term of the correct sort. The sort of a variable term is
  that stated in the *variable declaration* component of the specification (the FORALL
  section in an Axis specification).
- A *heterogeneous algebra*, $\mathscr{A} = [A, \Omega]$ consists of a family of N carrier sets $A = \{A_i\}$ with
  $i = 1, 2, \ldots, N$ together with a collection of operations Ω, whose domain and range

belong to the family of carriers. A *homogeneous algebra* is an algebra whose carrier set consists of a single set of values. Algebras provide *models* of specifications.

- Given a signature Σ, then any algebra $\mathscr{A} = [A, \Omega]$ such that
  - each term belonging to the sort of Σ maps to a member of A
  - each function symbol $\sigma \in \Sigma$ maps to an operation $\omega \in \Omega$ of the appropriate arity, domain and range

  is said to *interpret* that signature.
- A *signature* can denote many algebras, and the class of algebras which are models of a given signature is broad and very general. Some models may have undesirable properties.
- *Homomorphisms* are special mappings between the carrier sets of two algebras which preserve the structure imposed by the operations of the algebra. If the mapping is one-to-one, the two algebras are said to be *isomorphic*.
- The strongest measure of similarity that can be found between two algebras $\mathscr{A}$ and $\mathscr{B}$ is that where an *isomorphism* exists between $\mathscr{A}$ and $\mathscr{B}$. For such algebras, there is a one-to-one correspondence between the members of the respective carrier sets. This means that if the function h maps values from $\mathscr{A}$ to $\mathscr{B}$, then an *inverse* function (often denoted by h^{-1}) will map values the other way, that is from $\mathscr{B}$ to $\mathscr{A}$. Isomorphic algebras are 'abstractly' identical in the sense that the only possible difference between them is that their carrier sets differ in name.

10.15.2 Theory presentations and their interpretations

- Extending a signature, Σ, with a set of axioms, E, has the effect of 'constraining' the resulting specification to describe more precisely the required properties of an abstract data type. The resulting specification is known as a *presentation*, and can be written as the tuple $\langle \Sigma, E \rangle$.
- Given the presentation $\langle \Sigma, E \rangle$, the set of all algebras which is denoted by Σ and which satisfy E is called the *variety* over the presentation.
- Use of the axioms together with the inference rules of *equational logic* allows equivalences between terms to be established and the set of all axioms which can be derived from a given set of axioms E is known as the *closure* of E.
- The closure defines all the 'theorems' (equivalences between terms) provable within the presentation and we consider the closure as presenting a *theory*.
- A presentation together with the closure of its axioms is called a *theory presentation*.
- An algebra $\mathscr{A}$ is a *model* of a theory presentation if $\mathscr{A}$ is denoted by the signature of the presentation and if the axioms of the presentation are satisfied by $\mathscr{A}$.
- At least one model can always be found—the *quotient term algebra* in which the elements of the carrier set are the equivalence classes of terms constructed from the strings of symbols that are used to denote terms of the theory. The advantage of the term algebra is that it provides a symbolic representation of the theory which can be manipulated and treated as a model in its own right.
- There are many algebras which, with appropriate interpretations of the values and function symbols in a specification, provide models of an algebraic specification. The algebras which make up this family of models are related in that *each* member of the family can be derived from the *initial* algebra by a unique mapping (*homomorphism*).

- The *initial* algebra approach uses the unique (up to isomorphism) *initial* algebra as the standard representative model of the theory presentation. Initial models have the desirable properties of having *no junk*, and *no confusion*.
- The quotient term algebra is an initial algebra. All initial models of a presentation are isomorphic to each other and importantly, are therefore isomorphic to the quotient term algebra.
- *Canonical terms* are a subset of the terms generated by the term algebra such that each term in the subset is a member of a different equivalence class. The resulting algebra of canonical terms is called the *canonical term algebra* and this algebra is isomorphic to the quotient term algebra and is therefore initial.
- Identification of an appropriate set of atomic constructors for an abstract data type provides a useful bridge between the canonical term algebra and the perceived behaviour of the operations of that abstract data type.
- The difference between *initial* and *final* semantics is also discussed with the aid of an example
  - With *initial* semantics, two ground terms of the same sort denote *different* values unless it can be proved from the axioms that they denote the same value
  - With *final* semantics, two ground terms of the same sort denote the *same* value unless it can be proved from the axioms that they denote a *different* value

Crudely speaking, proofs of equivalence with initial semantics involve applying the constructor operations whereas proofs of non-equivalence with final semantics involves application of accessor operations.

10.15.3 Axioms as rewrite rules

- The axioms of an algebraic specification can be treated as a set of *left* to *right rewrite* or *production* rules which permits any term matching the left-hand side of an axiom to be replaced by the corresponding right-hand side. These term-rewriting systems have a number of important applications:
  - Initial algebra semantics can be implemented by an *operational* semantics based on rewrite rules.
  - A computation which uses rewrite rules produces a sequence of terms whereby instances of left-hand sides of axioms are replaced by the corresponding right-hand side until a *normal* or *reduced form* is obtained. If the sequence of rewrites always terminates and produces a unique normal form, the set of rewrite rules is *finitely convergent*.
  - If a set of rewrite rules is finitely convergent, term rewriting provides a feasible decision procedure for determining whether two variable-free terms are equal, and so provides an operational semantics for executable algebraic specification languages such as OBJ and Axis.

ADDITIONAL PROBLEMS

10.1 Consider the following operations zero, succ, pred, add with domain and range sorts shown below

```
zero : → nat

succ : nat → nat
```

```
pred : nat → nat

add : nat nat → nat
```

One obvious interpretation is the Σ-algebra $\mathscr{A}_{Natural} = [\mathbb{N}, \{0_\mathbb{N}, Succ_\mathbb{N}, Pred_\mathbb{N}, Add_\mathbb{N}\}]$ where $\mathbb{N}$ denotes the set of natural numbers and

(a) $0_\mathbb{N}$ is the natural number 0
(b) $Succ_\mathbb{N}:\mathbb{N}\to\mathbb{N}$ is defined by $Succ_\mathbb{N}(n)=n+1$
(c) $Pred_\mathbb{N}:\mathbb{N}\to\mathbb{N}$ is defined by $Pred_\mathbb{N}(0)=0$; $Pred_\mathbb{N}(n+1)=n$
(d) $Add_\mathbb{N}:\mathbb{N}^2\to\mathbb{N}$ is defined by $Add_\mathbb{N}(m, n)=m+n$

where $+$ is the conventional mathematical 'plus' operation.
Let *Tuple* denote $\mathbb{N}^2$, that is the set of ordered pairs of natural numbers $\langle m, n \rangle$ where $m, n \in \mathbb{N}$, then the Σ-algebra $\mathscr{A}_{Tuple}$

$$\mathscr{A}_{Tuple} = [Tuple, \{0_{Tuple}, Succ_{Tuple}, Pred_{Tuple}, Add_{Tuple}\}]$$

where the operations are defined by

(a') $0_{Tuple} = \langle 0, 0 \rangle$
(b') $Succ_{Tuple}(\langle m, n \rangle) = \langle m+1, n+1 \rangle$
(c') $Pred_{Tuple}(\langle 0, n \rangle) = \langle 0, 0 \rangle$; $Pred_{Tuple}(\langle m+1, n \rangle) = \langle m, 0 \rangle$
(d') $Add_{Tuple}(\langle m, n \rangle, \langle m', n' \rangle) = \langle m+m', n+n' \rangle$

is also an interpretation of Σ over the set of tuples. (Note that the function $Pred_{Tuple}$ decrements the first slot if possible but always reduces the second to zero).

(e) Let $h : Tuple \to \mathbb{N}$ defined by $h(\langle m, n \rangle)=m$ be a mapping between the carriers of $\mathscr{A}_{Tuple}$ and $\mathscr{A}_{Natural}$. Show that h is a *homomorphism*.
(f) Is the mapping h an *isomorphism*?
(g) Let $h': Tuple \to \mathbb{N}$ defined by $h'(\langle m, n \rangle)=n$ be a mapping between the carriers of $\mathscr{A}_{Tuple}$ and $\mathscr{A}_{Natural}$. Determine whether h' is a *homomorphism*.

10.2 An algebra $\mathscr{A}_{Natural}$ where

$$\mathscr{A}_{Natural} = [\mathbb{N}, \{0, Succ, +, \times, Pred, -\}]$$

includes the unary operation $Pred:\mathbb{N}\to\mathbb{N}$ defined by

$$Pred(n)=n-1$$

and the binary operation minus $(-)$ in addition to the familiar successor (*Succ*), addition $(+)$ and multiplication $(\times)$ operations. This algebra is to provide a model of the natural numbers. What complication does the inclusion of the predecessor operation (*Pred*) and subtraction operation $(-)$ introduce into a model of the natural numbers?

10.3 Show that the algebra

$$\mathscr{A}_{NatOdd} = [\mathbb{N}_{Odd}, \{1, Succ_{Odd}\}]$$

where $\mathbb{N}_{Odd} = \{1, 3, 5, \dots\}$ is the set of odd natural numbers and $Succ_{Odd}:\mathbb{N}_{Odd}\to\mathbb{N}_{Odd}$ defined by $Succ_{Odd}(n)=n+2$ $(\forall n \in \mathbb{N}_{Odd})$ provides an interpretation for the signature of Fig. 10.1.

10.4 Consider the algebra $\mathscr{A}_{Nat}$ introduced at the start of this chapter and $\mathscr{A}_{NatOdd}$ of the previous problem (Problem 10.3). Show that the mapping $h: \mathbb{N} \to \mathbb{N}_{Odd}$ from the natural numbers to the odd natural numbers defined by $h(n) = 2n + 1$ for all $n \in \mathbb{N}$ is a homomorphism.

10.5 Show that the algebras $\mathscr{A}_{Nat}$ and $\mathscr{A}_{NatOdd}$ are isomorphic.

10.6 Show that the algebra $\mathscr{A} = [A, \Omega]$ where

$$A = \{0, 1\} \quad \Omega = \{0, 1, \neg, \wedge\}$$

with

```
true ⟶ 0; false ⟶ 1
```

and

$$\neg 0 = 1 \; ; \; \neg 1 = 0$$

$$0 \wedge 0 = 0 \; ; \; 0 \wedge 1 = 1$$

$$1 \wedge 0 = 1 \; ; \; 1 \wedge 1 = 1$$

is a model of `Boolean` given in Fig. 10.4. Is this model an initial one?

10.7 A rather simple but elegant illustration of 'junk' and 'confusion' in models of a specification can be derived by considering the specification `Natural` for natural numbers given in Fig. 10.3. One model of the specification is the algebra $[\mathbb{Z}, \{0, +1, +\}]$ where $\mathbb{Z}$ is the set of *integers*, '+1' denotes the successor function and we use the interpretation

```
nat ⟶ ℤ
```

```
succ ⟶ +1
```

```
add ⟶ +
```

$$\{\texttt{zero} \to 0, \texttt{succ(zero)} \to 1, \texttt{succ(succ(zero))} \to 2, \dots\}$$

where $+$ is the familiar mathematical addition operator.

The axioms of the specification are easily seen to be satisfied with this interpretation. However, for this model, the negative integer values $-1, -2, -3, \dots$ are not denoted by any term which belongs to nat. In other words, these negative values are not denoted by terms which can be constructed using the operations of the specification `Natural`. This model has *junk*.

Another model of `Natural` is the algebra $[\mathbb{N}, \{0, +0, +\}]$ where $\mathbb{N}$ is the set of natural numbers, '+0' is the function which leaves the value of its input argument unaltered, $+$ is as before and we use the denotation

```
nat ⟶ ℕ
```

```
succ ⟶ +0
```

add $\longrightarrow$ +

$\{$zero $\longrightarrow 0$, succ(zero) $\longrightarrow 0$, succ(succ(zero)) $\longrightarrow 0, \ldots\}$

The axioms of Natural are satisfied with this interpretation with all reducing to '$0=0$' and this model has *confusion*. This model has the undesirable property of collapsing all the terms of the specification onto a single element of the carrier and so renders them indistinguishable. Terms such as zero and succ(zero), for example, which were intended to be distinct in the specification are denoted by the same value, 0, in this model. Junk and confusion in these models therefore debar them from being faithful interpretations of their corresponding specification Natural.

(a) When implementing a queue using an array, the queue tends to migrate through the available storage as data values are enqueued and dequeued and the bounds of the array can soon be reached even though the number of data values in the queue is less than the maximum size of the array. To avoid this problem, when a pointer (index) to the front/back of the queue is at a bound of the array and the queue is not full, we can 'wrap' the queue around by resetting that pointer to the lowest location in the array (if we are currently at the highest) and vice-versa. As an example, suppose an array of size *MaxSize* is used with an index in the range $1..MaxSize$. For this application, we might need a function $Succ_Q: \mathbb{N}_Q \rightarrow \mathbb{N}_Q$ with the property

$$Succ_Q(n) = (n+1) \ MOD \ MaxSize$$

where $\mathbb{N}_Q$ denotes the set $\{1, 2, 3, \ldots, MaxSize\}$ and MOD denotes the remainder when $(n+1)$ is divided by *MaxSize*. Create a specification ModMaxSize by using the specification Natural of Fig. 10.3 and including an additional axiom for an operation succQ which specifies the required 'wrap-around' property. (To keep the problem simple, assume $MaxSize=3$.)

(b) Does the resulting specification ModMaxSize preserve the initial properties of Natural? If not, explain why.

REFERENCE

Zilles, S.N. (1974) Algebraic Specification of Data Types, *MIT, Laboratory for Computer Science, Progress Report XI*, Cambridge, MA.

FURTHER READING

A gentle introduction to algebras with the associated concepts of homomorphism, isomorphism and quotient algebras is given in Chapter 7 of:
Stanat, D.F., and McAllister, D.F. (1977) *Discrete Mathematics in Computer Science*, Prentice-Hall, Englewood Cliffs, NJ.
   This text provides one of the best introductions to the structure and properties of algebraic systems. The book also provides a comprehensive account of the mathematics required for formal specification.

11

BUILDING LARGER SPECIFICATIONS

11.1 INTRODUCTION

One of the fundamental tools for managing the complexity of software systems is *modularity*, whereby large products are composed from smaller, simpler, and independent components using the glue of interfaces. One of the benefits that such an approach promotes is the reusability of software.

For algebraic specification languages, complex specifications are built up compositionally, in bottom-up fashion, from simpler algebraic specifications of abstract data types. Algebraic specifications developed this way have a hierarchical structure in the form of an acyclic graph of specification modules with the higher-level modules 'importing' the sorts and operations of lower-level modules. This concept is apparent even in the simple specifications developed already such as Stack, Queue, and Binary-tree where we have explicitly imported the (built-in) specification modules Boolean and Natural. The corresponding dependency graph for Queue is shown in Fig. 11.1. The statement which appears

USING Natural + Boolean

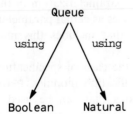

Figure 11.1 Illustration of the dependency of Queue on Natural and Boolean.

at the top of our specifications denotes that the predefined specification modules Natural and Boolean are available in those top-level specifications. The expression following the keywords USING is called a *module expression* and its signature consists of the *union* of the signatures of Natural and Boolean. We can think of USING as a 'read-only' type of import in the sense that the importing module cannot alter the properties of the imported specifications. Specifications (theories) can be *extended* or *enriched* by introducing new operations and/or axioms into an existing specification. Specifications can also include operations and/or sorts of other specifications, define new sorts and/or operations for the included specification, and then use them in conjunction with its own introduced sorts and operations.

In order to be able to reuse 'formal specification software components', it is essential that an algebraic specification language allows *generic* or *parameterized* theories to be developed. For example, if we want to manipulate stacks of natural numbers, stacks of Booleans and stacks of characters, we do not want to produce three different explicit specifications. The key concept here is that the characteristic operations of a stack are quite independent of the type of the data items it manipulates. In other words, the *type* of the items pushed onto a stack is quite irrelevant to the operations of the stack. This immediately suggests the possibility of producing a *generic* or *parametric* specification along the lines of

```
SPEC Stack(S : Specification-Class)
```

where S is a *formal* parameter that represents any SPEC module that is a member of a *class* of specifications Specification–Class, that class being characterized by some common property. That property could be a very general one such as requiring only the existence of a named sort. We could then supply an *actual* specification parameter such as Natural, Boolean, or Identifier in place of S, that is *instantiate* the parametric specification to create the desired instance of a specification. For example, a stack of natural numbers and a stack whose data elements are character strings could be generated using the two instantiations

```
Stack(Natural) ; Stack(Identifier)
```

respectively. This facility clearly promotes the reuse of theories but the way in which parameterization is handled does differ from one algebraic specification language to another. In the case of the early algebraic specification language *ACT ONE*, parameterized specifications can be derived that take both sorts and operations as actual parameters while the language *Clear* incorporates a more powerful form of parameterization in that it allows the production of *theory procedures* that take other theories as actual parameters. We will develop a framework for handling parameterization that includes this more powerful generic facility.

Following the style of Axis (© Hewlett-Packard Ltd 1988), the class of specifications Specification–Class will be denoted by so-called PROPS specification modules. PROPS modules will be introduced to define the class of specifications that can be used to *instantiate* a parameterized SPEC module. Unlike ordinary SPEC modules, generic specifications are not interpreted initially, because any given actual parameter (SPEC module) may have 'more properties' (for example, more operations) than specified in the formal parameter. A PROPS specification therefore defines the interface of a parameterized specification in the sense that it declares the structure and properties required of an *actual* parameter (a SPEC module) for meaningful instantiation. These ideas will be developed later.

To start, however, we expand upon the idea of building up larger specifications from simpler ones and illustrate the concept with two small case studies. First we derive an algebraic specification for the estate agent example that was developed earlier using VDM. We also produce a specification for a small control system that regulates the operations of filling and emptying petrochemical tanks. This case study will be developed and expanded by specifying a real-time monitoring system for a petrochemical plant that collects data from a number of petrochemical tanks and is responsible for conveying information about that data.

11.2 ESTATE AGENT EXAMPLE

We now derive an *algebraic* specification for the estate agent's record system, an example studied earlier in Chapter 3.

11.2.1 Status of a house

To start, we will specify a two-valued data type Mode which consists of the elements for-sale and under-offer which will be used to denote whether or not an offer has been made on a house. The specification is given in Fig. 11.2. For simplicity, we will treat a house address as a single identifier in which case we can use the 'built-in' specification module Identifier with a suitable renaming of its sort id to address. This is denoted in Axis by the statement

```
WITH id AS address
```

The specification Address is given in Fig. 11.3.

```
SPEC   Mode
SORT   mode
OPS
   for-sale      :   ->   mode
   under-offer   :   ->   mode
ENDSPEC
```

Figure 11.2 Specification of the two-valued abstract data type Mode.

```
SPEC   Address
USING  Identifier
   WITH id AS address
ENDSPEC
```

Figure 11.3 Specification of the abstract data type Address.

11.2.2 Operations for the database

The operations we require for the specification Houses-for-sale are:

- empty   creates an empty database.
- insert   inserts a *new* address into the database.
- add-house   adds an address into the database regardless of whether the address is already in the database.
- delete-house   removes a given house from the database.
- is-on-market?   checks whether a given address is in the database.
- make-offer   takes an address that is for sale and puts it under offer.
- is-under-offer?   checks whether a particular address is under offer.

We need two constructors insert and add-house because we have to restrict the values of the type. The operation add-house is too general in that it allows addresses to be entered into the database whether they are present or not, so we have introduced another constructor insert which only adds an address into the database if that address is *not* already present. The operation insert is to provide the only means for creating a valid database, so we insist that the constructor add-house must be inaccessible to any user of the specification. We therefore treat the operation add-house as *private* so that it cannot be exported and any user will view empty and insert as the atomic constructors. Following the convention introduced in Chapter 9, we declare the operation private (hidden) by prefixing it with an exclamation mark. (This idea of hidden operations was introduced in Chapter 9 when we looked at the specification of an ordered binary tree.)

Denoting the introduced sort of Houses-for-sale by house-db, the signature of these operations is shown in Fig. 11.4. A word of explanation is needed concerning the different domain sorts of the operations insert and !add-house. The operation !add-house adds a given address to the database *regardless* of whether the address is already in the database or not and *regardless* of its 'mode' (for-sale or under-offer). On the other hand, insert only adds a *new* address to the database, in which case the *mode* of that address is set to 'for-sale'.

If the database is empty, then 'inserting' any address addr is the same as 'adding' a new house to the database. This result is expressed by the axiom

```
insert(empty, addr) = !add-house(empty, addr, for-sale)
```

where it has been 'flagged' as being for-sale. For a nonempty database, we do not want to add an address if the address is already in the database. The outcome of attempting to

```
SORT   house-db
OPS
        empty :      ->  house-db
       insert :  house-db  address  ->  house-db
    !add-house :  house-db  address  mode  ->  house-db
  delete-house :  house-db  address  ->  house-db
    make-offer :  house-db  address  ->  house-db
  is-on-market? :  house-db  address  ->  bool
 is-under-offer? :  house-db  address  ->  bool
```

Figure 11.4 Signature of Houses-for-sale.

'insert' an address addr2 into a database hs to which the address addr1 has previously been added is given by the axiom

```
insert(!add-house(hs, addr1, m), addr2) =

        IF addr1 == addr2 THEN !add-house(hs, addr1, m)

        ELSE !add-house(insert(hs, addr2), addr1, m) ENDIF
```

where m ∈ mode.

Let us examine this axiom in more detail. When a *new* address addr2 is inserted, the statement

```
!add-house(insert(hs, addr2), addr1, m)
```

(which follows the ELSE delimiter) ensures that the updated value of the database expression will, after the appropriate number of recursive applications of insert, end up as the expression

```
!add-house(!add-house( ··· , insert(empty, addr2), ··· ))
```

The innermost subterm insert(empty, addr2) then terminates the recursion since it 'adds' the address (using !add-house) and flags it as being for-sale. It is worth expanding upon this idea a little by constructing some values of the sort house-db.

To start, consider the value of the database obtained by 'inserting' the address 'house1' into an empty database. (The quotes denote a string literal.) The resulting database hs1 ∈ house-db is

```
hs1 = insert(empty, 'house1')
```

and use of the axiom above gives

```
hs1 = !add-house(empty, 'house1', for-sale)
```

If we now insert a new address 'house2', the value of the database is the element hs2 where

```
hs2 = insert(hs1, 'house2')
    = insert(!add-house(empty, 'house1', for-sale), 'house2')
    = !add-house(insert(empty, 'house2'), 'house1', for-sale)
    = !add-house(!add-house(empty, 'house2', for-sale), 'house1', for-sale)
```

The reader is strongly encouraged to try inserting 'house1' again and then 'house2' again into the database hs2, and so confirm that the integrity of the database is preserved.

Exercise 11.1 Suppose a third new address 'house3' is to be inserted into the database hs2 above to produce a new database hs3. Express hs3 in terms of the atomic constructors empty and !add-house. Verify also that 'inserting' any of the existing addresses again into the database will not alter the value of hs3.

11.2.3 **Axioms for** delete-house

First we assert that removing an address from an empty database results in an empty database, which produces the axiom

```
delete-house(empty, addr) = empty
```

For the general nonempty database expression !add-house(hs, addr1, m), the effect of deleting the address addr2 is given by the expression

```
delete-house(!add-house(hs, addr1, m), addr2)
```

Clearly, if the two addresses are the same, the result is simply hs. If the two addresses addr1, addr2 are not the same, we need to reapply the operation delete-house to the ('truncated') database before addr1 is added, that is to hs. In order to preserve the existence of addr1 in the database, we must, however, then reinstate addr1 which is achieved by applying !add-house. These results are expressed in the axiom

```
delete-house(!add-house(hs, addr1, m), addr2) =

        IF addr1 == addr2 THEN hs

        ELSE !add-house(delete-house(hs, addr2), addr1, m) ENDIF
```

The reader may wonder why the operation !add-house appears following the ELSE rather than insert. The reason is that the entry addr1, which has to be reinstated, may be 'under-offer' (that is its associated value m is under-offer) and, if we then subsequently put addr1 back into the database using insert, its mode m will be reinitialized back to under-offer. Notice the similarity of this axiom to that for the operation remove given in the specification Queue of Chapter 9. As there, the effect of the 'delete' operation on an 'add' involves interchanging the positions of the two constructor operations. Note also that the effect of deleting an address that is not present in the database will leave the database unaltered.

Exercise 11.2 Delete the entry 'house2' from the database hs2 given in the previous exercise.

11.2.4 **Axioms for** is-on-market?

The operation is-on-market? tests whether a given address is in the database, *regardless* of whether that address is 'for sale' or 'under offer'. (We have a further operation is-under-offer? which tests whether a specified address has had an offer made). It is evident that if the database is empty, the result of the query will return false, so that

```
is-on-market?(empty, addr) = false
```

In the case of the query

```
is-on-market?(!add-house(hs, addr1, m), addr2)
```

if the addresses addr1 and addr2 are equal, then is–on–market? returns true. If the addresses are not equal, we then need to repeat the enquiry on the database hs. This result is expressed in the axiom

```
is-on-market?(!add-house(hs, addr1, m), addr2) =

          IF addr1 == addr2 THEN true

          ELSE is-on-market?(hs, addr2) ENDIF
```

Exercise 11.3 Given the database hs2 defined above, use the axioms for is–on–market? to show that:

(a) is–on–market?(hs2, 'house1') = true
(b) is–on–market?(hs2, 'house3') = false

11.2.5 Axioms for is–under–offer?

The operation is–under–offer? tests whether a given address is 'under offer' in the database. To start, we assert that the outcome of the query will return false if the database is empty

```
is-under-offer?(empty, addr) = false
```

Consider now the result of

```
is-under-offer?(!add-house(hs, addr1, m), addr2)
```

If the addresses addr1 and addr2 are the same, the house will be under offer if the value of m is under–offer. If the addresses are not the same, we need to check the rest of the database, that is is–under–offer?(hs, addr2). The axiom that expresses this statement is

```
is-under-offer?(!add-house(hs, addr1, m), addr2) =

          IF addr1 == addr2 THEN

            IF m == under-offer THEN true

            ELSE false ENDIF

          ELSE is-under-offer?(hs, addr2) ENDIF
```

(It is important to realize that this operation will also return false if the specified address is *not* in the database.)

11.2.6 Axioms for make–offer

The operation make–offer needs to search through the database for the specified address and then check its status. If the house is not yet under offer, the operation can change the status of the address by first deleting that address from the database and then adding it into the database with its status flagged as under-offer. If the database is empty or the house is already under offer, the state of the database should remain unchanged and, if the specified address is not in the database, the value of the database should also be unaltered. The axioms for make-offer therefore take the form

$$\texttt{make-offer(empty, addr)} = \texttt{empty}$$

make-offer(!add-house(hs, addr1, m), addr2) =

   IF addr1 == addr2 THEN

      IF m == for-sale THEN

         !add-house(delete-house(hs, addr1), addr1, under-offer)

     ELSE !add-house(hs, addr1, m) ENDIF

    ELSE

     !add-house(make-offer(hs, addr2), addr1, m) ENDIF

Although the second axiom appears complicated, some explanation should help to clarify matters. Firstly, if the two addresses are the same and the address is already under offer, then we require make-offer to leave the state of the database unchanged (that is the application of make-offer to the database on the left-hand side of the axiom will return that same database). This situation is expressed by the statement following the first ELSE.

If, on the other hand, the two addresses are not the same, we need to repeat the operation make-offer on the database hs before address addr1 is added. As with the case of the operation delete-house, we must preserve the entries in the database, so we must reinsert the address addr1 (and its associated status m) into the database. This is expressed by the statement following the final ELSE. The complete specification Houses-for-sale is shown in Fig. 11.5.

Exercise 11.4 Use the axioms derived above to show that:

(a) is-under-offer?(hs2, 'house1') = false
(b) is-under-offer?(make-offer(hs2, 'house2'), 'house2') = true

11.3 COMPOUND MODULES

Algebraic specifications can be built up hierarchically whereby larger theories are developed as *enrichments* or *extensions* of others. All algebraic specification languages provide certain theory building operations, or *combinators*, which allow theories to be amalgamated and extended. We should alert the reader to the fact that there is no standard terminology used in this area.

```
SPEC   Houses-for-sale
USING  Address  +  Mode  +  Boolean
SORT   house-db
OPS
            empty  :    ->  house-db
           insert  :  house-db  address    ->  house-db
      !add-house   :  house-db  address  mode  ->  house-db
    delete-house   :  house-db  address    ->  house-db
      make-offer   :  house-db  address    ->  house-db
    is-on-market?  :  house-db  address    ->  bool
   is-under-offer? :  house-db  address    ->  bool
FORALL
               hs  :   house-db
addr, addr1, addr2 :   address
                m  :   mode
```

AXIOMS:

(1)   insert(empty, addr) = !add-house(empty, addr, for-sale)

(2)   insert(!add-house(hs, addr1, m), addr2) =
              IF addr1 == addr2 THEN
              !add-house(hs, addr1, m) ELSE
              !add-house(insert(hs, addr2), addr1, m) ENDIF

(3)   delete-house(empty, addr) = empty

(4)   delete-house(!add-house(hs, addr1, m), addr2) =
             IF addr1 == addr2 THEN hs ELSE
             !add-house(delete-house(hs, addr2), addr1, m) ENDIF

(5)   is-on-market?(empty, addr) = false

(6)   is-on-market?(!add-house(hs, addr1, m), addr2) =
              IF addr1 == addr2 THEN true
              ELSE is-on-market?(hs, addr2) ENDIF

(7)   is-under-offer?(empty, addr) = false

(8)   is-under-offer?(!add-house(hs, addr1, m), addr2) =
              IF addr1 == addr2 THEN
                  IF m == under-offer THEN true
                  ELSE false ENDIF
              ELSE is-under-offer?(hs, addr2) ENDIF

(9)   make-offer(empty, addr) = empty

(10)   make-offer(!add-house(hs, addr1, m), addr2) =
           IF addr1 == addr2 THEN
           IF m == for-sale THEN
               !add-house(delete-house(hs, addr1), addr1, under-offer)
           ELSE !add-house(hs, addr1, m) ENDIF
         ELSE
              !add-house(make-offer(hs, addr2), addr1, m) ENDIF
```

**Figure 11.5**  Specification Houses-for-sale.

## 11.3.1 Combinators

Axis provides two theory-building constructs by which algebraic specifications can be built on top of other specifications, namely the combinators USING and INCLUDING. The combinator USING permits 'read only' access to a specification while INCLUDING permits
```

part or all of an existing specification to be imported and so allows it to be modified. The specification that is accessed or imported is given by a *module expression*. More precisely, USING and INCLUDING are defined as follows:

- USING—if a module S accesses a module T by means of a USING combinator, it is illegal for S to introduce any new values of T or make any distinct values of T equal.
- INCLUDING—if a module S imports a module T by means of the INCLUDING combinator, then S can modify the sort(s) of T (for example, by introducing new values of the imported sort through the use of nullary operations) and can introduce additional axioms to compel distinct values of T to be equal.

The USING construct therefore provides an extension that does not invalidate any of the previous properties of the accessed specification and so avoids introducing *junk* and *confusion* if the original specification is an initial model. On the other hand, INCLUDING provides a means of importing module expressions that does not require them to be protected. In essence, we can think of the text of an 'INCLUDED' module as being copied in with the result that the sorts that are consequently copied in and that are now 'owned' by the (larger) 'INCLUDING' module can be modified. For example, the enlarged specification may introduce new values for an existing specification (and so destroy the initial semantics of that imported specification).

11.3.2 Module expressions

Module expressions can be used to build complex specifications which are then included in a specification by means of the USING or INCLUDING combinators.

A module expression can be any one of the following:

1. The identifier of an unparameterized SPEC module
2. The instantiation of a parameterized SPEC module
3. The recursive application of the building operation '+' (the *sum* or *union*) or renaming (WITH) to module expressions

The following points should be noted:

- Given two specifications M1 and M2, the specification sum (or union) M1 + M2 combines the sorts, operations, and axioms of the two specifications to form an enlarged specification with duplicated components included only once.
- With USING, regardless of how many times a module T is imported by a module M, module M inherits one and only one copy of the *signature* of T. (We use the term *signature* in this context to denote the collection of sorts and operations with their associated domain and range sorts.) For example, if a module S1 imports T, a module S2 imports S1 + T, and a module S3 imports S1 + S2 + T, then only *one* copy of T is imported into module S3.
- As part of the process of constructing larger specifications, we follow standard practice by providing a feature whereby existing specification modules can be renamed to reflect their intended use. This feature is provided by the WITH combinator which allows part or all of a module's *owned* signature to be renamed.

11.4 PETROCHEMICAL PLANT EXAMPLE

This example will illustrate the concept of module expressions and combinators.

Suppose a piece of software is needed to control the operation of a petrochemical plant which consists of a number of similar petrochemical storage tanks containing different petrochemicals. Suppose further that an individual component of the software system is required to control the filling and emptying of the tanks. Let us assume that any petrochemical tank can contain one of five petrochemicals *pc1*, *pc2*, *pc3*, *pc4*, *pc5* and each has the same maximum capacity denoted by *max-vol*. A useful abstract data type for such a computer program is Tank.

11.4.1 Petrochemical tank—version 1

An appropriate set of operations for the abstract data type Tank is:

- new   an operation that corresponds to an empty tank.
- add-chem   an operation that adds a specified amount of petrochemical to a tank such that the amount added does not cause the tank to overflow and the petrochemical added is the same as that currently in the tank.
- fill   an operation that adds a specified amount of a given petrochemical to a tank regardless of the amount or type of petrochemical in the tank.
- remove   an operation that removes a specified amount of petrochemical from a tank. If the tank is empty, the operation should return an empty tank, while an attempt to remove a quantity in excess of the current contents should also return an empty tank.
- empty-tank   an operation that takes a tank and 'empties' the entire contents of the tank.
- change-pc   an operation that fills a nonempty tank with a specified amount of a given petrochemical. The existing contents of the tank must first be removed before filling with the specified petrochemical. The amount added must not exceed *max-vol*.
- is-empty?   an operation that returns true if the tank is empty, false otherwise.
- is-full?   an operation that returns true if the tank is full, false otherwise.
- chem   an operation that returns the petrochemical contained in a nonempty tank.
- level   an operation that returns the amount of petrochemical in a tank.

To start, we need to specify an abstract data type PetroChemical which specifies the five petrochemicals. The specification is given in Fig. 11.6 where chemical denotes the

```
SPEC   PetroChemical
SORT   chemical
OPS
    pc1  :   ->   chemical
    pc2  :   ->   chemical
    pc3  :   ->   chemical
    pc4  :   ->   chemical
    pc5  :   ->   chemical
ENDSPEC
```

Figure 11.6   Specification of the petrochemicals.

corresponding sort. We assume also the availability of a specification Real with sort real to represent the *nonnegative* amount of petrochemical in the tank. (To be more faithful to the spirit of the algebraic approach, we could specify an abstract data type Amount with associated operations to 'add' and 'subtract' amounts, but, to keep the example simple, we 'cheat' by using a standard data type specification with provided operations '+' and '−').

The domain and range sorts of the operations are given in Fig. 11.7 where tank denotes the sort of Tank and ne-tank in a subsort of tank that denotes the collection of nonempty tank values. In the discussion of Tank that follows, we use the variables

- c, c1, c2 ∈ chemical to denote petrochemical values
- q, q1, q2 ∈ real to denote the quantity of petrochemical in a tank

```
      new  :   -> tank
 add-chem  :   tank  chemical  real  ->  tank
    !fill  :   tank  chemical  real  ->  ne-tank
   remove  :   tank  real  ->  tank
empty-tank :   tank  ->  tank
change-pc  :   tank  chemical  real  ->  tank
 is-empty? :   tank  ->  bool
  is-full? :   tank  ->  bool
     chem  :   ne-tank  ->  chemical
    level  :   tank  ->  real
  max-vol  :   -> real
```

Figure 11.7 The syntax of the operations of Tank.

11.4.2 The constructors add-chem and !fill

To preserve the integrity of the values of our data type tank, we need the constructor add-chem since the operation fill adds a petrochemical without checking either the existing contents of the tank or the amount added. The operation add-chem provides the 'proper' way of adding the petrochemical, where 'proper', in this sense, means that, if the tank is originally empty, the amount added must not exceed max-vol. If the tank is not empty, the petrochemical to be added must be the *same* as that in the tank *and* the quantity added must not cause the tank to overflow. We require the operation add-chem to provide the *only* means for creating well-formed values of the sort tank. We therefore declare the operation fill as private (by prefixing '!' to its name) to signify that it cannot be exported and any *user* will view new and add-chem as the atomic constructors.

In the case of adding a specified petrochemical to an empty tank, the only constraint is that the amount added should not exceed max-vol. If the quantity to be added exceeds the maximum, we stipulate, for the purposes of this version of the example, that the operation should return a full tank. This is expressed in the axiom

```
add-chem(new, c, q) =

        IF q == 0.0 THEN new

        ELSEIF q < max-vol THEN

        !fill(new, c, q)

        ELSE !fill(new, c, max-vol) ENDIF
```

In the case of a nonempty tank containing an amount q_1 of petrochemical c_1, adding an amount q_2 of the same petrochemical will result in a tank containing the quantity $q_1 + q_2$ provided $q_1 + q_2 \leqslant$ max-vol. An attempt to add an excessive quantity of c_1 is to leave a full tank and we stipulate that an attempt to add a different petrochemical c_2 is to leave the contents of the tank unaltered. These properties are described by the axiom

```
add-chem(!fill(new, c1, q1), c2, q2) =

        IF c1 == c2 THEN

          IF (q1 + q2) < max-vol

            THEN !fill(new, c1, q1 + q2)

          ELSE !fill(new, c1, max-vol) ENDIF

        ELSE !fill(new, c1, q1) ENDIF
```

The axioms for the operation add–chem ensure that the values of tank conform to the well-formed expressions we require. (In VDM, such constraints would be expressed by the pre- and post-conditions attached to each operation and by the data type invariant.) These two axioms for add–chem ensure that all well-formed expressions of sort tank take one of the forms

- new
- !fill(new, c, q) with $c \in$ chemical and $0.0 < q \leqslant$ max-vol.

Note that the result of an add–chem operation will be either an empty tank new or a *nonempty* tank !fill(new, c, q) where $q > 0$. For this reason, we take the range of add–chem to be tank (which includes both the empty tank new and nonempty tank values), while the range of !fill is ne–tank.

In practice, we would also require operations to warn of attempts being made to add too much chemical or mix chemicals. This extension is left as an exercise and is described in the additional problems (Problem 11.6) that appear at the end of the chapter.

11.4.3 Axioms for remove, empty-tank **and** change-pc

In the case of remove acting upon an empty tank, we return the empty tank so that

```
remove(new, q) = new
```

while removing an amount q_2 from a tank containing q_1 will result in a tank with contents $q_1 - q_2$ (provided $q_1 > q_2$). If $q_1 \leqslant q_2$, we specify that the result returned should be new. The corresponding axiom is therefore

```
remove(!fill(new, c1, q1), q2) =

        IF q1 > q2 THEN add-chem(new, c1, q1 − q2)

        ELSE new ENDIF
```

The axioms satisfied by empty-tank are immediately seen to be

```
empty-tank(new)          = new

empty-tank(!fill(new, c, q)) = new
```

For the operation change-pc, we must first remove the entire contents of the tank (if any) and then 'add' the given petrochemical. If the tank is initially empty, we specify that the operation change-pc is equivalent to add–chem. This leads to the axioms

```
change-pc(new, c, q)                = add-chem(new, c, q)

change-pc(!fill(new, c1, q1), c2, q2) =

        add-chem(empty-tank(!fill(new, c1, q1)), c2, q2)
```

Note that the right-hand sides of the axioms for remove and change-pc use the constructor add–chem to ensure that the resulting values of the sort tank are well-formed.

11.4.4 Axioms for Boolean-valued operations

The axioms for is–empty? and is–full? are derived immediately

```
is-empty?(new)          = true

is-empty?(!fill(new, c, q)) = false

is-full?(new)           = false

is-full?(!fill(new, c, q))  = (q = = max-vol)
```

11.4.5 Axioms for chem **and** level

The remaining operations chem and level are accessors that 'select' the kind of petrochemical (for a nonempty tank) and the quantity of that petrochemical respectively. The corresponding axioms are

```
chem(!fill(new, c, q)) = c

    level(new) = 0.0

level(!fill(new, c, q)) = q
```

The complete specification Tank is shown in Fig. 11.8.

Before leaving this example, the reader may wonder whether the second axiom for is–empty? should be

```
is-empty?(!fill(new, c, q)) = (q == 0.0)
```

```
SPEC   Tank
USING   PetroChemical  +  Real  +  Boolean
SORTS   ne-tank  tank
SUBSORT  ne-tank  <  tank
OPS
         new  :  ->  tank
   add-chem  :  tank  chemical  real  ->  tank
      !fill  :  tank  chemical  real  ->  ne-tank
     remove  :  tank  real  ->  tank
 empty-tank  :  tank  ->  tank
  change-pc  :  tank  chemical  real  ->  tank
  is-empty?  :  tank  ->  bool
   is-full?  :  tank  ->  bool
       chem  :  ne-tank  ->  chemical
      level  :  tank  ->  real
    max-vol  :  ->  real


FORALL
   c, c1, c2  :  chemical
   q, q1, q2  :  real


AXIOMS:
  (1)   add-chem(new, c, q)  =
                   IF  q == 0.0  THEN  new
                   ELSEIF  q < max-vol  THEN
                   !fill(new, c, q)
                   ELSE  !fill(new, c, max-vol)  ENDIF
  (2)   add-chem(!fill(new, c1, q1), c2, q2)  =
                   IF  c1 == c2  THEN
                       IF  (q1 + q2) < max-vol
                           THEN  !fill(new, c1, q1 + q2)
                         ELSE  !fill(new, c1, max-vol)  ENDIF
                       ELSE  !fill(new, c1, q1)    ENDIF
  (3)   remove(new, q)  = new
  (4)   remove(!fill(new, c1, q1), q2)  =
                   IF  q1 > q2  THEN  add-chem(new, c1, q1 - q2)
                       ELSE  new  ENDIF
  (5)   empty-tank(new)              = new
  (6)   empty-tank(!fill(new, c, q))  = new
  (7)   change-pc(new, c, q)          = add-chem(new, c, q)
  (8)   change-pc(!fill(new, c1, q1), c2, q2)  =
               add-chem(empty-tank(!fill(new, c1, q1)), c2, q2)
  (9)   is-empty?(new)  = true
 (10)   is-empty?(!fill(new, c, q))  = false
 (11)   is-full?(new)  = false
 (12)   is-full?(!fill(new, c, q))  = (q == max-vol)
 (13)   chem(!fill(new, c, q))  = c
 (14)   level(new)  = 0.0
 (15)   level(!fill(new, c, q))  = q


ENDSPEC
```

Figure 11.8 Algebraic specification of a small petrochemical control system—version 1.

In fact, study of the 'constructor' axioms that define add-chem, remove, empty-tank, and change-pc reveals that the term !fill(new, c, 0.0) cannot result from the application of any of these operations.

Exercise 11.5 Use the axioms of Tank to reduce the following expressions:

(a) remove(add-chem(add-chem(new, pc1, 50.0), pc1, 60.0), 30.0)
(b) level(change-pc(!fill(new, pc1, 70.0), pc2, 40.0))

where pc1, pc2 ∈ chemical. (Note that (a) corresponds to adding a quantity 50.0 of petrochemical pc1, then adding a further quantity 60.0, and then removing a quantity 30.0—so we should end up with an amount 80.0!)

For this example, we have handled the (potential) problems that can arise, such as overfilling a tank or adding a different petrochemical to a tank, by demanding that add-chem should return a full tank or leave the value of the tank unaltered respectively. This treatment is very much in the spirit of 'damage limitation' but leaves us with the concern that these potentially dangerous situations should be treated as alarm or danger values and signalled as such. One way of handling this is to introduce an error value together with a Boolean operation alarm? which returns true if either (or both) of the above situations arises. This approach will now be examined as we develop a second version of the specification Tank.

11.5 PETROCHEMICAL TANK—VERSION 2

The interesting feature of the abstract data type Tank is that it is a *bounded* structure (bound by the *finite* size of a petrochemical tank). Were we to place no restrictions on the size of a tank and to allow the mixing of petrochemicals, then every tank value could be generated using the atomic constructors new and add-chem (the operation !fill being superfluous). What we have, however, is the situation in which the set of allowable sort values is characterized by having a *quantity* not exceeding max-vol and containing a *single* petrochemical. This situation is analogous to a *bounded* stack in which the constructor operation push is now a *partial* operation. In the case of a bounded stack, stack values for which push is a valid operation cannot be expressed directly as a set generated by an arbitrary number of applications of push and init. The values of the sort stack are now characterized by the condition that the 'length' of the stack (that is the number of items on the stack) must not exceed the bound. The values of the sort stack are therefore constrained in the sense of being restricted to a subset of those for the unbounded stack. Such 'sort constraints' do require subtle handling but can be encompassed within an initial algebra semantics.

Without going into elaborate detail, we present a second version of the specification Tank. This is similar to the previous specification, but we now include a *supersort* err-tank (of the sort tank) which contains the exceptional value error together with the additional operation alarm? which returns true if an attempt is made to add too much petrochemical or mix two petrochemicals. The sort of nonempty tank values ne-tank is a subsort of tank which is itself a subsort of err-tank. We express these subsort relations as

SUBSORTS ne-tank < tank < err-tank

As before, we need the two constructors add–chem and !fill

```
add-chem : err-tank chemical real → err-tank

  !fill : tank chemical real → ne-tank
```

together with the operation alarm? and the nullary operation error with syntax

```
alarm? : err-tank → bool

error : → err-tank
```

The domain and range sorts of the other operations are as given previously except for the operation change–pc which now has the signature

```
change-pc : tank chemical real → err-tank
```

The operation add–chem will produce an error value if the amount of petrochemical added causes the tank to overflow or if two different petrochemicals are mixed. This is expressed by the axioms

```
add-chem(new, c, q) = IF q = = 0.0 THEN new

                  ELSEIF q <= max-vol THEN

                  !fill(new, c, q) ELSE error ENDIF
add-chem(!fill(new, c1, q1), c2, q2) =

                  IF (c1 = = c2) and (q1 + q2 <= max-vol) THEN

                  !fill(new, c1, q1 + q2) ELSE error ENDIF
add-chem(error, c, q) = error
```

The axioms satisfied by alarm? follow directly

```
alarm?(new)           = false

alarm?(!fill(new, c, q)) = false

alarm?(error)          = true
```

The complete specification is shown in Fig. 11.9.

11.6 PETROCHEMICAL PLANT DATA-STORE

Let us extend this example by specifying a real-time monitoring system that is responsible for collecting data from all the tanks in the petrochemical plant. Apart from showing how large specifications can be built up from smaller ones, this case study illustrates the use of

```
SPEC   Tank
USING  Petrochemical  +  Real  +  Boolean
SORTS  ne-tank  tank  err-tank
SUBSORTS  ne-tank  <  tank  <  err-tank
OPS
        new  :   ->  tank
   add-chem  :   err-tank  chemical  real  ->  err-tank
      !fill  :   tank  chemical  real  ->  ne-tank
     remove  :   tank  real  ->  tank
 empty-tank  :   tank  ->  tank
  change-pc  :   tank  chemical  real  ->  err-tank
      error  :   ->  err-tank
     alarm?  :   err-tank  ->  bool
  is-empty?  :   tank  ->  bool
   is-full?  :   tank  ->  bool
       chem  :   ne-tank  ->  chemical
      level  :   tank  ->  real
    max-vol  :   ->  real
FORALL
c, c1, c2  :  chemical
q, q1, q2  :  real
AXIOMS:
  (1)  add-chem(new, c, q)  =  IF  q == 0.0  THEN  new
                                ELSEIF  q <= max-vol  THEN
                                  !fill(new, c, q)  ELSE  error  ENDIF
  (2)  add-chem(!fill(new, c1, q1), c2, q2)  =
                IF  (c1 == c2)  and (q1 + q2 <= max-vol)  THEN
                  !fill(new, c1, q1 + q2)  ELSE  error  ENDIF
  (3)  add-chem(error, c, q)  =  error
  (4)  remove(new, q)          =  new
  (5)  remove(!fill(new, c1, q1), q2)  =
                IF  q1 > q2  THEN  add-chem(new, c1, q1 - q2)
                ELSE  new  ENDIF
  (6)  empty-tank(new)                 =  new
  (7)  empty-tank(!fill(new, c, q))    =  new
  (8)  change-pc(new, c, q)            =  add-chem(new, c, q)
  (9)  change-pc(!fill(new, c1, q1), c2, q2)  =
                add-chem(empty-tank(!fill(new, c1, q1)), c2, q2)
  (10)  alarm?(new)                =  false
  (11)  alarm?(!fill(new, c, q))   =  false
  (12)  alarm?(error)              =  true
  (13)  is-empty?(new)             =  true
  (14)  is-empty?(!fill(new, c, q)) =  false
  (15)  is-full?(new)              =  false
  (16)  is-full?(!fill(new, c, q)) =  (q == max-vol)
  (17)  chem(!fill(new, c, q))     =  c
  (18)  level(new)                 =  0.0
  (19)  level(!fill(new, c, q))    =  q

ENDSPEC
```

Figure 11.9 Algebraic specification of a small petrochemical control system—version 2.

the INCLUDING construct for importing existing specifications, a topic introduced earlier in this chapter.

We will assume that each petrochemical tank is fitted with a detector device that conveys information on which petrochemical that particular tank contains and the amount it contains. In particular, suppose that each time an amount of petrochemical is added to or removed from a tank or the petrochemical contents of a tank are changed, the updated data on the status of that tank is added to the data-store. Let us assume also that several tanks may contain the same petrochemical.

We require the system to provide information on the current state of the plant and, in particular, it should supply data in response to the following operations:

- isolate   an operation that takes a data-store together with a named tank and returns a data-store that contains *only* the readings from that named tank.
- global-max   an operation that returns the *overall* maximum recorded amount of petrochemical in the data-store.
- global-min   an operation that returns the *overall* minimum recorded amount of petrochemical in the data-store.
- max-level   an operation that returns the maximum recorded amount of petrochemical contained in a specified tank.
- min-level   an operation that returns the minimum recorded amount of petrochemical contained in a specified tank.
- any-values?   an operation that returns true if a specified tank has had any data recorded and false if no data on that tank has been recorded.
- pc-contents   an operation that returns the current type of petrochemical contained in a given tank, provided data has been recorded from that tank.
- pc-level   an operation that returns the current amount of petrochemical contained in a given tank, provided data has been recorded from that tank.
- full-warning?   an operation that returns true if *any* tank has been recorded as full, false otherwise.
- count   an operation that returns the number of readings that have been recorded for an *individual* tank.
- total   an operation that returns the total number of readings that have been recorded for the plant.

11.6.1 The sensor devices

To start, we assume that the plant contains *five* tanks, each of which is associated with a uniquely named corresponding detector device. (The specification is easily extended to allow for any number of tanks.) An algebraic specification for the abstract data type Tank-Detector which specifies five named detector devices is given in Fig. 11.10 where the five devices are denoted by the nullary (constant) operations dev-1, dev-2, dev-3, dev-4, dev-5.

11.6.2 The petrochemical readings

Readings from each detector device consist of two values, namely the type and the quantity of the petrochemical contained. Our first task is to introduce an abstract data

```
SPEC   Tank-Detector
SORT   name
OPS
    dev-1  :   ->   name
    dev-2  :   ->   name
    dev-3  :   ->   name
    dev-4  :   ->   name
    dev-5  :   ->   name
ENDSPEC
```

Figure 11.10 Algebraic specification of the detector devices.

type Reading with sort reading which specifies this required property of our data. We therefore require a constructor operation make which takes a petrochemical value and a quantity (nonnegative real value) and produces a composite reading value. What we have here is an abstraction of a 'record' type data structure with two *fields*. The signature of make is

```
make : chemical real → reading
```

As an example, the reading that corresponds to an amount 90.0 of petrochemical pc1 is

```
make(pc1, 90.0)
```

In order to 'get at' the individual components of a reading value, we also need the accessor operations p–chem and amount with individual signatures

```
p-chem : reading → chemical ; amount : reading → real
```

If c denotes a petrochemical value and q denotes a quantity of petrochemical, the axioms satisfied by these accessors are

```
p-chem(make(c, q)) = c
amount(make(c, q)) = q
```

Finally, we need to compare different amounts of petrochemical. In particular, we must be able to order quantities and determine which is the larger or smaller of two quantities. An appropriate pair of operations is:

- smaller : real real → real an operation that takes two quantities and returns the smaller value of the two petrochemical quantities.
- larger : real real → real an operation that takes two quantities and returns the larger value of the two petrochemical quantities.

The corresponding specification Reading is shown in Fig. 11.11. Note that 'COMM' which appears to the right of the range of smaller and larger expresses the fact that these operations are commutative, which means that, for any two quantities $q1$ and $q2$,

```
SPEC   Reading
USING  Petrochemical  +  Real
SORT   reading
OPS
        make     :  chemical  real  ->  reading
        p-chem   :  reading  ->  chemical
        amount   :  reading  ->  real
        smaller  :  real  real  ->  real    (COMM)
        larger   :  real  real  ->  real    (COMM)
FORALL
     c           :  chemical
     q, q1, q2   :  real
AXIOMS:
   (1)   p-chem(make(c, q))  =  c
   (2)   amount(make(c, q))  =  q
   (3)   smaller(q1, q2)  =  IF  q1 > q2 THEN
                                      q2
                               ELSE  q1   ENDIF
   (4)   larger(q1, q2)   =  IF  q1 > q2  THEN
                                      q1
                               ELSE  q2  ENDIF
ENDSPEC
```

Figure 11.11 Algebraic specification Reading.

smaller(q1, q2) = smaller (q2, q1) and larger(q1, q2) = larger(q2, q1). This commutativity could be expressed by including these results as additional axioms and this issue will be taken up in the following chapter.

11.6.3 Specification of the data-store

We now turn our attention to the specification of the data-store itself. The corresponding abstract data type will be denoted by DataStore. To start, we need the constructor operations empty and add which will allow us to construct our data-store of readings:

- empty an operation that returns an empty data-store from which all other data-store values can be created.
- add an operation that adds a reading (a petrochemical type and a quantity) together with the name of the appropriate detector device (tank) to create a new data store.

Requesting the maximum or minimum amounts of petrochemical from a data-store to which no data has been added is an error, so that the operations max-level and min-level will be defined only over nonempty data-stores. A similar comment applies to the operations pc-level and pc-contents which return the current quantity and type of petrochemical in a stated tank respectively. Furthermore, it is only meaningful to apply these operations if the database contains at least one reading from the specified tank. We therefore have to impose a condition that states the circumstances under which the operation can be applied. Hence, we introduce the sort ne-datastore of nonempty data-stores which is a subsort of the other introduced sort datastore (which includes the empty data-store value empty). The signature of the operations of DataStore can now be stated and is shown in Fig. 11.12. The specification DataStore will use values from the sorts reading, name and chemical which are supplied by the independent modules Reading, Tank-Detector, and PetroChemical respectively.

```
SORTS  ne-datastore  datastore
SUBSORT  ne-datastore  <  datastore
OPS
      empty  :  ->  datastore
        add  :  datastore   name   reading   ->  ne-datastore
    isolate  :  datastore   name   ->  datastore
 global-max  :  ne-datastore   ->  real
 global-min  :  ne-datastore   ->  real
  max-level  :  ne-datastore   name   ->  real
  min-level  :  ne-datastore   name   ->  real
any-values?  :  datastore   name   ->  bool
pc-contents  :  ne-datastore   name   ->  chemical
   pc-level  :  ne-datastore   name   ->  real
full-warning?  :  datastore   ->  bool
      count  :  datastore   name   ->  nat
      total  :  datastore   ->  nat
```

Figure 11.12 Signature of the specification DataStore.

In the ensuing discussion, we use variable names:

- s to denote a data-store
- r to denote a reading
- n, n1 and n2 to denote detector device names (tanks)

11.6.4 Axioms for any-values?

We look firstly at the axioms associated with the operations with ranges of sort bool and start with any-values?. The derivation of the axioms that describe whether any reading exists in the data-store for a named detector (corresponding to an individual petrochemical tank) is straightforward.

If the data-store is empty, then obviously *no* readings will have been recorded for *any* detector. Thus

```
any-values?(empty, n) = false
```

and this holds for any detector device n. This is the first axiom of the specification DataStore as given in Fig. 11.13.

Furthermore, if the data-store has been formed by adding a reading from a named detector, then the enquiry asking whether there are any readings in the data-store from this same detector will obviously return true, that is

```
any-values?(add(s, n, r), n) = true
```

```
       SPEC  DataStore
       USING  Reading  +  Tank-Detector  +  Tank  + Boolean + Natural
       INCLUDING  PetroChemical  +  Real
       SORTS  ne-datastore  datastore
       SUBSORT  ne-datastore  <  datastore
       OPS
            empty  :   ->  datastore
              add  :   datastore   name   reading  ->  ne-datastore
         isolate  :   datastore   name   ->  datastore
      global-max  :   ne-datastore  ->  real
      global-min  :   ne-datastore  ->  real
       max-level  :   ne-datastore   name   ->  real
       min-level  :   ne-datastore   name   ->  real
     any-values?  :   datastore   name   ->  bool
     pc-contents  :   ne-datastore   name   ->  chemical
        pc-level  :   ne-datastore   name   ->  real
   full-warning?  :   datastore   ->  bool
           count  :   datastore   name  ->  nat
           total  :   datastore   ->  nat
       FORALL
             s  :   datastore
     n, n1, n2  :   name
             r  :   reading
       AXIOMS:
       (1)   any-values?(empty, n)  =  false
       (2)   any-values?(add(s, n2, r), n1)  =  IF  n1 == n2  THEN true
                                                 ELSE any-values?(s, n1) ENDIF
       (3)   full-warning?(empty)  =  false
       (4)   full-warning?(add(s, n, r))  =
                         IF  amount(r) == max-vol  THEN  true
                         ELSE  full-warning?(s)  ENDIF
       (5)   pc-contents(add(s, n2, r), n1)  =
                      ( IF  n1 == n2  THEN  p-chem(r)
                        ELSE  pc-contents(s, n1)  ENDIF )
                        IF  any-values?(add(s, n2, r), n1)
       (6)   pc-level(add(s, n2, r), n1)  =
                      ( IF  n1 == n2  THEN  amount(r)
                        ELSE  pc-level(s, n1)  ENDIF )
                        IF  any-values?(add(s, n2, r), n1)
       (7)   isolate(empty, n)  =  empty
       (8)   isolate(add(s, n2, r), n1)  =
                        IF  n1 == n2  THEN  add(isolate(s, n1), n1, r)
                        ELSE  isolate(s, n1)  ENDIF
       (9)   global-max(add(s, n, r))  =
                        IF  s == empty  THEN  amount(r)
                        ELSE  larger(amount(r), global-max(s))  ENDIF
      (10)   global-min(add(s, n, r))  =
                        IF  s == empty  THEN  amount(r)
                        ELSE  smaller(amount(r), global-min(s))  ENDIF
      (11)   max-level(add(s, n2, r), n1)  =
                        global-max(isolate(add(s, n2, r), n1))
                        IF any-values?(add(s, n2, r), n1)
```

Figure 11.13 Algebraic specification of a data-store.

```
(12)    min-level(add(s, n2, r), n1)  =
                    global-min(isolate(add(s, n2, r), n1))
                    IF any-values?(add(s, n2, r), n1)
(13)    count(empty, n)  =  0
(14)    count(add(s, n2, r), n1)  =  IF n1 == n2  THEN  1 + count(s, n1)
                                       ELSE  count(s, n1)  ENDIF
(15)    total(empty)  =  0
(16)    total(add(s, n, r))  =  1 + total(s)


ENDSPEC
```

Figure 11.13—*Contd.*

If, however, the reading was added to the data-store by another detector, then further study is needed

```
any-values?(add(s, n2, r), n1) = any-values?(s, n1)
```

These two axioms can be combined into one and the corresponding result is given by axiom (2) of Fig. 11.13, that is

```
any-values?(add(s, n2, r), n1) = IF n1 = = n2 THEN true

                              ELSE any-values?(s, n1) ENDIF
```

11.6.5 Axioms for full-warning?

We now turn our attention to the operation full-warning? which returns true if any tank has been recorded as full, false otherwise. If the datastore is empty, then full-warning? will return false. For the data-store add(s, n, r), in which the reading r is added to the data-store s, application of full-warning? will return true if the quantity of petrochemical contained in r is equal to max-vol. If this is not the case, we must repeat the operation on the rest of the data-store s. These results are expressed in axioms (3) and (4) of Fig. 11.13 where we have used the operation amount defined in Reading to select the *amount* of petrochemical from the composite data value r.

```
full-warning?(empty) = false

full-warning?(add(s, n, r)) =

                    IF amount(r) = = max-vol THEN true

                    ELSE full-warning?(s) ENDIF
```

11.6.6 Axioms for pc-contents and pc-level

The operation pc-contents is required to return the current type of petrochemical contained within the tank denoted by detector n1. It is only meaningful to apply this operation if the data-store is nonempty and has some existing data from that particular tank. We need to consider the outcome of the expression

```
pc-contents(add(s, n2, r), n1)
```

If n1 and n2 denote the same detector, then the value returned is simply p–chem(r) where the operation p–chem was introduced in Reading and accesses the petrochemical component from the reading r. If n1 and n2 denote different detectors, we must repeat the operation on the data-store s.

Although pc-contents is only defined over the subsort ne–datastore, we still have to consider the situation of a nonempty data-store that contains *no* readings from the required detector n1. Clearly, it is only meaningful to apply the operation pc-contents *if* the data-store already contains readings from n1, that is to say if any-values?(add(s, n2, r), n1) is true. We can impose this requirement by introducing the *conditional* axiom

```
pc-contents(add(s, n2, r), n1) =

        ( IF n1 = = n2 THEN p-chem(r)

        ELSE pc-contents(s, n1) ENDIF )

        IF any-values?(add(s, n2, r), n1)
```

A conditional axiom is one of the form l=r IF c and can only be applied when the pattern on its left-hand side l is matched and when the Boolean condition c evaluates to true for those same variables determined by the match. (It follows that all variables that occur in the condition c must also occur on the left-hand side l.)

A *conditional* axiom of the form l=r IF c presents no added problems with regards to equational logic since such an axiom can always be transformed into the *unconditional* axiom

```
l = IF c THEN r ELSE l ENDIF
```

This now raises the question of what we are to make of *syntactically* legal terms such as

```
pc-contents(add(new, dev-1, make(pc1, 20.0)), dev-2)
```

which returns a value of sort chemical. For this term, the data-store contains just the one reading from tank 1 (characterized by the detector dev–1) with tank 1 containing an amount 20.0 of petrochemical pc1. Requesting the current contents of tank 2 from this database (corresponding to the term above) is clearly a meaningless operation. This is reinforced by the fact that such a term *cannot* be reduced to one of the values of the sort chemical (that is to one of the values pc1, pc2, ..., pc5) using the axioms of the specification. The specification DataStore is therefore introducing a *new* value of sort chemical and, for this reason, the existing specification PetroChemical must be imported by means of the INCLUDING construct.

The conditional axiom satisfied by pc-level is structurally similar to that for pc-contents so we have

```
pc-level(add(s, n2, r), n1) =

        ( IF n1 = = n2 THEN amount(r)

        ELSE pc-level(s, n1) ENDIF )

        IF any-values?(add(s, n2, r), n1)
```

These axioms are (5) and (6) of Fig. 11.13. Note that the corresponding specification Real must also be imported using the INCLUDING construct for *initial* models of DataStore since we are extending Real with new values such as pc-level(add(new, n2, r), n1) when n1 and n2 denote *different* sensors (tanks).

11.6.7 Axioms for isolate

In the case of an empty data-store, we will define the outcome of isolate(empty, n) to be the empty data-store, so that for any tank n

```
isolate(empty, n) = empty
```

Consider next the outcome of isolate(add(s, n1, r), n1) where the most recently added reading comes from the *same* named tank whose readings we want to isolate. This last reading r from n1 needs to be added to the 'previous' isolated data-store which leads to the axiom

```
isolate(add(s, n1, r), n1) = add(isolate(s, n1), n1, r)
```

Finally, we need to consider the result of isolate(add(s, n2, r), n1) where n1 and n2 refer to *different* tanks. In this case, we do *not* add the reading from n2 so that

```
isolate(add(s, n2, r), n1) = isolate(s, n1)
```

These last two axioms can be combined to give

```
isolate(add(s, n2, r), n1) = IF n1 = = n2 THEN add(isolate(s, n1), n1, r)

                ELSE isolate(s, n1) ENDIF
```

The corresponding axioms for isolate are (7) and (8) of Fig. 11.13.

11.6.8 Axioms for global-max **and** global-min

These operations are defined for nonempty data-stores. If only one reading r has been added to the data-store, this single value will correspond to both the overall maximum and overall minimum quantity of petrochemical. The overall maximum and minimum are therefore given by amount(r) in this case, which leads to the axioms

```
global-max(add(empty, n, r)) = amount(r)

global-min(add(empty, n, r)) = amount(r)
```

For a data-store containing more than one reading, we simply need to compare the most recently added reading with the overall maximum (minimum) of the previously added readings. This produces the axioms

```
global-max(add(s, n, r)) = larger(amount(r), global-max(s))

global-min(add(s, n, r)) = smaller(amount(r), global-min(s))
```

The two axioms for each of these operations can be combined into one using the IF THEN ELSE construct and the corresponding axioms are (9) and (10) of Fig. 11.13.

11.6.9 Axioms for max-level and min-level

We now turn our attention to the two remaining operations with range sort real. The data-store will contain readings from potentially *all* the detectors and we need axioms for max-level and min-level which return the maximum and minimum quantities, respectively, recorded by a *given* detector device. We have to consider the outcome of expressions such as

```
max-level(add(s, n2, r), n1)
```

The values of max-level and min-level can be obtained directly from the appropriate 'isolated' data-stores that contain readings from a *given* tank. We simply need to apply the operations global-max and global-min to the relevant isolated data-store. This leads directly to the *conditional* axioms

```
max-level(add(s, n2, r), n1) =

                global-max(isolate(add(s, n2, r), n1))

                IF any-values?(add(s, n2, r), n1)

min-level(add(s, n2, r), n1) =

                global-min(isolate(add(s, n2, r), n1))

                IF any-values?(add(s, n2, r), n1)
```

which correspond to (11) and (12) of Fig. 11.13. Observe that it is only meaningful to apply these operations if the data-store contains at least one reading from the named tank. Note also that these terms can define new 'real' terms (sort values) in certain situations.

11.6.10 Natural-valued operations

The outcomes of both count(empty, n) and total(empty) are zero since no readings have been added to the data-store. In the case of total, adding a reading from *any* detector device will increment the previous value of total by one. These results are expressed in axioms (15) and (16)

$$total(empty) = 0$$

$$total(add(s, n, r)) = 1 + total(s)$$

Finally, the result of count(add(s, n2, r), n1) must be examined. If n1 and n2 refer to the one detector, the value of count(s, n1) is incremented, otherwise the outcome is count(s, n1). The corresponding axioms are (13) and (14).

The specification for DataStore is now complete and presented in Fig. 11.13.

Exercise 11.6 Produce axioms for an operation first-reading which takes a data-store and returns the first reading from *any* named tank (detector).

Exercise 11.7 Develop further operations for DataStore and produce axioms for your operations.

Exercise 11.8 Identify the atomic constructor, nonatomic constructor, and accessor operations for the specification DataStore.

Exercise 11.9 Use the axioms of DataStore to reduce the term d where

```
d = full-warning?(add(empty, dev-4, make(pc2, larger(3, max-vol))))
```

and hence determine whether a warning should be sounded!

11.7 PARAMETERIZATION

We now discuss in more detail, the production of generic specifications. Parameterization allows many different specifications to be derived as instances of one single parameterized specification. Our treatment of parameterization will focus on the production of SPEC modules as instances of a single parameterized SPEC module. Our specifications will be parameterized by module rather than simply by sort or operation. Required instances of a module are then obtained by supplying module expressions as actual arguments.

11.7.1 PROPS **modules and instantiation**

Initial models of SPEC modules have the property that all values of the carrier set of the algebra that interprets the specification can be expressed as ground terms, and terms that the axioms cannot show to be equivalent denote distinct values of the sort. On the other hand, PROPS modules do not enforce an initial interpretation, so the fact that two terms cannot be shown to be equivalent as a consequence of the axioms does *not* imply inequality.

Syntactically, PROPS modules are similar to SPEC modules in that they consist of sorts and (possibly) operations that satisfy some axioms; but, semantically, they define the properties of *all* algebras that satisfy the axioms (not just initial algebras). The important feature of PROPS modules is that they are used as *formal* parameter 'types' in parameterized specifications.

We declare a parameterized specification by incorporating a *formal parameter list* which occupies a distinguished position at the head of the declaration of the specification, so that, for the parameterized specification Generic-Spec with two formal parameters, we write

```
SPEC Generic-Spec(E1 : PROP1 && E2 : PROP2)
```

The formal parameters E1 and E2 are identifiers that stand for a SPEC module 'value' that is supplied to the parameterized specification on *instantiation*. The identifiers PROP1 and PROP2 denote PROPS modules.

We can think of a parameterized specification as a template. These templates must be *instantiated* with actual parameters (SPEC modules) 'plugged into them' in order to produce a normal SPEC module. As part of the instantiation process, we must match the generic parameters with actual parameters, just as we match actual and formal parameters in procedure subprograms. In the latter case, we must supply an actual parameter with the 'property requirement' that it is of the correct *data type*. For parameterized specifications, the actual parameter is a SPEC module that must *satisfy* the property requirements given in the PROPS module. The PROPS specification module therefore imposes a semantic interface requirement that any actual (SPEC) module must satisfy.

11.7.2 Three examples of PROPS specifications

The PROPS modules considered in this subsection all declare structure and property requirements. The first is the theory Elem (also called the trivial theory) whose only requirement is the existence of a sort named element and the corresponding PROPS module is shown in Fig. 11.14. The theory Elem specifies the class of *all* algebras and hence is extremely broad and general.

A second example is presented in Fig. 11.15 where we have included one constant (the nullary operation e) in the sort. The PROPS module Elem-with-e describes the class of all algebras with a nonempty carrier set. As a final example, we present a PROPS module Poset which requires that models have a binary infix Boolean-valued operation * which is reflexive and transitive. This is shown in Fig. 11.16 and corresponds to the theory of

```
PROPS  Elem
SORT   element
ENDPROPS
```

Figure 11.14 The class of all algebras.

```
PROPS   Elem-with-e
SORT    element
OP   e  :  ->  element
ENDPROPS
```

Figure 11.15   The class of all algebras with a nonempty carrier set.

```
PROPS   Poset
USING   Boolean
SORT    element
OPS
   _ * _  :  element  element  ->  bool
FORALL
e, e1, e2 : element
AXIOM  for reflexive law :
(1)  e * e  =  true
AXIOM  for transitive law :
(2)  e * e2  =  (e * e1) and (e1 * e2)

ENDPROPS
```

Figure 11.16   Class of partially ordered sets.

partially ordered sets. Note that the SPEC module Natural can satisfy Poset with the familiar binary operation '$\leqslant$' (*less than or equal to*). Natural can also satisfy Poset with the ordering relation '$\geqslant$' (*greater than or equal to*). A SPEC module can therefore satisfy a PROPS module in more than one way and each corresponds to what we call a *view*. This idea will be examined in more detail shortly.

Exercise 11.10 The *initial* interpretation of Elem is a sort with an empty carrier. Explain why.

Exercise 11.11 Explain why the SPEC modules Mode (Fig. 11.2) and PetroChemical (Fig. 11.6) both satisfy Elem-with-e.

11.8 PARAMETERIZED SPECIFICATIONS

We now develop two generic specifications, one describing a *list* of arbitrary elements, the other a *tuple* (or *ordered pair*) with first and second slots taken from arbitrary sort elements.

11.8.1 Generic list module

First, we present a parameterized list module List(E : Elem). The semantic interface here is the PROPS module Elem which demands only that the actual argument should possess a sort to be used as the elements for the list. The operations for our list are:

- [ ] an operation that denotes the empty list.
- −·− an operation that takes an element and inserts it into an existing list to produce a new list.
- _ app _ an operation that appends one list to another to produce a new list.

Note that all three operations are constructors and that [ ] and _._ are atomic constructors. The values of the sort list are terms of the form

   [ ], e1.[ ], e2.(e1.[ ]), ...

which are isomorphic to the lists [ ], [e1], [e2, e1], and so on. The first axiom

   [ ] app l1 = l1

expresses the fact that the empty list is a left identity for _app_ while the second axiom

   (e . l1) app l2 = e . (l1 app l2)

states that inserting an element e into a list l1 and concatenating the resulting list with a list l2 is the same as concatenating the lists l1 and l2 and then inserting e into that concatenated list.

Lists of natural numbers, Booleans, and characters are then obtained by instantiation in which appropriate module expressions are supplied as actual arguments for the formal parameter E. The specification is shown in Fig. 11.17.

We can then create a specification List-of-natural for a list of natural numbers as follows. First, we instantiate the parameterized specification List(E : Elem) by replacing the formal parameter E with the SPEC module Natural (which satisfies Elem). On instantiation,

```
SPEC   List ( E : Elem )
SORT   list
OPS
       [ ]   :   ->  list
     _ . _   :   element list  ->  list
   _ app _   :   list list  ->  list
FORALL
     l1,l2   :   list
         e   :   element
AXIOMS:
(1)    [ ] app l1  =  l1
(2)    (e . l1) app l2  =  e . (l1 app l2)
ENDSPEC
```

Figure 11.17 Parameterized specification for a generic list.

we create the *anonymous* module List(Natural) which is then 'USEd' (that is imported) by List-of-natural. The corresponding specification module List-of-natural is shown in Fig. 11.18.

```
SPEC   List-of-natural
USING  List(Natural)
ENDSPEC
```

Figure 11.18 Specification of a list of naturals.

Note that, on instantiation, the sort element of Elem is mapped to the sort nat of Natural. Following the Axis style, we use List(Natural) as an abbreviation that is equivalent to the longer, but more informative, expression

```
List(Natural FIT element AS nat)
```

An enlarged specification is presented in the Additional Problems in which 'head', 'tail', and 'postaffixing' operations are included together with subsorts.

Exercise 11.12 Use the axioms of List-of-natural to show that

$$(1.[\ ])\,app\,(2.[\ ]) == 1.2.[\ ]$$

is true whereas

$$(1.[\ ])\,app\,(2.[\ ]) == 2.1.[\ ]$$

is false.

Exercise 11.13 Enrich the parameterized specification List(E : Elem) by including an operation length which returns the number of items in a list.

11.8.2 Generic specification of a tuple (ordered pair)

As a second example, consider the specification of a tuple < f ; s > whose first (f) and second (s) slots are values drawn from arbitrary and possibly different sorts. By parameterizing the specification, we can introduce a generic 'record' data type whose fields can be constructed from any two specified data types. Using the formal parameters F and S to denote the first and second slots, the header of the parameterized specification is

```
SPEC Tuple( F : Elem && S : Elem )
```

so that Tuple requires two parameters, each of which satisfy Elem. We need the following three mixfix operations:

- < _ ; _ >   an operation that takes two values f ∈ element and s ∈ element and forms the tuple < f ; s >.

- 1-st _ an operation that takes a tuple and returns the first slot of the tuple, so that 1-st < f ; s > returns the value f.
- 2-nd _ an operation that takes a tuple and returns the second slot of the tuple, so that 2-nd < f ; s > returns the value s.

In order to 'disambiguate' the two sort identifiers element within the body of Tuple (because the formal parameters F and S are both of 'class' Elem), we express the signature of < _ ; _ > as

```
< _ ; _ > : F's element  S's element → tuple
```

where tuple is the sort introduced by the specification.

The corresponding parameterized specification is given in Fig. 11.19. The parameterized specification can be used to specify a two-dimensional co-ordinate pair < x ; y >, where x and y are natural numbers, corresponding, for example, to the position of a pixel on a graphics screen. The corresponding specification Pixel-Coordinate is shown in Fig. 11.20 where the sort tuple has been renamed pixel. A generic module List-of-tuple which specifies a list of tuples whose components (fields) are taken from arbitrary sorts is then given in Fig. 11.21. Note that when an instantiation occurs *inside* a parameterized module, such as is indicated in the second line of Fig. 11.21, formal parameters can be used as actual arguments. It is by means of this construct that, on instantiation with an actual parameter, *both* generic modules use the same actual arguments.

We will make use of some of these parameterized specifications in Chapter 14 when we develop an algebraic specification for a neural network.

```
SPEC   Tuple( F :  Elem   &&   S :  Elem )
SORT   tuple
OPS
   < _ ; _ >  :   F's element    S's element   ->   tuple
         1-st  :   tuple    ->   F's element
         2-nd  :   tuple    ->   S's element
FORALL
           f  :   F's element
           s  :   S's element
AXIOMS:
         1-st < f ; s >  =  f
         2-nd < f ; s >  =  s
ENDSPEC
```

Figure 11.19 Specification of a parameterized tuple.

```
SPEC   Pixel-Coordinate
USING   Tuple( Natural  &&  Natural )
        WITH   tuple  AS  pixel
ENDSPEC
```

Figure 11.20 Specification of a pixel coordinate.

```
SPEC  List-of-tuple( F : Elem  &&  S : Elem )
USING  List(Tuple( F  &&  S ))
ENDSPEC
```

Figure 11.21 Specification of a parameterized list of tuples.

11.9 FITTING MORPHISMS AND VIEWS

We have seen that entire algebraic specifications (with associated sorts, operations, and axioms) may be passed as parameters and their sorts and operations used in a new (instantiated) specification module. Instantiating a parameterized module means supplying actual SPEC modules which *satisfy* corresponding PROPS modules. The interface declarations contain not only syntactic requirements that an actual module must satisfy but also semantic interface requirements that actual SPEC modules must satisfy before they can be meaningfully substituted.

A specification S (which can be a SPEC or another PROPS module) is said to *satisfy* a PROPS module P if the family of algebras denoted by S is contained within the class of algebras denoted by P. As we saw with the PROPS module Poset, a SPEC module (in that case Natural) can satisfy a PROPS module in more than one way, each corresponding to a different *view*. We therefore need to be able to state precisely which particular view is required in an application and this can be achieved using a *fitting morphism*.

To match an actual parameter (a SPEC module) with a formal parameter (a PROPS module), we have to match the sorts and operations of the PROPS module with some (or all) of the sorts and operations from the SPEC module. A fitting morphism therefore provides a mapping from the sort and operation symbols in the PROPS module P to those in the actual SPEC module S, in such a manner that all the axioms of the PROPS module are satisfied.

Informally, a SPEC module S *satisfies* a PROPS module P if the axioms of S imply the axioms of P. Hence, when instantiating a module, the user will normally supply a fitting morphism that is the pair of mappings:

sorts of P → sorts of S

operations of P → operations of S

which fits P onto S. In Axis, this mapping of sorts is expressed as

```
p AS s
```

where the sort p, which belongs to the PROPS module P, is mapped to sort s of the SPEC module S, while the operation mappings will be written

```
op_i : d_i → r_i AS op_j
```

where the operation op_i with domain d_i and range r_i specified in the PROPS module is mapped to the identifier or mixfix template op_j. The components of a fitting morphism are applied simultaneously so that the order in which operations are listed is of no significance. It is precisely the *owned* signature of the PROPS module P that must be fitted.

Axis allows part or all of the fitting morphism from a PROPS module to be omitted through the use of default fitting morphisms when the mapping between sort(s) and/or operations can be completely determined. For example, as stated earlier, the instantiation List(Natural) is equivalent to

```
List(Natural FIT element AS nat)
```

11.10 SUMMARY

This chapter introduced the following concepts:

- Larger specifications can be built up hierarchically in bottom-up fashion from simpler algebraic specifications using certain *theory-building constructs*. In our specification language, these constructs include the *combinators*:
  - USING which imports an existing specification and permits 'read-only' access to that introduced module.
  - INCLUDING which provides a means of importing a specification without requiring it to be protected.
- *Module expressions* can be used to build complex specifications which are then incorporated into a specification by means of the USING or INCLUDING combinators. A module expression can be any one of:
  - the identifier of an unparameterized SPEC module
  - the instantiation of a parameterized SPEC module.
  - the recursive application of the *sum (union)* operation + to module expressions
- The production of *generic* specifications is discussed and PROPS modules introduced.
- A PROPS module specifies a collection of models and defines the properties of *all* algebras which satisfy the axioms and not just the *initial* algebra.
- PROPS modules are used as formal parameter types in parameterized specifications and *instantiating* a parameterized SPEC module means supplying actual SPEC modules which *satisfy* the corresponding PROPS modules.
- A specification S *satisfies* a PROPS module P if the family of algebras denoted by S is contained within the class of algebras denoted by P.
- A SPEC module can satisfy a PROPS module in more than one way, each corresponding to what is termed a *view*. We therefore need to state precisely which particular view is required in an application and this is accomplished by supplying a *fitting morphism*.

Three examples are developed which demonstrate how specifications can be built up hierarchically from smaller ones. In particular:

- An algebraic specification is developed for the estate agent's database which was specified earlier in Chapter 3 using VDM.
- A specification is also developed for a small control system which regulates the operations of filling and emptying petrochemical tanks.
- As a larger case study, the specification of a petrochemical storage plant monitoring system is built up.

ADDITIONAL PROBLEMS

11.1 Suppose the estate agent's database contains four houses, 'house1', 'house2', 'house3', 'house4', all of which are up for sale and that subsequently offers are made for 'house1', 'house2' and 'house3'. Write down the value of the corresponding database expression in terms of the constructors empty and !add-house. Use the axioms of Houses-for-sale to verify that:
   (a) 'house3' and 'house4' are in the database.
   (b) 'house3' is under offer.
   (c) 'house4' is for sale.

11.2 Amend the specification Houses-for-sale so that the price of a house is also added to the database when it is initially put up for sale.

11.3 Enrich the specification of the previous exercise by introducing an operation change-price which takes an address and a price and amends the sale price of the specified address to the amount given.

11.4 Introduce operations number-for-sale and number-under-offer which return the number of houses *for sale* and the number of houses *under offer* respectively.

11.5 Use the axioms of Tank to reduce each of the following expressions:
   (a) is-empty?(remove(add-chem(new, pc1, 30.0), 25.0))
   (b) is-empty?(remove(add-chem(new, pc2, 60.0), 60.0))
   (c) is-full?(change-pc(add-chem(new, pc1, 80.0), pc2, max-vol))

11.6 The specification Tank can be developed by including the additional Boolean-valued operations overflow-danger?, underflow-danger?, and mixing-danger? which return true in the event of attempting to add too much petrochemical, to remove too much petrochemical, and to add a different petrochemical to an existing tank respectively. Produce a revised specification that incorporates these extra operations.

11.7 Produce a VDM specification for Tank.

11.8 Suppose the data-store for the petrochemical plant specified by DataStore has *one* reading from each of three tank detectors dev-1, dev-2, and dev-3 containing 30.0 of pc1, 60.0 of pc2, and 15.0 of pc1 respectively, together with *two* readings from dev-4 with amounts 25.0 and 20.0 of petrochemical pc3. Produce an expression d for the corresponding value of the data-store and use the axioms of DataStore to evaluate the following terms:
   (a) max-level(d, dev-1)
   (b) min-level(d, dev-2)
   (c) any-values?(d, dev-4)
   (d) pc-level(d, dev-3)

11.9 A richer version of the parameterized list specification is provided by including the operations head, tail, and length together with a postaffixing operation

   _._ : list element → list

which overloads the existing 'cons' operation _._ : element list → list and so allows the operation of adding an element to a list to be defined for both ends of the list. Since head and tail are not defined for an empty list, we introduce the subsort ne-list of nonempty list values. The complete specification is given in Fig. 11.22.

(a) Identify the accessor and constructor operations.

(b) Suppose an application requires that the tail of an empty list should be an empty list. Amend the specification to include this requirement.

(c) Suppose an application requires a list whose elements are lists of natural numbers, for example, [[1,3], [3,6,2], [4]]. How can such a specification be derived from List(E : Elem)?

```
SPEC   List( E : Elem )
USING   Natural
SORTS   list   ne-list
SUBSORT   ne-list   <   list
OPS
    [ ]      :                        ->  list
    _ . _    :  element  list    ->  ne-list
    _ . _    :  list   element   ->  ne-list
    head _   :  ne-list          ->  element
    tail _   :  ne-list          ->  list
    _ app _  :  list  list       ->  list     (ASSOC)
    length _ :  list             ->  nat
FORALL
        e    :  element
    l, ll    :  list
AXIOMS for appending :
    [ ] app l  =  l
    (e . l) app ll  =  e . (l app ll)
AXIOM for post-affixing :
    l . e  =  l app (e . [ ])
AXIOMS for head and tail :
    head (e . l)  =  e
    tail (e . l)  =  l
AXIOMS for length :
    length [ ]  =  0
    length e . l  =  succ length l
ENDSPEC
```

Figure 11.22 Parameterized specification for a list.

11.10 Derive a generic specification Ordered-tree which specifies a binary tree with elements taken from an arbitrary sort. Produce SPEC modules Tree-of-natural, Tree-of-identifier whose elements are (a) natural numbers, (b) identifiers.

11.11 Produce a parameterized SPEC module Triple with header

```
Triple ( F : Elem && S : Elem && T : Elem )
```

with the four operations < _;_;_ >, 1-st, 2-nd, and 3-rd which construct a triple < f;s;t > (given three values f, s, t ∈ element); select the first slot (argument) the second slot, and the third slot of a given triple respectively.

11.12 Enrich Triple with an operation equals? which takes two triples and returns true if the values in corresponding slots are equal, false otherwise.

11.13 Instantiate the parameterized specification Tuple to produce a SPEC module for a record data type where the first field (slot) corresponds to a user-name and the second field corresponds to a user-number (a natural) and which possesses the field selectors get-name and get-number. State the fitting morphism explicitly.

11.14 Explain why the SPEC module Tank-Detector satisfies the PROPS module Elem-with-e and write down four possible fitting morphisms.

11.15 Given the PROPS module Elem-2

```
PROPS Elem-2

SORT element

OPS

    a : → element

    b : → element

ENDPROPS
```

explain why Tank-Detector satisfies Elem-2 and determine the number of different views and produce fitting morphisms for each view, for example

```
element AS name,
a : → element AS dev-1
b : → element AS dev-2
```

11.16 Use the axioms of the parameterized List module given in Fig. 11.17 to show that

$$(a.[\ ])\, app\, (b.[\ ]) = = a.b.[\ ]$$

where $a, b \in$ element.

11.17 The signature of a set of constructor operations that specifies the syntax of an abstract data type String of alphanumeric characters is given below

```
SORT string

OPS

    empty : → string

     make : alphanumeric string → string

    concat : string string → string
```

where the set of alphanumerics consists of the collection of readable ASCII characters. The operation make takes a single alphanumeric and forms the corresponding string of length 1, while concat joins together a left and right string to form a single string.

(a) The operation concat is associative. Give the right-hand side of the axiom that expresses this property, that is

```
concat(s1, concat(s2, s3)) =
```

where s1, s2, s3 ∈ string.

(b) Give the right-hand sides of the axioms that state that empty is a left and right identity for concat, that is

```
concat(s, empty) =   and   concat(empty, s) =
```

(c) Suppose an application requires two operations r-add and l-add which allow a character to be added at either end of a string. If the signatures of r-add and l-add are

```
r-add : string alphanumeric → string
```

```
l-add : alphanumeric string → string
```

produce axioms that define these operations in terms of the two other constructors make and concat.

(d) Enrich your specification by including an appropriate collection of accessor operations.

11.18 This extended problem develops an algebraic specification for the symbol table which was specified using VDM in Chapter 4. The operations for Symbol-Table are:

- init   sets up a new symbol-table.
- enter-block   prepares a new local naming scope.
- add   adds an identifier and its attribute(s) to the current block.
- insert   adds an identifier and its attribute(s) to the current block provided that identifier is *not* already present in the block.
- leave-block   discards entries from the current block and re-establishes the next outer scope.
- retrieve   returns the attribute(s) of an identifier from the innermost declaration.
- is-in-block?   returns true if a specified identifier has already been declared in the current block, false otherwise.

We have included the additional operation is-in-block? which is required to test for duplicate declarations within the same block. We also need an operation insert which adds an identifier and its attribute to the current block provided the identifier is not already in the current block. Our specification differs from the original one of Guttag (1977) in that the original did not preclude adding the same identifier more than once in the same block. The operation add will be declared as *hidden* and so will not be available to any *user* of the specification. We also include the Boolean-valued operation is-in-table? which checks whether it is meaningful to apply the operation retrieve.

Consider the notional program T1 which contains no variable declarations

```
  program T1;
  begin
*     write("limiting case")
  end.
```

The value of the symbol table st1 at the point marked ∗ is

```
st1 = enter-block(init)
```

since we must first prepare a local naming scope in anticipation of inserting variable identifiers and their attributes into the outermost block. If we now declare a single variable x : real in this outermost block, the value of the corresponding symbol table st2 at the point marked ∗ becomes

```
st2 = insert(enter-block(init), x, real)
    = !add(enter-block(init), x, real)
```

since the operations !add and insert have an identical semantics when inserting an identifier and its attribute into a freshly prepared (empty) block. Inserting an identifier and its attribute into an *empty* symbol table requires firstly the creation of a new empty block into which the identifier can be added. This result is expressed by the axiom

```
insert(init, id, a) = !add(enter-block(init), id, a)
```

where id belongs to the sort identifier and a belongs to the sort attribute. In the ensuing discussion, we assume id1, id2 ∈ identifier and a1, a2 ∈ attribute.

To add an identifier and its attribute to the current block, we need to check first whether that identifier has already been declared in the block. The operation is-in-block? provides the means for testing this. The axioms satisfied by

```
is-in-block? : symbol-table identifier → bool
```

are

```
is-in-block?(init, id1) = false

is-in-block?(enter-block(st), id1) = false

is-in-block?(!add(st, id1, a1), id2) = IF id1 = = id2 THEN true

                                  ELSE is-in-block?(st, id2) ENDIF
```

where st $\in$ symbol-table, the sort introduced by the specification Symbol-Table. The last axiom compares the specified identifier id2 with the most recently added identifier id1, returning true if they are the same with further enquiry needed of the remaining entries if they are not.

Having specified the semantics of is-in-block?, we can now produce axioms that relate insert and !add with

```
!add : symbol-table identifier attribute → ne-symbol-table
```

```
insert : symbol-table identifier attribute → ne-symbol-table
```

where ne-symbol-table is a subsort of symbol-table and denotes the set of nonempty symbol tables. (Note that we include enter-block(init) as a member of ne-symbol-table). As we observed earlier, if a new local naming scope has just been prepared, the operations insert and !add are equivalent, so that for any symbol table st

```
insert(enter-block(st), id1, a1) = !add(enter-block(st), id1, a1)
```

When adding an identifier to an existing block, we must ensure that it is not already in scope. This result is expressed by the axiom

```
insert(!add(st, id1, a1), id2, a2) =

          IF id1 = = id2 THEN !add(st, id1, a1)

          ELSE !add(insert(st, id2, a2), id1, a1) ENDIF
```

We now come to the axioms for the constructor

```
leave-block : ne-symbol-table → symbol-table
```

If the current value of the symbol table is st and we then prepare a new local naming scope st' = enter-block(st) and subsequently re-establish the next outer scope st" = leave-block(st'), we will recover the original value of the symbol-table st. This result is conveyed by the axiom

```
leave-block(enter-block(st)) = st
```

We now need to consider the outcome of leave-block(!add(st, id1, a1)). In this situation, we discard *all* entries from the current scope, then re-establish the next outer scope and this is described by the axiom

```
leave-block(!add(st, id1, a1)) = leave-block(st)
```

We therefore apply leave-block recursively to discard all the entries in the current block until we eventually reach the *base* case leave-block(st'), say, where the previous axiom applies.

Finally, we consider the axioms satisfied by

```
retrieve : ne-symbol-table identifier → attribute
```

where `retrieve` returns the attribute(s) associated with an identifier in the most local scope in which it occurs. Clearly this operation is only meaningful if the stated identifier exists somewhere in the symbol table. We therefore need to introduce another Boolean-valued operation

```
is-in-table? : symbol-table identifier → bool
```

which returns `true` if the specified identifier is in the symbol-table, `false` otherwise. The axioms satisfied by `is-in-table?` are seen to be

```
is-in-table?(init, id1) = false

is-in-table?(enter-block(st), id1) = is-in-table?(st, id1)

is-in-table?(!add(st, id1, a1), id2) = IF id1 == id2 THEN true

                                ELSE is-in-table?(st, id2) ENDIF
```

and we can now produce *conditional* axioms for `retrieve`, guarded by the predicate `is-in-table?`

```
retrieve(enter-block(st), id1) =

                    retrieve(st, id1) IF is-in-table?(st, id1)

retrieve(!add(st, id1, a1), id2) =

                    ( IF id1 == id2 THEN a1

                    ELSE retrieve(st, id2) ENDIF )

                    IF is-in-table?(!add(st, id1, a1), id2)
```

The complete specification is shown in Fig. 11.23.

(a) Given the program EX1 below

```
program EX1;
var
    x : real;
    procedure john;
    var
        y : char;
 *        .
          .
    end;
      .
      .
  end.
```

```
SPEC   Symbol-Table
USING  Identifier + Attribute + Boolean
SORTS  symbol-table  ne-symbol-table
SUBSORT ne-symbol-table  <  symbol-table
OPS
  init        :  -> symbol-table
  enter-block :  symbol-table -> ne-symbol-table
  leave-block :  ne-symbol-table -> symbol-table
  !add        :  symbol-table identifier attribute -> ne-symbol-table
  insert      :  symbol-table identifier attribute -> ne-symbol-table
  retrieve    :  ne-symbol-table identifier -> attribute
  is-in-block? :  symbol-table identifier -> bool
  is-in-table? :  symbol-table identifier -> bool
FORALL
        st   :  symbol-table
    idl, id2 :  identifier
      al, a2 :  attribute
AXIOMS:
 (1) insert(init, idl, al) = !add(enter-block(init), idl, al)
 (2) insert(enter-block(st), idl, al)  =  !add(enter-block(st), idl, al)
 (3) insert(!add(st, idl, al), id2, a2)  =
                      IF  idl == id2  THEN  !add(st, idl, al)
                      ELSE  !add(insert(st, id2, a2), idl, al)  ENDIF
 (4) leave-block(enter-block(st))  =  st
 (5) leave-block(!add(st, idl, al))  =  leave-block(st)
 (6) is-in-block?(init, idl)  =  false
 (7) is-in-block?(enter-block(st), idl)  =  false
 (8) is-in-block?(!add(st, idl, al), id2)  =
                      IF  idl == id2  THEN  true
                      ELSE  is-in-block?(st, id2)  ENDIF
 (9) is-in-table?(init, idl)  =  false
(10) is-in-table?(enter-block(st), idl)  =  is-in-table?(st, idl)
(11) is-in-table?(!add(st, idl, al), id2)  =
                      IF  idl == id2  THEN  true
                      ELSE  is-in-table?(st, id2)  ENDIF
(12)  retrieve(enter-block(st), idl)  =
                      retrieve(st, idl)  IF  is-in-table?(st, idl)
(13)  retrieve(!add(st, idl, al), id2)  =
                      ( IF  idl == id2  THEN  al
                      ELSE  retrieve(st, id2)  ENDIF )
                      IF  is-in-table?(!add(st, idl, al), id2)
ENDSPEC
```

Figure 11.23 Specification for a symbol table.

show that the value of the symbol table st1 at the point * is

```
insert(enter-block(insert(init, x, real)), y, char)
```

which rewrites to

```
!add(enter-block(!add(enter-block(init), x, real)), y, char)
```

(b) Use the axioms of Symbol-Table to show that:
   (i) is-in-block?(st1, x) = false
   (ii) is-in-block?(st1, y) = true
   (iii) is-in-block?(st1, z) = false
   (iv) is-in-table?(st1, x) = true
   (v) is-in-table?(st1, y) = true
   (vi) is-in-table?(st1, z) = false
   (vii) retrieve(st1, y) = char
   (viii) retrieve(st1, x) = real
   (ix) leave-block(st1) = !add(enter-block(init), x, real)

(c) Consider now the program EX2 shown below

```
    program EX2;
    var
        x : real;
 *      y : integer;
        procedure lee;
        var
            x : boolean;
**          y : char;
            .
            .
        end;
        .
        .
    end.
```

The expressions corresponding to the values st2 and st22 of the symbol table at the points marked * and ** respectively are

```
st2 = insert(insert(init, x, real), y, integer)
```

```
st22 = insert(insert(enter-block(st2), x, boolean), y, char)
```

Use the axioms to show firstly that

```
st2 = !add(!add(enter-block(init), y, integer), x, real)
```

```
st22 = !add(!add(enter-block(!add(!add(enter-block(init),

       y, integer), x, real)), y, char), x, boolean)
```

and also to show that:
  (i) is-in-block?(st2, x) = true
  (ii) is-in-block?(st2, y) = true
  (iii) is-in-table?(st22, x) = true
  (iv) is-in-table?(st22, y) = true
  (v) leave-block(st22) = st2
  (vi) retrieve(st2, x) = real
  (vii) retrieve(st2, y) = integer
  (viii) retrieve(st22, x) = boolean
  (ix) retrieve(st22, y) = char

REFERENCE

Guttag, J. (1977) Abstract Data Types and the Development of Data Structures, *Communications of the ACM*, **20**, 396–404.

12

CANONICAL TERMS AND PROOF OBLIGATIONS

12.1 INTRODUCTION

This chapter considers the proof obligations that should be discharged both prior to and as part of the process of validating an algebraic specification.

For VDM specifications, we have seen that the proof obligations concern *satisfiability* whereby, for each operation, we must prove that an output state exists given that the operation's pre-conditions have been met and that all output states are valid. In the case of the algebraic approach, discharging the relevant proof obligations often involves *structural induction* and this proof technique is examined. We also look more formally at the notions of *completeness* and *consistency* in the context of algebraic specification.

An important aspect of proof obligations for algebraic specifications concerns the verification that an identified collection of terms, drawn from the term algebra, constitutes a set of *canonical terms* (*forms*) for a specification. These ideas were introduced in Chapter 10 along with the *quotient term* and *canonical term* algebras. We recall that the canonical term algebra is important because it is an initial model and can often be generated directly from a subset of the constructor operations (that is from the *reduced expressions* that involve compositions of the atomic constructors). Initial models are widely used for algebraic specifications because they provide precisely what the specification requires and nothing more. Initial models have no superfluous elements (*no junk*) and do not force two values of the data type to be equal that were meant to be distinct (*no confusion*). They therefore provide faithful interpretations of a specification and so are often used as the standard representational model of a specification.

Discharging the proof obligations for algebraic specifications involves structural induction and we should say at the outset that although the method of proof follows a well-trodden path, proofs for even small specifications can involve lengthy manipulations. The aim of this chapter, therefore, is to inform the reader how we would expect them to *use* these formal ideas and techniques. We would not expect the reader to prove *everything* formally, but to understand the principles involved in discharging the proof obligations. This should give a better understanding of the nature of the algebraic approach itself.

The purpose of this chapter, therefore, is to give the reader an insight into this more formal aspect of algebraic specification. We discuss also the *attributes* that operations may possess such as *associativity* and *commutativity* and show that such attributes can often be proved as a direct consequence of the axioms. The proof of such properties often provides a valuable check on the *validity* of the specification with respect to its proposed interpretation. The chapter concludes with a summary of the main results.

12.2 PROOF OBLIGATION: CANONICAL TERMS

We recall from Chapter 10 that given a specification S, then an algebra whose carrier set contains the entire set of ground (variable-free) terms generated using the signature of S is the *term algebra* of S. The effect of the axioms of S is to partition these terms into a number of different equivalence classes with each equivalence class containing all those terms that the axioms identify as 'equal'. The resulting algebra whose carrier set consists of these equivalence classes is the *quotient term algebra*, which is an *initial* model. For the quotient term algebra, each element of its carrier set is an equivalence class of terms.

If we now isolate *one* term from each of the different equivalence classes (that is choose one member from each class as a 'representative' of that class), then the collection of all such terms constitutes a set of *canonical terms* (*forms*). The algebra whose carrier set is made up from this collection of canonical terms is called the *canonical term algebra*, which is isomorphic to the quotient term algebra and is, therefore, also an *initial* model. These ideas are illustrated in Fig. 12.1.

The importance of canonical forms is that every term that can be generated using the signature is equivalent to one of these canonical forms. The collection of canonical terms therefore provides a representation of all the distinct symbolic values of the sort. These observations lead us directly to identify the following proof obligation for an algebraic specification:

- The assertion that a set of terms constitutes a set of canonical forms must be proved by demonstrating that every (ground) term generated from the signature is equivalent to one and only one of the canonical forms.

To prove this result, we use *structural induction* over the axioms.

12.2.1 Canonical terms and reduced expressions

From the very outset, we have built up specifications by supplying a collection of constructor (and accessor) operations and then dividing the constructor operations into two groups, namely *atomic* and *nonatomic* constructors. We can now let the cat out of the bag—the collection of atomic constructors provides us immediately with a means of generating a set of canonical forms. The collection of reduced terms, that is terms involving

Carrier set of the term algebra

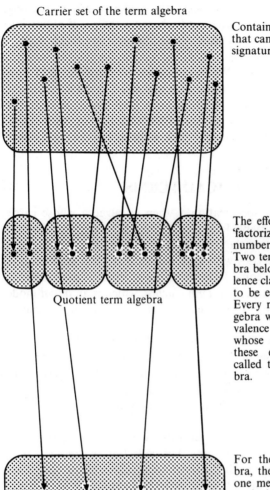

Contains all the ground terms that can be generated using the signature of the specification.

Quotient term algebra

The effect of the axioms is to 'factorize' all the terms into a number of equivalence classes. Two terms from the term algebra belong to the same equivalence class if they can be shown to be equal using the axioms. Every member of the term algebra will belong to one equivalence class. The algebra whose carrier set consists of these equivalence classes is called the quotient term algebra.

Canonical term algebra

For the canonical term algebra, the carrier set consists of one member from each of the equivalence classes. Such a collection of terms constitutes a set of canonical forms. The cardinality of this set gives the number of distinct values of the abstract data type.

Figure 12.1   The relation between the term, quotient term and canonical term algebras.

legal compositions of the atomic constructors, often provides us with a set of canonical forms. For example, with the stack, we have asserted that a set of canonical forms is given by the set of terms

{init, push(init, e1), push(push(init, e1), e2), ...}

for all e1, e2, ... ∈ nat. Clearly, this assertion should be proved and will be demonstrated shortly.

We must emphasize that, with the examples we have looked at, it has been our intuitive understanding of the required properties of an abstract data type that has helped us to identify a set of atomic constructors. It is this knowledge that provides the vital bridge between our perceived model of the data type and the identification of an appropriate set of atomic constructors that realizes this model. Having identified the atomic constructors, we can then systematically generate a set of canonical forms and so construct an abstract implementation in the form of an initial canonical term algebra. A rather useful analogy here is to think of atomic constructors as operations that create values of the abstract data type while nonatomic constructors describe how these values can be transformed to other values of the type (that is describe their functional behaviour).

Of course, intuition can lead us astray by producing, for example, a set of reduced terms (involving what is perceived to be a set of atomic constructors) that are *not* canonical forms. We will explore this aspect shortly by considering the specification of a *set* data type. These issues emphasize the importance of recognizing the appropriate proof obligation and knowing how to discharge it.

12.3 PROOF OBLIGATIONS: CONSISTENCY AND COMPLETENESS

Two fundamental concepts associated with *any* formal theory concern the *consistency* and *completeness* of the theory. We need to look briefly at these ideas in the context of algebraic specifications as *theory presentations*.

12.3.1 Consistency

Consistency requires that at least one model of the specification can be found. In other words, no contradictory theorems can be derived. For algebraic specifications, consistency presents no problem since one model can always be constructed from the specification, namely the quotient term algebra.

12.3.2 Completeness

Completeness, in the context of algebraic specification, demands that all the required properties of our data type can be deduced from the axioms of the presentation, so that any model of the theory will satisfy those properties. Completeness therefore demands that axioms are included that allow terms that are *intended* to be equivalent to be identified as such.

The proof obligation for *completeness*, therefore, is

- Every expression that can be made up from the constructors is equivalent to one in the proposed set of canonical forms.

which essentially restates our first proof obligation above.

12.3.3 Sufficient completeness

In the context of algebraic specifications, completeness therefore requires that terms that are 'intended' to be equivalent should be recognized as such. In other words, the axioms of a specification need to state what we expect of the behaviour of an abstract data type and we say that the specification is *sufficiently complete* if these expectations are met. It was

Guttag (1977) who introduced the qualifier 'sufficiently' in order to emphasize this 'expectational' aspect of completeness. It is worth expanding on this concept a little.

When a new data type is being specified that uses *existing* specifications as a basis (in the sense of importing sorts and/or operations and/or values from those existing data types), the results of all well-formed expressions that can be constructed using the operations of the new type (constructor and accessor) should *either* belong to the new type *or* be reducible by the axioms (of the new specification) to values of the existing types. A specification that has this property is said to be *sufficiently complete*. Identification of a set of canonical forms for a data type and the construction of axioms showing how each accessor and nonatomic constructor acts upon the atomic constructors provides a systematic and adequate procedure for constructing sufficiently complete theories.

12.3.4 Extensibility (conservative extension)

As we saw in the previous chapters, theory presentations generally 'use' or 'import' other existing theories in the sense of including references to separately defined theories. In this manner, hierarchical specifications are built up in bottom-up fashion. For example, the specification DataStore of Fig. 11.13 uses the theories Natural and Boolean and so allows the definition of the operations total and any-values? which return the number of readings in the data-store and whether any readings have been recorded from a named tank respectively. The construction of such hierarchical specifications promotes *reusability* at the specification level. It follows that, in order to reap the benefits of this hierarchical approach, each new level of the specification hierarchy should preserve the structure of the algebras introduced at the previous (lower) levels. The desirability of promoting reusability will therefore impose constraints at each level of the hierarchy.

A specification that 'extends' an existing specification in this way should therefore preserve the properties of the original specification and so it should be proved that the operations of the new specification introduce no *junk* and no *confusion*.

12.3.5 Validating an algebraic specification

We made the point earlier that the axioms of a specification need to state what we expect regarding the behaviour of an abstract data type. It follows that, as part of the process of *validating* an algebraic specification, we should ensure that the axiomatization has no undesired consequences such as identifying as equivalent terms that were meant to be different. Hence, as part of the process of *validating* a specification, we need to recognize the following proof obligation for *consistency*.

- No two terms in the designated set of canonical forms will be forced to be equivalent as a consequence of the axioms.

12.3.6 Termination

One further issue that should be considered concerns the termination of a term rewriting system. For example, the pair of rewrite rules

```
john → lee
lee → john
```

will result in an infinite sequence of rewrites. In Chapter 10, we observed that a set of rewrite rules is *finitely convergent* if it is both

1. *Church–Rosser*—the order of applying the rules does not affect the result.
2. *Noetherian*—the set of rewrite rules is terminating.

Such a set of rewrite rules is also called *canonical*.

In general, it is undecidable whether an *arbitrary* set of rewrite rules is terminating, although methods have been devised for proving termination for certain types of sets of rewrite rules. The methods involve mathematical ideas which are beyond the scope of this book and the interested reader is referred to Huet and Oppen (1980) for a comprehensive survey of term rewriting systems.

Suffice it to say that in the case of typical term rewriting systems for abstract data types, it is possible to produce rules which are both Church–Rosser and terminating. In practice, following the approach we have adopted in this book, it is comparatively straightforward to ensure that a set of axioms will be finitely convergent. On this point, it is worth repeating an observation made by Goguen and Winkler (1988), who developed the executable algebraic specification language OBJ3. They remarked that they had run thousands of reductions (of terms) on hundreds of examples (of specifications) and had hardly ever encountered problems with canonicity (finite convergence).

12.4 SPECIFICATION OF A SET

Before embarking on the formal aspects of structural induction and its application to discharging proof obligations, we examine the specification of a *set* data type. We have seen that identification of a set of atomic constructors leads us immediately to a set of canonical forms composed from those atomic constructors. However, as we remarked at the time, intuition might lead us astray, as we now show with the specification Funny-Set for a 'set' of natural numbers. This example demonstrates that having identified (what is apparently) a set of atomic constructors, the corresponding set of reduced expressions composed from these atomic constructors does *not* constitute a set of canonical forms.

12.4.1 Requirement

To keep the discussion as simple as possible, we include just four operations:

- empty   a nullary operation that returns an empty set $\{\ \}$ ($\emptyset$).
- add   an operation that adds a natural number to an existing set to produce a new set.
- delete   an operation that removes a specified natural number from a set to produce a new set.
- is-in?   an operation that returns true if a specified natural number is a member of a set and false otherwise.

Of course, a more useful specification would include the operations of set union ($\cup$) and intersection ($\cap$) and this is developed in the additional problems at the end of the chapter.

The two atomic constructors for this abstract data type are empty and add. The operation delete is nonatomic, a result we will formally prove later, while the operation is-in? is an accessor, so that a sufficiently complete specification is given by version 1 in Fig. 12.2. The reduced expressions of this specification are terms of the form

    add(... add(add(empty,e1),e2) ... ,en)

where $e1, e2, \ldots, en \in$ nat. Using standard mathematical notation, this reduced form corresponds to the set with n elements $\{e_1, e_2, \ldots, e_n\}$.

```
SPEC Funny-Set
USING  Natural  +  Boolean
SORT set
OPS
    empty  :   -> set
     add   :  set  nat  -> set
   delete  :  set  nat  -> set
    is-in? :  set  nat  -> bool
FORALL
        s  :  set
  n1, n2   :  nat
AXIOMS:
  (1)  is-in?(empty, n1)  =  false
  (2)  is-in?(add(s, n1), n2)  =  IF  n1 == n2  THEN  true
                                  ELSE  is-in?(s, n2)  ENDIF
  (3)  delete(empty, n1)  =  empty
  (4)  delete(add(s, n1), n2)  =  IF  n1 == n2  THEN  delete(s, n2)

                                  ELSE  add(delete(s, n2), n1)  ENDIF
ENDSPEC
```

Figure 12.2 Algebraic specification of a set – version 1.

Consider now the two reduced expressions s1 and s2 where

    s1 = add(add(empty, 3), 2)

    s2 = add(add(empty, 2), 3)

Using the axioms of Fig. 12.2, it is *not* possible to derive the theorem s1 = s2 from the specification because there are no axioms whose left-hand sides have add as their leftmost outermost operation. It follows that s1 and s2 denote different terms.

However, this is incompatible with one of the fundamental properties of sets, namely that the order of insertion of elements into a set is irrelevant (that is the sets $\{3,2\}$ and $\{2,3\}$ are identical). This is alarming since expressions that the specification identifies as *different* are intended to denote the *same* set. This problem did not arise with the previous specifications such as the stack, queue and binary tree. In those examples, it happens that each reduced form is also a canonical term so that the algebra whose carrier set consists of this collection of reduced expressions will be a canonical term algebra.

In the case of the stack, every reduced expression (such as push(push(init, 2), 3)) has a *unique* stack value (a stack with the value 2 on the bottom and 3 on the top) associated with it. Also, every required stack value has a unique reduced term that denotes it. The basic difference between stacks (queues) and sets is that whereas the order in which elements are pushed onto a stack (added to a queue) is important, the order in which elements are added to a set is of no consequence.

A further problem with the above specification is that it does *not* meet a second fundamental property of sets, namely that inserting an element more than once will leave the value of the set unaltered, that is add(add(s, n), n) = add(s, n). The equivalence of such terms cannot be shown using the axioms of Fig. 12.2. The specification is therefore not complete since it fails to identify terms that were intended to be equivalent as such. Hence, for the specification Funny-Set, the set of reduced expressions does *not* provide a set of canonical forms.

12.4.2 Additional axioms

The basic problem with our specification Set is that, while it defines an abstract data type, it does not adequately capture the entire mathematical concept of a 'set'. The axiomatization is sufficiently complete as defined earlier but extra axioms are needed that embrace the two additional properties of sets described above.

The property that the order of insertion of elements into a set is not important is expressed by the axiom

add(add(s, n1), n2) = add(add(s, n2), n1)

while the requirement that an element may be added to a set more than once without altering its value is expressed by

add(add(s, n), n) = add(s, n)

where s ∈ set and n, n1, n2 ∈ nat. The above axioms can be combined into one and the revised specification, with the additional axiom (5), is shown in Fig. 12.3 (version 2). It is important to observe that these additional axioms present problems when treated as rewrite rules. The introduction of axiom (5) results in a nonfinitely convergent set of rewrite rules since it results in a nonterminating sequence of rewrites. Inclusion of axiom (5) leads to an infinite loop of rewrites and so cannot appear in any prototype of the specification that uses term rewriting for its operational semantics.

Axiom (5) states that the set denoted by a reduced expression is independent of the order in which different elements are inserted. We now have the situation that there are many equivalent reduced expressions that correspond to a single set value—for example, the set $\{e_1, e_2, \ldots, e_n\}$ (with n distinct values) will have $n!$ *equivalent* reduced expressions that denote the set. We therefore have a one-to-one correspondence between an equivalence class of reduced expressions and the set value it denotes. Hence, two reduced set expressions s_1, s_2 ∈ set will denote the same set value if they belong to the same equivalence class of reduced expressions.

We can still derive a set of canonical terms by selecting *one* member of each equivalence class of reduced expressions as a 'standard' canonical term. A suitable set of

```
SPEC Set
USING  Natural  +  Boolean
SORT set
OPS
   empty  :   ->  set
    add   :  set  nat  ->  set
  delete  :  set  nat  ->  set
   is-in? :  set  nat  ->  bool
FORALL
       s  :  set
  n1, n2  :  nat
AXIOMS:
  (1)  is-in?(empty, n1)  =  false
  (2)  is-in?(add(s, n1), n2)  =  IF  n1 == n2  THEN   true
                                  ELSE  is-in?(s, n2)  ENDIF
  (3)  delete(empty, n1)  =  empty
  (4)  delete(add(s, n1), n2)  =  IF  n1 == n2  THEN  delete(s, n2)
                                  ELSE  add(delete(s, n2), n1)  ENDIF
  (5)  add(add(s, n1), n2)  =  IF  n1 == n2  THEN  add(s, n1)
                               ELSE  add(add(s, n2), n1)  ENDIF
ENDSPEC
```

Figure 12.3 Algebraic specification of a set – version 2.

canonical terms for Set would be terms involving empty and add in which the elements are inserted using some *ordering relation* on the natural numbers and with no duplicates.

A simple example should help focus these ideas. Given the set {1,2,3}, the corresponding equivalence class of reduced expressions includes the six members

```
add(add(add(empty, 1), 2), 3) ,  add(add(add(empty, 1), 3), 2),
add(add(add(empty, 2), 1), 3) ,  add(add(add(empty, 2), 3), 1),
add(add(add(empty, 3), 1), 2) ,  add(add(add(empty, 3), 2), 1)
```

and a suitable 'standard' canonical form is add(add(add(empty, 1), 2), 3) where we use the ordering relation '<' whereby the elements are inserted in ascending order. Each member belonging to the carrier set of the canonical term algebra would then be a reduced expression involving only the atomic constructors add and empty in which elements are inserted in order and with duplicates removed. Later, we will use structural induction to *prove* that such a collection of reduced expressions, with the elements inserted in ascending order, does indeed constitute a set of canonical forms.

12.4.3 Use of hidden operations

We could have followed the example of the specification Ordered-tree of Chapter 9 and introduce the exportable constructor build : set nat → set which constructs set expressions that conform to the above 'standard' form in which elements are inserted in ascending order with no duplicates. The constructor add would then be *hidden* so that it could not be used outside the specification Set and users of Set would view empty and build as their atomic constructors. By direct analogy with the specification Ordered-tree, the two additional axioms for build that must be added to Set are

```
build(empty, n)      = !add(empty, n)

build(!add(s, n1), n2) = IF n1 = = n2 THEN !add(s, n1)

                         ELSEIF n1 < n2 THEN !add(build(s, n1), n2)

                         ELSE !add(build(s, n2), n1) ENDIF
```

Exercise 12.1 Use the above axioms for build to show that

```
build(build(build(empty, 3), 1), 2) = !add(!add(!add(empty, 1), 2), 3)
```

Exercise 12.2 Use axiom (5) of version 2 of Set to show that

```
add(add(add(add(add(empty, 3), 1), 2), 1), 4) = add(add(add(add(empty, 3), 2), 4), 1)
```

12.4.4 Specification of a bag

It is interesting to observe that if axioms (4) and (5) of Fig. 12.3 were replaced by

```
delete(add(s, n1), n2) = IF n1 = = n2 THEN s ELSE add(delete(s, n2), n1) ENDIF
```

and

```
add(add(s, n1), n2) = add(add(s, n2), n1)
```

respectively, then Fig. 12.3 would specify a *bag* data type. Although, like sets, the order of insertion of elements into a bag is not important, the value of a bag is altered if an existing element is added more than once, for example, the bags [1,2] and [1,1,2] are not the same.

12.4.5 Other atomic constructors for a set data type

The specification of a set data type has a number of other interesting features that are worth exploring. Firstly, although we chose empty and add as the atomic constructors, other atomic constructors could be chosen. For example, the three constructors:

- empty : → set
- { _ } : nat → set
- _ U _ : set set → set

form a collection of atomic constructors. The second operation takes a natural number n and produces the corresponding singleton set {n} while the third operation U is the familiar set union operation ∪. With this collection of atomic constructors, the mathematical set {1,5,3} is represented by the expression {1} U {5} U {3}. A sufficiently complete specification results by considering the outcomes of the operations is-in? and delete acting on these three atomic constructors. The corresponding axioms are

```
is-in?(empty, n) = false
  is-in?({n1}, n2) = IF n1 = = n2 THEN true ELSE false ENDIF
is-in?(s1 U s2, n) = is-in?(s1, n) or is-in?(s2, n)
delete(empty, n) = empty
  delete({n1}, n2) = IF n1 = = n2 THEN empty ELSE {n1} ENDIF
delete(s1 U s2, n) = delete(s1, n) U delete(s2, n)
```

where n, n1, n2 $\in$ nat and s, s1, s2 $\in$ stack.

On a point of some subtlety, although this may appear at first sight to specify a set, it is unfortunately deficient with regards to the expected mathematical properties of a set in four respects!

1. With reference to set union, the empty set ($\emptyset$) is an *identity* element, that is the empty set has the property:

    empty U s = s   and   s U empty = s

2. The union operation is *commutative*:

    s1 U s2 = s2 U s1

3. The union operation is *associative*:

    s1 U (s2 U s3) = (s1 U s2) U s3

4. The union operation is *idempotent*:

    s U s = s

These results cannot be derived as a consequence of the six axioms given above and need to be added to the specification. The resulting specification with its eleven axioms is shown in Fig. 12.4 (version 3).

12.5 STRUCTURAL INDUCTION

Discharging the proof obligations for algebraic specifications usually involves structural induction and there is no doubt that the proofs, even for small specifications, can be cumbersome. The aim of the rest of this chapter, therefore, is to inform readers how we would expect them to *use* these formal ideas and techniques. We would not expect them to prove *everything* formally, but to understand the principles involved in discharging the proof obligations. This should give a better understanding of the nature of the algebraic approach itself.

To keep the discussion as simple as possible, we will use the example of the specification Stack of Fig. 9.7 for an unbounded stack of natural numbers and prove that:

1. The collection of reduced expressions constitutes a set of canonical forms.
2. The specification is *sufficiently complete*.

```
SPEC Set
USING  Natural  +  Boolean
SORT set
OPS
   empty   :   ->  set
   { _ }   :   nat  ->  set
   _ U _   :   set  set  ->  set
   delete  :   set  nat  ->  set
   is-in?  :   set  nat  ->  bool
FORALL
   s, s1, s2, s3  :  set
   n, n1, n2      :  nat
AXIOMS:
   (1)  is-in?(empty, n)    =  false
   (2)  is-in?({n1}, n2)    =  IF  n1 == n2  THEN  true  ELSE  false  ENDIF
   (3)  is-in?(s1 U s2, n)  =  is-in?(s1, n) or is-in?(s2, n)
   (4)  delete(empty, n)    =  empty
   (5)  delete({n1}, n2)    =  IF  n1 == n2  THEN  empty  ELSE  {n1}  ENDIF
   (6)  delete(s1 U s2, n)  =  delete(s1, n)  U  delete(s2, n)
   (7)  empty U s  =  s
   (8)  s U empty  =  s
   (9)  s1  U  s2  =  s2  U  s1
   (10) s1 U (s2 U s3)  =  (s1 U s2) U s3
   (11) s U s  =  s
ENDSPEC
```

Figure 12.4 Algebraic specification of a set – version 3.

The formal reasoning used to prove these properties is based on *structural induction* (also known as *data type induction*) and the arguments used can similarly be applied to prove corresponding properties for the specifications of the previous chapters. Structural induction is an extension of one of the classical proof techniques in mathematics known as *mathematical induction*. This idea was introduced at the end of Chapter 2 and used informally in Chapter 5 where the technique was applied to prove that an explicit specification satisfied an implicit one. The idea of structural induction is not always immediately accessible, so we use the example of the stack to ease the analysis and give the reader confidence with the approach. The analysis scales up for larger examples without too much difficulty apart from the increased notation involved.

Structural induction is similar to the principle of mathematical induction over the integers. In the case of algebraic specifications, in order to prove that some property (predicate) P holds for all values of the data type, we have to demonstrate that the property is valid for all syntactically legal applications of the operations that produce values of the data type.

Suppose the specification of an abstract data type T has v constructor operations $C_1, C_2, \ldots, C_v$ where the first m of them are nullary operations (constant values). Furthermore, let t_n denote a well-formed term formed from a syntactically legal composition (application) of n of these operations, so that $t_n = C_{t_1} C_{t_2} \ldots C_{t_n}$ where n denotes the *length* of the expression t_n. For brevity of notation, we have omitted the other arguments of the constructors.

The principle of structural induction can be informally stated as follows:

1. **If** we can establish the truth of $P(C_i)$ for *all* nullary operations C_i where $1 \leqslant i \leqslant m$ and $m \leqslant v$ (the base case)
2. **And** that the truth of P for the term t_n implies the truth of P for *all* terms $C_j t_n$ where $C_j t_n$ is the term of length $(n+1)$ obtained by the syntactically legal application of the constructor operation C_j to the term t_n
3. **Then** we can infer the truth of P for all values of the data type.

With structural induction, the base case that must be established is to demonstrate that P is true for all nullary constructor operations.

Basically, since the data values t of an abstract data type T are only modified to other values of type t by constructor operations, they must have attained their values as a result of a finite sequence of applications of these constructors, with the *first* operation creating a new instance of the data type (init and new in the case of the stack and queue respectively). The truth of some property P about the data type can then be inferred as a direct consequence of induction on the length of the sequence of operation applications.

There is a parallel here with proving 'valid' output states in VDM, described in Chapter 5. The 'property' P in this case is VDM's data type invariant and the 'constructors' C_i ($1 \leqslant i \leqslant v$) are VDM operations which change the state.

12.5.1 Canonical forms for the stack

From the outset we have asserted that any stack value of sort stack can be 'constructed' using just the atomic constructors init and push. In other words, the set of reduced expressions

$$\{\text{init, push(init, e1), push(push(init, e1), e2), ...}\}$$

for all e1, e2, ... $\in$ nat constitutes a set of canonical forms. This assertion will now be proved using structural induction.

To start, we define more precisely what we mean by the *length* of a sequence of operation applications (for this example, expressions whose results are of type stack). The length *len* of a stack expression is defined as the number of occurrences of the constructor names init, push, and pop which appear as the leftmost outermost part of a stack expression. In other words, the function *len* is defined recursively as

- $len\,(\text{init}) = 1$
- $len\,(\text{push(s, n)}) = 1 + len\,(\text{s})$
- $len\,(\text{pop(s)}) = 1 + len\,(\text{s})$

where s $\in$ stack and n $\in$ nat. Hence, for example:

1. $len\,(\text{init}) = 1$
2. $len\,(\text{push(push(init, 3), 6)}) = 3$

3. $len\,(\text{push}(\text{pop}(\text{push}(\text{init}, 2)), 4)) = 4$
4. $len\,(\text{pop}(\text{pop}(\text{push}(\text{push}(\text{init}, 1), 2)))) = 5$
5. $len\,(\text{push}(\text{init}, \text{top}(\text{push}(\text{init}, 1)))) = 2$

Note that in the last example (5), the subterm top(push(init,1)) (which produces a value that belongs to nat), does not contribute to the length of the *outer* expression—we are concerned only with the length of expressions constructed from compositions of the constructor operations. (In other words, expressions returning values other than of sort stack must be evaluated before *len*).

We recall that a *reduced* stack expression is one that is either the empty stack, init, or an expression of the form push(s, e) where $e \in$ nat and s is itself a *reduced* expression. (That is reduced expressions are terms involving only the atomic constructors of Stack.) Hence, a general reduced expression of length n is given by

$$\text{push}(\,\ldots\,\text{push}(\text{push}(\text{init}, e_1), e_2)\,\ldots\,,\, e_{n-1})$$

where $e_i \in$ nat $(1 \leqslant i \leqslant (n-1))$.

12.5.2 Proof of canonical property for Stack

In order to show that the above collection of reduced forms constitutes a set of canonical forms, we must demonstrate that *any* stack expression is equivalent to one of the above forms. In other words, we first have to prove the following theorem.

Theorem Any well-formed stack expression $s \in$ stack is equivalent to one of the forms:

1. init
2. push(s', e) where s' is a reduced expression and $e \in$ nat

Base case From our stated theorem, the base case s = init, corresponding to an expression of length 1, is true. (For this example, init is the only nullary constructor).

Hypothesis Suppose that any given stack expression s of length n is equivalent to push(s', e) or init, where s' is itself a reduced expression (of length $(n-1)$). What we must do now is show that the above theorem also holds for all stack expressions obtained from s of length $(n+1)$, that is for the terms push(s, e_n) and pop(s), where $e_n \in$ nat.

Inductive step Given that $s \in$ stack (of length n) is a reduced expression

1. Consider the application of push to s. Then push(s, e_n) = push(push(s', e), e_n) and since s' is a reduced expression, push(s, e_n) is immediately of form 2.
2. Consider now the expression pop(s), defined for all nonempty stack values s. We can use the axioms of Stack to reduce pop(s). In particular, pop(s) = pop(push(s', e)) = s' by axiom (3) of Fig. 9.7. But from our hypothesis, s' is a reduced expression (of length $n-1$), so the fact that s is a reduced expression implies that pop(s) is also a reduced expression.

Hence, by induction on the length of the sequence of operation applications, we have proved that all stack expressions can be expressed in terms of just the atomic constructors init and push. What we have shown is that since the stack expression init of length 1 is a reduced expression, so is any term of length 2 obtained by applying a legal constructor operation to init. Hence, $t_2 = push(init, e_1)$ is also a reduced expression. (Remember pop is only defined for nonempty stack values.)

Continuing the inductive proof, since all stack expressions of length 2 are reduced expressions, so are all stack expressions of length 3 derived by applying legal constructor operations to t_2. Hence, the two terms $push(t_2, e_2)$ and $pop(t_2)$ are also reduced expressions. Starting from these reduced expressions, any stack expression of length 4 derived from the terms of length 3 by applying the constructors push and pop will also be reduced expressions and so the inductive proof goes on.

To prove that the set of reduced expressions is a canonical set of terms, we must now show that every well-formed stack expression s is equivalent to one and only one of these reduced terms. We have already shown that every well-formed expression s is equivalent to a reduced expression. Furthermore, it *cannot* be shown using the axioms of Stack that any one member of the set of reduced expressions is equivalent to another. The only way such a result could be derived was if an axiom were included that related two of the reduced expressions directly, that is an axiom whose outermost leftmost operation were an atomic constructor—which is not the case here. Hence each member of the set of reduced expressions is in a different equivalence class.

We have therefore proved that every term is equivalent to a reduced term and that each reduced term is in a different equivalence class. Hence, by definition, the collection of reduced terms constitutes a set of canonical forms.

12.5.3 Proof of the sufficient completeness of Stack

The claim that Stack is sufficiently complete can now be proved using the theorem just derived. The proof involves verifying that *all* possible outcomes of the *accessor* operations top and is-empty? applied to any stack value s are defined by the axioms.

From the theorem just proved, we know that any stack value s is equivalent to a canonical form (that is s reduces either to init or to a composition of push operations). Hence, if the axioms show how top and is-empty? act on init and on push(s, n) (where s ∈ stack and n ∈ nat), then the axiomatization is sufficiently complete. Indeed, this is precisely the systematic procedure we have been adopting so far to generate our axioms and its fundamental importance is now clear.

In Sec. 12.6 we will prove the corresponding result for the specification Set of Fig. 12.3.

Exercise 12.3 Show formally that remove is a nonatomic constructor operation for the specification Queue and that the collection of reduced expressions involving compositions of the atomic constructors new and add constitutes a set of canonical forms. Deduce that the axiomatization is sufficiently complete. (If you find this difficult, see the discussion on the specification of a *set* data type that follows, where structural induction is used to prove corresponding results for that specification.)

12.6 PROOF OF CANONICAL PROPERTY FOR Set

To prove that the set of terms

```
{empty, add(empty, n1), add(add(empty, n1), n2), ...
        add( ... add(empty, n1), n2) ... , np), ... }
```

with the ordering $n1 < n2 < \cdots < np$ constitutes a set of canonical terms we must first demonstrate that each such term belongs to a different equivalence class. This result follows immediately by observing first that no two terms of this set can be proved to be equivalent as a result of the axioms. We must next show that any reduced set expression s is equivalent to one of these canonical forms.

Given a *general* set of expression s of the form

```
add( ... add(add(empty, v1), v2) ... , vp)
```

where $v1, v2, \ldots, vp \in$ nat are not necessarily ordered and may include duplicate values, then repeated application of axiom (5) of Fig. 12.3 will 'reduce' the above expression to a canonical form in which the values $v1, v2, \ldots$ are ordered with all duplicates removed. This result follows since the ELSE clause of axiom (5) can be applied to interchange two adjacent values, for example, add(add(... , vi), vj) is equivalent to add(add(... , vj), vi) and repeating this process, the subterms can be arranged with the $v1, v2, \ldots, vp$ values arranged in ascending order. The procedure is nothing more than a *bubble sort*. (With a bubble sort, a sequence of values can be placed in ascending or descending order by systematically comparing adjacent pairs of values and interchanging their position if the two values are not in the required order. This procedure is repeated on each new sequence of values until every pair of adjacent values is in the correct order).

Identical values will be brought together and they can then be removed using the THEN clause of axiom (5). This idea is explained further in the next section when we discuss the use of hidden operations.

We have shown that any *reduced expression* is equivalent to a term in our proposed set of canonical terms. However, to prove that our set of terms is indeed a canonical set, we must now show that *any* set term s can be reduced to one of the proposed canonical forms. Just as with the stack example, we prove this result using structural induction.

Theorem: All well-formed set expressions s ∈ set can be reduced to one of the forms:

1. empty
2. add(add(... add(add(empty, e1), e2) ... , ek), em) where $e1 < e2 < \ldots < ek < em$.

Base case From our stated theorem, the base case when s has the value empty, corresponding to an expression of length 1, is true. (For this example, empty is the only nullary constructor).

Hypothesis Suppose that any given set expression s of length n can be reduced to

```
add(add( ... add(add(empty, e1), e2) ... , ek), em)
```

where $e1 < e2 < \cdots < ek < em$ (and $m = n - 1$).

What we must do now is show that the above theorem also holds for all set expressions obtained from s of length $(n+1)$, that is for the terms add(s, en) and delete(s, en) (en ∈ nat).

Inductive step   Given that s ∈ set is of length n

1. Consider the application of add to s. Then

$$\text{add(s, en) = add(add(add(... add(add(empty, e1), e2) ... , ek), em) ,en)}$$

We have just seen that applying axiom (5) allows us to interchange adjacent subterms since add(add(... , em), en) is equivalent to add(add(... , en), em), so that the subterm involving en will 'gravitate' to the left and arrive at its appropriate place in the ordering. If the value en is already in the set, it can be removed using axiom (5) once it has 'arrived' and become adjacent to its duplicate. The resulting expression add(s, en) is, therefore, also a member of our proposed set of canonical forms if s is a canonical form.

2. Consider now the expression delete(s, en). We can use the axioms of Set to reduce the term delete(s, en). In particular

$$\text{delete(s, en) = delete(add(add(... add(add(empty, e1), e2) ... , ek), em), en)}$$

There are three cases to consider.

(a) Case 1. Suppose first that en = em, then application of axiom (4) gives

$$\text{delete(s, en) = delete(add(... add(add(empty, e1), e2) ... , ek), en)}$$

since the replacement is given by the expression following the THEN clause of axiom (4). Applying axiom (4) again produces

$$\text{delete(add(... add(add(empty, e1), e2) ... , ek), en) =}$$

$$\text{add(delete(... add(add(empty, e1), e2), ... en), ek)}$$

where ek < en (since by hypothesis ek < em and em = en). Axiom (4) is then repeatedly applied with the ELSE clause on the right-hand side of axiom (4) always providing the replacement expression. The effect, therefore, is to move delete 'inwards' until it eventually arrives at the centre of an equivalent expression given by

$$\text{add(... add(add(delete(empty, en), e1), e2) ... , ek)}$$

Use of axiom (3) then allows us to replace delete(empty, en) by empty, so that we end up with the reduced term

$$\text{add(... add(add(empty, e1), e2) ... , ek)}$$

with e1<e2<···<ek. This final equivalent expression is, therefore, a canonical term. Hence, we have shown that if s is a canonical form then the term delete(s, en) is also a canonical form since it can be expressed in terms of the atomic constructors empty and add with no duplicates and the elements inserted in increasing order.

(b) Case 2. If the element en is a member of the set s but not the largest element, a similar result can be proved. In this case, the subterm involving delete(... , en) will again 'move inwards' because the ELSE clause of axiom (4) will apply for the replacement term until we arrive at the equivalent expression

$$add(... delete(add(...,en), en), ... , em)$$

where the en values 'meet up'. This now corresponds to Case 1 and the analysis proceeds as above. We again end up with a canonical term with the element en removed.

(c) Case 3. Finally, if the value en is not a member of the original set s, the ELSE clause of axiom (4) will apply for each reduction and eventually the innermost subterm will be delete(empty, en). Use of axiom (3) then produces the result

$$delete(s, en) = add(add(... add(add(empty, e1), e2) ... , ek), em)$$

with e1<e2<···<ek<em.

In other words, delete(s, en) = s since en is not a member of s and since, by hypothesis, s is a canonical term, so is delete(s, en).

Use of structural induction over the axioms has therefore shown that any set expression s is equivalent to a reduced expression in which the elements are inserted in increasing order with duplicates removed.

At this point, the reader may be thinking 'but wait a minute, VDM gives us sets for free!' We should point out that this discussion of the *set* data type has been presented to enable the reader to *understand* the concepts and principles involved with proof obligation for algebraic specifications. In an application, the reader can start by importing sets into an algebraic specification and then use a similar analysis on the user's own data type specification.

12.7 ATTRIBUTES OF AN OPERATION

Properties, such as those expressed by axioms (7) to (11) of Fig. 12.4, are *attributes* that are possessed by the operations of many data types. For example, in the case of the Boolean data type, the operations ∧ (*and*) and ∨ (*or*) are both associative and commutative. Furthermore, the value *false* is an *identity* element for the operation ∨ since for any Boolean value b

$$false \vee b = b \vee false = b$$

(Similarly, *true* is an identity element for the operation ∧.)

Suppose we identify the need for an abstract data type with operation(s) that are required to possess some attribute and proceed to produce an algebraic specification for that abstract data type. Then, obviously, that attribute *must* either appear as an *explicit* axiom of the specification or be derivable from the axioms using equational logic and structural induction. In the latter case, the attribute is *implicit* in the axiomatization. Note that the use of explicit axioms to express such a property may result in axioms whose left-hand sides contain *atomic* constructors as their *outermost* operation.

We will allow the associativity and commutativity attributes of operations to be explicitly declared in the signature, following the range sort of the appropriate operation. For example, following the style of Axis, we will declare that the operation U is both associative and commutative by means of the statement

```
OPS
 _ U _ : set set → set (ASSOC COMM)
```

The corresponding axioms that state these attributes do not then need to be included in the specification.

12.8 DERIVATION OF ATTRIBUTES FROM AXIOMS

The requirement that the operations in an interpretation of an abstract data type possess attributes such as commutativity or associativity can be expressed directly by means of explicit axioms. What is not always immediately apparent is the fact that such attributes can often be *derived* from the axioms of a specification using equational inference and structural induction, in which case the attributes are implicit in the axiomatization. An illuminating example which exploits these ideas is given in the small specification Natural for natural numbers, first introduced in Chapter 10 (Fig. 10.3) and repeated for reference in Fig. 12.5, which consists of the three constructor operations zero, succ and add together with the two axioms satisfied by the nonatomic constructor add. From this 'lean' specification, we will prove a number of interesting properties, including the commutativity of the operation add. The atomic constructors for this specification are zero and succ and the proof of this result will be looked at in the additional problems at the end of this chapter (Prob. 12.11).

```
SPEC   Natural
SORT   nat
OPS
   zero  :  ->  nat
   succ  :  nat  ->  nat
   add   :  nat  nat  ->  nat
FORALL
   m , n :  nat
AXIOMS:
 (1)  add(zero, n)  =  n
 (2)  add(succ(m), n)  =  succ(add(m, n))
ENDSPEC
```

Figure 12.5 Small specification of natural numbers.

Before embarking on such proofs, it is important to realize that, when developing algebraic specifications, the operations in the intended interpretation may often be expected to possess attributes such as commutativity and associativity, so the proof of such properties provides a valuable check on the *validity* of the specification with respect to that interpretation. For this reason, the reader is strongly encouraged to undertake such proofs.

As in Chapter 10, we will denote the ground term consisting of m applications of succ to zero by $\text{succ}^m(\text{zero})$. Before proving that the operation add is commutative, we derive the following property which will be used subsequently in the proofs that the operation add is commutative and nonatomic.

Property 1

$$\text{add}(\text{succ}^m(\text{zero}), n) = \text{succ}^m(n)$$

where $n \in \text{nat}$. We will prove this result using structural induction (over m).

Base case   The base case ($m = 0$) of **Property 1** asserts that $\text{add}(\text{zero}, n) = n$, which is true from axiom (1).

Hypothesis   Assume now that **Property 1** is true for the term $\text{succ}^m(\text{zero})$. We then need to show that this result will also hold for the term $\text{succ}^{m+1}(\text{zero})$, that is we have to prove that the truth of **Property 1** implies the truth of

$$\text{add}(\text{succ}^{m+1}(\text{zero}), n) = \text{succ}^{m+1}(n)$$

Inductive step   The left-hand side of this last result can be expressed as

$$\text{add}(\text{succ}(\text{succ}^m(\text{zero})), n) \tag{12.1}$$

and use of axiom (2) allows us to transform this expression to

$$\text{succ}(\text{add}(\text{succ}^m(\text{zero}), n))$$

From our original hypothesis, the subterm $\text{add}(\text{succ}^m(\text{zero}), n)$ in the above expression is equal to $\text{succ}^m(n)$ so that Expression (12.1) becomes

$$\text{succ}(\text{succ}^m(n))$$

which is equal to $\text{succ}^{m+1}(n)$ as required. We are now ready to prove that the operation add is commutative.

Property 2

$$\text{add}(\text{succ}^m(\text{zero}), \text{succ}^n(\text{zero})) = \text{add}(\text{succ}^n(\text{zero}), \text{succ}^m(\text{zero}))$$

We will prove the *commutativity* property of the operation add using structural induction over *n*, although the result could also be proved by induction over *m*.

Base case   The base case $(n=0)$ that must first be proved is

$$add(succ^m(zero), zero) = add(zero, succ^m(zero))$$

For $m=0$, the above result obviously holds since both terms reduce to the same term add(zero, zero). For general *m*, the left-hand side is $add(succ^m(zero), zero)$ and, from **Property 1** with n replaced by zero, we have that the left-hand side

$$add(succ^m(zero), zero)$$

transforms to

$$succ^m(zero)$$

The right-hand side of the base case, $add(zero, succ^m(zero))$, reduces immediately to $succ^m(zero)$ using axiom (1). Both terms therefore reduce to $succ^m(zero)$ and the base case is established.

Hypothesis   Assume **Property 2** holds. We must now prove that if **Property 2** holds then

$$add(succ^m(zero), succ(succ^n(zero))) = add(succ(succ^n(zero)), succ^m(zero)) \quad (12.2)$$

Inductive Step   From **Property 1**, the left-hand side of Expression 12.2 is equal to

$$succ^m(succ(succ^n(zero))).$$

which is equal to $succ^{m+1+n}(zero)$. The right-hand side of Expression 12.2 can be transformed using axiom (2) and gives

$$succ(add(succ^n(zero), succ^m(zero)))$$

We can again use **Property 1** to transform this expression to

$$succ(succ^n(succ^m(zero)))$$

which reduces to $succ^{1+n+m}(zero)$. Since *m* and *n* are any nonnegative integers, $m+1+n=1+n+m$, so that both sides of Expression 12.1 reduce to the same term $succ^{m+n+1}(zero)$. The commutative property of add has therefore been established and has been shown to be implicit in the axioms of the specification.

Exercise 12.4   For both the natural numbers and the integers, confirm that 0 is an identity element for the binary addition operation '+' and that 1 is an identity element for the binary multiplication operation '×'.

12.9 SUMMARY

The principal results are presented in the summaries below.

- During the various phases of software development, the software engineer must produce arguments, using the appropriate mathematical formalism, to demonstrate:
  - how the various features of the design relate to the goals set for it in the specification, that is *identify* the *proof obligations*
  - that these features *do* indeed achieve these goals—that is *discharge* the proof obligations
- For algebraic specifications, the following proof obligations need to be discharged:
  - *Consistency* requires that a model of the specification exists. Since at least one model can always be constructed (the *quotient term algebra*), consistency does not present a problem. However, a presentation may still have undesirable features, such as identifying as equivalent terms that were meant to be distinct. The proof obligation for *consistency* is then that *no two terms in the intended set of canonical forms should be forced to be equivalent as a consequence of the axioms.*
  - The assertion that a collection of terms built up from a subset of constructor operations constitutes a set of canonical forms must be proved by demonstrating that each equivalence class in the carrier set of the quotient term algebra contains exactly one canonical form. The proof of this property uses structural induction over the axioms.
  - *Completeness* requires that all the desired properties of our data type can be deduced from the axioms of the presentation. Completeness demands, therefore, that terms that are intended to be equivalent are identified as such. The proof obligation for *completeness* is then that *every term is equivalent to one in the proposed set of canonical forms.*
  - *Conservative extension*—specifications that build upon other existing specifications must preserve the properties of those original specifications. In particular, it should be proved that the enlarged specification introduces *no junk* and *no confusion*.

  Proofs of these properties often rely on *structural induction*
- When a new abstract data type is specified that uses as a basis existing specifications of abstract data types, the new specification is *sufficiently complete* if the values of all syntactically-legal expressions that can be constructed using the signature of the new type *either* belong to that new type *or* are reducible by the axioms of the new type to values of the existing types.
- A subset of the constructor operations, the atomic constructors, can often be identified, which are necessary and sufficient for constructing terms that denote all the required values of the data type. All such values of the data type are then denoted by compositions of these atomic constructors and such compositions of atomic constructors are called *reduced* expressions (terms).
- Canonical terms can often be derived directly from the subset of atomic constructors in that the collection of reduced terms immediately provides a set of canonical terms.
- Operations may possess intrinsic properties such as associativity and commutativity. These properties can be stated explicitly using axioms or derived from the set of axioms using equational logic and structural induction. The proof of such properties affords a check on the validity of the specification with regards to its intended interpretation.

ADDITIONAL PROBLEMS

12.1 Use mathematical induction to show that the sum of the cubes of the first n natural numbers

$$1^3 + 2^3 + 3^3 + \cdots + (n-1)^3 + n^3$$

is given by $[n(n+1)/2]^2$.

12.2 Use structural induction to show that delete is a nonatomic constructor for versions 1 and 2 of the specification for a set given in Figs 12.2 and 12.3.

12.3 Enrich the specification Funny-Set given in Fig. 12.2 (version 1) by including the operations of set union and set intersection. Produce axioms for these two operations and prove formally that these two constructors are nonatomic.

12.4 Enrich the specification Set given in Fig. 12.4 (version 3) by including an operation for set intersection and derive axioms satisfied by this operation. Demonstrate formally that the intersection operation is a nonatomic constructor.

12.5 For the specification Boolean given in Fig. 10.3, identify the atomic and nonatomic constructors and formally verify your results.

12.6 Derive a parameterized specification for a set data type with header SPEC Set(E : Elem), which specifies a generic set data type. Base your specification on the unparameterized specification Set of Fig. 12.4.

12.7 Extend the generic specification of Prob. 12.6 to include the set difference operation '−'. What attributes, if any, does the set difference operation possess?

12.8 Demonstrate formally that the set difference operation introduced in Prob. 12.7 is a nonatomic constructor.

12.9 Given a commutative binary operation opc with domain and range sorts s where opc : s s → s and s1, s2 ∈ s, what problem does the axiom

    opc(s1, s2) = opc(s2, s1)

present for term rewriting systems where the axioms are interpreted as rewrite rules? In particular, is the resulting set of rewrite rules Noetherian?

12.10 Consider the specification Natural of Fig. 12.5. Extend this specification by including the infix *multiplication* operation.

    ∗ : nat nat → nat

If m, n ∈ nat

(a) Complete the axiom whose left-hand side is zero ∗ n.
(b) Complete the axiom whose left-hand side is succ(m) ∗ n. (You will need to make use of the existing operation add.)
(c) Use structural induction to show that the operation ∗ is commutative.
(d) What other attributes does the operation ∗ possess? Show that these properties can be derived from your axioms.

12.11 This problem uses structural induction to show that for the specification Natural of Fig. 12.5 the operation add is a nonatomic constructor. The proof makes use of the result **Property 1** which we derived earlier. The problem then looks at adapting the specification to provide a formal specification for the integers.

We have to show that the operations zero and succ are atomic constructors. In other words, we have to prove that all ground terms (variable-free terms) will consist of applications of succ to the nullary operation zero. We need to prove that every $m \in$ nat can be denoted by either zero or succ(succ(...(zero) ...)) and this will be done using structural induction.

As before, let us express the term consisting of n applications of succ to zero by $\text{succ}^n(\text{zero})$. We refer to such terms as being *reduced* or in *reduced form*.

Base case   The result obviously holds for the nullary operation zero.

Hypothesis 1 If $n \in$ nat is in reduced form, then so is succ(n)

Hypothesis 2 If m and $\in$ nat are in reduced form, then add(m, n) can be expressed as a reduced form.

Inductive step In the case of Hypothesis 1, since n is in reduced form, it will be of the form $\text{succ}^{n'}(\text{zero})$ for some positive integer n'. It follows that succ(n) is equal to $\text{succ}(\text{succ}^{n'}(\text{zero}))$ which reduces immediately to $\text{succ}^{n'+1}(\text{zero})$ which is itself a reduced expression. It follows that if n is in reduced form, so is succ(n).

In the case of Hypothesis 2, since m and n are reduced expressions, the term add(m, n) can be expressed as

$$\text{add}(\text{succ}^{m'}(\text{zero}), \text{succ}^{n'}(\text{zero}))$$

with appropriate nonnegative values of m' and n'. Using **Property 1** derived earlier, which states

$$\text{add}(\text{succ}^m(\text{zero}), n) = \text{succ}^m(n)$$

we can transform the expression above into

$$\text{succ}^{m'}(\text{succ}^{n'}(\text{zero}))$$

which is equal to $\text{succ}^{m'+n'}(\text{zero})$. This is again a reduced expression, so we have shown that if m and n are reduced expressions, so is add(m, n). This completes the proof using structural induction.

(a) Produce a specification for the *integers* by adapting the specification Natural of Fig. 12.4 to include the unary operation pred : int $\rightarrow$ int which satisfies the axioms

$$\text{pred}(\text{succ}(i)) = i \ ; \ \text{succ}(\text{pred}(i)) = i$$

for all $i \in$ int, where int is the introduced sort.

(b) Complete the axiom whose left-hand side is add(pred(i), j).

(c) Show formally that pred is a nonatomic constructor.

REFERENCES

Goguen, J.A., and Winkler, T. (1988) Introducing OBJ3, *SRI International Computer Science Laboratory Report SRI-CSL-88-9*, 333 Ravenswood Avenue, Menlo Park, California.

Guttag, J. (1977) Abstract Data Types and the Development of Data Structures, *Communications of the ACM*, **20**, 396–404.

Huet, G., and Oppen, D. (1980) Equations and Rewrite Rules: A Survey. In R. Book, (ed.) *Formal Language Theory. Perspectives and Open Problems*, Academic Press, London.

13
PROTOTYPING ALGEBRAIC SPECIFICATIONS

13.1 INTRODUCTION

In this chapter the prototyping of algebraic specifications is examined. The refinement of an algebraic specification into an implementation is no easy task in general. Therefore, instead of describing specification refinement, we will concentrate on specification prototyping. This is entirely consistent with our emphasis on specification construction rather than program design. We will focus our attention on prototyping and in particular on the use of the executable algebraic specification language OBJ3 as a means of producing a correct implementation. We also comment on some of the differences between the two executable specification languages OBJ3 and Axis.

We remind the reader that the operational semantics of algebraic specification languages immediately provides a prototyping mechanism. In our case, the semantics of a SPEC module is prescribed by its axioms which are interpreted operationally as left-to-right rewrite rules in which instances of left-hand sides of axioms are replaced by their corresponding right-hand sides until a value is obtained that contains no instance of any left-hand side.

The chapter concludes with examples of OBJ3 prototypes for some of the small case studies that were specified in Chapter 11, including the estate agent database, the petrochemical plant and the symbol table manager.

13.2 INITIAL MODELS AND PROTOTYPING

Throughout our treatment of the algebraic approach to specification, we have focused on *initial* algebra semantics. Initial algebra semantics are important for four main reasons:

- The mathematical foundations of initial algebra semantics are well established (Goguen 1978, Ehrig and Mahr 1985).

- The initial algebra approach provides a very appropriate framework for defining specification correctness criteria such as *sufficient completeness*.
- Initial models have the 'no junk, no confusion' property.
- Specifications with an initial semantics can be directly implemented. Indeed, specification prototyping is only possible with *initial* algebra semantics.

We noted in Chapter 7 that the main difference between a specification language and a programming language is that the latter is executable, in that it can accept input data and should output data. Given a specification S and a corresponding implementation P, then, if that implementation is correct, the input–output relationship will always conform to the specification S.

When an algebraic data type specification is implemented, an appropriate representation for values of the data type is chosen from the various models of the theory, with each operation of the specification being defined as a function over the chosen representation. We stressed the importance of initial algebras as models of algebraic specifications in Sec 10.10. We reiterate that they provide the 'best' model for a given specification since they contain no junk and no confusion and so provide a faithful interpretation of the specification. Executability demands also that we confine our attention to initial models. We therefore concentrate on the quotient term algebra since this initial algebra provides a 'standard model' which is unique (up to isomorphism).

Any implementation must therefore be able to evaluate terms in this model and among other things should be able to accomplish tasks such as the following:

- Given as input any syntactically legal ground term (that is one that conforms to the signature and so belongs to the term algebra), compute and output its value. In other words, reduce any given term to a canonical form.
- Given two ground terms (terms containing no variables), determine whether they denote the same value.

Any algorithm that implements an algebraic specification must therefore be able to handle *term equality*, a fundamental concept for algebraic specification. In the case of our specification language, this means implementing the Boolean-valued operation

```
_ == _ : s s → Bool
```

where s is any arbitrary sort.

One approach is to use the term algebra in the implementation. Each ground term can then be represented in the machine by a tree with different sites where rewrite rules may apply. Each time a rewrite rule is used, the tree will be transformed until a point is reached where no further rules can be applied. The resulting term will be in a *normal* or *canonical* form. The equivalence of two ground terms is then determined by reducing each term to normal form and comparing the two resulting forms. If the normal forms are identical, the two ground terms denote the same value.

We now look briefly at four different approaches for prototyping algebraic specifications. These are the use of executable algebraic specification languages, functional programming languages, Prolog and imperative programming languages.

13.3 PROTOTYPING SPECIFICATIONS USING OBJ3

The first approach and the one of most interest to us is to interpret the specification directly as a term rewriting system where the set of axioms is treated as a collection of one-way rewrite rules. The executable algebraic specification languages Axis and OBJ adopt this stance. Although Axis (© Hewlett-Packard 1988) is itself an executable specification language, it does not support the concept of subsorts and supersorts and it is primarily for this reason that we have chosen OBJ3 as a vehicle for prototyping our specifications. The Axis term rewriting interpreter is also very much slower than its OBJ3 counterpart.

The executable algebraic specification language OBJ has undergone a number of changes since 1976 when Goguen designed the original version of the language. Goguen's aim was to encompass error handling and partial operations within the framework of the algebraic theory of abstract data types in a straightforward and uniform manner. The resulting algebraic structures were known as *error-algebras* and the first implementations, OBJ0 and OBJT, were produced by Tardo and Goguen. The former was based on unsorted equational logic while OBJT included a construct for producing parameterized specifications. The next version, OBJ1, based on OBJT, was implemented by Plaisted in 1983 and included the handling of associative/commutative rewrite rules together with a highly interactive environment. In 1985 OBJ2 was developed by Futatsugi and Jouannaud in collaboration with Meseguer and Goguen. Although it used parts of OBJ1, it discarded the error-algebra approach in favour of *order-sorted algebras*. We can think of an order-sorted algebra as a generalization of a many-sorted algebra and this concept is looked at briefly at the very end of this chapter. The latest version, OBJ3, was developed (as was OBJ2) at the SRI International Computer Science Laboratory in California by Winkler, Meseguer, Goguen, Kirchner and Megrelis (Goguen and Winkler, 1988). The syntax of OBJ3 is similar to that of OBJ2 but its implementation uses a simpler approach to order-sorted rewriting and OBJ3 provides more powerful parameterization facilities. The mathematical semantics of OBJ2 and OBJ3 are both based on order-sorted equational logic but their operational semantics are different. OBJ2 used a translation of order-sorted into many-sorted algebra which reduced computation to standard term rewriting, whereas OBJ3 uses a more efficient approach through the direct application of order-sorted rewriting. A comprehensive and precise treatment of order-sorted equational logic can be found in Goguen *et al.* (1985). Interestingly, both OBJ2 and OBJ3 can be viewed as implementations of the early specification language Clear.

13.4 OVERVIEW OF OBJ3

We present a brief account of the main features of OBJ3 and how these features relate to Axis. We do not aim to provide an exhaustive manual of the OBJ3 programming language here—for more details, the reader is referred to Goguen and Winkler (1988). OBJ3 is a wide spectrum programming language which consists of an interpreter and an environment for a powerful functional programming language. It has a rigorous mathematical semantics based on *order-sorted equational logic*. This logic uses the concept of *subsorts*, which provides a simple, yet mathematically precise, way of handling errors and operation overloading.

The rigorous semantics allows specifications to be written as programs that are declarative in style and mirror the structure of an algebraic specification. This permits

OBJ3 to be used not only for validating and implementing algebraic specifications but also as a theorem prover. The three top-level programming structures that support the specification of abstract data types are *object* modules, *theory* modules and *views*. In the discussion which follows, we use a serif typewriter face to denote OBJ3 keywords, specification fragments and complete OBJ3 specifications.

- **Objects**—these encapsulate executable code and correspond to the SPEC modules of Axis. They are delimited by the keywords obj and endo, which correspond to our SPEC and ENDSPEC respectively.
- **Theories**—these define the syntax and semantic properties of modules and module interfaces. They specify properties that may (or may not) be satisfied by another object or theory. They are structurally similar to object modules in that they consist of a collection of sorts, subsorts, operations, variable declarations, and axioms (not necessarily all), but they do not enforce an initial interpretation. They correspond to the PROPS modules of Axis.
- **Views**—these are a concept we discussed in the context of parameterized specifications in Chapter 11 (Sec. 11.9). We recall that a *view* is a binding of the sorts and/or operations declared in some theory to sorts and/or operations in some other module together with an assertion that this other module satisfies the properties stated in the theory. Views are delimited by the keywords view and endv.

As with Axis, both types of module (object and theory) can be parameterized where the parameter types are modules. Modules can also import existing modules which supports multiple inheritance at the module level. Large specifications can then be built up in bottom-up fashion using *module expressions*, which consist of unparameterized object modules, instantiated parameterized modules, renamed modules and the sum combinator operator +, in much the same way as discussed in Chapter 11.

With regards to the importing of modules, OBJ3 handles this feature differently from Axis. Whereas Axis identifies *two* ways that modules can be imported, namely USING which preserves the initial semantics of the imported module and INCLUDING which guarantees nothing, OBJ3 provides *three* means for importing modules, protecting, extending and using. The meanings of these types of import are connected with the initial semantics of objects as described below. Assume that a module S imports a module T. The importation is:

1. *Protecting* if and only if S adds no new data values of sorts from T and does not force two distinct values of T to be equal. In other words, S does not introduce junk or confusion. This is equivalent to the USING construct of Axis.
2. *Extending* if and only if the axioms of S do not force two distinct values of T to be equal. In other words, the enlarged specification preserves the 'no confusion' property. This type of importation has no equivalent in Axis.
3. *Using* if there are no guarantees at all. This is equivalent to our INCLUDING construct.

OBJ3 has a built-in binary infix equality operation $\_==\_:S\ S\rightarrow Bool$ for every sort S and also has a number of built-in predefined data types such as BOOL, NAT, INT, FLOAT corresponding to the theories of Boolean values, natural numbers, integers and floating point values respectively. The polymorphic function if _ then _ else _ fi is provided by BOOL.

The axioms of an OBJ3 specification are referred to as *equations* and are prefixed by one of the keywords eq or cq which denotes an *unconditional* or *conditional* axiom respectively. Also OBJ3 supports prefix, postfix, infix and mixfix syntax for operations, in addition to the mathematical parenthesized prefix form. The reader should be aware of the terminology used in OBJ3 for the domain and range sorts of an operation. Given an operation op

```
op : s1 s2 ... sn → s
```

the domain s1 $\times$ s2 $\times$ ... $\times$ sn is known as the *arity* and the range sort s is known as the *value sort* or *co-arity*. The pair (*arity, co-arity*) is called the *rank* of an operation. OBJ3 employs the convention that an expression is well-formed if and only if it has a unique parse of least sort.

One further distinguishing feature of OBJ3 is its use of *retracts* to parse terms that on first inspection look as though they are not well-formed. When subterms are not of the anticipated sort, they can sometimes be *coerced* to that sort, and this is a simple task from a subsort to a supersort. For instance, consider the two sorts Nat and Rat corresponding to the sorts of natural numbers and rational numbers respectively. Suppose the addition operation _ + _ :Rat Rat → Rat is only defined over the rational numbers, then 1 + 2 can be made to conform to the pattern laid down by that signature because 1 and 2 are natural numbers and Nat < Rat, that is the sort of natural numbers is a subsort of the sort of rationals. Put another way, any natural number can be represented as a rational. For example, 1 + 2 can be expressed as 1/1 + 2/1 and so conforms to the signature of the original operation +.

Coercions from supersorts to subsorts are more subtle, however, and one distinguishing feature of OBJ3 is its use of *retracts* to handle such coercions. As an illustration, suppose the factorial function is defined for natural numbers only, and that the parser is presented with the expression $(-6/-3)!$. The parser must treat the subterm $-6/-3$ (which is strictly a rational) as a natural number since at parse time it cannot ascertain whether $-6/-3$ will evaluate to a natural number. In OBJ3, such subterms are 'given extra breathing space' by having the parser introduce a *retract* which for this example is denoted by the special operation symbol r:Rat>Nat. The effect of a retract is to lower the sort and the retract is then withdrawn if the subterm evaluates to a natural number. In the event of the subterm not evaluating to a natural number, the retract is left behind where it then serves as an instructive error message. For our example, the parser will transform the expression $(-6/-3)!$ into the expression (r:Rat>Nat(-6/-3))! which at run-time first evaluates to (r:Rat>Nat(2))! and subsequently to (2)! using the built-in equation r:Rat>Nat(X) = X where X is any variable that belongs to Nat.

Finally, the period character '.' is somewhat special in OBJ3, as it is used to terminate operation, variable, and axiom declarations among other duties. Care has to be taken when using periods in any other context, for example, as an operation symbol, since the interpreter will think a 'loose' period within an axiom denotes the end of the axiom. OBJ3 is very tetchy on this point as the authors discovered to their cost when prototyping some of the specifications. Expeditious use of brackets is the order of the day in these situations!

We conclude this summary with a specimen OBJ3 program for a parameterized queue module. The requirement theory is ELEM which simply requires the existence of a sort and corresponds exactly to our PROPS module Elem given in Fig. 11.14. The parameterized

```
    th  ELEM  is
       sort  Element .
    endth
*** ================================================
    obj QUEUE[E :: ELEM]  is
       sorts  Queue  NeQueue       .
       protecting  BOOL            .
       subsort  NeQueue  <  Queue .
       op   new       :                      -> Queue    .
       op   add       : Queue Element  -> NeQueue .
       op   remove    : NeQueue        -> Queue    .
       op   front _   : NeQueue        -> Element .
       op   is-empty? _ : Queue             -> Bool     .
       var          q : Queue    .
       var          e : Element  .
       eq   front add(q,e)       = if is-empty? q  then  e
                                     else  front q  fi          .
       eq   is-empty? new        = true                         .
       eq   is-empty? add(q,e)   = false                        .
       eq   remove(add(q,e))     = if is-empty? q  then  new
                                     else  add(remove(q),e)  fi  .
    endo
```

Figure 13.1 Specification of a generic queue using OBJ3.

specification is then instantiated to produce a specification for a queue of natural numbers. The resulting program is shown in Fig. 13.1. Observe that we have chosen to write the accessor operations in prefix form while the constructors are expressed in parenthesized prefix format. This is done merely to display the features of OBJ3 and is no requirement of OBJ3 itself. Note also that comments in OBJ3 are introduced by ***> or ***. The former print during execution while the latter do not. We can then instantiate the formal parameter E with the (built-in) module NAT to produce a specification of a queue of natural numbers. We rename the sorts and the accessor operations to reflect this application and the resulting specification is shown below.

```
    obj QUEUE-OF-NAT is

       protecting QUEUE[NAT] *

                  (sort Queue to QueueNat,

                   sort NeQueue to NeQueueNat,

                   op front _ to first _ ,

                   op is-empty? _ to empty-queue? _ ).

    endo
```

We have used a default view in the instantiation QUEUE[NAT] which is equivalent to the explicitly stated form

```
QUEUE[view to NAT is sort Element to Nat . endv]
```

where Nat is the sort corresponding to the built-in module NAT.

Given an object (specification module) together with an expression ⟨*Expr*⟩ (the input to the prototype program), the expression can be evaluated (that is reduced by applying an appropriate sequence of axioms in the form of rewrite rules) by using the command

```
reduce ⟨Expr⟩ .
```

and such an expression is evaluated with respect to the last module entered into the system. If it is required to reduce an expression with respect to a different module, ⟨*ModName*⟩ say, the appropriate command is

```
reduce in ⟨ModName⟩ : ⟨Expr⟩ .
```

As an example, evaluation of the expression

```
first add(add(new, 2), 9)
```

is accomplished by the command

```
reduce in QUEUE-OF-NAT : first add(add(new, 2), 9) .
```

and the corresponding output from this program is

```
reduce in QUEUE-OF-NAT : first add(add(new, 2), 9)
rewrites: 6
result NzNat: 2
```

where NzNat denotes the type (sort) of the result, a nonzero natural number.

Similarly, to find the canonical form of the term remove(add(add(new, 1), 4)), use the command

```
reduce in QUEUE-OF-NAT : remove(add(add(new, 1), 4)) .
```

which produces the result

```
reduce in QUEUE-OF-NAT : remove(add(add(new, 1), 4))
rewrites: 6
result NeQueueNat: add(new, 4)
```

To determine whether two ground terms are equal, say, for example, the terms remove(add(add(new, 1), 4)) and add(new, 4), we use the command

```
reduce in QUEUE-OF-NAT : remove(add(add(new, 1), 4)) = = add(new, 4) .
```

which produces the output

```
reduce in QUEUE-OF-NAT : remove(add(add(new, 1), 4)) = = add(new, 4)
rewrites : 7
result Bool : true
```

13.4.1 Some OBJ3 prototypes

In appendix 2 we present OBJ3 prototypes of the case studies developed in Chapter 11. All these prototypes were run on a Sun4 workstation using version 2.03 of OBJ3. The examples include the estate agent database (HOUSES-FOR-SALE), the petrochemical tank—version 2 (TANK-2), the petrochemical plant monitor (DATASTORE) and the symbol table manager (SYMBOL-TABLE). At the end of each OBJ3 program, the results of some evaluations are presented.

13.5 PROTOTYPING WITH FUNCTIONAL LANGUAGES

A second approach is to translate the specification directly into a functional programming language such as ML, Miranda, pure Lisp. The affinity between functional and algebraic specification languages has already been discussed in Chapter 9. Programs written in a functional language contain functions and type declarations that are defined by pattern-matching rules on the *type constructors* of their argument sorts. These type constructors in a language such as Miranda essentially correspond to the atomic constructors of an algebraic specification. An example of the functional approach can be seen in the Miranda implementation of the abstract data type Queue given in Fig. 9.6. Indeed, the algebraic specification language OBJ3 is, in essence, a broad spectrum functional programming language based on many-sorted equational logic and this is discussed below.

13.6 PROTOTYPING WITH PROLOG

This approach is included for completeness and also to contrast with the use of Prolog in Chapter 7 as a prototyping language for VDM. With this approach, the specification is translated into a logical programming language such as Prolog. For specifications with a set of rewrite rules that is finitely convergent, a simple algorithm can be used for the translation process.

1. For each *nullary* operation symbol op, introduce the Prolog rule (clause)

    ```
    reduce(op, R) :-
      canonise(op, R) .
    ```

2. For each operation symbol op with arity n ($n \geq 1$), introduce the Prolog rule

    ```
    reduce(op(X1, X2, ... , Xn), R) :-
      reduce(X1, E1),
      reduce(X2, E2),
      ...........
      reduce(Xn, En),
      canonise(op(E1, E2, ..., En), R) .
    ```

3. For each rewrite rule (axiom) $L = R$, add the fact

```
axiom(left, right).
```

where 'left' and 'right' represent the translation of the terms L and R into Prolog syntax.

4. Finally, append the following two rules to the Prolog program in the order shown

```
canonise(X, Z) :-
  axiom(X, Y),
  reduce(Y, Z) .
canonise(X, X) .
```

For this scheme, a leftmost innermost strategy is used to evaluate terms. To reduce (that is to transform to canonical form) any term $t(a_1, a_2, \ldots, a_n)$ with n arguments $a_1, a_2, \ldots, a_n$, its leftmost argument a_1 is first put into canonical (normal) form, then its second argument a_2 is reduced and so on until a_n is reduced. If any argument $a_i (1 \leqslant i \leqslant n)$ itself contains subterms, this procedure is recursively applied. *Only* when the term t has *all* its subterms reduced to normal form will the predicate canonise use an appropriate axiom to reduce t itself, unless the term t is already in normal form. Remember, for a finitely convergent set of rewrite rules, the term will be in normal form if no further axiom can be applied. Hence, if the resulting term cannot be pattern matched with the left-hand side of any axiom, no further reductions are possible and the term will be in a normal form.

In Fig. 13.2 we present a Prolog implementation of the specification Houses-for-sale which was derived earlier for the case study of the estate agent database (Fig. 11.5). Several points are worth noting about this Prolog program:

1. Standard Edinburgh Prolog does not support the modularization of software, so that the 'imported' specifications Address, Mode, and Boolean with their associated nullary operations adr1, adr2, adr3, adr4 ; for_sale, under_offer ; true and false are transformed, also using the above algorithm, and appear as an integral part of the Prolog program.
2. The axioms for the operations of Houses-for-sale require case analysis to define their semantics (since the right-hand sides of the axioms contain IF _ THEN _ ELSE _). We can easily recast such axioms into Prolog by employing *pattern matching* with appropriate alternative forms for each axiom (rule).
3. The variable R which appears as the second slot in the predicates reduce and canonise is essentially a 'place-holder' for the result of the reduction of the term held in the first slot. Looking at the two rules for canonise, if no axiom can be applied to reduce a term, that term must be a normal form. In that case the first rule cannot be applied and canonise(X, X) will fire. (This is the base case which terminates the recursion). The outcome of this is simply to copy the value in the first slot (which is now a normal form) across to the second slot. It is worth emphasizing at this point that Prolog does not *evaluate* anything! (Well, unless forced to by a side effect.)
4. The predicate equivalent(T1, T2) will be true if the terms T1 and T2 are equivalent, that is if they have the same normal form. This predicate essentially corresponds to the equality operation = = which is required for every sort.

The Prolog program of Fig. 13.2 will terminate for all queries of the form

```
?- reduce(T, Nf).
```

and

```
?- equivalent(Term1, Term2).
```

In the first case, after termination, Nf is instantiated to the canonical form of the term T, where T is any ground term, expressed in Prolog syntax. In the second case, equivalent will succeed if Term1 and Term2 are 'equal' under equational inference (using the axioms of Houses-for-sale). Some examples of such queries are

```
?- reduce(insert(insert(empty, adr1), adr2), Nf1).

?- reduce(make_offer(insert(insert(empty, adr1), adr2), adr1), Nf2).

?- reduce(delete_house(insert(insert(empty, adr1), adr2), adr1), Nf3).

?- equivalent(insert(empty, adr1), add_house(empty, adr1, for_sale)).
```

All four queries succeed, the last one because the two terms

```
insert(empty, adr1)  and  add_house(empty, adr1, for_sale)
```

are 'equal' with respect to the axioms of the specification. In the case of the first three queries, the results of the computations are that Nf1, Nf2 and Nf3 are, respectively, instantiated to

1. `add_house(add_house(empty, adr2, for_sale), adr1, for_sale)`
2. `add_house(add_house(empty, adr2, for_sale), adr1, under_offer)`
3. `add_house(empty, adr2, for_sale)`

The pros and cons of using Prolog to prototype VDM specifications have been discussed in Chapter 7 so it suffices here to say that two disadvantages of using Standard Edinburgh Prolog for prototyping algebraic specifications are:

- Prolog does not support modularity.
- Prolog is not strongly typed. The main advantage of a strongly typed ('strongly sorted') programming language is that the compiler can trap meaningless expressions before they are executed. The trouble with Prolog is that it is too permissive. For instance, in the above example

```
reduce(insert(insert(empty, under_offer), true), R)
```

is a well-formed expression in Prolog, although the arguments of the predicate insert do not conform to the expected sort of the corresponding operation of Houses-for-sale. Moreover, the query

```
?- reduce(insert(insert(empty, under_offer), true), R).
```

will succeed for this meaningless expression.

```
reduce(true,R) :-
    canonise(true,R) .
reduce(false,R) :-
    canonise(false,R) .
reduce(adr1,R) :-
    canonise(adr1,R) .
reduce(adr2,R) :-
    canonise(adr2,R) .
reduce(adr3,R) :-
    canonise(adr3,R) .
reduce(adr4,R) :-
    canonise(adr4,R) .
reduce(for_sale,R) :-
    canonise(for_sale,R) .
reduce(under_offer,R) :-
    canonise(under_offer,R) .
reduce(empty,R) :-
    canonise(empty,R) .
reduce(insert(D,A),R) :-
    reduce(D,D1),
    reduce(A,A1),
    canonise(insert(D1,A1),R) .
reduce(add_house(D,A,M),R) :-
    reduce(D,D1),
    reduce(A,A1),
    reduce(M,M1),
    canonise(add_house(D1,A1,M1),R) .
reduce(delete_house(D,A),R) :-
    reduce(D,D1),
    reduce(A,A1),
    canonise(delete_house(D1,A1),R) .
reduce(make_offer(D,A),R) :-
    reduce(D,D1),
    reduce(A,A1),
    canonise(make_offer(D1,A1),R) .
reduce(is_on_market(D,A),R) :-
    reduce(D,D1),
    reduce(A,A1),
    canonise(is_on_market(D1,A1),R) .
reduce(is_under_offer(D,A),R) :-
    reduce(D,D1),
    reduce(A,A1),
    canonise(is_under_offer(D1,A1),R) .


axiom(insert(empty,Addr), add_house(empty,Addr,for_sale)) .
axiom(insert(add_house(Hs,Addr1,M),Addr1), add_house(Hs,Addr1,M)) .
axiom(insert(add_house(Hs,Addr1,M),Addr2),
                        add_house(insert(Hs,Addr2),Addr1,M)) :-
    Addr1 \== Addr2 .
axiom(delete_house(empty,Addr), empty) .
```

Figure 13.2 Prolog implementation of the algebraic specification Houses-for-sale.

```
axiom(delete_house(add_house(Hs,Addr1,M),Addr1), Hs) .
axiom(delete_house(add_house(Hs,Addr1,M),Addr2),
                        add_house(delete_house(Hs,Addr2),Addr1,M)) :-
    Addr1 \== Addr2 .
axiom(is_on_market(empty,Addr), false) .
axiom(is_on_market(add_house(Hs,Addr1,M),Addr1), true) .
axiom(is_on_market(add_house(Hs,Addr1,M),Addr2), is_on_market(Hs,Addr2)) :-
    Addr1 \== Addr2 .
axiom(is_under_offer(empty,Addr), false) .
axiom(is_under_offer(add_house(Hs,Addr1,under_offer),Addr1), true) .
axiom(is_under_offer(add_house(Hs,Addr1,for_sale),Addr1), false) .
axiom(is_under_offer(add_house(Hs,Addr1,M),Addr2), is_under_offer(Hs,Addr2)) :-
    Addr1 \== Addr2 .
axiom(make_offer(empty,Addr), empty) .
axiom(make_offer(add_house(Hs,Addr1,for_sale),Addr1),
                        add_house(delete_house(Hs,Addr1),Addr1,under_offer)) .
axiom(make_offer(add_house(Hs,Addr1,under_offer),Addr1),
                        add_house(Hs,Addr1,under_offer)) .
axiom(make_offer(add_house(Hs,Addr1,M),Addr2),
                        add_house(make_offer(Hs,Addr2),Addr1,M)) :-
    Addr1 \== Addr2 .
canonise(X,Z) :-
    axiom(X,Y),
    reduce(Y,Z).
canonise(X,X) .
equivalent(T1,T2) :-
    reduce(T1,Nf),
    reduce(T2,Nf) .
```

Figure 13.2–*contd.*

Exercise 13.1 Demonstrate that the well-formed Prolog query

```
?- reduce(insert(insert(empty, under_offer), true), R) .
```

succeeds with R instantiated to the (meaningless) expression

```
add_house(add_house(empty, true, for_sale), under_offer, for_sale)
```

13.6.1 Use of an imperative programming language

Another means of implementing an algebraic specification is to translate the specification into a general-purpose imperative procedural programming language such as Modula-2 or Ada. A fundamental difficulty here is the complexity of the translation process. While it is true that program modules (units) can be written in Modula-2 and Ada which are strikingly similar in style to algebraic specifications (especially if only *function* subprograms are used and a 'functional' style is used consistently throughout—see Harrison (1989), moving in the opposite way from an algebraic specification to a Modula-2 implementation module or Ada package, though feasible, is a much weightier task in practice (Priestley, (1989)).

Priestley developed a system that enables algebraic specifications to be integrated into an Ada programming environment. An algebraic specification is expressed as an Ada package specification and automatically transformed into an executable Ada package that implements the corresponding abstract data type. The resulting Ada package interprets the axioms as left-to-right rewrite rules. One of the design aims of the system was to use the information-hiding capabilities of Ada so that the derived package could be totally interchangeable with a conventional (and correct) hand-coded implementation of the same abstract data type. One key task in the process is to redefine the built-in equality operator = which is available in Ada for every nonlimited data type so that it equates two objects of the data type if the terms implementing them are the same. For example, in the case of stacks, the terms

push(init, 2) and pop(push(push(init, 2), 1))

represent the same data value, but the corresponding expression

push(init, 2) = pop(push(push(init, 2), 1))

would evaluate to false with the standard definition of =, assuming the stacks are implemented by some dynamic data structure. This is so because = is based on the identity of the objects used to implement the data type and not on the values represented by its arguments. What has to be done is to export the equality operation == which equates two objects if the terms that implement them are identical. This can be effected if the operation always compares the corresponding *normal forms* of each object.

A major problem arises if the correctness of the translation process has to be established entirely formally. To do this, we would have to rely on being able to describe our implementation as an algebra and then prove that this algebra is an initial model of the specification. A formal semantics, in the form of these 'implementation algebras' (as Goguen calls them), is rarely available for imperative programming languages, so that the correctness of the translation process from specification to implementation is very hard to establish.

13.7 MANY-SORTED AND ORDER-SORTED ALGEBRAS

To conclude this chapter, we return to the idea of *subsorts* and examine their mathematical semantics and how the associated concept of an *order-sorted algebra* (OSA) is related to *many-sorted algebra* (MSA). The major difference between OBJ3 and Axis is that OBJ3 is based on OSA while Axis is founded upon MSA. The principal advantage of OSA is that it directly supports the concept of subsorts.

Implementing *strong typing* (or to be pedantic *strong sorting*) using many-sorted logic can be too rigid and is also not always sufficiently flexible when dealing with errors. Our discussion of errors in Chapter 9 highlighted the problems that can arise when many-sorted algebras are used to handle exceptions. Subsorts were introduced in order to confront these difficulties and we have seen that the use of subsorts provides a powerful, yet simple way of handling errors. This is the principal reason for using OBJ3 as a prototyping language rather than Axis.

13.7.1 Mathematical semantics of OSA

Order-sorted algebra or OSA was developed to deal with situations where items of one sort are also of another sort (for example, all natural numbers are also integers) and where operations or expressions may have more than one sort. OSA is different from many-sorted algebra or MSA in that a partial ordering exists in the collection of sorts, in the form of an inclusion relation (denoted by $<$ in our pseudocode), which is interpreted semantically as subset inclusion among the carrier sets of the intended model. For example, the *subsort* relation nat $<$ int where nat and int are sorts associated with the theory of natural numbers and integers, respectively, is interpreted as the *subset* relation $\mathbb{N} \subseteq \mathbb{Z}$. The great advantage of OSA is that it overcomes the difficulties arising from exceptions and partial operations.

Order-sorted type structures allow multiple inheritance (in the sense that a given sort may be a subsort of two or more other sorts), operation overloading, and error handling to be encompassed within standard equational logic. OSA also allows operations that would otherwise have to be *partial* to be made *total*, which is achieved by the simple device of restricting them to the appropriate subsort.

An OSA is a generalization of standard MSA which leads directly to the question of which constructions, ideas and results from many-sorted initial algebra carry over and are valid for OSA. In fact, it turns out that although OSA differs from MSA in that a partial ordering exists among the carriers, many of the concepts of MSA can be immediately and easily generalized to OSA provided we confine ourselves to what are called *regular* signatures. This is pleasing since it means that the algorithms and results we have developed to date within the framework of (standard) MSA can be applied without modification.

The requirement that a signature is *regular* places mild and natural constraints on the form of an order-sorted signature and ensures that any order-sorted term will always have a well-defined *least sort*. In this context, such a term is then said to be *well-formed*. In essence, regularity requires that overloaded operations must be consistent (that is must agree in their results) when restricted to arguments in the same subsorts.

If we take the example above, with the subsort relation nat $<$ int interpreted as the inclusion $\mathbb{N} \subseteq \mathbb{Z}$, the operation symbol $+$ can be overloaded, for example

```
+ : nat nat → nat ; + : int int → int
```

and regularity requires that the two should agree when restricted to arguments in the same subsorts.

For the interested reader, we present a short and informal account of how order-sorted algebra can be reduced to many-sorted algebra in Sec. 13.7.2. This subsection is included just for the mathematically curious.

13.7.2 An operational semantics for order-sorted algebra

Our aim is to outline, in as simple and direct a way as possible, how order-sorted algebra can be translated into standard many-sorted algebra. The description is not intended to be detailed or exhaustively rigorous but simply to convey the principal ideas and amplifies the discussion in Goguen *et al.* (1985).

The difference between order-sorted algebra and standard (many-sorted) algebra is that the former has an inclusion (subset) relation between the carriers which interprets the subsort relation of the corresponding specification. We can model this subsort relation by introducing so-called *embedding functions* or *coercions* $c_{s,s'}$ for each subsort relation $s < s'$ together with a collection of equations (axioms) satisfied by these embedding functions. To keep the discussion as simple as possible, suppose we have four sorts *NzNat*, *Nat*, *Int*, and *Bool*, where *NzNat* is a subsort of *Nat* which is itself a subsort of *Int* corresponding to the sorts of *nonzero* natural numbers, natural numbers, integers and Boolean values respectively). The subsort relations are expressed by

$$NzNat < Nat < Int$$

which is a statement of the fact that the subsort relation is *transitive*. Each subsort relation can be translated into standard equations (axioms) by viewing a subsort pair $s < s'$ as a mapping from s to s', that is to say as a (unary) operation (function) $c_{s,s'}$ with

$$c_{s,s'} : s \to s'$$

We now examine the equations that need to be supplied for each subsort pair.

1. Since, by definition, $s < s$, that is *each sort s includes itself*, we introduce the embedding function $c_{s,s} : s \to s$ for each sort s together with the (conditional) equation

$$c_{s,s}(x) = x \quad \forall x \in s$$

So, for our small example, we would introduce the four embedding functions $c_{NzNat,NzNat}$, $c_{Nat,Nat}$, $c_{Int,Int}$, $c_{Bool,Bool}$.

2. The conditional equation

$$c_{s,s'}(x) = c_{s,s'}(y) \text{ implies } x = y \quad \forall x \in s \text{ and for all subsorts } s \text{ of } s'$$

models the injective property that must hold for embedding functions. This equation ensures that two distinct values that belong to the sort s are not mapped to the same element in s'. Hence, for our example, this equation ensures that the (distinct) natural numbers 3 and 7, say, are not mapped to the same integer value using the embedding function $c_{Nat,Int}$.

3. The transitive property $s < s' < s''$ is expressed by the equation

$$c_{s',s''}(c_{s,s'}(x)) = c_{s,s''}(x) \quad \forall x \in s$$

which for our example becomes

$$c_{Nat,Int}(c_{NzNat,Nat}(x)) = c_{NzNat,Int}(x) \quad \forall x \in NzNat$$

4. Finally, whenever an operation symbol *op* of arity n is defined for two sorts s and s' with s a subsort of s' ($s < s'$), that is

$$op_s : s_1 s_2 \ldots s_n \to s$$

$$op_{s'} : s_{1'} s_{2'} \ldots s_{n'} \to s'$$

we must ensure that

$$op_{s'}(c_{s,s'}(x_1), c_{s,s'}(x_2), \ldots, c_{s,s'}(x_n)) = c_{s,s'}(op_s(x_1, x_2, \ldots, x_n))$$

where $x_i \in s_i$. This equation looks rather fearsome, perhaps even more so when we state that this result expresses the fact that all subsort relations must be homomorphisms! If we refer back to Chapter 10, and in particular Eq. (10.1) of Sec. 10.6.1, we see that the above equation defines a homomorphism. Our concrete example should help us understand this result and should also sharpen our understanding of the meaning and importance of homomorphisms.

If we consider the binary infix addition operation '+', defined for both *Nat* and *Int* as our operation *op*, where $Nat < Int$, the above 'homomorphism' equation becomes

$$c_{Nat,Int}(x) +_{Int} c_{Nat,Int}(y) = c_{Nat,Int}(x +_{Nat} y)$$

where $+_{Nat}: Nat\ Nat \to Nat$ and $+_{Int}: Int\ Int \to Int$ denote the addition operation for the two levels and $x, y \in Nat$. We can interpret this result as follows. Since the sort of natural numbers is a subsort of the integers, any two natural numbers x and y will also be members of the sort of integers. Furthermore, if we add two natural numbers the result will be a natural number that will also be a member of the sort of integers. Hence, if we add two natural numbers using the 'natural +' operation ($+_{Nat}: Nat\ Nat \to Nat$) and then 'coerce' the result to an integer using the embedding function $c_{Nat,Int}$ (which is the right-hand side of the above equation), we must get the same result when we 'coerce' each of the natural numbers x and y to an integer first and then add the integer values using the 'integer +' operation ($+_{Int}: Int\ Int \to Int$) (which is the left-hand side of the above equation).

This process defines a translation from order-sorted algebra notation to standard equational notation. Thus if E is a set of axioms defining a SPEC module, we obtain a translation E^* in which the equations given in (1) to (4) above have been added. The pleasing result, from our point of view, is that an *equivalence* exists between the class of order-sorted algebras satisfying E and the class of standard algebras satisfying E^* under which the *initial* algebras of each class correspond. This result is important since it means that we can translate back and forth between E and E^* without loss of information.

The particular translation under which the initial algebras of the two classes correspond involves mapping an overloaded operation in the order-sorted algebra (such as the operation + in our example) to *one* of its forms in the standard algebra (that is $+_{Nat}$ or $+_{Int}$). The translation is done by selecting the operation with the smallest *range* sort such that the resulting expression is well-formed. This resulting expression is referred to as the *lowest parse*.

13.8 SUMMARY

- Use of the executable algebraic specification language *OBJ3* as a vehicle for *prototyping* specifications is explored and a summary of the main features of OBJ3 presented.
- The issue of implementing algebraic specifications using *functional* languages, *Prolog*, and *imperative* languages is examined.

ADDITIONAL PROBLEMS

13.1 Use Prolog to produce prototypes for the algebraic specifications Stack and Queue of Figs 8.2 and 9.2 respectively.

13.2 Use Prolog to produce a prototype for the algebraic specification Symbol-Table of Fig. 11.23 (Additional Problem 11.18).

REFERENCES

Ehrig, H., and Mahr, B. (1985). *Fundamentals of Algebraic Specification 1: Equations and Initial Semantics*, Springer-Verlag, Berlin.

Goguen, J.A., Jouannaud, J.-P., and Meseguer, J. (1985). Operational Semantics of Order-sorted Algebra. In *Proceedings of the 12th. International Conference on Automata, Languages and Programming*, published in *Lecture Notes in Computer Science*, vol. 194, Springer-Verlag, Berlin, pp. 221–231.

Goguen, J.A., Thatcher, J.W., and Wagner, E.G. (1978). An Initial Algebra Approach to the Specification, Correctness and Implementation of Abstract Data Types. In R.T. Yeh (ed.) *Current Trends in Programming Methodology*, vol. 3, Prentice-Hall, Englewood Cliffs, NJ, pp. 80–149.

Goguen, J.A., and Winkler, T. (1988). Introducing OBJ3, *SRI International Computer Science Laboratory Report SRI-CSL-88-9*, 333 Ravenswood Avenue, Menlo Park, California.

Harrison, R. (1989). *Abstract Data Types in Modula-2*, John Wiley, Chichester.

Priestley, M. (1989). Implementing Structured Algebraic Specifications in Ada *Proceedings of the 8th. Ada UK Conference*, Peter Peregrinus, Oxford.

14

JOINT CASE STUDY: DEVELOPMENT OF A NEURAL NETWORK SPECIFICATION

14.1 INTRODUCTION

This chapter includes an introduction to and a discussion of the requirements of a neural network system. A formal specification of the network will be developed using first the algebraic style and then the VDM style.

14.2 NEURAL NETWORKS

Our first task is to give an overview of the principal features of neural networks. Our aim is to present a brief yet adequate overview of this aspect of computing and *no* previous knowledge of this field is assumed.

A *neural network* is a parallel distributed information processing structure which consists of a collection of simple processing *elements* which are interlinked by means of signal channels or *connections*. The processing elements are often referred to as *units* or *neurons* and each such element has a local memory which can perform localized information processing. Each neuron in a neural network has a *single* output connection that *spreads* (*fans*) out into as many collateral connections as required. The *output signal* from a neuron is then carried by each such collateral connection. Neural networks are seen as providing an alternative method for implementing parallel (distributed) information processing systems and their main applications up to now have been in classification and image processing.

14.2.1 A simple model of neurons

One of the earliest models of a neuron was propounded by McCulloch and Pitts (1943), who considered neurons as *binary threshold units*. In other words, the neuron computes a (linear) weighted sum of its 'incoming' input signals and outputs a '0' if this weighted sum is below a certain threshold or a '1' if the weighted sum is equal to or above that threshold. When the output is 1 (0), the state of the neuron is represented as *firing* (*not firing*) respectively.

As an example, consider a neuron i with threshold T_i and three 'incoming' signals n_1, n_2, n_3 with corresponding weights w_{1i}, w_{2i}, w_{3i}. Neuron i will then fire with output $n_i = 1$ if

$$w_{1i}n_1 + w_{2i}n_2 + w_{3i}n_3 \geqslant T_i$$

Note that the expression $w_{1i}n_1 + w_{2i}n_2 + w_{3i}n_3$ is the *weighted sum* for this particular neuron and this example is illustrated in Fig. 14.1. The weights for each neuron can be considered as local data stored by that neuron. The individual weight w_{ji} is a measure of the strength of the connection from neuron j to neuron i. The weight w_{ji} can be positive in which case the signal from neuron j is said to be *excitatory*, negative in which case the signal is said to be *inhibitory*, or the weight can be zero which indicates there is no connection from neuron j to neuron i. The weights w_{ji} for neuron i can be considered as local data stored by that neuron.

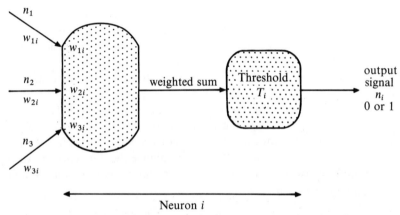

Figure 14.1 *Binary threshold* model for a neuron.

An interconnection *from* neuron j to neuron i is therefore characterized by two properties, its *type*, that is whether it is excitatory or inhibitory, and the relative influence that neuron j has on neuron i. Changing the weights w_{ji} associated with a connection alters the degree of 'interconnectedness' and in this manner the neural network can be made to adapt to new situations. For the McCulloch–Pitts model, the *threshold function* (also referred to as the *transfer function*) is a *step function*[1] and variations on this model exist

---

[1] We can express the output n_i as

$$n_i = H(w_{1i}n_1 + w_{2i}n_2 + w_{3i}n_3 - T_i)$$

where $H(x-a)$ is the *Heaviside step function* defined by

$$H(x-a) = \begin{cases} 1 & \text{if } x \geqslant a \\ 0 & \text{otherwise} \end{cases}$$

which use different transfer functions such as *sigmoid functions* which output a continuously varying value between 0 and 1. More generally, each individual neuron in a neural network has a *transfer function* which operates on the incoming input signals to the neuron and generates the corresponding output signal from that neuron. As part of this process, the transfer function may make use of and change the data values (weights) stored in the neuron's local memory.

The McCulloch–Pitts model of a neuron, although simple, is computationally a potent device in the sense that, for appropriately chosen weights w_{ji}, a multi-layer network of neurons can accomplish any computation that can be performed by a conventional von Neumann machine (although not necessarily as fast or efficiently as the latter). For more information, see Rumelhart and McClelland (1986).

14.2.2 Applications of neural networks

Neural networks are a particular type of *multiple instruction multiple data* (*MIMD*) architecture and two important applications have been their development as 'pattern recognition' and 'learning' machines.

Of interest here is the problem of how to select the weights w_{ij} in order to carry out a given computation. One technique involves 'teaching' the network to perform the required task by allowing the net to modify the weights in accordance with some *learning law*. This learning law is often embodied as a subfunction of a neuron's transfer function. The role of this component is to adapt the input–output behaviour of the neuron's transfer function by modifying its weights w_{ij} in response to the training examples (input/output pairs).

The method involves 'training', whereby the net is presented with a *training set* of *correct* input–output pairs as examples. A 'training' input is applied to the network and the output produced by the network is compared with the correct value ('learning with a teacher'). The connection strengths w_{ij} are then altered to minimize the difference between the actual and correct output values. The main network architecture used for this type of learning is the *backpropagation* neural network.

14.2.3 Types of neural networks

Basically, we can classify neural networks according to their connection geometries and one of the simplest architectures is the *layered feed-forward network*. Such structures are characterized by a collection of input neurons ('terminals') whose sole purpose is to supply input signals from the outside world into the rest of the network. Following this can come one or more intermediate layers of neurons and finally an output layer where the output of the computation can be communicated to the outside world. The intermediate layers which have no direct contact with the outside world are called *hidden layers*. For this class of networks, there are no connections from a neuron to neuron(s) in previous layers, other neurons in the same layer, or to neurons more than one layer ahead. An example of such a layered feed-forward network is shown in Fig. 14.2, which is an example of a *three-layered* network and we have labelled the individual neurons 1 to 5. For feed-forward networks, every neuron in a given layer receives inputs from layers below its own (that is from layers nearer the output layer) and sends output to layers above its own (that is to layers nearer

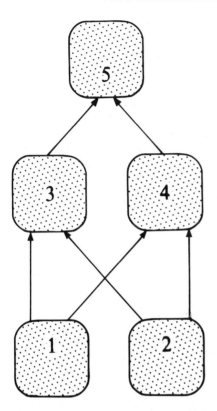

Figure 14.2   Example of a three layered feed-forward neural network.

the output layer). For such networks, given a set of inputs (the *input vector*) from the neurons in the input layer, the output vector is computed by a succession of forward passes, which compute the intermediate output vectors of each layer in turn using the previously computed signal values in the earlier layers. One of the simplest such networks consists of a single layer and is called a *perceptron*.

A more general class of network extends the feed-forward topology by allowing the *output signal* of each neuron in a given layer to be connected not only to the layer ahead but also to that same neuron as an *input signal*. Such networks are called *associative recurrent networks*.

Backpropagation networks not only have feed-forward connections but each layer also receives an *error feedback* connection from each of the neurons above it. For neural networks, in general, the only restriction on the type of information processing that can be undertaken by a neuron is that it must be *entirely local*. In other words, it must depend solely on the values stored in the neuron's local memory and on the current values of the input signals reaching that neuron through the linked connections.

14.3 SPECIFYING A NEURAL NETWORK

For the purposes of our discussion, we can define a neural network as a parallel distributed information processing structure that can be represented by a *directed graph* (*digraph*) with the following features:

- The nodes of the graph are neurons.
- The arcs (links) of the graph are connections and behave as one-directional paths along which signals can travel.
- Apart from 'input' neurons, each neuron can be the recipient of an arbitrary number of incoming ('impinging') connections.
- The set of 'input' neurons (or 'terminals') originates in the outside world and the only function of such 'input' neurons is to feed input signals into the rest of the network.
- Each neuron has one output connection but the associated signal can branch or 'shoot' out into copies and so form multiple output connections. By this means, each neuron can have a number of outgoing ('emergent') connections, but the signals along all these emergent paths will be the same.
- The result of a whole network computation is read off from connections that leave the network.
- Neurons can possess local memory (at least a threshold) and undertake localized information processing.
- Each neuron has a local processing capability which is prescribed by a *transfer* or *gain* function. The *only* permissible inputs to a neuron's transfer function are the current values of the impinging ('incoming') signals received by the neuron *and* the values (weights) stored in the neuron's local memory. The *only* permissible outputs from a neuron's transfer function are the neuron's output signal.
- Neurons can respond to their input either at *discrete* time intervals or in a *continuous* manner. In the discrete case, a neuron's transfer function operates in response to an 'activate' input signal which makes the neuron process its current impinging (incoming) signals and local memory values to produce an updated output signal. The outputs are updated either *synchronously*, usually one layer at a time, or *asynchronously* (in random order at random times). The transfer functions of continuous-time neurons are always active.

14.4 ALGEBRAIC SPECIFICATION OF A NEURAL NETWORK

We now develop an algebraic specification for a *general* neural network. The specification will be built up from smaller individual specifications using the theory-building operators and the parameterization mechanism introduced in Chapter 11. The following assumptions are made:

- We adopt what is essentially the McCulloch–Pitts model of a neuron in which a neuron n_i with threshold T_i fires when the weighted sum of its incoming input signals equals or exceeds T_i.
- For simplicity, we do not incorporate any learning law.
- We assume synchronous discrete firing.
- The weights, input/output signals and thresholds are discrete values.

We therefore need to specify abstract data types whose values denote discrete values such as input and output signals, thresholds and weights. As stated above, we assume the weights, input/output signals, and thresholds are discrete values and so assume the availability of appropriate specifications Signal, Weighting, and Threshold with corresponding sorts signal, weighting, and thresh. We will also need a specification Name with sort name to specify neuron identifiers. (For simple neuron models, the signals, weights, and threshold values are all drawn from the set of values $-1, 0, 1$.)

When a neuron fires, we need to 'inform' all neurons with connections from n_i that n_i has fired. This will be specified using a two-valued data type consisting of the (constant) values on and off. The corresponding specification Activation is shown in Fig. 14.3.

```
SPEC   Activation
SORT   activation
OPS
    on  :   ->   activation
    off :   ->   activation
ENDSPEC
```

Figure 14.3 The specification Activation.

14.5 STRUCTURE OF A NEURAL NETWORK

Conceptually, we can think of a neural network as a *collection* of neurons, with *each* neuron characterized by a 4-tuple with the following components:

1. A name that identifies the neuron
2. A threshold
3. A *collection* of impinging ('incoming') neuron connections
4. A *collection* of emergent ('outgoing') neuron connections

In view of the emphasis on 'collections' of data items, it makes sense to utilize a specification for a *generic* collection of items. Sets and lists immediately spring to mind as possible specification modules that could be utilized for the collection of neuron structures. The principal reason for choosing the list rather than the set to describe the collections of neurons and their individual connections is that the elements in a list have an explicit ordering. When we come to develop axioms that describe the behaviour of the operations for a network, we need to be able systematically to 'process' each neuron (or connection) in turn. While this is straightforward with a list structure, the lack of any ordering in the elements of a set can lead to problems of indeterminacy. For this reason, we will use a parameterized list module and the corresponding specification is given in Fig. 14.4 where the atomic constructors are the empty list, [ ], and the *cons* operation _ . _ which takes an element and a list and inserts the element at the front of the existing list to produce a new list. The operation _ app _ is the familiar (associative) concatenation operation while the Boolean-valued operation is-in? _ _ returns true if a specified element is a member of the set and false otherwise.

A neural network can then be specified in terms of a *list* of neurons, with each neuron specified as a 4-tuple in which the third and fourth slots are themselves *lists* of neuron connections.

```
SPEC  List (E : Elem)
USING  Boolean
SORTS  list  ne-list
SUBSORT  ne-list < list
OPS
    []          :                        -> list
    _ . _       : element  list   -> ne-list
    _ app _     : list  list       -> list      [ASSOC]
    is-in? _ _  : element  list    -> bool
FORALL
    e, e1, e2 : element
    s, s1, s2 : list

AXIOMS for list concatenation:
    [] app s          = s
    ( e . s1 ) app s2 = e . ( s1 app s2 )
AXIOMS for determining whether an element e1 is present in a list:
    is-in? e1 []      = false
    is-in? e1 (e2 .s) = IF  e1 == e2   THEN   true  ELSE  is-in? e1 s  ENDIF
ENDSPEC
```

Figure 14.4 Parameterized specification of a list.

14.5.1 Specification of incoming and outgoing connections

For each connection that transmits a signal *to* a given neuron, we need three pieces of data about each *incoming* signal:

1. The value of the incoming signal
2. Whether the source neuron from which the signal emanates 'is activated'. We will use the value on ∈ activation to denote this state
3. The name of the source neuron

The connections to a given neuron can therefore be specified by a *list* of 3-tuples (triples). For input neurons ('terminals') whose only role is to feed information into the network from the outside world, the list of incoming connections will consist of the single 3-tuple < input signal; on ; 0 > where we use a dummy value '0' in the third slot to flag that the incoming signal is from an 'input' neuron.

Turning to the connections that feed out *from* a given neuron, three pieces of information are necessary:

1. The value of the output signal
2. The weight with respect to a given destination neuron
3. The name of the destination neuron

For 'output' neurons which transmit information to the outside world, the list of outgoing connections will consist of the single 3-tuple < output signal ; weight ; 0 >. In this case the dummy value '0' is used to signify that this neuron transmits information to the outside world.

Of immediate use, therefore, will be a specification for a 3-tuple whose individual components are values drawn from arbitrary sorts. Such a specification for an unconstrained 3-tuple is given by the generic specification Triple of Fig. 14.5. The operation < _ ; _ ; _ > takes three values drawn from arbitrary sorts and returns the corresponding 3-tuple, while 1-st, 2-nd and 3-rd are accessor operations that select the first, second, and third components of a 3-tuple respectively. A parameterized specification describing a list of unconstrained 3-tuples can be derived immediately from the parameterized specifications List and Triple and the resulting specification List-of-Triple is shown in Fig. 14.6.

```
SPEC  Triple( S1 : Elem  &&  S2 : Elem  &&  S3 : Elem )
SORT triple
OPS
     < _ ; _ ; _ > : S1's element  S2's element  S3's element
                                             ->  triple
     1-st _           :  triple  ->  S1's element
     2-nd _           :  triple  ->  S2's element
     3-rd _           :  triple  ->  S3's element
FORALL
     a : S1's element
     b : S2's element
     c : S3's element
AXIOMS:
     1-st < a ; b ; c >  =  a
     2-nd < a ; b ; c >  =  b
     3-rd < a ; b ; c >  =  c
ENDSPEC
```

Figure 14.5 Specification for an unconstrained 3-tuple.

```
SPEC  List-of-Triple( F : Elem  &&  M : Elem  &&  E : Elem )
USING List ( Triple ( F && M && E ) )
ENDSPEC
```

Figure 14.6 Specification of a list of unconstrained 3-tuples.

14.5.2 Specification of a neuron

As noted earlier, we can specify a neuron as a 4-tuple with the following components:

1. An identifier (name) for the neuron
2. A threshold for the neuron
3. A list of incoming ('input') neuron connections from which signals can be received
4. A list of outgoing ('output') neurons to which signals can be sent

so that an *individual* neuron is specified by the 4-tuple

< identifier ; threshold ;

list of < input value ; on *or* off ; source neuron > ;

list of < output value ; weight ; destination neuron > >

We can produce a generic specification for such a 4-tuple immediately by direct analogy with the specification Triple of Fig. 14.5. We denote the four selector operations that access the components of a 4-tuple by identifier, threshold, input, and output respectively and the corresponding specification is given in Fig. 14.7. The complete neural network will then be specified as a *list* of neurons (4-tuples) where the collections of input and output connections are both *lists* of 3-tuples.

```
SPEC   Neuron (S1 : Elem && S2 : Elem && S3 : Elem && S4 : Elem)
SORT neuron
OPS
    < _ ; _ ; _ ; _ > :  S1's element  S2's element  S3's element
                         S4's element  ->  neuron
      identifier _       :  neuron  ->  S1's element
      threshold _        :  neuron  ->  S2's element
      input _            :  neuron  ->  S3's element
      output _           :  neuron  ->  S4's element
FORALL
    a : S1's element
    b : S2's element
    c : S3's element
    d : S4's element
AXIOMS:
    identifier < a ; b ; c ; d >  =  a
    threshold  < a ; b ; c ; d >  =  b
    input < a ; b ; c ; d >       =  c
    output < a ; b ; c ; d >      =  d
ENDSPEC
```

Figure 14.7 Specification of a neuron as a parameterized 4-tuple.

14.5.3 Overview of the specification for the network

We begin to see the overall form that our specification Neural-Network will take. First we will have specification modules Info and Outfo corresponding to the list of incoming (impinging) 'input' connections and the list of outgoing (emergent) 'output' connections respectively. These are obtained immediately by instantiating the generic specification List-of-Triple given by Fig. 14.6. The *headers* for the resulting specifications Info and

Outfo are

> SPEC Info
>
> USING List-of-Triple (Signal && Activation && Name)
>
>> WITH list AS info,
>>
>>> ne-list AS ne-info

where we have renamed the sort list as info and ne-list as ne-info, and

> SPEC Outfo
>
> USING List-of-Triple (Signal && Weighting && Name)
>> WITH
>>> 1-st _ : triple → signal   AS value-of _ ,
>>> 2-nd _ : triple → weighting   AS weight _ ,
>>> 3-rd _ : triple → name   AS to-neuron _ ,
>>> list AS outfo

where the operations of Triple and the sort list of List have been suitably renamed. The specifications Info and Outfo will be developed shortly.

From our description above of the neural network as a list of neurons (4-tuples), we can create a specification Neural-Network by instantiating the parameterized specifications List and Neuron as shown in the specification *header* below

> SPEC Neural-Network
>
> USING List (Neuron (Name && Threshold &&
>>>> Info FIT element AS info &&
>>>> Outfo FIT element AS outfo))
>
>> WITH list AS network

where the sort list has been renamed network. Consider the three-layer network shown in Fig. 14.8 which has two 'input' neurons (1, 2) and one 'output' neuron (5). For this network, the thresholds of all five neurons are -1, all neurons are off ('deactivated') apart from the 'input' neurons 1 and 2, and the weights of connections w_{ij} are shown enclosed in curly brackets (for example $\{-1\}$). For this perceptron, the corresponding term, which is a member of the sort network, is given by the expression

$< 1 ; -1 ; < 1 ; \text{on} ; 0 > . [\ ] ; < 0 ; 1 ; 3 > . < 0 ; -1 ; 4 > . [\ ] > .$

$< 2 ; -1 ; < 0 ; \text{on} ; 0 > . [\ ] ; < 0 ; -1 ; 3 > . < 0 ; 1 ; 4 > . [\ ] > .$

$< 3 ; -1 ; < 0 ; \text{off} ; 1 > . < 0 ; \text{off} ; 2 > . [\ ] ; < 0 ; 1 ; 5 > . [\ ] > .$

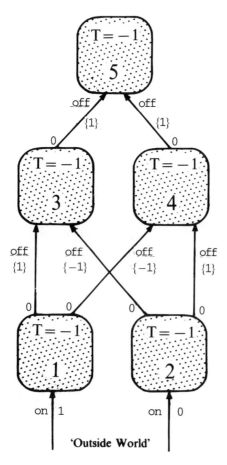

Figure 14.8   Example of a three-layer neural network.

$$< 4 ; -1 ; < 0 ; off ; 1 > . < 0 ; off ; 2 > . [ ] ; < 0 ; 1 ; 5 > . [ ] > .$$

$$< 5 ; -1 ; < 0 ; off ; 3 > . < 0 ; off ; 4 > . [ ] ; < 0 ; 1 ; 0 > . [ ] > . [ ]$$

Our next task is to develop the specification by looking at the operations and associated axioms of Neural-Network and its concomitant subspecifications Info, Outfo and Neuron.

14.6 SPECIFICATIONS FOR THE COMPONENT ABSTRACT DATA TYPES

Having established the constituent abstract data types for a neural network, we proceed to examine, in more detail, the required operations and associated axioms for the specifications Outfo, Info, Neuron and Neural-Network.

14.6.1 The specification `Outfo`

To start, we complete the specification for the list of 'outgoing' (emergent) neuron connections from a single neuron. Apart from the selector operations value–of, weight and to–neuron (already introduced) which recover the values corresponding to the *output signal*, *weight* and *destination neuron* respectively for an individual connection, one further operation fire–out is needed

```
fire-out _ _ : signal outfo → outfo
```

Given an arbitrary signal value m (an integer value) and an output list of emergent connections (3-tuples), this operation copies the given value m into the first slot of *all* 3-tuples in the output list. The axioms satisfied by fire–out are immediately seen to be

```
fire-out m [ ] = [ ]
```

```
fire-out m < n ; w ; p > .1 = < m ; w ; p > .(fire-out m 1)
```

where m, n, $\in$ signal, w $\in$ weighting, p $\in$ name, and 1 $\in$ outfo. The second axiom simply says replace the first slot of the leading triple in the list by m and repeat this action for all subsequent triples in the list. This operation will be used later in Neural–Network (in conjunction with others) to specify the behaviour of a *firing* neuron. The completed specification Outfo is given in Fig. 14.9.

Exercise 14.1 Derive axioms for a Boolean-valued operation has–output? : outfo → bool which returns true if the list of outgoing connections corresponds to an 'output' neuron (that is one which transmits information to the 'outside world') and false otherwise.

```
SPEC   Outfo
USING List-of-Triple(Signal  &&  Weighting  &&  Name)
   WITH
        1-st _ :  triple -> signal      AS   value-of _,
        2-nd _ :  triple -> weighting   AS   weight _,
        3-rd _ :  triple -> name        AS   to-neuron _,
        list  AS   outfo
OPS
   fire-out _ _ :  signal  outfo  ->  outfo
FORALL
   1     :   outfo
   m, n  :   signal
   w     :   weighting
   p     :   name
AXIOMS for fire-out:
   fire-out m []   =   []
   fire-out m < n ; w ; p > . 1   =   < m ; w ; p > . (fire-out m 1)
ENDSPEC
```

Figure 14.9   The algebraic specification Outfo.

14.6.2 The specification Info

The list of impinging (incoming) inputs to an individual neuron consists of triples whose first, second, and third slots correspond to the input signal value, the activation state (on or off), and the neuron source respectively. The operations required for the specification Info are:

- all-active? _ : ne-info → bool an operation that takes a nonempty list of incoming neuron connections and returns true if *all* the incoming connections are activated, that is if the second slots of *all* the 3-tuples in the list have the value on.
- sum-active _ : info → signal an operation that, given a list of input triples for a particular neuron, finds the sum of the incoming input signals coming from *activated* neurons (that is those 3-tuples whose second slots have the value on).
- make-passive _ : info → info an operation that takes a list of incoming neuron connections and replaces each activation value (that is the value in the second slot of each 3-tuple in the list) with the value off.
- change-weight _ _ _ : signal name info → info an operation that takes a signal value s (the first argument), a neuron identifier id1 (the second argument), and a list of incoming neuron connections, and amends the 3-tuple of the named neuron id1 by:
  - replacing the input signal of the corresponding 3-tuple (the value in its first slot) by s and
  - activating that same neuron id1, that is setting the value of the second slot in that same 3-tuple to on.

Axioms for all-active? The axioms for all-active? can be derived immediately by observing that for a list containing a single 3-tuple, all-active? will return true if its second slot has the value on. In general, all-active? returns true if the second slot of the 3-tuple at the head of the list has the value on and the second slots of all remaining 3-tuples have the value on. These results are expressed in the axioms

    all-active? < n ; a ; m > .[ ] = a = = on

    all-active? < n ; a ; m > .l = a = = on and all-active? l

where n ∈ signal, m ∈ name, l ∈ info, and a ∈ activation (that is takes one of the values on or off).

Axioms for sum-active Although for our chosen model, neurons will only fire if *all* their 'incoming' neuron connections are activated, we have chosen to introduce this less restrictive operation (in which not all the incoming connections have to be activated) to make the specification more general . For our application, we will use the Boolean-valued operation all-active? in conjunction with sum-active as a guard to ensure the required behaviour of our 'firing' operation is produced.

The operation sum-active finds the sum of the first slots of those 3-tuples in the list whose second slots have the value on. The axioms satisfied by sum-active follow by noting that, for an empty list, the sum is zero, while, for a non-empty list, we need to search through the 3-tuples in the list in turn and, if a 3-tuple t is activated (that is 2-nd t = = on), then add its signal (1-st t) to the result of repeating the operation on the remaining 3-tuples in the list. These observations lead immediately to the axioms

```
sum-active [ ] = 0
```

```
sum-active t . l = IF 2-nd t = = on THEN 1-st t + sum-active l
                      ELSE sum-active l ENDIF
```

where t ∈ triple and l ∈ info.

Exercise 14.2 Produce an axiom for the operation active? : triple → bool that takes an individual 3-tuple < n ; a ; m > where n ∈ signal, a ∈ activation, and m ∈ name, and returns true if its second slot has the value on and false otherwise. Rewrite the right-hand side of the second axiom for sum-active to incorporate the operation active?.

Axioms for make-passive The axioms for make-passive follow by noting that we can set the activation slots of every 3-tuple in the list to off by placing off in the second slot of the 3-tuple at the head of the list and then reapplying the operation make-passive to the remaining 3-tuples in the list. The result of applying make-passive to an empty list will result in an empty list. These results are expressed by the axioms

```
make-passive [ ] = [ ]
```

```
make-passive < n ; a ; m > . l = < n ; off ; m > . make-passive l
```

where n ∈ signal, m ∈ name, l ∈ info and a ∈ activation.

Axioms for change-weight The operation change-weight will be needed later in the specification Neural-Network when we consider the operation of firing a neuron. When a neuron *N* fires, it needs to notify this fact to all those neurons that have *N* in their list of incoming 3-tuples. In other words, *N* needs to 'communicate ahead' to all those neurons to which it is connected that it has fired. When *N* fires, it must also copy its output signal into the *input* value slot of those same neuron connections. We therefore introduce the operation

```
change-weight _ _ _ : signal name info → info
```

which takes an *arbitrary* signal value s (which will later correspond to the appropriate output signal), an *arbitrary* neuron identifier id1 (which will later correspond to a firing neuron *N*), and an *arbitrary* list of incoming neuron connections and seeks out that 3-tuple connection that has id1 as its destination neuron. Having found that 3-tuple, the given value s is placed in its first slot and that 3-tuple is activated by setting the value of its second slot to on.

Axioms for change-weight follow by noting that the operation achieves its task by scanning through the list of 3-tuples, checking in turn whether the neuron name in the most recently inserted triple matches the given neuron name.

Starting with the list of 3-tuples $< n ; a ; m > . 1$, the 3-tuple at the head of the list is $< n ; a ; m >$ (where $n \in$ signal, $a \in$ activation, $m \in$ name, and $1 \in$ info). If m matches the neuron identifer id1, the triple is immediately updated to $< s ; on ; id1 >$ and appended to the end of the list. This leads directly to the axiom

```
change-weight s id1 < n ; a ; m > . 1 = 1 app < s ; on ; id1 > . [ ]
```

On the other hand, if the specified neuron identifier does not match m, we reapply the operation change-weight to the tail of the list and append the unaffected 3-tuple $< n ; a ; m >$ to the end of the list. Finally, we define the outcome of change-weight applied to an empty list to be the empty list, which leads to the axioms

```
change-weight s id1 [ ] = [ ]

change-weight s id1 < n ; a ; m > . 1 =
   IF id1 = = m THEN 1 app < s ; on ; id1 > . [ ]
   ELSE (change-weight s id1 1 ) app < n ; a ; m > . [ ]
   ENDIF
```

The specification Info is now complete and is given in Fig. 14.10.

We can demonstrate the behaviour of the operation change-weight by considering the application

```
change-weight 1 3 < 0 ; off ; 2 > . < 0 ; off ; 3 > . < 1 ; on ; 4 > . [ ]
```

which results in the 'input' list

```
< 1 ; on ; 4 > . < 1 ; on ; 3 > . < 0 ; off ; 2 > . [ ]
```

where the second 3-tuple has been amended. Note that this operation changes the order of the 3-tuples in the list.

Exercise 14.3 Verify this result. You should show first that the operation change-weight is applied twice with the result

```
(< 1 ; on ; 4 > . [ ] app < 1 ; on ; 3 > . [ ] ) app ( < 0 ; off ; 2 > . [ ] )
```

Application of the axioms satisfied by the concatenation operation app from the parameterized list specification in Fig, 14.4 leads to the final result.

Exercise 14.4 Show that if the list of 3-tuples does not contain the given neuron id1, the operation change-weight will not amend any of the 3-tuples in the given list but will reverse the order of the 3-tuples that make up the list.

Exercise 14.5 Derive axioms for the Boolean-valued operation is-input? : info → bool which returns true if the list of incoming connections corresponds to an 'input' neuron (one that feeds information into the network from the 'outside world') and false otherwise.

```
SPEC   Info
USING  List-of-Triple(Signal  &&  Activation  &&  Name)
   WITH  list  AS  info, ne-list  AS  ne-info
OPS
   sum-active _          : info  ->  signal
   all-active? _         : ne-info  ->  bool
   make-passive _        : info  ->  info
   change-weight _ _ _   : signal  name  info  ->  info
FORALL
   t      :   triple
   l      :   info
   a      :   activation
   idl, m :   name
   n, s   :   signal
AXIOMS for sum-active:
   sum-active [] = 0
   sum-active t . l  =  IF 2-nd t == on  THEN
                        1-st t +  sum-active l
                        ELSE  sum-active l  ENDIF
AXIOMS for all-active?:
   all-active? < n ; a ; m > . []  =  a == on
   all-active? < n ; a ; m > . l   =  a  ==  on and all-active? l
AXIOMS for make-passive:
   make-passive [] = []
   make-passive < n ; a ; m > . l =
                               < n ; off ; m > . make-passive l
AXIOMS for change-weight:
   change-weight s idl [] = []
   change-weight s idl < n ; a ; m > . l  =
      IF  idl == m THEN  l app < s ; on ; idl > . []
      ELSE  (change-weight s idl l) app < n ; a ; m > . []
      ENDIF
ENDSPEC
```

Figure 14.10 The algebraic specification Info.

14.7 SPECIFICATION OF THE NEURAL NETWORK

As a prelude to the final part of the development of the specification for the neural network, it will be instructive to summarize the component specifications we have constructed to date.

Thus far, we have concentrated on the construction of specification modules that characterize *individual neurons* and *neuron connections*. A neuron is specified by a 4-tuple < a ; b ; c ; d > where a identifies the neuron, b denotes its threshold, c denotes the list of impinging ('input') connections, and d denotes the 'output' list of emergent connections.

We have developed algebraic specifications that describe the connections emanating from an individual neuron and the connections impinging on (entering) an individual neuron. The emergent connections have been described in terms of a list of 3-tuples with each tuple containing the value of the output signal, its weight, and the name of a destination neuron. This abstract data type is specified by the module Outfo.

The incoming connections to a particular neuron are specified by the module `Info`. These connections have also been specified in terms of a list of 3-tuples with each tuple containing the value of the input signal, whether the source neuron is activated or not, and the source neuron from where the signal originates.

Hence, we have descriptions of isolated neurons, each with their own incoming and outgoing connections so that, figuratively speaking, we have the constituent components of a network. Our task now is to 'assemble' these isolated components (specifications) and 'join' up these connections into a single coherent network and specify operations that describe the behaviour of this network.

14.8 THE OPERATIONS OF Neural-Network

Basically, we can think of a neural network as a parallel system of processors (or neurons as we have chosen to call them) with each neuron containing a simple program that computes a weighted sum of the input data from 'incoming' neuron connections and then outputs a single value (or 'signal') that is a (nonlinear) function of the weighted sum. This output is then sent on to other neurons which are continually doing the same kind of computation. For the McCulloch–Pitts model of a neuron, the nonlinear function used is a unit *step function* (threshold function). With this concept of the kind of processing involved in a neural network, we need to supply an operation

```
settle _ : network → network
```

which takes a neural network ns and repeatedly:

- Looks for a neuron whose list of 'incoming' 3-tuples are *all* 'activated', that is the value of the second slot of *all* the 3-tuples in its list of incoming signals has the value on. If there are no such neurons, then settle is to return an unaltered network ns.
- If there is such an 'activated' neuron and the weighted sum of its input signals *is equal to or exceeds* the threshold:
  (a) *fire* the neuron, then
  (b) *spread* its output, and
  (c) *deactivate* the neuron
- If there is such an *activated* neuron but the weighted sum of the incoming 'input' signals *is less than* the threshold of that neuron, then deactivate that neuron (that is set the value of the second slot of *all* the 3-tuples in its list of incoming signals to off).

The operation settle is required to perform the above task until there are no neurons in the network whose list of 'incoming' 3-tuples are *all* 'activated'. Clearly, we need a Boolean-valued operation

```
all-settled? _ : network → bool
```

which takes a neural network (that is a list of neurons) and returns false if any neuron in the network has all its inputs 'activated'. When this operation returns true, no further processing by the network can take place.

Our immediate task is to define the operations fire, spread, and sleep, corresponding to (a), (b), and (c) above, and, to this end, we first introduce two auxiliary operations each of which takes a neuron as input and returns a neuron as a result. The first operation, sleep, 'deactivates' a neuron while the second, fire, 'fires' a neuron.

14.8.1 The operation sleep

The operation sleep _ : neuron → neuron takes a neuron and replaces the value in the activation slot of *every* 3-tuple in the neuron's list of 'input' connections by the value off. This is achieved by simply applying the operation make-passive of Info to the third slot of the 4-tuple specifying the neuron. Hence, the axiom for sleep is

sleep < a ; b ; c ; d > = < a ; b ; make-passive c ; d >

where a∈ name, b∈ thresh, c∈ info, and d∈ outfo.

14.8.2 The operation fire

The operation fire _ : neuron → neuron takes a neuron and copies the sum of its *activated* incoming signals across into the first slot (the output signal) of *all* its outgoing (emergent) connections. For example, given a neuron N with name n, threshold T, two activated incoming connections (from neurons 1 and 3 with signals s1 and s3 respectively), and two outgoing connections (to neurons 2 and 5), that is

N = < n ; T ; < s1 ; on ; 1 > . < s3 ; on ; 3 > . [ ] ; < 0 ; 1 ; 2 > . < 0 ; −1 ; 5 > . [ ] >

the outcome of the operation fire acting on N will be given by

fire N = < n ; T ; < s1 ; on ; 1 > . < s3 ; on ; 3 > . [ ] ;

< s1 + s3 ; 1 ; 2 > . < s1 + s3 ; −1 ; 5 > . [ ] >

Two pre-conditions have to be met for a neuron to fire, namely *all* its incoming connections must be activated and the *weighted* sum of the incoming signals must equal or exceed the threshold of that neuron. When those conditions are satisfied, a signal is copied across to all the neuron's outgoing connections. Rather than combine all these different actions into a single operation, we have introduced fire which is essentially concerned with just transmitting the sum of the activated incoming signals to a neuron across to all the neuron's outgoing connections. Appropriate use of existing operations such as all-active? will ensure that the neurons in a network fire as required.

We can express the behaviour of fire in terms of the operation sum-active of Info, which computes the sum of the activated input signals in a list of incoming neuron connections, and fire-out of Outfo, which copies a given signal into the first slot (the output signal) of all the 3-tuples of a list of outgoing connections. This leads immediately to the axiom

```
fire < a ; b ; c ; d > = < a ; b ; c ; (fire-out (sum-active c) d) >
```

Having fired a neuron, our next task is to spread its signal out to the appropriate connections in the network. The three operations one-shot, spread-out, and spread are concerned with this task.

14.8.3 The operation one-shot

Readers may now be thinking 'wait a minute, when a neuron fires, it is the *weighted* sum of the incoming signals that is copied across, not just the sum'. We can ensure that the weighted sum is indeed copied across using our existing operation fire by simply replacing the input signal for each incoming connection to a neuron by the product $w \times f$ where w denotes the weighting of the connection and f the *output* signal that has emanated from the corresponding sending (source) neuron. We therefore introduce an operation

```
one-shot _ _ _ _ : name signal name network → network
```

whose behaviour is as follows. The application one-shot id1 v id2 ns, where id1, id2 ∈ name, v ∈ signal, and ns ∈ network, seeks out the neuron with name id2 in the network ns and seeks out the 3-tuple in that neuron's list of 'incoming' connections whose third slot (that is 'source' neuron) has the value id1. The operation then changes the input value of this 3-tuple (that is its first slot) to the given value v (the second argument of one-shot) *and* sets the value in the second slot of this 3-tuple to on (that is 'activates' id1). If no neuron identifier id2 is present in the given network, the operation is to return the value of the original network.

The individual 4-tuple (neuron) corresponding to id2 will be given by < id2 ; b ; c ; d > where b ∈ thresh, c ∈ info, and d ∈ outfo. From the specification Info, we recall that the application change-weight v id1 c amends the input signal value emanating from neuron id1 to the value v and activates id1. Hence, after application of one-shot, the value of the above 4-tuple is

```
< id2 ; b ; (change-weight v id1 c) ; d >
```

Remember, the operation one-shot must first search through the list of neurons that makes up the network to look for id2 and then apply change-weight to achieve its task. This leads to the axioms

```
one-shot id1 v id2 [ ] = [ ]

one-shot id1 v id2 < a ; b ; c ; d > . ns =
        IF a = = id2 THEN
        < id2 ; b ; (change-weight v id1 c) ; d > . ns
        ELSE
        (one-shot id1 v id2 ns) app < a ; b ; c ; d > . [ ]
        ENDIF
```

(Note that if the neuron identifier id2 is not present in the network, the resulting network will be the list of 4-tuples of the original network but in a different order). We then observe that, if f denotes the output signal from a neuron named id1 and w denotes the weight w_{12} of the connection from id1 to id2, we can change the input signal to the required weighted value $w_{12} \times f$ by means of the application

```
one-shot id1 (w * f) id2 ns
```

where $*$ is the multiplication operation supplied by Signal. This application will be used shortly. We can show the behaviour of one-shot diagrammatically and this is shown in Fig. 14.11.

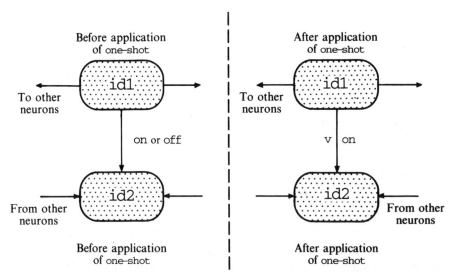

Figure 14.11 The behaviour of the operation one-shot.

14.8.4 The operations spread-out and spread

We noted above that the application one-shot id1 (w*f) id2 ns takes a network ns and returns a new network value in which the input signal value of the connection (if any) from neuron id1 to the *individual* neuron id2 is given the value w*f and the connection activated (the value in the second slot of the same connection's 'input' 3-tuple is set to on). We now require an operation that extends this process so that *all* the neurons that have connections from id1 have the input signals in their list of input 3-tuples assigned a specified value and are activated. In other words, generalize the above operation from a *single* destination neuron id2 to a *collection* of outgoing connections. We therefore introduce the operation

```
spread-out ___ : name outfo network → network
```

to accomplish this task. We can express an *arbitrary* list of output neuron connections as < f ; w ; id2 > .o where f is an output signal value, w is the weight of the connection to the destination neuron id2, and o is the tail of the list of remaining neuron connections.

If the output list contains only the single 3-tuple < f ; w ; id2 > (that is o is the empty list [ ]), then clearly the results of the operations spread-out and one-shot are 'equivalent' in the sense that

```
spread-out id1 < f ; w ; id2 > . [ ] ns = one-shot id1 (w*f) id2 ns
```

where ns ∈ network. For the general case when o is not the empty list, we need to reapply the operation spread-out with arguments id1, the tail of the list of output 3-tuples, o, and the network one-shot id1 (w*f) id2 ns. If the list of output 3-tuples is empty, we require the outcome of spread-out id1 [ ] ns to return an unchanged network ns. This leads to the axioms

```
spread-out id1 [ ] ns = ns

spread-out id1 ( < f ; w ; id2 > . o ) ns =

        (spread-out id1 o (one-shot id1 (w*f) id2 ns) )
```

It is important to realize that the second argument of spread-out is an *arbitrary* list of output 3-tuples and so does not necessarily correspond to the list of 'outgoing' connections of neuron id1 (its first argument).

In order to achieve our aim of changing the input values of all those neurons contained *expressly* in the output list of neuron id1, we introduce the operation

```
spread _ _ : neuron network → network
```

Given a neuron and a network, this operation returns as its result, the network produced by amending the input values of all those neurons contained within the output list of the specified neuron. This operation can be specified directly in terms of the operation spread-out by constraining it to operate expressly on the output list of the specified neuron id1. Hence, for a neuron < id1 ; b ; c ; d >, where b is its threshold, c is its list of input 3-tuples, d its list of output 3-tuples, and ns is a network, we have the axiom

```
spread < id1 ; b ; c ; d > ns = spread-out id1 d ns
```

The behaviour of the operation spread is shown schematically in Fig. 14.12 where f is the output signal from id1 and the weights w_{ij} are enclosed within curly braces. Note that the neurons will have other incoming connections and that id2, id3 and id4 will have outgoing connections but these are omitted to avoid unnecessary detail.

14.9 THE OPERATIONS all-settled? AND settle

We recall that the operation all-settled? takes a network (a list of neuron 4-tuples) and returns true if *no* neuron in the network has the second slot of *all* its list of input 3-tuples set to on. The operation returns false otherwise. For an empty network, the operation is required to return the value true.

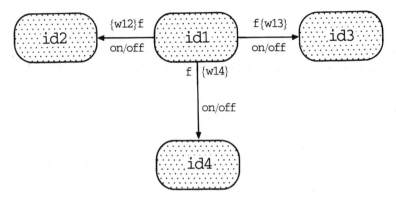

Before application of spread

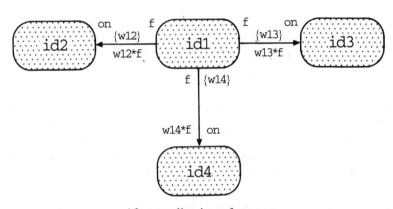

After application of spread

Figure 14.12   The behaviour of the operation spread.

From the specification Neuron of Fig. 14.7, the selector operation input applied to a neuron 4-tuple n returns the list of 'incoming' input neuron connections of n. Also from Info (Fig. 14.10), the application all-active? (input n) returns true if all the 3-tuples in the list of incoming 3-tuples have the value on. The axioms for all-settled? are therefore

```
all-settled? [ ] = true

all-settled? n . ns = IF all-active? input n THEN false

                  ELSE all-settled? ns ENDIF
```

where ns ∈ network. Our concluding task is to derive axioms for the operation settle and we now analyse the four cases A, B, C and D that can arise.

Case (A) First, if there is no neuron that has all of its inputs activated (that is all-settled? n . ns has the value true), the operation settle returns an unchanged network, which leads directly to the conditional axiom

```
settle n . ns = n . ns IF all-settled? n . ns                    (14.1A)
```

Case (B) Suppose now that the 3-tuples in the list of incoming connections of n are all activated. This neuron will then fire if, additionally, the (weighted) sum of the input values of these activated neurons (given by the expression sum-active input n) is equal to or exceeds the threshold value of neuron n, (that is threshold n). If both of these conditions are met, then neuron n will *fire*. The network that results when n *fires* and *spreads* its output to its outgoing connected neurons is given by the network spread (fire n) ns. Having fired, n needs to be deactivated, which is achieved by applying the operation sleep to the 'fired' neuron, that is sleep (fire n). This deactivated neuron is now appended to the end of the list of other neurons that make up the network using the concatenation operation app. The resulting network will be given by the expression

spread (fire n) ns app (sleep (fire n) . [ ])

We now need to repeat the application of settle to this resulting network. This leads to the (conditional) axiom

settle n . ns =

  settle ((spread (fire n) ns) app (sleep (fire n) . [ ]))

    IF all-active? input n

    and threshold n <= sum-active input n   (14.1B)

Case (C) Suppose now, that the 3-tuples in the list of incoming connections of n are all activated but the sum of the input values of these activated neuron connections is less than the threshold value of n. In this case, n is simply deactivated and reinserted into the list of neurons and the subsequent behaviour of the network is determined by applying settle to the resulting network. This leads immediately to the conditional axiom

settle n . ns =

  settle (ns app sleep n . [ ])

    IF all-active? input n

    and sum-active input n < threshold n   (14.1C)

Case (D) In the remaining case, n will not have all input neurons activated and so is incapable of firing, in which case its 4-tuple is simply removed from the head of the list, appended to the end, and the operation repeated on the remaining neurons of the network, so that we have

settle n . ns = settle (ns app n . [ ])   for all other cases   (14.1D)

The four results (14.1A), (14.1B), (14.1C) and (14.1D) can be expressed in the single unconditional axiom

```
settle n . ns =

IF all-settled? n . ns THEN n . ns

ELSEIF all-active? input n and ( threshold n <= sum-active input n)

  THEN settle ( (spread (fire n) ns ) app (sleep (fire n) . [ ] ) )

ELSEIF all-active? input n THEN

  settle ( ns app sleep n . [ ] )

ELSE

  settle ( ns app n . [ ] )

ENDIF
```

The complete specification Neural-Network is given in Fig. 14.13 and an OBJ3 prototype presented in Appendix 2.

```
***
*** The trivial data-type property
***
    PROPS Elem
    SORTS   element
    ENDPROPS
*** **************************************************
***
*** Simple parameterised list
***
    SPEC  List (E : Elem)
    USING  Boolean
    SORTS  list  ne-list
    SUBSORT  ne-list < list
    OPS
      []          :                  -> list
      _ . _     : element  list  -> ne-list
      _ app _   : list list      -> list      [ASSOC]
      is-in? _ _ : element   list  -> bool
    FORALL
      e, e1, e2 : element
      s, s1, s2 : list
    AXIOMS for list concatenation:
      [] app s         = s
      ( e . s1 ) app s2   = e . ( s1 app s2 )
```

Figure 14.13 The complete algebraic specification Neural-Network

```
AXIOMS for determining whether an element el is present in a list:
   is-in? el []       = false
   is-in? el (e2 . s) = IF el == e2 THEN true ELSE is-in? el s END
ENDSPEC
```

```
*** *****************************************************
***
*** Unconstrained 3-tuples
***
   SPEC  Triple( S1 : Elem  &&  S2 : Elem  &&  S3 : Elem )
   SORT triple
   OPS
      < _ ; _ ; _ > : S1's element  S2's element  S3's element
                                                -> triple

      1-st _         :  triple  ->  S1's element
      2-nd _         :  triple  ->  S2's element
      3-rd _         :  triple  ->  S3's element
   FORALL
      a : S1's element
      b : S2's element
      c : S3's element
   AXIOMS:
      1-st < a ; b ; c >  =  a
      2-nd < a ; b ; c >  =  b
      3-rd < a ; b ; c >  =  c
ENDSPEC
```

```
*** *****************************************************
***
*** List of 3-tuples
***
   SPEC  List-of-Triple( F : Elem  &&  M : Elem  &&  E : Elem )
   USING List ( Triple ( F && M && E ) )
   ENDSPEC
```

```
*** *****************************************************
***
*** on/off activation state
***
   SPEC  Activation
   SORT  activation
   OPS
      on   :  ->  activation
      off  :  ->  activation
   ENDSPEC
```

```
*** *****************************************************
***
*** List of output (emergent) neuron connections
***
   SPEC  Outfo
   USING List-of-Triple(Signal  &&  Weighting  &&  Name)
      WITH
         1-st _ : triple -> signal    AS  value-of _,
         2-nd _ : triple -> weighting AS  weight _,
```

Figure 14.13—*Contd.*

```
        3-rd _ : triple -> name         AS  to-neuron _,
        list    AS  outfo
    OPS
        fire-out _ _ : signal  outfo  -> outfo
    FORALL
        l    :   outfo
        m, n :   signal
        w    :   weighting
        p    :   name
    AXIOMS for fire-out:
      fire-out m [] =   []
      fire-out m < n ; w ; p > . l =  <m ; w ; p > . (fire-out m l)
    ENDSPEC
*** *************************************************
***
*** List of input (incoming) neuron connections
***
    SPEC  Info
    USING List-of-Triple(Signal  &&  Activation  &&  Name)
    WITH  list  AS  info,  ne-list  AS  ne-info
    OPS
        sum-active _          : info  ->  signal
        all-active? _         : ne-info  ->  bool
        make-passive _        : info  ->  info
        change-weight _ _ _   : signal name  info  ->  info
    FORALL
        t    :   triple
        l    :   info
        a    :   activation
        idl, m : name
        n, s :   signal
    AXIOMS for sum-active:
        sum-active [] =  0
        sum-active t . l = IF  2-nd t == on   THEN
                              1-st t +  sum-active l
                              ELSE   sum-active l ENDIF
    AXIOMS for all-active?:
        all-active? < n ; a ; m > . [] =  a == on
        all-active? < n ; a ; m > . l  =  a  ==  on and all-active? l
    AXIOMS for make-passive:
        make-passive [] =  []
        make-passive < n ; a ; m > . l =
                                < n ; off ; m > . make-passive l
    AXIOMS for change-weight:
        change-weight s idl [] =  []
        change-weight s idl < n ; a ; m > . l =
            IF  idl == m  THEN  l app < s ; on ; idl > . []
            ELSE  (change-weight s idl l) app < n ; a ; m > . []
            ENDIF
    ENDSPEC
*** *************************************************
```

Figure 14.13—*Contd.*

```
***
*** Individual neuron as a 4-tuple
***
    SPEC   Neuron (S1 : Elem && S2 : Elem && S3 : Elem && S4 : Elem)
    SORT neuron
    OPS
        < _ ; _ ; _ ; _ > : S1's element   S2's element   S3's element
                            S4's element  ->   neuron
          identifier _         :  neuron  ->  S1's element
          threshold _          :  neuron  ->  S2's element
          input _              :  neuron  ->  S3's element
          output _             :  neuron  ->  S4's element
    FORALL
        a : S1's element
        b : S2's element
        c : S3's element
        d : S4's element
    AXIOMS:
        identifier < a ; b ; c ; d >  =  a
        threshold  < a ; b ; c ; d >  =  b
        input < a ; b ; c ; d >       =  c
        output < a ; b ; c ; d >      =  d
    ENDSPEC
*** *****************************************************
***
*** Neural network as a list of neurons
***
    SPEC   Neural-Network
    USING List ( Neuron ( Name   &&   Threshold  &&
                          Info  FIT  element  AS  info  &&
                          Outfo  FIT  element  AS  outfo ) )
      WITH   list  AS   network
    OPS
        sleep _          :  neuron  ->  neuron
        fire _           :  neuron  ->  neuron
        spread _ _       :  neuron  network  ->  network
        spread-out _ _ _ :  name  outfo  network  ->  network
        one-shot _ _ _ _ :  name  signal  name  network  ->  network
        all-settled? _   :  network  ->  bool
        settle _         :  network  ->  network
    FORALL
        a, id1, id2 :   name
        f, v        :   signal
        b           :   thresh
        w           :   weighting
        c           :   info
        d, o        :   outfo
        n           :   neuron
        ns          :   network
    AXIOM for sleep:
        sleep < a ; b ; c ; d > = < a ; b ; make-passive c ; d >
```

Figure 14.13—*Contd.*

```
AXIOM for fire:
   fire < a ; b ; c ; d >  =
                       < a ; b ; c ; (fire-out (sum-active c) d) >
AXIOM for spread:
   spread < idl ; b ; c ; d >  ns  =  spread-out idl d ns
AXIOMS for spread-out:
   spread-out idl [] ns  =  ns
   spread-out idl ( < f ; w ; id2 > . o )  ns  =
          (spread-out idl o  (one-shot idl (w * f) id2 ns) )
AXIOMS for one-shot:
   one-shot idl v id2 []  =  []
   one-shot idl v id2 < a ; b ; c ; d > . ns  =
              IF  a == id2   THEN
                 < id2 ; b ; (change-weight v idl c) ; d > . ns
              ELSE
                 (one-shot idl v id2 ns) app < a ; b ; c ; d > . []
              ENDIF
AXIOMS for all-settled?:
   all-settled? []       =  true
   all-settled? n . ns   =  IF  all-active? input n THEN false
                            ELSE all-settled? ns   ENDIF
AXIOM for settle:
   settle []      =  []
   settle n . ns  =
   IF  all-settled? n . ns  THEN  n . ns
   ELSEIF  all-active? input n and (threshold n <= sum-active input n)   THEN
              settle ( (spread(fire n) ns ) app (sleep (fire n).[]) )
        ELSEIF  all-active? input n THEN
              settle ( ns app sleep n.[] )
              ELSE                 .
              settle ( ns app n.[] )
   ENDIF
ENDSPEC
*** **************************************************
```

Figure 14.13—*Contd.*

14.10 EXAMPLE EVALUATION OF A NEURAL NETWORK

It will be instructive to look at the neural network shown in Fig. 14.8 and consider the
network that results from applying the operation settle, that is

```
settle < 1 ; -1 ; < 1 ; on ; 0 > . [ ];
        < 0 ;1 ;3 > . < 0 ; -1 ; 4 > . [ ] > .

  < 2 ; -1 ; < 0 ; on ; 0 > . [ ];
        < 0 ; -1 ; 3 > . < 0 ; 1 ; 4 > . [ ] > .

  < 3 ; -1 ; < 0 ; off ; 1 > . < 0 ; off ; 2 > . [ ];
        < 0 ; 1 ; 5 > . [ ] > .
```

```
< 4 ; −1 ; < 0 ; off ; 1 > . < 0 ; off ; 2 > . [ ] ;
        < 0 ; 1 ; 5 > . [ ] > .

< 5 ; −1 ; < 0 ; off ; 3 > . < 0 ; off ; 4 > . [ ] ;
        < 0 ; 1 ; 0 > . [ ] > . [ ]
```

This example was run using the OBJ3 prototype given in Appendix 2 and a corresponding OBJ3 program EXAMPLE-NEURON-NETWORK is presented at the end of that prototype. In that program, the neural network of Fig. 14.8 is expressed as the nullary operation network-before and the result of the application settle to network-before is denoted by the nullary operation network-after. As a check, the Boolean terms all-settled? network-before and all-settled? network-after (denoted by settled-before? and settled-after? respectively) are also evaluated. These terms should reduce to false and true respectively. Note that the lists of input and output neuron connections for each neuron j have been written as infoj and outfoj respectively. This was done to avoid including yet more brackets, necessary for each occurrence of the insertion operation '.' (as noted earlier, OBJ3 is very unforgiving on this point!). We used the built-in specification INTEGER with sort integer for our specifications Name, Signal, Weighting, and Threshold, and have represented the empty list constructor [ ] by #.

The output network, network-after is

```
< 3 ; −1 ; < 1 ; off ; 1 > . < 0 ; off ; 2 > . [ ] ;
        < 1 ; 1 ; 5 > . [ ] > .

< 2 ; −1 ; < 0 ; off ; 0 > . [ ] ;
        < 0 ; −1 ; 3 > . < 0 ; 1 ; 4 > . [ ] > .

< 4 ; −1 ; < −1 ; off ; 1 > . < 0 ; off ; 2 > . [ ] ;
        < −1 ; 1 ; 5 > . [ ] > .

< 1 ; −1 ; < 1 ; off ; 0 > . [ ] ;
        < 1 ; 1 ; 3 > . < 1 ; −1 ; 4 > . [ ] > .

< 5 ; −1 ; < 1 ; off ; 3 > . < −1 ; off ; 4 > . [ ] ;
        < 0 ; 1 ; 0 > . [ ] > . [ ]
```

The program was run on a Sun 4 workstation using version 2.03 of OBJ3 and took under one minute to compile and execute. Observe that the output from the network is given by the final slot of the output neuron 5, that is the output list

```
< 0 ; 1 ; 0 > . [ ]
```

containing a single triple. In other words an output signal of 0 to the dummy neuron '0'.

The number of rewrites taken to reduce the terms settled-before?, settled-after?, and network-after were as follows:

- settled-before? took 17 rewrites
- settled-after? took 748 rewrites
- network-after? took 712 rewrites

14.11 SOME COMMENTS ON THE ALGEBRAIC SPECIFICATION

There are several important observations to be made about the specification Neural-Network of Fig. 14.13. The first concerns the use of *lists* to represent the input and output connections to an individual neuron and the collection of neurons that make up the network itself. Axioms describing the behaviour of the operations of Info, Outfo, and Neural-Network were obtained by systematically 'looking through' the constituent elements of the associated list and 'processing' the appropriate element or elements. This requirement to methodically examine each neuron (or connection 3-tuple) in turn can be satisfied when lists are used. The element at the *head* of the list can be isolated, transformed, or left unaltered as required and the 'processing' repeated (recursively) with the remaining elements that make up the *tail* of the list. Such a procedure cannot be undertaken with a *set* structure since the elements of a set have no ordering. We can illustrate the sort of problem that could have arisen, had we elected to use sets, by considering, as an example, the behaviour of the operation settle _ : network →
network. We can easily adapt the parameterized List specification (Fig. 14.4) to a generic Set specification by replacing the empty list [ ] by the empty set { }, reinterpreting the *cons* operation _ . _ as the insertion operation that places a given element into a set provided that element is not already in the set (the operation _ . _ is then identical with the operation add of the specification Set given in Fig. 12.2) and replacing the associative concatenation operation app by the associative–commutative operation of set union U. The axioms of the generic set specification would then take the form

$$e1 . (e2 . s) = \text{IF } e1 == e2 \text{ THEN } e1 . s \text{ ELSE } e2 . (e1 . s) \text{ ENDIF}$$

$$\{ \} \, U \, s = s$$

$$(e . s1) \, U \, s2 = e . (s1 \, U \, s2)$$

$$s1 \, U \, s2 = s2 \, U \, s1$$

$$\text{is-in? } e \, \{ \} = \text{false}$$

$$\text{is-in? } e1 \, (e2 . s) = \text{IF } e1 == e2 \text{ THEN true ELSE is-in? } e1 \, s \text{ ENDIF}$$

where e, e1, e2 ∈ element and s, s1, and s2 are members of the sort set (the counterpart of the sort list). If we carry this correspondence between the specifications List and Set through, the axiom for settle corresponding to case (14.1D) above would take the form

$$\text{settle } n . ns = \text{settle} (ns \, U \, n . \{ \})$$

and since set union is commutative, we have on subsequently applying the second and third axioms above

$$ns \, U \, n . \{ \} = (n . \{ \}) \, U \, ns = n . (\{ \} \, U \, ns) = n . ns$$

which leads to the result settle n . ns = settle (n . ns)!

The next observation leads on from this use of lists and concerns the algebras that provide models of our specification. A requirement of our description of a neural network is that the *order* in which the constituent neurons of the network (and the individual incoming and outgoing neuron connections) appear is of no importance. For example, 'listing' the individual neuron 4-tuples of the network network-before in reverse order should specify exactly the same network. However, under an *initial* interpretation, these two network expressions will denote *different* values in any intended model (since the axioms of List cannot be used to show they are equal). On the other hand, if *final* algebra semantics are used for the instantiated List specifications, two neural network expressions are equal unless application of the operation is-in? produces a different result, which will only occur if one neural network contains a neuron (or neural connection) that is not included in the other network.

The final comment concerns adapting Neural-Network, which specifies a network with a *general* connection geometry, to specify particular classes of networks such as *feed-forward* and *recurrent networks*. This problem forms the basis of the following exercises.

Exercise 14.6 Adapt Neural-Network so that it specifies a simple *feed-forward* neural network. You could, for example, consider treating the constructor _._ of List as a *hidden* operation and introduce a new constructor that builds terms ('networks') that are well-formed in the sense that they conform to a feed-forward network geometry. Would such a strategy enable you to continue using a *generic list* module for the neural connections and the network itself?

Exercise 14.7 Repeat Exercise 14.6 for a layered network in which a neuron in any given layer can have connections to neurons one layer above and one layer below, no other types of connection being permitted.

14.12 VDM SPECIFICATION OF THE NEURAL NETWORK

In this section we derive a model-based specification of the neural network, making comparative observations of the differing specification styles as we progress. The same network model will be used as in Sec. 14.3, in that the principal function will be *settle*, which inputs a network and 'evaluates' it to a settled state. Initially, the VDM network representation will also image the algebraic one, but consideration of the resulting data type invariant forces a shift in representation, and the resulting network is modelled chiefly in terms of maps.

14.12.1 Requirements

We require a specification of neural network as discussed in Sec. 14.3.

14.12.2 Creation of a data model: first attempt

As a first attempt, a 'neuron-centred' representation will be used that follows closely the algebraic formalization

Each neuron is identified by a natural number:

Neuron_name $= \mathbb{N}$

Following Sec. 14.5.1, a single input to a neuron is a structure consisting of an input signal (*is*), the source neuron of the signal (*nfrom*), and a flag that captures whether the input is activated. As in Fig. 14.3, we capture this with a type consisting of two constants:

Activation = *on* | *off*

and the input structure is then:

Neuron_input :: *is*   : $\mathbb{Z}$
                 act   : *Activation*
                 nfrom : *Neuron_name*

No particular ordering is required, so the input connections to a neuron can be modelled as a set:

All_Neuron_inputs = *Neuron_input*-set

Observations:

- Compare the way the simple type *Activation* is declared in both languages. In the algebraic style it is explicit that the type has two constructors that return a constant, and the VDM notation is in a sense a shorthand for this.
- Notice how in the algebraic specification the parameterized Triple structure mirrors VDM's composite with three slots. Whereas in Sec. 14.5.1 the constructor is $< \_ ; \_ ; \_ >$, in VDM it is the *mk-* function. Thus, once types have been defined in an algebraic specification language, they can be used rather like 'built-in' types in VDM. For example, in the network of Fig. 14.8, the input connection from neuron 3 to neuron 5 would be represented by the VDM composite as

    mk-Neuron_input(0, *off*, 3)

and using the Triple structure represented as:

    $< 0 ; off ; 3 >$

Following Sec. 14.5.1, we store the neuron output information as a structure containing: the output signal (*os*), weight (*wt*) and connecting neuron's name (*nto*)

Neuron_output :: *os* : $\mathbb{Z}$
                   wt : $\mathbb{Z}$
                   nto : *Neuron_name*

In the same way as with the inputs, we represent the output connections as a set:

All_Neuron_outputs = *Neuron_output*-set

In Sec. 14.5.2 the neuron was modelled as the composition of its identifier (*id*), threshold (*thrd*), and in and out connections. In a similar fashion, we use VDM's composite structure to represent a neuron:

$$Neuron :: \begin{array}{ll} id & : \mathbb{N} \\ thrd & : \mathbb{Z} \\ ins & : All\_Neuron\_inputs \\ outs & : All\_Neuron\_outputs \end{array}$$

Finally, following the discussion earlier in the chapter on this point, the network is modelled as a *sequence* of neurons, to facilitate sequential processing:

$$Network = Neuron*$$

14.12.3 Creation of the data type invariant: first attempt

The constraints we need to place on the network to make it valid are essentially integrity constraints; for example, each neuron contains sets of information with references to the names of other neurons. Therefore, one constraint should be:

• Every neuron referenced by another neuron actually exists.

Consideration of these constraints leads us to realize that the representation we have chosen is not apt: there is redundancy in the way neuron identifiers are stored, and to compensate for this the invariant would have to express the fact that all the neuron identifiers referenced in the inputs and outputs of each neuron appear elsewhere in the network. In summary, we would do better to choose a representation that has less redundancy and implicitly holds the connections between neurons.

14.12.4 Creation of a data model: second attempt

As we saw in the Symbol Table example of Chapter 4, a shift in representation (usually involving the Map type) may be useful in reducing the size or complexity of the invariant. In our second attempt, we will create a more 'connection' oriented model of the network, storing the neuron identifiers separately from their inputs and outputs:

$$Neuron\_name = \mathbb{N}$$

$$Neuron\_names = Neuron\_name*$$

The nature of the network suggests that connections in the network might be better represented explicitly as arcs between two neurons. A composite type captures the start and end of an arc as follows:

$$Arc :: \begin{array}{ll} start : Neuron\_name \\ end \;\; : Neuron\_name \end{array}$$

$$\text{inv } mk\text{-}Arc(start, end) \triangleq start \neq end$$

The invariant on arcs can be used to constrain the kind of topologies allowed; here we have simply excluded those networks whose neurons have connections back to themselves. Collecting the arcs together, we have a set of connections representing the network's topology:

$Connections = Arc\text{-set}$

As a running example, we will use the network in Fig. 14.8. The connections there can be represented as:

$\{mk\text{-}Arc(1, 3), mk\text{-}Arc(1, 4), mk\text{-}Arc(2, 3), mk\text{-}Arc(2, 4),$

$mk\text{-}Arc(3, 5), mk\text{-}Arc(4, 5), mk\text{-}Arc(5, 0)\}$

Neuron '0' has been added so that the output signal can be recorded from the output neuron numbered '5' (the reason for this will become clear below).

Each neuron has associated with it a *unique* threshold, and we can use the Map type to model this:

$Threshold = Neuron\_name \xrightarrow{m} \mathbb{Z}$

The network example's thresholds would be stored as follows:

$\{1 \mapsto -1, 2 \mapsto -1, 3 \mapsto -1, 4 \mapsto -1, 5 \mapsto -1, 0 \mapsto 0\}$

The threshold of the dummy neuron is set to '0' although it will soon become apparent that this value is purely arbitrary. Each connection has a unique weight associated with it:

$Weight = Connections \xrightarrow{m} \mathbb{Z}$

The network example's weights would be stored as the following:

$\{mk\text{-}Arc(1, 3) \mapsto 1, mk\text{-}Arc(1, 4) \mapsto -1, mk\text{-}Arc(2, 3) \mapsto -1, mk\text{-}Arc(2, 4) \mapsto 1,$
$mk\text{-}Arc(3, 5) \mapsto 1, mk\text{-}Arc(4, 5) \mapsto 1, mk\text{-}Arc(5, 0) \mapsto 0\}$

Also, each connection will have associated with it a unique activation value and a Boolean-valued activation level:

$Value = Connections \xrightarrow{m} \mathbb{Z}$

$Activation = Connections \xrightarrow{m} \mathbb{B}$

Similarly, the network example's values and activation level, respectively, would be stored:

$\{mk\text{-}Arc(1, 3) \mapsto 1, mk\text{-}Arc(1, 4) \mapsto 1, mk\text{-}Arc(2, 3) \mapsto 0,$
$mk\text{-}Arc(2, 4) \mapsto 0, mk\text{-}Arc(3, 5) \mapsto 0, mk\text{-}Arc(4, 5) \mapsto 0, mk\text{-}Arc(5, 0) \mapsto 0\}$

$\{mk\text{-}Arc(1, 3) \mapsto true, mk\text{-}Arc(1, 4) \mapsto true, mk\text{-}Arc(2, 3) \mapsto true,$
$mk\text{-}Arc(2, 4) \mapsto true, mk\text{-}Arc(3, 5) \mapsto false, mk\text{-}Arc(4, 5) \mapsto false, mk\text{-}Arc(5, 0) \mapsto false\}$

This example shows up the difference in a 'connection-oriented' representation: the neurons numbered 1 and 2 in Fig. 14.8 have thresholds that are meant always to allow the incoming signals to pass, therefore there is no need to represent a level of neurons below them (in effect they are the input neurons). This also means that we initialize the network by activating all the connections from these input neurons.

The output neurons, however, have thresholds, and in our connection-oriented representation we must represent the connections to the 'outside world' from them, so that any output they give will be stored there. To do this, we simply connect them to the dummy neuron called '0'. The dummy neuron will *never* be processed, because its inputs are the outputs of the whole network.

Putting all these components together we form the network as a composite data structure:

$$Network :: ns : Neuron\_names$$
$$t \;\; : Threshold$$
$$w : Weight$$
$$v \;\; : Value$$
$$a \;\; : Activation$$

14.12.5 Creation of data type invariant: second attempt

The invariant for the *Network* composite has to capture integrity constraints on the maps. In the weight map, all the arcs in the domain must be between valid neuron identifiers in the network:

$$\forall x \in \text{dom } w \cdot \exists n, m \in \text{elems } ns \cdot x.start = n \land x.end = m$$

The other maps using the 'Connection' type can be equated to the weight map:

$$\text{dom } w = \text{dom } v \land$$
$$\text{dom } w = \text{dom } a$$

Putting these constraints together we have

$$\text{inv } mk\text{-}Network(ns, t, w, v, a) \triangleq$$
$$\quad \forall x \in \text{dom } w \cdot \exists n, m \in \text{elems } ns \cdot$$
$$\quad x.start = n \land x.end = m \land$$
$$\quad \text{dom } w = \text{dom } v \land$$
$$\quad \text{dom } w = \text{dom } a$$

14.12.6 The network operation

VDM allows the specifier to choose between two types of specification:

1. Operations centred around a system state.
2. Functions defined purely in terms of parameters.

The former option is preferable when the central object in the model is highly structured, complex, and a number of operations are required that access different parts of it. We only require one operation on the network, and the network itself is not highly structured, so in this case we will rely on a purely functional approach. Moreover, an implicit post-condition for the network operation *settle* is not apparent, so the nature of the application forces us to make the specification in an executable form. It is also interesting that the structure of *settle*'s definition is identical to its algebraic counterpart in Fig. 14.13.

We will first develop the auxiliary functions. For a neuron to fire in our model, as we pointed out in Sec. 14.6, all its input connections must be active. We therefore need the following function, which corresponds to the algebraically defined all-active? operation in Sec. 14.6.2:

$active : Neuron\_name \times Activation \rightarrow \mathbb{B}$
$active(nm, a) \triangleq$
   $\{a(mk\text{-}Arc(z, nm)) \mid mk\text{-}Arc(z, nm) \in \text{dom } a\} = \{true\}$

The *active* function inputs a neuron name and an activation mapping, and returns *true* if and only if *all* the neuron's inputs are active (that is the activation map evaluates all the input connections to *true*). It uses set comprehension to build up a set of Boolean activation values of all the connections that input neuron *nm*. If the value *false* does not belong to this set, then all the activation values are *true*, and *active* therefore returns *true*. For example

$active(3, \{mk\text{-}Arc(1, 3) \mapsto true, mk\text{-}Arc(1, 4) \mapsto true, mk\text{-}Arc(2, 3) \mapsto true,$
$mk\text{-}Arc(2, 4) \mapsto true, mk\text{-}Arc(3, 5) \mapsto false, mk\text{-}Arc(4, 5) \mapsto false, mk\text{-}Arc(5, 0) \mapsto false\})$

will evaluate to *true*. Note that *active* deals with input neurons (which have no input connections) in the way that we would like: in their case the set comprehension expression evaluates to the empty set and *active* returns *false*.

Next, we require a function to sum a neuron's inputs, in preparation for this sum being compared with the neuron's threshold. Again, we use set comprehension, this time building up a set of (weights × values) from the neuron's inputs. Consider the expression

$n\_set = \{w(mk\text{-}Arc(z, nm)) \times v(mk\text{-}Arc(z, nm)) \mid mk\text{-}Arc(z, nm) \in \text{dom } w\}$

If a neuron has *n* inputs, then *n_set* is the set of *n* values obtained by multiplying each input signal's value with its weight. For our example network, for neuron 3 ($= nm$), *n_set* evaluates to

$\{1, 0\}$

We need to combine this with a function *sumset* which inputs a set of numbers and outputs their sum. Its definition below uses the let construct that we originally introduced in Chapter 4

$sumset : \mathbb{Z}\text{-set} \rightarrow \mathbb{Z}$
$sumset(ns) \triangleq$
if $ns = \{ \}$
then 0
else let $x = takeone(ns)$ in $x + sumset(ns \setminus \{x\})$

Also, an auxiliary function *takeone* is used, which inputs a nonempty set and returns an element of that set (the function MAX_IN defined in Chapter 3 could be used for this purpose).

Putting these definitions together, the function *sum*, which produces the weighted sum of a neuron's inputs, is defined thus

> $sum : Neuron\_name \times Weight \times Value \rightarrow \mathbb{Z}$
> $sum(nm, w, v) \triangleq$
>   let $n\_set = \{w(mk\text{-}Arc(z, nm)) \times v(mk\text{-}Arc(z, nm)) | mk\text{-}Arc(z, nm) \in \text{dom } w\}$
>   in $sumset(n\_set)$

The corresponding algebraic function is sum-active defined in Sec. 14.6.2 (assuming a neuron only sums its inputs when *active* is true). If the *sum* of the weighted inputs of a neuron is equal to or above its threshold, then that neuron will 'fire'. We require a function to fire the neuron, and spread its 'pulse' to the adjoining neurons

> $spread : Neuron\_name \times Value \times \mathbb{Z} \rightarrow Value$
> $spread(nm, v, pulse) \triangleq$
> $v \dagger \{mk\text{-}Arc(nm, z) \mapsto pulse | mk\text{-}Arc(nm, z) \in \text{dom } v\}$

The *spread* function uses map comprehension to define the set of maplets forming a map. It overwrites the old values of the network connections from the fired neuron with the new pulse. Assuming an output pulse of 1 for neuron 3 in the example, the map comprehension expression in *spread* evaluates to the maplet

> $\{mk\text{-}Arc(3, 5) \mapsto 1\}$

As well as firing out the pulse, we also need to activate the out connections, and put the incoming connections to sleep:

> $activate : Neuron\_name \times Activation \rightarrow Activation$
> $activate(nm, a) \triangleq$
> $a \dagger \{mk\text{-}Arc(nm, z) \mapsto true | mk\text{-}Arc(nm, z) \in \text{dom } a\}$

> $sleep : Neuron\_name \times Activation \rightarrow Activation$
> $sleep(nm, a) \triangleq$
> $a \dagger \{mk\text{-}Arc(z, nm) \mapsto false | mk\text{-}Arc(z, nm) \in \text{dom } a\}$

Finally, we need a function *allsettled* to return *true* when the network eventually settles down—that is when no more neurons can fire.

> $allsettled : Neuron\_names \times Activation \rightarrow \mathbb{B}$
> $allsettled(ns, a) \triangleq$
> $true \notin \{active(n, a(n)) | n \in \text{elems } ns\} \vee active(0, a)$

The extra 'or'ed condition $active(0, a)$ is necessary because the network is also deemed to have settled if all the output neurons have fired. In this case the output value is stored in the connections between the output neurons and the dummy neuron '0'.

The *settle* operation As in the algebraic specification, we create *settle* as a recursive function. In fact, the structure of this function is identical to the algebraic version, following Case (A), Case (B), and so on in Sec. 14.9. The differences lie with the auxiliary functions explained above:

settle : *Network* → *Network*
settle(*mk-Network*(*ns*, *t*, *w*, *v*, *a*)) ≜
    let *p* = *sum*(hd *ns*, *w*, *v*) in
    let *ac* = *activate*(hd *ns*, *sleep* (hd *ns*, *a*)) in
    if *allsettled*(*ns*, *a*)
    then *mk-Network*(*ns*, *t*, *w*, *v*, *a*)

    elseif *active*(hd *ns*, *a*) ∧ *p* ⩾ *t*(hd *ns*)
    then *settle*(*mk-Network*((tl *ns*) ⌢ [hd *ns*], *t*, *w*, *spread* (hd *ns*, *v*, *p*), *ac*))

    elseif *active*(hd *ns*, *a*) ∧ *p* < *t*(hd *ns*)
    then *settle*(*mk-Network*((tl *ns*) ⌢ [hd *ns*], *t*, *w*, *v*, *sleep* (hd *ns*, *a*)))

    else *settle*(*mk-Network*((tl *ns*) ⌢ [hd *ns*], *t*, *w*, *v*, *a*))

Exercises 14.8

(a) As its stands, our invariant could still do with more conditions to ensure the integrity of the input network. Formalize the following condition within our second attempt's representation above, and thus create an expanded invariant: 'all output neurons must be connected to a dummy neuron identified as 0'.

(b) Our first attempt at a network representation involved the following invariant: 'for every neuron, every one of its input and output structures references a neuron existing in the network.' Formalise this condition within the representation given, and continue on to specify the whole network and its operation *settle*.

(c) Create an invariant for *Arc*-set that effectively disallows networks having connections that feedback on themselves (this should turn out a similar invariant to that of the *poset* in Chapter 5).

14.13 Summary

- An overview of neural networks is given as a prelude to deriving an algebraic specification.
- In simple terms, a neural network is a collection of neurons, which are information processing units, where each processing unit can have any number of outgoing connections but the signals in all these outgoing connections must be the same.
- For the purposes of the specification, we treat a neural network as a collection of neurons. Each neuron is characterized by a collection of incoming connections and a collection of outgoing connections.
- The specification Neural-Network is built up step by step from smaller specification components. Each individual neuron is represented as a 4-tuple that contains the name of the neuron, its threshold, a collection of incoming connections, and a collection of

outgoing connections. The collections of incoming and outgoing connections both consist of 3-tuples:

- In the case of the incoming connections, each connection is characterized by a signal value, whether the incoming signal has come from an activated or deactivated neuron, and the source (neuron name) of the incoming signal.
- In the case of the outgoing connections, each connection is characterized by a signal value, a weight, and the name of the destination neuron to which the signal is being sent.

The emphasis on *collections* and *3-tuples* leads to the use of lists to represent the collections and triples to represent the individual elements of the connections. Generic specifications List and Triple are therefore utilized in the specification of the neural network.

- Specifications Info and Outfo are produced for the collections of incoming and outgoing neuron connections respectively, while the specification Neuron describes an individual neuron in terms of a 4-tuple.
- An OBJ3 prototype of Neural-Network is presented in Appendix 2.
- Finally, we build up corresponding specifications in VDM of the network neural.

ADDITIONAL PROBLEMS

14.1 Leading on from the theme of the exercises at the end of the algebraic treatment, there is a 'physical' constraint on the structure of the neuron connections in the sense that, if there is an *outgoing* connection from neuron N_i to neuron N_j, then there is also an *incoming* connection at neuron N_j from neuron N_i. What are the implications of this with regards to the specification Neural-Network?

14.2 Work through, by hand, the sequence of neuron firings for the three-layered network of Fig. 14.8 and so confirm that when, initially, the input neurons 1 and 2 have signals of 1 and 0 respectively, the final state of the network is as specified by network-after in the OBJ3 prototype of Appendix 2. (Note that this can be done in a few minutes so do not attempt to trace through the sequence of rewrites directly from the specification!)

14.3 Repeat Prob. 14.2 in the case when both input neurons carry the same input signal (0 or 1). In this situation, you will find that, regardless of which common value the input neurons 1 and 2 have, the incoming neuron connections to the output neuron 5 wll consist of the 3-tuples < 0 ; off ; 3> and < 0 ; off ; 4 >.

14.4 Produce a prototype of the specification Neural-Network using Prolog and try it out with the neural network of Fig. 14.8 when the signals from the input neurons 1 and 2 are respectively:
   (a) 0, 0
   (b) 0, 1
   (c) 1, 0
   (d) 1, 1
   Comment on the four results.

14.5 Use an informal argument to show that a feed-forward neural network specified using Neural-Network will eventually 'settle down', in that it will reach a state of 'equilibrium' in which no more neurons will have all their incoming neuron connections activated and so will not fire. (For such a state, application of the operation all-settled? to the state will return the value true.)

REFERENCES

McCulloch, W.S., and Pitts, W., (1943), A Logical Calculus of the Ideas Immanent in Nervous Activity, Bulletin of Math. Bio., Vol. 5, pp. 115–133.

Rumelhart, D.E., and McClelland, J.L., (1986). Parallel Distributed Processing: Explorations in the Microstructure of Cognition, I & II, MIT Press, Cambridge, MA.

A text which provides a useful introduction to the subject of neural computation is the collection of lecture notes:

Hertz, J., Krogh, A., and Palmer, R.G., (1991), *An Introduction to the Theory of Neural Computation* Addison-Wesley, Reading, MA.

15

BACKGROUND, COMPARISON AND SUMMARY

15.1 INTRODUCTION

In this final chapter we start by giving a brief comparison between different specification styles, particularly the two developed in this book. The reader has already had an opportunity to contrast styles, with comparative material appearing in Chapters 9 and 14. Following this, we give some idea of the history of formal specification languages and the applications to which they have been put. We will not attempt to give a survey of formal specification languages (the reader could consult Cohen *et al.* (1986) Chapter 7 for a systematic although somewhat dated survey).

As this chapter focuses on the overall context of specification, pragmatic concerns such as applicability of languages will be discussed. Although these issues are important, we feel that the study of formal specification has a much more fundamental role than its consequent use in software development. The study itself should increase our understanding of what it means to be able to capture a system within a computational framework using abstract mathematical structures.

15.1.1 Likely applications for formal specification

Which language or development method to use depends primarily on the application being undertaken. For example, so called 'structured' development methods have been applied successfully to business data processing for a number of years, and the current favoured British methodology is SSADM (Longworth (1992)), a combination of several more specific structured methods. In a well-trodden, well-understood application area such as data processing, little benefit may be gained from the use of a formal approach. More specifically, in applications that centre around relational databases and related 'applications generators', the use of a formal specification technique might be compared with using a hammer to crack a nut.

Systems whose requirements involve many nonfunctional aspects, such as characteristics of interfaces and peripherals, are not easy to capture within the languages taught in this book. This is because formal specification has been predominantly associated with the functional side of software—in other words, the specification of data and algorithms.

On the other hand, applications that seem to be the most likely candidates for a formal approach as proposed in this book can be characterized as having one or more of the following features:

- They require the creation of highly structured or complex computational models, such as in the fields of intelligent systems or requirements capture.
- They have a safety-critical aspect to them, such as in monitoring and control software, in which people's lives are at stake if the software fails.
- They involve the creation of and subsequent *standardization* of a commonly-used computer tool such as a compiler. This is an attractive application because the formal specification can be used to create the standard, and reused whenever a new implementation is needed.

15.1.2 Which type of formal specification?

Assume you are part of a development team that decides to use formal specification to capture the requirements of an application. A useful criterion in helping select a formalism is the development team's *stage of understanding* of the application area. Are you still trying to understand the system requirements, at an early stage of the development cycle, or has the system already been well researched? For these early stages in understanding and for very abstract system capture, the team would perform a *domain analysis*, which throws up the most important objects in the application. If the results of this were to be captured in a formalism, what type of language would you choose?

Rather than rushing to model the objects identified in the domain analysis with VDM-like data types, languages that allow one to pose axioms representing *constraints* on the properties of an object are more useful. These axioms could be posed in some very expressive, abstract language such as full first-order logic. Such a language, with the addition of *sorts*, resembles the algebraic approach, except that the axioms can be formulae in logic rather than being committed to equations (see Meinke and Tucker (1993) for a survey of many sorted logic). Certainly, first-order logic without the extra baggage of set theory is well suited to capturing requirements of a system at an early stage of development, where these requirements might evolve or build up incrementally. An overcommitment to a model at this stage may mean that as the application area becomes clearer, hasty design decisions will have to be undone, with the consequent waste of effort.

The algebraic approach put forward in this book is also very abstract, in the sense that we can write down exactly those axioms that we need to capture the application, without being tempted to overcommit ourselves to a model. In fact, the built-in data structures of VDM can be defined using equational axioms, and this suggests that the algebraic approach allows one to write more abstract specifications. One possible disadvantage is the commitment to expressing axioms as equations. Although this allows rapid prototyping (as is shown in Chapter 13 and Appendix 2), it results in a less expressive language than full first-order logic. For example, requirements are sometimes stated as rules, and in this case trying to translate them into equations results in an unnecessary loss of their natural form.

At the other extreme, the development team may be experts in the area and there may be little likelihood of any surprises. Application areas that have already been well thought out and require a 'design level' specification are ideal for the model-based approach. The platform offered by sets and related structures allows one quickly to build up a mathematically-precise specification, which nevertheless is close to a working prototype. The non-linear planner of Chapters 6 and 7 in this book is such an example; its model-based specification was based on years of research into planning, and it was derived from a more abstract specification written in a form of *modal logic* appearing in Chapman (1987).

15.2 COMPARISON OF SPECIFICATION LANGUAGES

15.2.1 General

Comparing the two styles of specification we have used in this book is a difficult task, as there are a number of criteria and viewpoints to consider. The novice to the two styles will initially find them very different: the reliance on sets as the basic data structure, and the use of pre- and post-conditions for operation definition gives VDM a very different flavour than the 'purist' algebraic approach as introduced in Chapter 8. A study of the neural network example developed in the last chapter, however, shows some startling similarities. Most noticeably, it became clear that the built-in types of VDM can be built by the user of an algebraic language, and reused in building up a specification. That a VDM specification can be made to resemble an algebraic one was shown in Chapter 9: the facility to use recursive type construction in VDM, as used in the binary tree specification, shows that it is possible to build up a data type in VDM algebraically! (see also Exercise 15.2 below).

15.2.2 Operator definition

The most significant difference between the two approaches is apparent when an external *system state* is used in VDM. The need for the system state device seems to be essential with very complex specifications, although the composing of two specifications with their own local state has been something we have sidestepped (as noted in the introduction to Chapter 5).

The crucial benefit of the system state is that we can access and change a (small) part of it, without referring to the rest; in other words, no part of the state changes by the action of an operation, unless it is explicitly specified to do so. This is summed up by what is called the 'default persistence' assumption:

- If a VDM operation has the effect of changing part of the system state, it is implicitly assumed that the rest of the state remains completely unchanged.

Exactly the same idea of default persistence underpinned the action representation that we built up in the planning case study of Chapter 6.

In contrast, an operation defined algebraically on a complex object, which produces a new value of the object by accessing a small part of it, must explicitly return the rest of the object untouched. In other words, parts of an object that do not change have to be somehow declared as such; this is not a problem in small specifications, but becomes enormously inefficient in large ones. Of course, if the value of an operation depends on *and only on* the value of its parameters, this does make clearer specifications.

To help in the comparison of operations, we divide them into the three kinds identified in the algebraic approach: atomic constructor, nonatomic constructor and accessor. For examples of specification in both styles, the Stack data type will be used. Although an extremely simple application, the main differences (including use of an external state) can be illustrated using it. As a useful correspondence, we will consider values of an abstract data type to be abstractions of the distinct 'states' generated within a corresponding VDM definition. Thus the 'state space' will be identified with the set of values in an abstract data type.

Atomic constructors generate the values of a type in an algebraic specification. The application of a constructor creates a new type value, and therefore corresponds in VDM to an operation that changes the state. An example 'state' of the stack from Chapter 8 is:

```
push(push(init, 5), 4)
```

Application of push, with input value '3', creates a new value of the state:

```
push(push(push(init, 5), 4), 3)
```

The new value of the stack can be written down by consulting its signature, in the heading of the algebra. In contrast, the new VDM state value is specified by writing the property the new state must satisfy, in the post-conditions of *PUSH* (taken from Chapter 9):

$PUSH(n : \mathbb{N})$
ext wr $s : Stack$
pre *true*
post $s = [n] \frown \overleftarrow{s}$

push(push(init, 5), 4) is an abstraction of the corresponding 'unbounded stack' representation from Chapter 9, modelled by the sequence '[4,5]'. Application of *PUSH*, with input value '3', means finding a new state that satisfies the post-condition. The only state within the confines of the stack model that satisfies it is of course '[3,4,5]'.

Nonatomic constructors are not dealt with any differently in VDM. For example, given the *POP* operation:

$POP(\ )$
ext wr $s : Stack$
pre len $s > 0$
post $s = $ tl $\overleftarrow{s}$

the output state is one that satisfies the post-condition, as with *PUSH*. The definition of the pop operation in the algebraic notation, with the use of subsorts, is:

```
pop: ne-stack → stack
AXIOM for pop:
pop(push(s,n)) = s
```

Thus, a nonatomic constructor is defined by showing how pop rewrites typical type values. Using our correspondence between states and type values, the axiom for pop could be read as 'if the state has the form push(s, n), then the output 'state' is s'. Notice how the exceptional case of the empty stack is dealt with: in VDM using a pre-condition, while in the algebraic approach using a subsort (in fact there are a number of different ways of dealing with exceptions—in Chapter 8 we used an error value stack-error).

Accessor operations in the algebraic formulation are defined very much like nonatomic constructors—in terms of the structure of the stack value. The operation is-empty?, which finds out if a stack is empty or not, is:

```
is-empty?: stack → bool
AXIOMS for is-empty?:
is-empty?(init) = true
is-empty?(push(s,n)) = false
```

Its VDM counterpart is:

IS_EMPTY?( ) $b : \mathbb{B}$
ext rd $s : Stack$
pre *true*
post $b \Leftrightarrow (s = [\ ])$

Accessors output values that are not members of the abstract data type being constructed. In VDM they correspond to operations that only have read access to the state, they do not change it. Accordingly, the heading only contains ext rd variables. In the algebraic approach they are defined in the same manner as nonatomic constructors: they give an output value depending on the structure of the input value.

Exercise 15.1 It is possible for VDM post-conditions to make their operators nondeterministic in the sense that more than one output state can satisfy them. On the other hand, our interpretation of equational axioms is deterministic. How do you think our algebraic language could be extended so that one could write nondeterministic specifications? (*Hint*: think about introducing a *choice* in the process of rewriting terms.)

Exercise 15.2 Consider the following example of an unbounded stack operation, written in explicit form, but using the same sequence model for the Stack:

$pop : Stack \rightarrow Stack$
$pop(s) \triangleq$
   if $s \neq [\ ]$
   then tl s

As witnessed in the joint case study of Chapter 14, the distinction between languages is not so great when one uses explicit function definitions in VDM. The function *pop* can be given a rewrite rule interpretation in the same way as an algebraic axiom for pop, and the only major difference between the two definitions is in the use of the built-in data type Sequence.

Using VDM's type constructor technique introduced in Chapter 9 to create the binary tree specification, we can create a Stack type without using the Sequence type, as follows:

$Stack = \text{INIT} \mid Stackpush$
$Stackpush :: rest : Stack$
$\qquad\qquad val\ : \mathbb{N}$

The representation in VDM of the stack example '[4,5]' given above would then be

$mk\text{-}Stackpush(mk\text{-}Stackpush(\text{INIT}, 5), 4)$

(a) Represent '[3,4,5]' in the same way.
(b) Create all the Stack operations as explicit functions on this new Stack representation.
(c) Compare your resulting specification with the algebraic specification. Apart from the purely syntactic, do any differences between specification methods remain?

15.2.3 Building up specifications

As you would have gathered by reading this book, the platform that VDM supplies in the shape of its built-in types allows the developer to build up complex specifications quite concisely. As the joint case study in Chapter 14 shows, the algebraic approach is more verbose, and the developer seems to have to start virtually from first principles. This does have the advantage, however, that only those axioms that capture the characteristics of the model need to be written down. Also, importing from a library of existing specifications may overcome the apparent 'low platform' problem of the algebraic approach. Unfortunately, it may also leave the developer open to choosing particular algebras for *convenience* (that is because they have already been defined) rather than for their natural fit. The disadvantage of choosing a model with more detail than necessary is certainly one that is apparent in a model-based approach.

A major advantage of the algebraic approach is the ease with which one can build up hierarchical objects and the disciplined way that importing and exporting of type specifications is handled. The approach seems to encourage one to build bottom-up, performing validation on individual objects as they are specified. VDM is certainly lacking in this area. As previously mentioned, standard VDM now has the facility of modules, but it remains to be seen how effective their use will be. In fact the problem of building up larger specifications, when this involves combining subspecifications with their own state, seems to be an inherent problem in the model-based approach.

15.2.4 The data type invariant

As a final point of comparison, it is instructive to consider the role of the data type invariant in VDM. When a model is built up from built-in data types, it is expected that the *fit* with what is desired may not be quite right. The data type invariant is there to tailor the fit, to invalidate any values of the original model that have no counterpart in the requirements.

For the algebraic approach, an understanding of the required properties of an abstract data type is often a useful prelude to identifying an appropriate collection of atomic constructors. We must be careful to create those atomic constructors that will result in exactly the set of values required. However, we may have to resort to introducing additional operations to 'constrain' the values of a data type in the sense that the atomic constructors are too general (this idea was discussed in Chapter 9 in the context of *hidden* (*private*) operations). The additional operations are constructor operations, which are defined (using axioms) in terms of atomic constructors and which allow 'valid' values of the data type to be constructed. Any external specification that wants to use this specification then views these additional constructors as the atomic constructors for that imported type. This means that the original atomic constructors cannot be exported with the specification and must be treated as hidden. The binary search tree of Chapter 9 and the petrochemical tank of Chapter 11 were two such examples.

15.2.5 Specification versus high-level programming languages

Notations for formally capturing specifications that allow a more abstract level of expression than that offered by a programming language are undoubtably essential in software engineering. But programming languages *are* formal languages, in that they have a precise syntax and semantics. The difference is that program languages are conceived primarily to express algorithms and to do so efficiently with respect to computer space and time.

As VDM was developed in the 1970s, it is not surprising that some programming languages have data structuring facilities at least as powerful. For example, modern functional programming languages contain list comprehension, algebraic types, polymorphism, and so on. If we limit VDM to explicitly defined functions, then specifications are made executable by interpreting them as if they were expressions in a functional language. The main difference, of course, is in the use of implicit specifications, which abstract away procedural details and therefore have no parallel in programming.

In a similar fashion, executable algebraic specification languages can be compared with modern functional programming languages. Both use a rewrite rule model to execute functions; both allow types to be built up using constructor operations. The main difference is that specification language component data types can be structured in a way that emphasizes the formal properties of the specification, with the emphasis on axioms as mathematical objects rather than executable statements.

Exercise 15.3 Specifications have much in common with *scientific theories*:

(a) An (inductive) theory can never in itself be *correct*, it has to be validated using experiment and observations. When experimental results are found that are not consistent with the theory, it has to be modified.
(b) An equation (or, more generally, an assertion) within a theory that holds over all the 'observables' is centrally important. This is known as an *invariant*.
(c) For theories to be respectable, they must be self-consistent and have no redundant axioms.

(d) Many theories are written in mathematics (for example relativity, Newtonian mechanics, electromagetism) although some are not (evolution, Marxism).

(e) Good theories predict future results and observations. For example, it is claimed that the famous 'black hole' phenomenon was predicted theoretically *before* it was actually observed.

Taking each point in turn, discuss the connections between scientific theory and software specification.

15.3 HISTORY AND APPLICATIONS

15.3.1 VDM and model-based specification

VDM evolved within an industrial environment in the early seventies, and it has continued to have a steady following. VDM is best known as a *software development method* and for this one should consult Jones (1990) or Andrews and Ince (1991) for a detailed description. The development method combines specification construction (using VDM-SL) with a rigorous method for refining the specification through a series of software design levels, each level more concrete than the last. The crucial point is that after a new refinement of the design has been created, proof obligations must be discharged which assert that the new concrete level is an adequate refinement of the last level. This involves the construction of a *homomorphism*, called the retrieve function, which maps the concrete level into the abstract (the reader may notice a parallel with the algebraic approach here: in Chapter 10 we described how *homomorphisms* are used to relate algebras, in a similar way). If one considers the case study in Chapter 6, it should be possible to relate the concrete specification of Sec. 6.4 to the abstract one in Sec. 6.3 in this way.

Composition of design levels using the refinement proofs gives us confidence that the final implementation conforms to the initial specification. Although the VDM school has always stressed that the level of formality is up to the developer, mathematical skill and the effort needed to perform rigorously these refinement steps (including discharging the proof obligations resulting from refinement) is significantly greater than that required to construct the initial specification. This problem has led to the development of *proof assistants*, software tools that assist the developer perform the formal reasoning required. At their base is a theorem prover which can be adapted to perform the type of reasoning required, although invariably reasoning is human-assisted. One such proof assistant, called *Muffin*, is specified using VDM itself in Jones and Shaw (1990). Our view is that while specifying software formally is here to stay, eventually hand-performed program refinement will become redundant; either 'prototyping' languages will become efficient enough (through compiler optimization), or refinement itself will become largely automatic.

VDM was initially used in compiler definition and in the related area of writing standard implementation-independent semantics for programming languages. A number of typical applications are reported in Jones and Shaw (1990) including the specifications of a database management system, and garbage collection and heap storage in the implementation of a programming language.

Other languages similar to VDM-SL have been developed, and a more modern and arguably more comprehensive specification language is Z. It has a wide range of built-in mathematical types, and it also has the advantage of having an easy syntactic construction for including smaller specifications in larger ones, in the shape of the *Schema*. The Schema is a syntactic device with which one can both build up data types and their invariants, and also define states and their transformations. It is divided into two parts, a declaration part (for signatures) and a predicate part (for semantics). One can build up a large Schema *A* by using a smaller one *B*, simply by declaring *B* to be textually included in *A*. Also Z is equipped with a device called the schema calculus to formally combine Schemas. It is this relative ease of being able to build up specifications using the Schema that gives Z an advantage over VDM.

Z's use is widespread, but it does have the disadvantage that a Z standard does not yet exist, unlike VDM. Well-publicized applications include the specification of part of the IBM CICS system, and this and other examples can be found in Hayes (1986). A recent introduction to Z may be found in Potter *et al.* (1991).

15.3.2 Algebraic specification

The key feature in specifying abstract data types is to present a description of that data type precisely but independent both of any concrete representation of the data objects and any implementation details of the operations. Many-sorted algebras are mathematical structures that correspond to this viewpoint of an abstract data type.

As noted in Chapter 8, Zilles was one of the first to recognize the fundamental connection between abstract data types and algebraic systems in the early 1970s (Zilles, 1974). Around the same time, other pioneers such as the ADJ group of Goguen, Thatcher, Wagner and Wright (Goguen, 1974) and Guttag (1975) explored this idea and investigated the implications of treating an abstract data type as a many-sorted algebra.

One of the earliest algebraic specification languages developed was *Clear* (Burstall and Goguen, 1977, 1981) which introduced the notion of parameterized specifications. Other early languages include *AFFIRM* (Musser, 1979) and *OBJ0* (Goguen, 1978). Since those early days, a large number of algebraic specification languages have been developed of which the most widely known are *ACT ONE* (Ehrig and Mahr, 1985), *Larch* (Guttag *et al.*, 1985) and the various versions of OBJ. The specification languages AFFIRM, OBJ, ACT ONE, and *Axis* (Coleman *et al.*, 1988) are based on many-sorted initial algebras and implementations of AFFIRM and OBJ were first produced at the end of the 1970s.

Before leaving this brief survey of specification languages, it is worth expanding a little on Larch. Larch is different from most other algebraic specification languages in that its specifications are two-tiered. Each Larch specification has one component written in an algebraic language together with a second component which is tailored to suit a particular target programming language. The first tier of a Larch specification uses a *common* language which permits the production of theories independent of any implementation detail. The second tier of a Larch specification is written in one (or possibly more) *interface* languages. Having decided on a target programming language for the implementation of a specification, an appropriate specification language is chosen from the set of *interface* languages and the second tier of the specification then produced. This has the advantage of permitting theories to be written which, although enrichments of those that belong to the *common* language, have a close affinity with the language(s) used in the final implementation.

The algebraic approach to specification has been successfully applied to the formal specification of a wide variety of systems, ranging from the smaller basic classical data structures to more elaborate software systems such as rewrite rule interpreters (Coleman *et al.*, 1987), relational databases (Hayes, 1988), hierarchical filing systems (Dollin, 1988) and the semantics of a small imperative programming language (Berghammer, *et al.*, 1988). For this last application, Berghammer and co-workers applied the algebraic approach to specify a compiler back-end. They showed how the task of code generation for a small language can be specified algebraically. Specifications of both the abstract syntax together with the semantics of the source and target language on the one hand and of the code generation on the other were constructed using hierarchical abstract data types.

The algebraic approach has also been extensively used to specify the term rewriting engines for executable specification languages. For the three executable languages mentioned, namely AFFIRM, OBJ and Axis, the implementation was designed using the language itself. Very much a case of 'the proof of the pudding is in the eating!'. Algebraic specifications techniques have also been used in graphics software applications, including the specification of computer graphics systems (Carson, 1983), the MacIntosh QuickDraw program (Nakagawa *et al.*, 1988) and the GKS graphics kernel system (Duce, 1989).

REFERENCES

Andrews, D., and Ince, D. (1991). *Practical Formal Methods with VDM*, McGraw-Hill, London.

Berghammer, R., Ehler, H., and Zierer, H. (1988). Towards an Algebraic Specification of Code Generation, *Science of Computer Programming*, vol. II, Elsevier North-Holland, Amsterdam, pp. 45-63.

Burstall, R.M., and Goguen, J.A. (1977). Putting Theories Together to Make Specifications. Invited paper in *Proceedings of the Fifth International Conference on Artifical Intelligence*, Cambridge, MA., pp. 1045–1058. See also Burstall and Goguen (1980).

Burstall, R.M., and Goguen, J.A. (1980). The Semantics of Clear, a Specification Language, *Lecture Notes in Computer Science*, vol. 86, Springer-Verlag, Berlin, pp. 294–331.

Burstall, R.M., and Goguen, J.A. (1981). An Informal Introduction to Specifications Using Clear, *The Correctness Problem in Computer Science*, R. Boyer, and J. Moore (eds), Academic Press, New York, pp. 185–213. Reprinted in N. Gehani and A. McGettrick (eds) *Software Specification Techniques* (1985) Addison-Wesley, Reading, MA., pp. 363–390.

Carson, G.S. (1988). The Specification of Computer Graphics Software, *IEEE Computer Graphics and Applications*, 27–41.

Chapman, D. (1987). Planning for Conjunctive Goals, *Artificial Intelligence*, **32**, July, 333–377.

Cohen, B., Harwood, W.T., and Jackson, M.I. (1986). *The Specification of Complex Systems*, Addison-Wesley, Wokingham.

Coleman, D., Dollin, C., Gallimore, R., Arnold, P., and Rush, T. (1988). An Introduction to the Axis Specification Language, *Hewlett-Packard Information Laboratory Report HPL-ISC-TR-88-031*, Software Engineering Department, Hewlett-Packard, Bristol.

Coleman, D., Gallimore, R., and Stavridou, V. (1987). The Design of a Rewrite Rule Interpreter from Algebraic Specifications, *Software Engineering Journal*, pp. 95–104.

Dollin, C. (1988). Axis Tutorial: A Simple Filing System, *Hewlett-Packard Information Laboratory Report* HPL-ISC-TM-88-18, Software Engineering Department, Hewlett-Packard, Bristol.

Duce, D. Concerning the Computability of PHIGS and GKS, article which was to appear in a book (unpublished as yet) on applications of OBJ.

Ehrig, H., and Mahr, B. (1985). *Fundamentals of Algebraic Specification 1: Equations and Initial Semantics*, Springer-Verlag, Berlin.

Goguen, J.A. (1974). Semantics of Computation, *Proceedings of the First International Symposium on Category Theory Applied to Computation and Control*, University of Massachusetts at Amherst, pp. 234–249. Also in Goguen, J.A. (1975). *Lecture Notes in Computer Science*, vol. 25, Springer-Verlag, pp. 151–163, Berlin.

Goguen, J.A. (1978). Some Design Principles and Theory for OBJ0: A Language for Expressing and Executing Algebraic Specifications of Programs, *Proceedings of the International Conference on Mathematical Studies of Information Processing*, Kyoto, pp. 425–473.

Guttag, J.V. (1975). The Specification and Application to Programming of Abstract Data Types, Ph.D. Thesis, Department of Computer Science, Toronto University.

Guttag, J.V., Horning, J.J., and Wing, J.M. (1985). The Larch Family of Specification Languages, *IEEE Software*, vol. 2, pp. 24–36.

Hayes, F. (1988). A Relational Algebra Specification Using Axis, *Hewlett-Packard Information Laboratory Report HPL-BRC-TM-88-019*, Software Engineering Department, Hewlett-Packard, Bristol.

Hayes, I. (1986). *Specification Case Studies*, Prentice-Hall, London.

Jones, C.B. (1990). *Systematic Software Development using VDM*, 2nd edn, Prentice-Hall, London.

Jones, C.B., and Shaw, R.C.F. (eds) (1990). *Case Studies in Systematic Software Development*, Prentice-Hall, London.

Longworth, G. (1992). *Introducing SSADM Version 4*, NCC Blackwell, Manchester.

Meinke, K., and Tucker, J.V. (eds). (1993). *Many Sorted Logic and its Application*, Wiley, Chichester.

Musser, D.R. (1979). Abstract Data Type Specification in the AFFIRM System, *Proceedings of Specifications of Reliable Software*, IEEE Catalog No. 79 CH1401-9C, IEEE Computer Society, pp. 47–57.

Nakagawa, A., Futatsugi, K., Tomura, S., and Shimizu, T. (1988). Algebraic Specification of Macintosh's QuickDraw Using OBJ2, *Proceedings of the Tenth International Conference on Software Engineering*, Singapore.

Potter, B., Sinclair, J., and Till, D. (1991). *An Introduction to Formal Specification and Z*, Prentice-Hall, London.

Zilles, S.N. (1974). Algebraic Specification of Data Types, *MIT, Laboratory for Computer Science, Progress Report XI*, Cambridge, MA.

One further article of interest with regards to applications of the algebraic approach is:

Hoffman, C.M., O'Donnell, M.J., and Strandh, R.I. (1985). Implementation of an Interpreter for Abstract Equations, *Software-Practice and Experience*, **15**(12), 1185–1204.

One final collection of articles, by different authors, which is well worth exploring and which fills in more of the detail on aspects of algebraic specification languages, such as prototyping algebraic specifications and the application of user-defined syntax in specification languages is:

Bergstra, J.A., Heering, J., and Klint, P. (eds) (1989). *Algebraic Specification*, ACM Press, Addison-Wesley, Reading, MA. This book is not intended as a tutorial for algebraic specification but can best be summarized as a progress report of research in these particular areas at that time.

THE PLANNER PROTOTYPE IN PROLOG

```
/*************** A SMALL VDM TOOLSET IN PROLOG ******************/
/******************** SET ****************************************/
/* element_of_set(E,Y)                     */
/* pre: Y is a set                         */
/* post: E is an element of Y              */
/*       iff element_of_set(E,Y) succeeds  */
element_of_set(E,[E|Y]).
element_of_set(E,[_|Y]) :-
    element_of_set(E,Y).
/* sub_set(X,Y)                            */
/* pre: X,Y sets                           */
/* post: X is a subset of Y                */
/*       iff sub_set(X,Y) succeeds         */
sub_set([First_Element|Rest],Y) :-
    element_of_set(First_Element,Y),
    sub_set(Rest,Y).
sub_set([],Y).
/* eq_set(X,Y)                             */
/* pre: X,Y sets                           */
/* post: X=Y iff eq_set(X,Y) succeeds      */
eq_set(X,Y) :-
    sub_set(X,Y),
    sub_set(Y,X).
/* union_set(X,Y,Z)                        */
/* pre: X,Y sets                           */
/* post: Z = X union Y                     */
union_set([E|X],Y,[E|Z]) :-
    not(element_of_set(E,Y)),
    union_set(X,Y,Z).
```

```
union_set([E|X],Y,Z) :-
    element_of_set(E,Y),
    union_set(X,Y,Z).
union_set([],Y,Y).
/* intersect_set(X,Y,Z)                          */
/* pre:  X,Y sets                                */
/* post: Z = X intersect Y                       */
intersect_set([E|X],Y,[E|Z]) :-
    element_of_set(E,Y),
    intersect_set(X,Y,Z).
intersect_set([E|X],Y,Z) :-
    not(element_of_set(E,Y)),
    intersect_set(X,Y,Z).
intersect_set([],Y,[]).
/* minus_set(X,Y,Z)                              */
/* pre:  X,Y sets                                */
/* post: Z = X minus Y                           */
minus_set([E|X],Y,Z) :-
    element_of_set(E,Y),
    minus_set(X,Y,Z).
minus_set([E|X],Y,[E|Z]) :-
    not(element_of_set(E,Y)),
    minus_set(X,Y,Z).
minus_set([],Y,[]).


/******************* SEQUENCE ******************/
/* tl_seq(List_in, List_out):                    */
/* post:  List_out = tl(List_in)                 */
tl_seq([H|T], T).
/* hd_seq(List_in, El_out):                      */
/* post:  El_out = hd(List_in)                   */
tl_seq([H|T], H).
/* concat_seq(List_inl,List_in2,  List_out):     */
/* post:  List_out = List_inl joined with List_in2 */
concat_seq([], List_in2,   List_in2).
concat_seq(List_in2,[],   List_in2).
concat_seq([H|T], List_in2,  [H|List]) :-
    concat_seq(T, List_in2,  List),!.


/******************* COMPOSITE ******************/
/* init_comp(Name, List_of_slot_names, List_of_slot_values,  Comp ): */
/* post: Comp is a composite structure with name Name, and a list    */
/* of component names given in List_of_slot_names, with corresponding */
/* values in List_of_slot_values                                     */
/* NB we can't just represent them as VDM since we've got to keep a   */
/* record of which field is which. We use a Prolog structure         */
/* str(Name,Body) corresponding to VDM's mk-Name(Body). Body in Prolog */
/* is represented by a list of Slot-Value pairs.                     */
init_comp(Name, Lsn, Lsv,   str(Name,Comp) ):-
    init_c(Lsn, Lsv,   Comp),!.
init_c([L|Lsn], [V|Lsv],  [c(L,V)| Comp]) :-
    init_c(Lsn, Lsv,   Comp),!.
init_c([], [],   []).
```

```
/* put_comp(Comp, Slot_name, Value,   NewComp):                      */
/* post: NewComp = Comp except Slot_name(NewComp) = Value            */
put_comp(str(Name,[c(N,Old_V)|R]), Name, N, V,   str(Name, [c(N,V)|R])) :- !.
put_comp(str(Name,[c(M,W)|R]), Name, N, V,   str(Name, [c(M,W)|R1])) :-
    put_comp(str(Name,R), Name, N, V,   str(Name,R1)),!.
/* get_comp(Comp, Slot_name,   Value):                               */
/* post: Value = Slot_name(Comp)                                     */
get_comp(str(Name, Body), Name, Slot_name,   Value):-
    element_of_set(c(Slot_name, Value),  Body),!.


/******************** MAP ***************************/
/*      To ensure map integrity we inbuild into the constructor the
        condition that each domain element maps to a unique range    */
/* init_map(  Map)                                                   */
/* post: Map is an empty map                                         */
init_map( [] ).
/* overwrite_map(Map, Dom, Value,   NewMap):                         */
/* post: NewMap = Map + [Dom -> Value]                               */
overwrite_map(Map, Dom, Value,   NewMap) :-
    dom_map(Map, DomM),
    element_of_set(Dom, DomM),
    overdo(Map, Dom, Value,   NewMap),!.
overwrite_map(Map, Dom, Value,   NewMap) :-  /* Dom is a new dom value */
    concat_seq([m(Dom, Value)],Map,   NewMap),!.
overdo([m(Dom,_)|T], Dom, Value,   [m(Dom, Value)|T]).
overdo([X|T], Dom, Value,   [X|T1]) :-
        overdo(T,Dom,Value,   T1),!.
/* apply_map(Map, Dom,   Value):                                     */
/* post: Value = Map(Dom)                                            */
apply_map(Map, Dom,   Value):-
        element_of_set(m(Dom,Value),Map),!.
/* dom_map(Map,   Dom_Map):                                          */
/* post: Dom_Map = dom(Map)                                          */
dom_map([],   []).
dom_map([m(D,_)|T],   [D|DT]) :-
        dom_map(T,DT),!.
/* ran_map(Map,   Ran_Map):                                          */
/* post: Ran_Map = ran(Map)                                          */
ran_map([],   []).
ran_map([m(_,R)|T],   RT) :-
        element_of_set(m(_,R),T),
        ran_map(T,RT),!.
ran_map([m(_,R)|T],   [R|RT]) :-
        ran_map(T,RT),!.


/* THE PLANNER PROTOTYPE ***********************************************/
/* N.B.
  (1) This planner can be made much more efficient with some simple
      changes:
        - The whole partial plan is 'carried' around in the achieve
          procedures below. The non-changeable bit - the planning problem
          itself, including all the action representations, should be made
          into global data by allowing it to be asserted as Prolog facts.
```

```
          - Some of the procedures in the ACHIEVE operations could be
            shuffled around to increase the speed of planning.
      (2) The top level loop is called from the drivers written
            separately for each World (below we give one for the Blocks
            World, and one for the Painting World).
      (3) Note one small change: although we used the sequence to model
            a literal, Prolog has as a data structure the literal itself,
            which we use instead: thus '[grasp,a]' is represented as
            'grasp(a)'. In fact since literals are propositions, they
            could be represented by single identifiers. To help future
            extension of the planner to accept literals with parameters,
            we will stick to Prolog's literal structure.
      (4) The prototype simply spews out a correct plan structure.
            Procedures are needed to present the completed plan to the user. */
continue_planning :-
retract( storedplan(Level, completed, PP) ),
nl,write('finished'),nl,write(PP),!.
continue_planning :-
 /* rather than simply retracting the first plan, one can write a
    heuristic function to pick the 'best' one to expand */
retract( storedplan(Level, partial, PP) ),
get_comp(PP, partial_plan, ps,    Ps),


 /* rather than simply picking the first goal in the unsovled (Ps),
      one can write heuristic function to pick the 'best' one to expand */
          element_of_set(Gi,   Ps),
achieve_all_ways(PP, Gi, Level),
continue_planning.
continue_planning :- nl,write('**no plans left**').
 /* This is the procedure that generates all the plans - NOTE
      that it does NOT generate all plans possible, for efficiency
      reasons, and so it will not solve some problems which have a
      solution. To make it generate all plans, the last clause of
      the first rule should finish with 'fail'. In this case, the
      user will have to add heuristics to the choice mechanisms
      to stave off an explosion of plans..                      */
achieve_all_ways(PPO, Gi, Level) :-
write(' in 1 '),
achieve1(PPO, Gi,    Plan),·
nl,write('Achieve1 Score '),
Level1 is Level +1,
score(Plan, Score),
write(Score),write(Level1),
assert(storedplan(Level1, Score, Plan)).
achieve_all_ways(PPO, Gi, Level) :-
write(' in 2 '),
achieve2(PPO, Gi,    Plan),
nl,write('Achieve2 Score '),
Level1 is Level +1,
score(Plan, Score),
write(Score),write(Level1),nl,
assert(storedplan(Level1, Score, Plan)),
fail.
```

```
achieve_all_ways(_, _, _).
/* a plan's 'score' is here simply 'completed' or 'partial'. */
score(Plan, completed) :-
    get_comp(Plan, partial_plan, ps, []).
score(Plan, partial).
/************* OPERATIONS on PARTIAL PLAN *********/
init(PPI,  PPO) :-
    get_comp(PPI, planning_problem, i,   IPP),      /* IPP = i(PPI) */
    get_comp(PPI, planning_problem, g,   GPP),      /* GPP = g(PPI) */
    init_comp(action, [name,pre,add,del], [init,[],IPP,[]],   INIT),
    init_comp(action, [name,pre,add,del], [goal, GPP,[],[]],   GOAL),
    init_map(  OS),
    overwrite_map(OS, init, INIT,   OS1),
    overwrite_map(OS1, goal, GOAL,   OS2),
    make_goal_instances(goal, GPP,   GIs),
    initPO(Ts),
    init_comp(partial_plan, [pp,os,ts,ps,as], [PPI,OS2,Ts,GIs,[]],  PPO).
achieve1(PlanI, Gi,   PlanO) :-
    get_comp(PlanI, partial_plan, os,   Os),
    get_comp(PlanI, partial_plan, ts,   Ts),
    get_comp(PlanI, partial_plan, ps,   Ps),
    get_comp(PlanI, partial_plan, as,   As),
    element_of_set(Gi, Ps),
    dom_map(Os,   DomOs),
    element_of_set(A, DomOs),
    achieve(Os,Ts,A,Gi,   Ts_new),
    minus_set(Ps, [Gi],   Ps_new),
    union_set(As, [Gi],   As_new),
    put_comp(PlanI, partial_plan, ts, Ts_new,   Plan1),
    put_comp(Plan1, partial_plan, ps, Ps_new,   Plan2),
    put_comp(Plan2, partial_plan, as, As_new,   PlanO).
achieve2(PlanI, Gi, PlanO) :-
    get_comp(PlanI, partial_plan, pp,   PP),
    get_comp(PlanI, partial_plan, os,   Os),
    get_comp(PlanI, partial_plan, ts,   Ts),
    get_comp(PlanI, partial_plan, ps,   Ps),
    get_comp(PlanI, partial_plan, as,   As),
    element_of_set(Gi, Ps),                    /* pre-condition */
    dom_map(Os,   DomOs),                      /* post-condition */
    newid(DomOs,   NewA),
    add_node(NewA,Ts,   Ts2),
    get_comp(PP,planning_problem, as,   ASpp),
    element_of_set(Action, ASpp),
    overwrite_map(Os,NewA,Action,   Os_new),

    achieve(Os_new,Ts2,NewA,Gi,   Ts3),
    for_all_elsIO(As, declobber(Os_new,NewA), Ts3,   Ts_new),

    get_comp(Action,action,pre,   PreA),
    make_goal_instances(NewA, PreA,   GIs),
    minus_set(Ps, [Gi],   Ps_new1),
    union_set(Ps_new1, GIs,   Ps_new2),
    union_set(As, [Gi],   As_new),
```

```
            put_comp(PlanI, partial_plan, os, Os_new,   Planl),
            put_comp(Planl, partial_plan, ts, Ts_new,   Plan2),
            put_comp(Plan2, partial_plan, ps, Ps_new2,  Plan3),
            put_comp(Plan3, partial_plan, as, As_new,   Plan0).
achieve(Os,Ts,A,GI,   New_Ts) :-
        get_comp(GI,goal_instance, ai,  O),
        get_comp(GI,goal_instance, gi,  P),
        apply_map(Os,A,    ActionA),                .
        get_comp(ActionA,action,add,   AddA),
        element_of_set(P,   AddA),               /* P is in A.add    */
        make_before(A,O,Ts,   Tsl),              /* before(A,O,Tsl) */
        dom_map(Os,   DomOs),
        for_all_elsIO(DomOs, declobber_achieve(P,A,O,Os), Tsl,   New_Ts).
declobber_achieve(P,A,O,Os,O,Ts,   Ts) :- !. /* C = O V */
declobber_achieve(P,A,O,Os,A,Ts,   Ts) :- !. /* C = A V */
declobber_achieve(P,A,O,Os,C,Ts,   Ts) :-
        before(O,C,Ts),!.                        /* before(O,C,Ts) V */
declobber_achieve(P,A,O,Os,C,Ts,   Ts) :-
        before(C,A,Ts),!.                        /* before(C,A,Ts) V */
declobber_achieve(P,A,O,Os,C,Ts,   Ts) :-
        apply_map(Os,C,   CA),
        get_comp(CA,action,del,   CAD),
        not(element_of_set(P,CAD)),!.            /* not( p in Os(C).del) */

declobber_achieve(P,A,O,Os,C, Ts,   New_Ts) :-
        make_before(O,C,Ts,   New_Ts).          /* make  before(O,C,Ts) */
declobber_achieve(P,A,O,Os,C, Ts,   New_Ts) :-
        make_before(C,A,Ts,   New_Ts).          /* make  before(C,A,Ts) */
/* declobber called from ACHIEVE2..*/
declobber(Os,NewA,GI,Ts,   Ts) :-
        get_comp(GI,goal_instance,ai,  C),
        before(C,NewA,Ts),!.
declobber(Os,NewA,GI,Ts,   Ts) :-
        get_comp(GI,goal_instance,gi,  Q),
        apply_map(Os,NewA,Os_NewA),
        get_comp(Os_NewA,action,del,  Del_Os_NewA),
        not(element_of_set(Q,Del_Os_NewA)),!.
declobber(Os,NewA,GI,Ts,   Ts) :-
        get_comp(GI,goal_instance,ai,  C),
        get_comp(GI,goal_instance,gi,  Q),
        element_of_set(W,Os),
        before(NewA,W,Ts),
        before(W,C,Ts),
        apply_map(Os,W,   Os_W),
        get_comp(Os_W,action,add,   add_Os_NewA),
        element_of_set(Q,add_Os_W),!.
newid(D,   act(Y)) :-
        element_of_set(act(X), D),
        Y is X+1,
        not(element_of_set(act(Y), D)),
        !.
newid(_,   act(1)).
/**********************************************************************/
```

```
/*  Implementation of Partial Ordering */
/* A is already before O */
make_before(A,O,Ts,    Ts) :-
    before(A, O, Ts),!.
/* otherwise put in constraint.. */
make_before(A,O,Ts,    [ARC|Ts]) :-
    poss_before(A,O,Ts),
    init_comp(arc, [source,dest], [A,O], ARC),!.
poss_before(A,O,Ts) :-
    not(A=O),
    not(before(O,A,Ts)).
before(A,O,Ts) :-
    init_comp(arc, [source,dest], [A,O],    ARC),
    element_of_set(ARC, Ts),!.
before(A,O,Ts) :-
    get_nodes(Ts,    Nodes),
    element_of_set(Y,    Nodes),
    init_comp(arc, [source,dest], [A,Y],    ARC),
    element_of_set(ARC,    Ts),
    before(Y,O,Ts),!.
get_nodes([],    []).
get_nodes([Arc|R],  S) :-
    get_comp(Arc,arc,source,    Val1),
    get_comp(Arc,arc,dest,    Val2),
    get_nodes(R, S1),
    union_set([Val1,Val2],S1,    S),!.
add_node(NewA,Ts, [ARC1,ARC2|Ts]) :-
    init_comp(arc, [source,dest], [init,NewA], ARC1),
    init_comp(arc, [source,dest], [NewA,goal], ARC2).
initPO([Ts]) :-
    init_comp(arc, [source,dest], [init,goal], Ts).


/* ************************** for all ********************/
/* post: for_all_els( Some_set, Proc) is true
 iff for all X in Some_set : Proc(X) is true */
for_all_els( [], Proc) :- !.
for_all_els( [E|L], Proc) :-
    Proc =.. OL,
    concat_seq(OL,[E], OL1),
    ProcE =.. OL1,
    call(ProcE),
    for_all_els( L, Proc),!.
/* ************************** for all ********************/
/* post: for_all_els( Some_set, Proc, I,O) is true
 iff for all X in Some_set : Proc(X,I,O) is true
 This is a simple generalisation of the above which allows
 an argument of Proc to change as each instance of Some_set
 is checked */
for_all_elsIO( [], _, I,I) :-!.
for_all_elsIO( [E|L], Proc,I,O) :-
    Proc =.. OL,
    concat_seq(OL,[E,I,I1], OL1),
    ProcE =.. OL1,
```

```
        call(ProcE),
        for_all_elsIO( L, Proc, Il, O),!.


/*************** make_goal_instances(A, Gs,   Gi)          */
/* pre: Gs is a literal set, A is an action identifier    */
/* post: Gi = {mk-Goal_instances(g,A) : g is in Gs}       */
make_goal_instances(Action_Id, [G|G_rest],   [Gi|Gi_rest]) :-
      init_comp(goal_instance, [gi, ai], [G, Action_Id],   Gi),
      make_goal_instances(Action_Id, G_rest,   Gi_rest),!.
make_goal_instances(_, [],   []).


/* BLOCKS PROBLEM ********************/
startblocks :-
/* This problem is the one built up as an example in the early
   part of chapter 6, and in Exercise 6.3.
   This first part of the program collects up the action
   representations, and computes the initial plan.
   Below we only list only a few Block's World actions; the reader
   is invited to write the rest (but see efficiency note at
   the beginning of the prototype).                        */

    init_comp(action, [name,pre,add,del],
   [ grasp(a),
   [clear_top(a),gripper_free],
   [gripper_grasps(a)],
   [clear_top(a),gripper_free] ],
  Action1),
   init_comp(action, [name,pre,add,del],
   [liftup(a,b),
   [gripper_grasps(a), on(a,b)],
   [ lifted_up(a), clear_top(b) ],
   [ on(a,b) ] ],
  Action2),
   init_comp(action, [name,pre,add,del],
   [liftup(a,table),
   [gripper_grasps(a), on(a,table) ],
   [lifted_up(a)],
   [on(a,table) ] ],
  Action3),
   init_comp(action, [name,pre,add,del],
   [put_down(a,c),
   [lifted_up(a), clear_top(c)],
   [on(a,c), gripper_free, clear_top(a) ],
   [lifted_up(a), gripper_grasps(a), clear_top(c)]],
  Action4),
   init_comp(action, [name,pre,add,del],
   [put_down(a,table),
   [lifted_up(a)],
   [on(a,table), gripper_free],
   [lifted_up(a),gripper_grasps(a)] ],
  Action5),
        /* form planning problem .. */
        init_comp(planning_problem, [as,i,g],
```

```
    [[Actionl, Action2, Action3, Action4, Action5],
     [on(a,b),on(c,table),on(b,table),on(d,table),
      clear_top(d),clear_top(a),clear_top(c),gripper_free],
     [on(a,c),clear_top(b)]],
PPI),

        /* execute the initial partial plan operator as specified in VDM */
init(PPI, PPO),
assert( storedplan(l,partial,PPO) ),
        continue_planning.
startpaint :-
/* This is the Painting World as described in chapter 5 and
   chapter 6.                                                */
    init_comp(action, [name,pre,add,del],
          [ paintceiling,
           [haveladder, functionalladder, havepaint],
           [paintedceiling],
           [] ],
                                        Actionl),
         init_comp(action, [name,pre,add,del],
           [paintwall,
           [havepaint, paintedceiling],
           [paintedwall],
           [] ],
                                        Action2),
         init_comp(action, [name,pre,add,del],
           [paintladder,
           [haveladder, havepaint],
           [paintedladder],
           [functionalladder] ],
                                        Action3),
         init_comp(action, [name,pre,add,del],
           [getpaint,
           [havecreditcard],
           [havepaint],
           [] ],
                                        Action4),
         init_comp(action, [name,pre,add,del],
           [getladder,
           [havecreditcard,ownlargecar],
           [haveladder,functionalladder],
           [] ],
                                        Action5),
/* form planning problem .. */
      init_comp(planning_problem, [as,i,g],
          [[Actionl, Action2, Action3, Action4, Action5],
           [ havecreditcard, ownlargecar],
           [ paintedladder, paintedceiling, paintedwall ]],
                PPI),
/* execute the initial partial plan operator as specified in VDM */
        init(PPI, PPO),
/* put it in a global store */
        assert( storedplan(l,partial,PPO) ),
```

```
/* start planning loop */
      continue_planning.

/* Planner Output:
This is the partial plan (pretty printed) that is output when
the planner is run with the input blocks problem.
*/
str(partial_plan, [
c(pp, str(planning_problem, [
   c(as, [
      str(action, [c(name, grasp(a)),
            c(pre, [clear_top(a), gripper_free]),
            c(add, [gripper_grasps(a)]),
            c(del, [clear_top(a), gripper_free])]),
      str(action, [c(name, liftup(a, b)),
            c(pre, [gripper_grasps(a), on(a, b)]),
            c(add, [lifted_up(a), clear_top(b)]),
            c(del, [on(a, b)])]),
      str(action, [c(name, liftup(a, table)),
            c(pre, [gripper_grasps(a), on(a, table)]),
            c(add, [lifted_up(a)]), c(del, [on(a, table)])]),
      str(action, [c(name, put_down(a, c)),
            c(pre, [lifted_up(a), clear_top(c)]),
            c(add, [on(a, c), gripper_free, clear_top(a)]),
            c(del, [lifted_up(a), gripper_grasps(a), clear_top(c)])]),
      str(action, [c(name, put_down(a, table)),
            c(pre, [lifted_up(a)]),
            c(add, [on(a, table), gripper_free]),
            c(del, [lifted_up(a), gripper_grasps(a)])])]),
    c(i, [on(a, b), on(c, table), on(b, table), on(d, table), clear_top(d),
                            clear_top(a), clear_top(c), gripper_free]),
    c(g, [on(a, c), clear_top(b)])])),
c(os, [
  m(act(3), str(action, [c(name, grasp(a)),
            c(pre, [clear_top(a), gripper_free]),
            c(add, [gripper_grasps(a)]),
            c(del, [clear_top(a), gripper_free])])),
  m(act(2), str(action, [c(name, liftup(a, b)),
            c(pre, [gripper_grasps(a), on(a, b)]),
            c(add, [lifted_up(a), clear_top(b)]),
            c(del, [on(a, b)])])),
  m(act(1), str(action, [c(name, put_down(a, c)),
            c(pre, [lifted_up(a), clear_top(c)]),
            c(add, [on(a, c), gripper_free, clear_top(a)]),
            c(del, [lifted_up(a), gripper_grasps(a), clear_top(c)])])),
  m(goal, str(action, [c(name, goal),
            c(pre, [on(a, c), clear_top(b)]), c(add, []), c(del, [])])),
  m(init, str(action, [c(name, init), c(pre, []),
               c(add, [on(a, b), on(c, table), on(b, table), on(d, table),
               clear_top(d), clear_top(a), clear_top(c), gripper_free]),
               c(del, [])]))]),
c(ts, [
  str(arc, [c(source, act(3)), c(dest, act(2))]),
```

```
        str(arc, [c(source, init), c(dest, act(3))]),
        str(arc, [c(source, act(3)), c(dest, goal)]),
        str(arc, [c(source, act(2)), c(dest, act(1))]),
        str(arc, [c(source, init), c(dest, act(2))]),
        str(arc, [c(source, act(2)), c(dest, goal)]),
        str(arc, [c(source, init), c(dest, act(1))]),
        str(arc, [c(source, act(1)), c(dest, goal)]),
        str(arc, [c(source, init), c(dest, goal)])])]),
c(ps, []),
c(as, [
        str(goal_instance, [c(gi, on(a, c)), c(ai, goal)]),
        str(goal_instance, [c(gi, clear_top(b)), c(ai, goal)]),
        str(goal_instance, [c(gi, lifted_up(a)), c(ai, act(1))]),
        str(goal_instance, [c(gi, clear_top(c)), c(ai, act(1))]),
        str(goal_instance, [c(gi, gripper_grasps(a)), c(ai, act(2))]),
        str(goal_instance, [c(gi, on(a, b)), c(ai, act(2))]),
        str(goal_instance, [c(gi, clear_top(a)), c(ai, act(3))]),
        str(goal_instance, [c(gi, gripper_free), c(ai, act(3))])])])])

/* Planner Output:
This is the partial plan (pretty printed) that is output when
the planner is run with the input Painting World problem.
*/
str(partial_plan, [
c(pp, str(planning_problem, [c(as, [
        str(action, [
            c(name, paintceiling),
            c(pre, [haveladder, functionalladder, havepaint]),
            c(add, [paintedceiling]), c(del, [])]),
        str(action, [
            c(name, paintwall),
            c(pre, [havepaint, paintedceiling]),
            c(add, [paintedwall]), c(del, [])]),
        str(action, [
            c(name, paintladder),
            c(pre, [haveladder, havepaint]),
            c(add, [paintedladder]), c(del, [functionalladder])]),
        str(action, [
            c(name, getpaint),
            c(pre, [havecreditcard]),
            c(add, [havepaint]), c(del, [])]),
        str(action, [
            c(name, getladder),
            c(pre, [havecreditcard, ownlargecar]),
            c(add, [haveladder, functionalladder]), c(del, [])])]),
    c(i, [havecreditcard, ownlargecar]),
    c(g, [paintedladder, paintedceiling, paintedwall])])]),
c(os, [
    m(act(5),  str(action, [c(name, getpaint),
                    c(pre, [havecreditcard]),
                    c(add, [havepaint]), c(del, [])])),
    m(act(4),  str(action, [c(name, getladder),
                    c(pre, [havecreditcard, ownlargecar]),
```

```
                        c(add,[haveladder,functionalladder]),c(del,[])])),
        m(act(3),  str(action,[c(name,paintwall),
                        c(pre,[havepaint,paintedceiling]),
                        c(add,[paintedwall]),c(del,[])])),
        m(act(2),  str(action,[c(name,paintceiling),
                        c(pre,[haveladder,functionalladder,havepaint]),
                        c(add,[paintedceiling]),c(del,[])])),
        m(act(1),  str(action,[c(name,paintladder),
                        c(pre,[haveladder,havepaint]),
                        c(add,[paintedladder]),c(del,[functionalladder])])),
        m(goal,  str(action,[c(name,goal),
                        c(pre,[paintedladder,paintedceiling,paintedwall]),
                        c(add,[]),c(del,[])])),
        m(init,  str(action,[c(name,init),
                        c(pre,[]),
                        c(add,[havecreditcard,ownlargecar]),c(del,[])])])),
c(ts,[
    str(arc,[c(source,act(2)),c(dest,act(3))]),
    str(arc,[c(source,act(5)),c(dest,act(3))]),
    str(arc,[c(source,act(5)),c(dest,act(2))]),
    str(arc,[c(source,act(2)),c(dest,act(1))]),
    str(arc,[c(source,act(4)),c(dest,act(2))]),
    str(arc,[c(source,act(5)),c(dest,act(1))]),
    str(arc,[c(source,init),c(dest,act(5))]),
    str(arc,[c(source,act(5)),c(dest,goal)]),
    str(arc,[c(source,act(4)),c(dest,act(1))]),
    str(arc,[c(source,init),c(dest,act(4))]),
    str(arc,[c(source,act(4)),c(dest,goal)]),
    str(arc,[c(source,init),c(dest,act(3))]),
    str(arc,[c(source,act(3)),c(dest,goal)]),
    str(arc,[c(source,init),c(dest,act(2))]),
    str(arc,[c(source,act(2)),c(dest,goal)]),
    str(arc,[c(source,init),c(dest,act(1))]),
    str(arc,[c(source,act(1)),c(dest,goal)]),
    str(arc,[c(source,init),c(dest,goal)])]),
c(ps,[]),
c(as,[
    str(goal_instance,[c(gi,paintedladder),c(ai,goal)]),
    str(goal_instance,[c(gi,paintedceiling),c(ai,goal)]),
    str(goal_instance,[c(gi,paintedwall),c(ai,goal)]),
    str(goal_instance,[c(gi,haveladder),c(ai,act(1))]),
    str(goal_instance,[c(gi,havepaint),c(ai,act(1))]),
    str(goal_instance,[c(gi,haveladder),c(ai,act(2))]),
    str(goal_instance,[c(gi,functionalladder),c(ai,act(2))]),
    str(goal_instance,[c(gi,havepaint),c(ai,act(2))]),
    str(goal_instance,[c(gi,havepaint),c(ai,act(3))]),
    str(goal_instance,[c(gi,paintedceiling),c(ai,act(3))]),
    str(goal_instance,[c(gi,havecreditcard),c(ai,act(4))]),
    str(goal_instance,[c(gi,ownlargecar),c(ai,act(4))]),
    str(goal_instance,[c(gi,havecreditcard),c(ai,act(5))])])]))
```

The material in this appendix can be accessed via remote ftp from 'ftp.wmin.ac.uk' in the path 'computing/published/turnerj/appendix 1'.

A2.1 OBJ3 PROTOTYPE OF ESTATE AGENT DATABASE

```
obj  MODE  is  sort  Mode          .
   op  for-sale     :  ->  Mode .
   op  under-offer  :  ->  Mode .
endo

*** ============================================
obj  ADDRESS  is  sort  Address                        .
   ops  adr1  adr2  adr3  adr4  :  ->  Address          .
endo

*** ============================================
obj  HOUSES-FOR-SALE  is  sort  House-db .
   protecting  ADDRESS  +  MODE  +  BOOL .
   op  empty          :                              -> House-db .
   op  insert         :  House-db  Address        -> House-db .
   op  add-house      :  House-db  Address  Mode  -> House-db .
   op  delete-house   :  House-db  Address        -> House-db .
   op  make-offer     :  House-db  Address        -> House-db .
   op  is-on-market?  :  House-db  Address        -> Bool     .
   op  is-under-offer? :  House-db  Address        -> Bool     .
   var                hs  :  House-db .
   vars  addr  addr1  addr2  :  Address  .
   var                m   :  Mode    .
   eq  insert(empty, addr)  =  add-house(empty, addr, for-sale) .
   eq  insert(add-house(hs, addr1, m), addr2)  =
        if  addr1 == addr2  then  add-house(hs, addr1, m)
```

387

```
                else  add-house(insert(hs, addr2), addr1, m)  fi      .
      eq  delete-house(empty, addr)  =  empty                         .
      eq  delete-house(add-house(hs, addr1, m), addr2)  =
            if  addr1 == addr2  then  hs
            else  add-house(delete-house(hs, addr2), addr1, m)  fi .
      eq  is-on-market?(empty, addr)  =  false                        .
      eq  is-on-market?(add-house(hs, addr1, m), addr2)  =
            if  addr1 == addr2  then  true
            else  is-on-market?(hs, addr2) fi                         .
      eq  is-under-offer?(empty, addr)  =  false                      .
      eq  is-under-offer?(add-house(hs, addr1, m), addr2)  =
                  if  addr1 == addr2  then
                        if  m == under-offer  then  true
                        else  false  fi
                  else  is-under-offer?(hs, addr2)  fi                .
      eq  make-offer(empty, addr)  =  empty                           .
      eq  make-offer(add-house(hs, addr1, m), addr2)  =
      if  addr1 == addr2  then

          if  m == for-sale  then
              add-house(delete-house(hs, addr1), addr1, under-offer)
          else  add-house(hs, addr1, m)  fi
        else
          add-house(make-offer(hs, addr2), addr1, m)  fi             .
endo

*** ====  Now evaluate some expressions
reduce is-on-market?(insert(insert(empty,adr1),adr2),adr1) .
***>  should be :  true
reduce delete-house(insert(insert(empty,adr1),adr2),adr2) .
***>  should be :  add-house(empty,adr1,for-sale)
reduce delete-house(insert(insert(empty,adr1),adr2),adr3) .
***>  should be :
***>       add-house(add-house(empty,adr2,for-sale),adr1,for-sale)
reduce make-offer(insert(insert(empty,adr1),adr2),adr2) .
***>  should be :  add-house(add-house(empty,adr2,under-offer),adr1,for-sale)
```

A2.2 OBJ3 PROTOTYPE OF PETROCHEMICAL TANK

```
obj PETROCHEMICAL  is  sort Chemical              .
    ops   pc1  pc2  pc3  pc4  pc5  :  ->  Chemical .
endo


*** ================================================
obj TANK-2 is sorts  NeTank  Tank  ErrTank                 .
    subsort  NeTank  <  Tank  <  ErrTank                   .
    protecting  PETROCHEMICAL + FLOAT + BOOL               .
    op   new        :                           ->  Tank     .
    op   add-chem   :  ErrTank  Chemical  Float  ->  ErrTank  .
    op   fill       :  Tank  Chemical  Float     ->  NeTank   .
    op   remove     :  Tank  Float               ->  Tank     .
    op   empty-tank :  Tank                      ->  Tank     .
    op   change-pc  :  Tank  Chemical  Float     ->  ErrTank  .
    op   error      :                            ->  ErrTank  .
```

```
op  alarm?         :  ErrTank                    ->  Bool      .
op  is-empty?      :  Tank                       ->  Bool      .
op  is-full?       :  Tank                       ->  Bool      .
op  chem           :  NeTank                     ->  Chemical .
op  level          :  Tank                       ->  Float     .
op  max-vol        :                             ->  Float     .
vars  c   c1  c2  :  Chemical .
vars  q   q1  q2  :  Float    .
eq  add-chem(new, c, q)  =
                  if  q == 0.0  then  new
                  else  if  q <= max-vol  then  fill(new, c, q)
                  else  error  fi  fi          .
eq  add-chem(fill(new, c1, q1), c2, q2)  =
                  if  (c1 == c2)  and  ((q1 + q2) <= max-vol)  then
                  fill(new, c1, q1 + q2)  else  error  fi .
eq  add-chem(error, c, q)       =  error          .
eq  remove(new, q)              =  new            .
eq  remove(fill(new, c1, q1), q2)  =  if  q1 > q2  then
                                      add-chem(new, c1, q1 - q2)
                                      else  new  fi          .
eq  empty-tank(new)             =  new .
eq  empty-tank(fill(new, c, q))  =  new .
eq  change-pc(new, c, q)         =  add-chem(new, c, q)           .
eq  change-pc(fill(new, c1, q1), c2, q2)  =
                  add-chem(empty-tank(fill(new, c1, q1)), c2, q2) .
eq  alarm?(new)                 =  false .
eq  alarm?(fill(new, c, q))     =  false .
eq  alarm?(error)               =  true  .
eq  is-empty?(new)              =  true  .
eq  is-empty?(fill(new, c, q))  =  false .
eq  is-full?(new)               =  false .
eq  is-full?(fill(new, c, q))   =  (q == max-vol) .
eq  chem(fill(new, c, q))       =  c     .
eq  level(new)                  =  0.0   .
eq  level(fill(new, c, q))      =  q     .
eq  max-vol                     =  (100.0) .
endo
```

```
*** ====  Now evaluate some expressions
reduce add-chem(add-chem(new, pc1, 23.0), pc1, 34.0) .
***>  should be : fill(new, pc1, 57.0)
reduce add-chem(add-chem(new, pc1, 45.0), pc1, 88.0) .
***>  should be : error
reduce add-chem(add-chem(new, pc1, 45.0), pc3, 5.0) .
***>  should be : error
reduce remove(add-chem(new, pc1, 33.0), 22.0) .
***>  should be : fill(new, pc1, 11.0)
reduce change-pc(add-chem(add-chem(new, pc1, 11.0), pc1, 22.0), pc4, 63.0) .
***>  should be : fill(new, pc4, 63.0)
reduce change-pc(add-chem(add-chem(new, pc1, 11.0), pc1, 22.0), pc4, 63.0) .
***>  should be : fill(new, pc4, 63.0)
reduce alarm?(add-chem(new, pc1, 23.0)) .
***>  should be : false
```

```
reduce alarm?(add-chem(new,pc1,123.0)) .
***>    should be : true
reduce alarm?(add-chem(add-chem(new,pc1,11.0),pc2,22.0)) .
***>    should be : true
reduce is-empty?(add-chem(add-chem(new,pc1,11.0),pc1,22.0)) .
***>    should be : false
reduce is-full?(add-chem(add-chem(new,pc1,11.0),pc1,22.0)) .
***>    should be : false
reduce is-full?(add-chem(add-chem(new,pc1,10.0),pc1,90.0)) .
***>    should be : true
reduce empty-tank(add-chem(add-chem(new,pc1,23.0),pc1,34.0)) .
***>    should be : new
reduce chem(add-chem(add-chem(new,pc3,52.0),pc3,48.0)) .
***>    should be : pc3
reduce level(add-chem(add-chem(add-chem(new,pc2,22.0),pc2,33.0),pc2,44.0)) .
***>    should be : 99.0
```

A2.3 OBJ3 PROTOTYPE OF PETROCHEMICAL PLANT DATA-STORE

```
obj READING  is  sort  Reading                              .
   protecting  PETROCHEMICAL + FLOAT                         .
   op  make    :  Chemical Float  ->  Reading               .
   op  p-chem  :  Reading          ->  Chemical             .
   op  amount  :  Reading          ->  Float                .
   op  smaller :  Float Float      ->  Float    [comm] .
   op  larger  :  Float Float      ->  Float    [comm] .
   var c       :  Chemical .
   vars q q1 q2 :  Float     .
   eq  p-chem(make(c, q))  =  c .
   eq  amount(make(c, q))  =  q .
   eq  smaller(q1, q2)  =   if  q1 > q2 then
                               q2
                            else q1 fi .
   eq  larger(q1, q2)   =   if  q1 > q2  then
                               q1
                            else q2  fi .
endo


*** =============================================
obj TANK-DETECTOR  is  sort  Name                    .
    ops dev-1 dev-2 dev-3 dev-4 dev-5 :  -> Name .
endo


*** =============================================
obj DATASTORE  is  sorts  Datastore NeDatastore                 .
   protecting  READING + TANK-DETECTOR + TANK-2 + BOOL + NAT    .
   extending  PETROCHEMICAL + FLOAT                             .
   subsort NeDatastore  < Datastore                             .
   op  empty    :                              -> Datastore   .
   op  add      :  Datastore  Name  Reading -> NeDatastore .
   op  isolate  :  Datastore  Name          -> Datastore   .
```

```
op   global-max   :  NeDatastore              ->  Float     .
op   global-min   :  NeDatastore              ->  Float     .
op   max-level    :  NeDatastore   Name       ->  Float     .
op   min-level    :  NeDatastore   Name       ->  Float     .
op   any-values?  :  Datastore     Name       ->  Bool      .
op   pc-contents  :  NeDatastore   Name       ->  Chemical  .
op   pc-level     :  NeDatastore   Name       ->  Float     .
op   full-warning? :  Datastore                ->  Bool      .
op   count        :  Datastore    Name        ->  Nat       .
op   total        :  Datastore                ->  Nat       .
var  s            :  Datastore .
vars n  n1 n2     :  Name     .
var  r            :  Reading  .
eq   any-values?(empty, n)            =  false              .
eq   any-values?(add(s, n2, r), n1)  =  if  n1 == n2  then true
                                           else any-values?(s, n1) fi .

eq   full-warning?(empty)          =  false        .
eq   full-warning?(add(s, n, r))   =
                      if  amount(r) == max-vol  then   true
                          else  full-warning?(s)  fi .
cq   pc-contents(add(s, n2, r), n1)  =
                       (if  n1 == n2  then  p-chem(r)
                        else  pc-contents(s, n1)  fi )
                        if  any-values?(add(s, n2, r), n1) .
cq   pc-level(add(s, n2, r), n1)  =
                       (if  n1 == n2  then  amount(r)
                        else  pc-level(s, n1)  fi )
                        if  any-values?(add(s, n2, r), n1)  .
eq   isolate(empty, n)          =  empty            .
eq   isolate(add(s, n2, r), n1)  =
                             if  n1 == n2  then  add(isolate(s, n1), n1, r)
                             else  isolate(s, n1)  fi   .
eq   global-max(add(s, n, r))      =
                             if  s == empty  then   amount(r)
                             else  larger(amount(r), global-max(s))  fi  .
eq   global-min(add(s, n, r))      =
                             if  s == empty  then  amount(r)
                             else  smaller(amount(r), global-min(s))  fi .
cq   max-level(add(s, n2, r), n1)  =
                             global-max(isolate(add(s, n2, r), n1))
                             if  any-values?(add(s, n2, r), n1) .
cq   min-level(add(s, n2, r), n1)  =
                             global-min(isolate(add(s, n2, r), n1))
                             if  any-values?(add(s, n2, r), n1) .
eq   count(empty, n)            =  0                .
eq   count(add(s, n2, r), n1)  =  if  n1 == n2  then  1 + count(s, n1)
                                    else  count(s, n1)  fi .
eq   total(empty)          =  0           .
eq   total(add(s, n, r))  =  1 + total(s) .
endo


***  ====  Now evaluate some expressions
reduce isolate(add(add(add(add(add(add(add(empty,dev-1,make(pcl,11.0)),
```

```
             dev-2,make(pc2,22.0)),  dev-3,make(pc3,33.0)),
               dev-4,make(pc4,44.0)),  dev-1,make(pc1,41.0)),
               dev-2,make(pc2,12.0)),  dev-3,make(pc3,13.0)), dev-1) .
***>   should be : add(add(empty,dev-1,make(pc1,11.0)),dev-1,make(pc1,41.0))
reduce isolate(add(add(add(add(add(add(add(empty,dev-1,make(pc1,11.0)),
               dev-2,make(pc2,22.0)),  dev-3,make(pc3,33.0)),
               dev-4,make(pc4,44.0)),  dev-1,make(pc1,41.0)),
               dev-2,make(pc2,12.0)),  dev-3,make(pc3,13.0)), dev-4) .
***>   should be : add(empty,dev-4,make(pc4,44.0))
reduce any-values?(add(add(add(add(add(add(add(empty,dev-1,make(pc1,11.0)),
                 dev-2,make(pc2,22.0)),  dev-3,make(pc3,33.0)),
                 dev-4,make(pc4,44.0)),  dev-1,make(pc1,41.0)),
                 dev-2,make(pc2,12.0)),  dev-3,make(pc3,13.0)), dev-4) .
***>   should be : true
reduce full-warning?(add(add(empty,dev-1,make(pc1,100.0)),
                     dev-2,make(pc2,40.0))) .
***>   should be : true
reduce pc-contents(add(add(empty,dev-1,make(pc1,100.0)),
                     dev-2,make(pc2,40.0)) ,dev-1) .
***>   should be : pc1
reduce pc-level(add(add(add(add(add(add(add(empty,dev-1,make(pc1,11.0)),
               dev-2,make(pc2,22.0)),  dev-3,make(pc3,33.0)),
               dev-4,make(pc4,44.0)),  dev-1,make(pc1,41.0)),
               dev-2,make(pc2,12.0)),  dev-3,make(pc3,13.0)), dev-2) .
***>   should be : 12.0
reduce global-max(add(add(add(add(add(add(add(empty,dev-1,make(pc1,11.0)),
                 dev-2,make(pc2,22.0)),  dev-3,make(pc3,33.0)),
                 dev-4,make(pc4,44.0)),  dev-1,make(pc1,41.0)),
                 dev-2,make(pc2,12.0)),  dev-3,make(pc3,13.0))) .
***>   should be : 44.0
reduce global-min(add(add(add(add(add(add(add(empty,dev-1,make(pc1,11.0)),
                 dev-2,make(pc2,22.0)),  dev-3,make(pc3,33.0)),
                 dev-4,make(pc4,44.0)),  dev-1,make(pc1,41.0)),
                 dev-2,make(pc2,12.0)),  dev-3,make(pc3,13.0))) .
***>   should be : 11.0
reduce max-level(add(add(add(add(add(add(add(empty,dev-1,make(pc1,11.0)),
                dev-2,make(pc2,22.0)),  dev-3,make(pc3,33.0)),
                dev-4,make(pc4,44.0)),  dev-1,make(pc1,41.0)),
                dev-2,make(pc2,12.0)),  dev-3,make(pc3,13.0)), dev-3) .
***>   should be : 33.0
reduce min-level(add(add(add(add(add(add(add(empty,dev-1,make(pc1,11.0)),
                dev-2,make(pc2,22.0)),  dev-3,make(pc3,33.0)),
                dev-4,make(pc4,44.0)),  dev-1,make(pc1,41.0)),
                dev-2,make(pc2,12.0)),  dev-3,make(pc3,13.0)), dev-3) .
***>   should be : 13.0
reduce count(add(add(add(add(add(add(add(empty,dev-1,make(pc1,11.0)),
            dev-2,make(pc2,22.0)),  dev-3,make(pc3,33.0)),
            dev-4,make(pc4,44.0)),  dev-1,make(pc1,41.0)),
            dev-2,make(pc2,12.0)),  dev-3,make(pc3,13.0)), dev-4) .
***>   should be : 1
reduce total(add(add(add(add(add(add(add(empty,dev-1,make(pc1,11.0)),
            dev-2,make(pc2,22.0)),  dev-3,make(pc3,33.0)),
            dev-4,make(pc4,44.0)),  dev-1,make(pc1,41.0)),
```

```
                dev-2,make(pc2,12.0)), dev-3,make(pc3,13.0))) .
***>    should be :  7
```

A2.4 OBJ3 PROTOTYPE OF SYMBOL TABLE MANAGER

```
obj  IDENTIFIER  is  sort  Identifier         .
   ops  x   y   z   s   t  :  -> Identifier .
endo


***  ============================================
obj  ATTRIBUTE  is  sort  Attribute           .
   ops  real  integer  char  boolean :  -> Attribute .
endo


***  ============================================
obj  SYMBOL-TABLE  is  sorts  Symbol-table  Ne-Symbol-table  .
   subsort  Ne-Symbol-table  <  Symbol-table         .
   protecting  IDENTIFIER  +  ATTRIBUTE  +  BOOL      .
   op  init       :                 -> Symbol-table      .
   op  enter-block :  Symbol-table    -> Ne-Symbol-table  .
   op  leave-block :  Ne-Symbol-table -> Symbol-table     .
   op  add     : Symbol-table Identifier Attribute -> Ne-Symbol-table .
   op  insert  : Symbol-table Identifier Attribute -> Ne-Symbol-table .
   op  retrieve : Ne-Symbol-table Identifier        -> Attribute       .
   op  is-in-block? : Symbol-table Identifier       -> Bool            .
   op  is-in-table? : Symbol-table Identifier       -> Bool            .
   var st       :  Symbol-table .
   vars  idl id2 : Identifier    .
   vars   al a2 : Attribute      .
   eq  insert(init, idl, al)              =  add(enter-block(init), idl, al) .
   eq  insert(enter-block(st), idl, al)  =  add(enter-block(st), idl, al)   .
   eq  insert(add(st, idl, al), id2, a2) =
                if  idl == id2  then  add(st, idl, al)
                else add(insert(st, id2, a2), idl, al)  fi     .
   eq  leave-block(enter-block(st))   = st     .
   eq  leave-block(add(st, idl, al))  =  leave-block(st) .
   eq  is-in-block?(init, idl)            =  false
   eq  is-in-block?(enter-block(st), idl)  =  false
   eq  is-in-block?(add(st, idl, al), id2) =  if  idl == id2  then  true
                                            else is-in-block?(st, id2) fi .
   eq  is-in-table?(init, idl)            =  false               .
   eq  is-in-table?(enter-block(st), idl)  =  is-in-table?(st, idl)
   eq  is-in-table?(add(st, idl, al), id2) =
                          if  idl == id2  then  true
                          else is-in-table?(st, id2)  fi      .
   cq  retrieve(enter-block(st), idl) =
                retrieve(st, idl)  if is-in-table?(st, idl)        .
   cq  retrieve(add(st, idl, al), id2) =
                ( if  idl == id2  then  al else  retrieve(st, id2)  fi )
                if  is-in-table?(add(st, idl, al), id2)           .
endo
```

```
***   ====   Now evaluate some expressions
reduce insert(enter-block(insert(init,x,real)),y,char) .
***>   should be : add(enter-block(add(enter-block(init),x,real)),y,char)
reduce is-in-block?(insert(enter-block(insert(init,x,real)),y,char),x) .
***>   should be : false
reduce is-in-block?(insert(enter-block(insert(init,x,real)),y,char),y) .
***>   should be : true
reduce is-in-table?(insert(enter-block(insert(init,x,real)),y,char),x) .
***>   should be : true
reduce is-in-table?(insert(enter-block(insert(init,x,real)),y,char),z) .
***>   should be : false
reduce retrieve(insert(enter-block(insert(init,x,real)),y,char),x) .
***>   should be : real
reduce leave-block(insert(enter-block(insert(init,x,real)),y,char)) .
***>   should be : add(enter-block(init),x,real)
```

A2.5 OBJ3 PROTOTYPE OF A NEURAL NETWORK

```
***
***   The PROPS or theory module ELEM imposes no requirement
***   apart from the need for a sort

 th ELEM is
    sort Element .
 endth
***   ==================================
***
***   Simple parameterised list
***
 obj LIST[E :: ELEM] is
    sorts  List  NeList
    subsort  NeList  <  List
    op   #            :                        -> List          .
    op   _ . _        : Element  List   -> NeList         .
    op   _ app _      : List  List      -> List    [assoc] .
    op   is-in? _ _   : Element  List   -> Bool           .
    vars  e  el  e2  : Element                            .
    vars  s  sl  s2  : List                               .
    ***     Axioms for list concatenation:
    eq   # app s          =  s                            .
    eq   (e . sl) app s2  =  (e . (sl app s2))            .
    ***     Axioms for determining whether an element el
    ***     is present in a list s
    eq   is-in? el #      =  false                        .
    eq   is-in? el (e2 . s) = (el == e2)  or  is-in? el s .
 endo


***   ===========================================
***
***   Unconstrained triples
***
```

```
obj TRIPLE[S1 :: ELEM, S2 :: ELEM, S3 :: ELEM] is
   sort  Triple .
   op  < _ ; _ ; _ >  :  Element.S1  Element.S2  Element.S3    ->       Triple .
   op  1-st _          :  Triple                            ->  Element.S1    .
   op  2-nd _          :  Triple                            ->  Element.S2    .
   op  3-rd _          :  Triple                            ->  Element.S3    .
   var          a  :  Element.S1                                       .
   var          b  :  Element.S2                                       .
   var          c  :  Element.S3                                       .
   eq   1-st < a ; b ; c >  =  a                                       .
   eq   2-nd < a ; b ; c >  =  b                                       .
   eq   3-rd < a ; b ; c >  =  c                                       .
endo


***    =================================================
***
***    List of unconstrained triples
***
obj LIST-OF-TRIPLE[F :: ELEM, S :: ELEM, T :: ELEM]  is
   protecting LIST[view to TRIPLE[F, S, T] is sort Element to Triple . endv]  .
endo


***    =================================================
***
***    on/off activation state
***
obj ACTIVATION is
   sort  Activation             .
   ops  on  off :  ->  Activation .
endo


***    ==================================================
***
***    List of output neurons
***
obj OUTFO is
   protecting  LIST-OF-TRIPLE[INT, INT, INT] *
                  ( sort List  to  Outfo ,
                        op  1-st _ to  value-of _ ,
                        op  2-nd _ to  weight _ ,
                        op  3-rd _ to  to-neuron _ )      .
   op  fire-out _ _ :  Int  Outfo  ->  Outfo        .
   var           l :  Outfo                         .
   vars  m n p w    :  Int                          .

   ***    Axioms for fire-out:
   eq   fire-out m #                      =  #    .
   eq   fire-out m (< n ; w ; p > . l)    =
                (< m ; w ; p > . (fire-out m l)) .
endo


***    ===================================================
***
```

```
***    List of incoming neurons
***
obj INFO is
    protecting  LIST-OF-TRIPLE[INT, ACTIVATION, INT] *
                    ( sort List  to  Info,
                      sort NeList  to  NeInfo )            .
    op   sum-active _            :  Info             -> Int  .
    op   all-active? _           :  NeInfo           -> Bool .
    op   make-passive _          :  Info             -> Info .
    op   change-weight _ _ _     :  Int Int Info  -> Info .
    var  t                       :  Triple     .
    var  l                       :  Info       .
    var  a                       :  Activation .
    vars s, idl, m, n            :  Int            .
    ***     Axioms for sum-active:
    eq   sum-active #        = O                    .
    eq   sum-active (t . l)  =  if 2-nd t == on  then  1-st t + sum-active l
                                else  sum-active l  fi .
    ***     Axioms for all-active?:
    eq   all-active? (< n ; a ; m > . #)  = a == on                    .
    eq   all-active? (< n ; a ; m > . l)  = a == on  and  all-active? l .
    ***     Axioms for make-passive:
    eq   make-passive #                       =  #                    .
    eq   make-passive (< n ; a ; m > . l)   =
                            (< n ; off ; m > . make-passive l)    .
    ***     Axioms for change-weight:
    eq   change-weight s idl #                =  #                .
    eq   change-weight s idl (< n ; a ; m > . l)  =
         if  idl == m  then  l app (< s ; on ; idl > . #)
         else  (change-weight s idl l) app (< n ; a ; m > . #)  fi   .
endo


***    ==============================================
***
***    Individual neuron as a 4-tuple
***
obj NEURON[S1 :: ELEM, S2 :: ELEM, S3 :: ELEM, S4 :: ELEM] is
    sort  Neuron .
    op   < _ ; _ ; _ ; _ >      :  Element.S1  Element.S2  Element.S3
                                   Element.S4  -> Neuron       .
    op   identifier _           :  Neuron     -> Element.S1 .
    op   threshold _            :  Neuron     -> Element.S2 .
    op   input _                :  Neuron     -> Element.S3 .
    op   output _               :  Neuron     -> Element.S4 .
    var  a :  Element.S1 .
    var  b :  Element.S2 .
    var  c :  Element.S3 .
    var  d :  Element.S4 .
    ***     Axioms:
    eq   identifier < a ; b ; c ; d >  =  a .
    eq   threshold < a ; b ; c ; d >   =  b .
    eq   input < a ; b ; c ; d >       =  c .
    eq   output < a ; b ; c ; d >      =  d .
endo
```

```
***      ================================================
***
***      Neural network as a list of neurons
***
obj NEURAL-NETWORK is
    protecting LIST[view to NEURON[INT, INT,
                        view to INFO is sort Element to Info . endv,
                        view to OUTFO is sort Element to Outfo . endv]
                    is sort Element to Neuron . endv] *
                            (sort List  to  Network)              .
    op   sleep _          : Neuron                    -> Neuron  .
    op   fire _           : Neuron                    -> Neuron  .
    op   spread _ _       : Neuron  Network           -> Network .
    op   spread-out _ _ _ : Int  Outfo  Network       -> Network .
    op   one-shot _ _ _ _ : Int  Int  Int  Network    -> Network .
    op   all-settled? _   : Network                   -> Bool    .
    op   settle _         : Network                   -> Network .
    var   a  b  w  f  v   : Int    .
    var      idl  id2     : Int    .
    var         c         : Info   .
    var       d   o       : Outfo  .
    var          n        : Neuron .
    var         ns        : Network .
***      Axiom for sleep:
eq   sleep < a ; b ; c ; d > = < a ; b ; make-passive c ; d >    .
***      Axiom for fire:
eq   fire < a ; b ; c ; d >  =
                        < a ; b ; c ; (fire-out (sum-active c) d) > .
***      Axiom for spread:
eq   spread < idl ; b ; c ; d > ns  =  spread-out idl d ns        .
***      Axioms for spread-out:
eq   spread-out idl # ns                         = ns             .
eq   spread-out idl (< f ; w ; id2 > . o) ns  =
        (spread-out idl o (one-shot idl (w * f) id2 ns))          .
***      Axioms for one-shot:
eq   one-shot idl v id2 #                        = #             .
eq   one-shot idl v id2 (< a ; b ; c ; d > . ns)      =
     if  a == id2  then
        (< id2 ; b ; (change-weight v idl c) ; d > . ns)
     else
        (one-shot idl v id2 ns) app (< a ; b ; c ; d > . #)  fi  .
***      Axioms for all-settled?:
eq   all-settled? #        = true
eq   all-settled? (n . ns)  =  if  all-active? (input n)  then  false
                                else  all-settled? ns  fi         .
***      Axiom for settle:
eq   settle #          = #                                        .
eq   settle (n . ns)  =
        if  all-settled? (n . ns)  then  (n . ns)
        else
            (if  all-active? (input n) and
                 (threshold n <= sum-active (input n))  then
                settle ((spread (fire n) ns) app (sleep (fire n) . #))
            else
```

```
                        (if  all-active? (input n)   then
                            settle (ns app ((sleep n) . #))
                        else  settle (ns app (n . #))  fi)
                    fi)
                fi
    endo


    ***    ==========================================
    ***
    ***    Example evaluation of a neural network
    ***
    obj EXAMPLE-NEURAL-NETWORK is
        protecting NEURAL-NETWORK                               .
        ops  info1  info2  info3  info4  info5      : -> Info   .
        ops  outfo1 outfo2 outfo3 outfo4 outfo5  : -> Outfo  .
        ops  network-before  network-after         : -> Network .
        ops  settled-before?  settled-after?        : -> Bool   .
        eq  info1  =  (< 1 ; on ; 0 > . #)                     .
        eq  info2  =  (< 0 ; on ; 0 > . #)                     .
        eq  info3  =  (< 0 ; off ; 1 > . (< 0 ; off ; 2 > . #))  .
        eq  info4  =  (< 0 ; off ; 1 > . (< 0 ; off ; 2 > . #))  .
        eq  info5  =  (< 0 ; off ; 3 > . (< 0 ; off ; 4 > . #))  .
        eq  outfo1  =  (< 0 ; 1 ; 3 > . (< 0 ; -1 ; 4 > . #))   .
        eq  outfo2  =  (< 0 ; -1 ; 3 > . (< 0 ; 1 ; 4 > . #))   .
        eq  outfo3  =  (< 0 ; 1 ; 5 > . #)                     .
        eq  outfo4  =  (< 0 ; 1 ; 5 > . #)                     .
        eq  outfo5  =  (< 0 ; 1 ; 0 > . #)                     .
        eq  network-before  =
                        (< 1 ; -1 ; info1 ; outfo1 > .
                        (< 2 ; -1 ; info2 ; outfo2 > .
                        (< 3 ; -1 ; info3 ; outfo3 > .
                        (< 4 ; -1 ; info4 ; outfo4 > .
                        (< 5 ; -1 ; info5 ; outfo5 > . #)))))  .
        eq  network-after  =
                    settle (< 1 ; -1 ; info1 ; outfo1 > .
                        (< 2 ; -1 ; info2 ; outfo2 > .
                        (< 3 ; -1 ; info3 ; outfo3 > .
                        (< 4 ; -1 ; info4 ; outfo4 > .
                        (< 5 ; -1 ; info5 ; outfo5 > . #)))))  .
        eq  settled-before? =  all-settled? network-before     .
        eq  settled-after?  =  all-settled? network-after      .
    endo


    ***    ==========================================
    ***  ====  Now evaluate some expressions
    reduce settled-before? .
    ***>  should be : false
    reduce settled-after? .
    ***>  should be : true
```

```
reduce network-after .
***>   should be :
   < 3 ; -1 ; < 1 ; off ; 1 > . < 0 ; off ; 2 > . # ;
                < 1 ; 1 ; 5 > . # > .
   < 2 ; -1 ; < 0 ; off ; 0 > . # ;
                < 0 ; -1 ; 3 > . < 0 ; 1 ; 4 > . # > .
   < 4 ; -1 ; < -1 ; off ; 1 > . < 0 ; off ; 2 > . # ;
                < -1 ; 1 ; 5 > . # > .
   < 1 ; -1 ; < 1 ; off ; 0 > . # ;
                < 1 ; 1 ; 3 > . < 1 ; -1 ; 4 > . # > .
   < 5 ; -1 ; < 1 ; off ; 3 > . < -1 ; off ; 4 > . # ;
                < 0 ; 1 ; 0 > . # > . #
***    =======================================================
```


The material in this apppendix can be accessed via remote ftp from 'ftp.wmin.ac.uk' in the path 'computing/published/turnerj/appendix2'.

GLOSSARY OF TERMS FOR
ALGEBRAIC SPECIFICATIONS

Accessor operation

An operation whose range (result sort) is not a principal sort (type of interest) is known as an *accessor* or *observer operation*. For example, in the specification Stack of Fig. 9.7, the operations top and is-empty? are both accessors since neither returns a result of sort stack or ne-stack (the principal sorts). The first returns a natural number while the second returns a Boolean value. See also **Type of interest** and **Constructor operation**.

ACT ONE

Algebraic specification language developed at the Technical University of Berlin. The acronym stands for **A**lgebraic **S**pecification **T**echniques for **C**orrect and **T**rusty **S**oftware **S**ystems.

AFFIRM

An early executable algebraic specification language.

Algebra

An algebra is a tuple $[A, \Omega]$ where A is a set of values, called the *carrier* set or *phylum*, and Ω is a collection of operations defined over the carrier. Such an algebra consisting of a single carrier set is called *homogeneous*. A *heterogeneous* algebra is the tuple $[A, \Omega]$ where $A = \{A_i\}$, $1 \leqslant i \leqslant n$, is a collection of carrier sets $A_1, A_2, \ldots, A_n$ and Ω is a collection of operations each of whose domain and range are drawn from the set of carriers $\{A_i\}$. Algebras provide *models* of algebraic specifications.

Arity

The *arity* of the *n*-ary operation f: $A^n \rightarrow A$ is equal to *n*. In general, a function of arity *n* will have *n* (input) arguments. In *OBJ*, the term arity is used to denote the domain sort of an operation, so the arity of the operation f : s1 s2 s3 $\rightarrow$ s is the Cartesian product s1 s2 s3.

Associativity
See **Attribute**.

Atomic constructor

If a subset of the *constructor* operations can be found that has the property that *all* values of the abstract data type can be denoted using compositions of these operations, the members of this subset are called *atomic constructors*.

Attribute (of an operation)

An *attribute* is an inherent property that an operation may have. Attributes that a binary operation $\_ * \_ : S\ S \rightarrow S$ may possess include *associativity* $((a*b)*c = a*(b*c) = a*b*c)$, *commutativity* $(a*b = b*a)$ and *idempotence* $(a*a = a)$ where $a, b, c \in S$.

Axiom

The *axioms* or *equations* of an algebraic specification formally prescribe the semantics of the operations for the abstract data type being specified. An axiom is a pair of terms *L*, *R* of the same sort that contains universally quantified variables. An axiom asserts that the left- and right-hand sides are equal for any legal substitution of values for variables.

Axis

An executable specification language developed at the Hewlett-Packard Laboratories, Bristol, UK (© Hewlett-Packard 1988).

Binary operation

An operation is said to be *binary* if it has two input arguments of the same sort (type). Operations such as $+$, $*$, and DIV over the integers are examples of binary operations. See also **Attribute**.

Binary relation

If *A* and *B* are sets, then a subset of the Cartesian product $A \times B$ defines a *binary relation* between *A* and *B*.

Canonical term

Canonical terms are a subset of the ground terms that have the property that each canonical term belongs to a different *equivalence class*. For *constructive* specifications, canonical terms can be generated systematically from the *atomic* constructors. An algebra whose carrier set(s) consist of canonical terms is called a *canonical term algebra*. Such an algebra is an *initial* model for the corresponding specification.

Canonical term algebra
See **Canonical term** and **Equivalence relation**.

Carrier
A *carrier*, *carrier set*, or *phylum* is a set of values. A single carrier taken together with a collection of operations defined over the carrier defines a *homogeneous algebra*. Carriers essentially provide interpretations of the sorts of an algebraic specification.

Cartesian product
Given two sets A and B, the Cartesian product of A and B, written $A \times B$ (or just $A\ B$) is the set of all *tuples* or *ordered pairs* (a, b) where $a \in A$ and $b \in B$. The Cartesian product of a set A with itself, $A \times A$, is usually written A^2. The definition extends to three or more sets. For example, $A \times B \times C$ is the set of all 3-tuples (a, b, c) where $a \in A$, $b \in B$, and $c \in C$.

Category
In its most general sense, a *category* of algebras with respect to a signature consists of a set of algebras that are denoted by the signature, together with a number of *homomorphisms* (including the identity homomorphism) between these algebras. Within the confines of our discussion, the category we use is the *variety* over the signature together with all possible homomorphisms between these algebras.

Church–Rosser
A set of *rewrite rules* is said to be *Church–Rosser* if every terminating sequence of rewrites from a given term t stops at a unique minimal form. This minimal form is known as the *normal form* of t.

Clear
An early algebraic specification language which has provided a basis for a number of more recent specification languages including *OBJ*.

Closure
See **Presentation**.

Coarity
In *OBJ*, the *range* of an operation is called the *coarity* or *value sort*.

Codomain
See **Function**.

Commutativity
See **Attribute**.

Confusion
An algebra that is a model of a specification has *confusion* if the interpretation enforces two terms to be equal that were intended to be *distinct*.

Constructive algebraic specification
Roughly speaking, specifications that can be implemented are said to be *constructive*. Constructive specifications have an initial semantics and these executable specifications can be used for *rapid prototyping* (assuming the correctness of the language interpreter).

Constructor operation

An operation whose range (result sort) is a principal sort (type of interest) is known as a *constructor operation* or *constructor*. The values of an abstract data type are built up using *constructors*. For all abstract data types, a constructor must be supplied to create an instance of the abstract data type. See also **Type of interest** and **Accessor operation**.

Denotation

A *denotation* is simply an assignment or interpretation of the sort(s) and operation symbols in a signature to carrier set(s) and operation names respectively in some intended (algebraic) model.

Domain

Given the operation $op : s1\ s2\ ...\ sn \rightarrow s$, the *domain* of op is the sequence of sort names between the colon and the arrow. See also **Function** and **Range**.

Equation
See **Axiom**.

Equational logic (inference)

This is a logical system that permits equational consequences to be deduced from a set of axioms using the symmetric, reflexive, and transitive properties of the equality relation together with substitution of equals for equals.

Equivalence class
See **Equivalence relation**.

Equivalence relation

An *equivalence relation* $\mathcal{R}$ over a set A is a *relation* that is symmetric, reflexive and transitive. It partitions the set A into *equivalence classes*. For an algebraic specification, the terms in each *carrier* set of the *term algebra* will be 'equivalent' to other terms in that carrier set, with the equivalence dictated by the axioms of the algebraic specification. The set of all terms equivalent to any given term forms an *equivalence class*. If we take the term algebra and with each carrier set factor out all the equivalence classes, we will have partitioned the terms of the term algebra into separate equivalence classes. The resulting algebra whose carrier set(s) consist of these different equivalence classes is known as the *quotient term algebra* or *quotient term structure*.

Expression
See **Term**.

Final semantics

The fundamental tenet of *final semantics* (also known as *terminal semantics*) is that two ground terms of the same sort denote the same value unless it can be shown, using the axioms of the specification, that they denote different values.

Fitting morphism

This expresses the idea of translating one signature Σ_1 into another Σ_2. A *fitting morphism* involves mapping some or all of the sorts from Σ_1 to the sorts of Σ_2 and mapping some or all of the operations of Σ_1 to the operations of Σ_2.

Function

Given two sets A and B, a *function f* (of one variable) from set A into set B, written $f: A \rightarrow B$, is a *relation* from set A into set B such that each member of A is related to exactly one member of the set B. The set A is called the *domain* of the function and the set B is called the *codomain* or *range*. The domain of a function can also be the *Cartesian product* of two or more sets, in which case the function is said to be a function of two, three, etc., variables. Functions return only a single result and provide mathematical models for the operations of algebraic specifications. Whereas functions may map many values from a domain onto the same range value, they cannot map a single domain value to more than one range value. See also **Operation**.

Ground term

A *ground* or *variable-free* term is one that does not contain any variables. For example, in the case of a stack of natural numbers, push(init,top(push(init,2))) is a ground term while push(s,top(push(init,n))) where $s \in$ stack and $n \in$ nat is a nonground term since it contains the variables s and n.

Heterogeneous algebra

See **Algebra**.

Homogeneous (many-sorted) algebra

See **Algebra**.

Homomorphism

A *homomorphism* from an algebra $\mathscr{A}$ to an algebra $\mathscr{B}$ is simply a function or mapping from the carrier set(s) of $\mathscr{A}$ to the carrier set(s) of $\mathscr{B}$ that preserves the structure of the original algebra $\mathscr{A}$.

Idempotent operation

The set union operation $\cup$ is an example of an *idempotent* operation since $S \cup S = S$ for all sets S. See also **Attribute**.

Initial algebra

Given a specification and the family of algebras that are models of that specification, an algebra that belongs to this family is *initial* if a *unique* homomorphism exists between it and *each* member of the family. All initial models of algebraic specifications are *isomorphic* to each other and so can be considered to be the 'same' to an extent that allows for algebras having sets that only differ in their name. Initial models are characterized by having *no junk* and *no confusion* and such models are often used as the 'standard' model of a specification.

Initial algebra semantics
Initiality implies that every value in the carrier set of an algebra can be denoted by *ground terms* of the specification; any two ground terms that cannot be shown to be equal using the axioms are unequal, that is they denote different values in the carrier.

Instantiation
This word describes the replacement of each formal parameter in a parameterized specification module by a module or module expression that satisfies the appropriate requirement which in Axis is a PROPS module.

Interpretation
See **Model**.

Isomorphism
A homomorphism $h: \mathscr{A} \to \mathscr{B}$ from algebra $\mathscr{A}$ to algebra $\mathscr{B}$ is called an *isomorphism* if h is a bijective mapping. If two algebras are isomorphic, then essentially they are the same in the sense that they are equivalent in all respects apart from the symbols that name the elements of their respective carrier sets and operations. Isomorphism expresses the key concept of the independence of representation necessary for values of abstract data types.

Junk
Given an algebra $\mathscr{A}$ that is a model of a presentation, the word *junk* is used to refer to those members of the carrier set of $\mathscr{A}$ that cannot be denoted by any term that belongs to the signature of the corresponding presentation.

Larch
A two-layered algebraic specification language.

Many-sorted algebra (MSA)
Another name for a *heterogeneous* algebra. See also **Algebra**.

Mapping
A *map* or *mapping m* from a set A to a set B, written $m: A \to B$ is a relation from A into B such that each element of A is related to exactly one element of B. If an element $a \in A$ is mapped to the element $b \in B$, we write $b = m(a)$ or $a \mapsto b$.

Model
An algebra is said to be a *model* of a specification if the algebra has a carrier set for each sort given in the signature and an operation for each operation symbol whose domain and range sets match exactly the pattern of domain and range sorts given in the signature. The sequence of mappings that denotes the correspondence between each sort name and carrier set and between each symbolic operation name of the signature and operation in the algebra is referred to as an *interpretation*.

Module expression
For our algebraic specification language, a *module expression* is defined recursively as follows. A module expression consists of the identifier of an unparameterized SPEC module

or the instantiation of a parameterized SPEC module or a composition of modules constructed using the building operators + (sum) applied to module expressions.

Noetherian

If a set of rewrite rules is such that every sequence of rewrites from a given term t terminates after a finite number of steps, the set of rewrite rules is said to be *Noetherian* or *finitely terminating*.

Nonatomic constructor
See **Atomic constructor**.

Normal form
See **Church–Rosser**.

n-tuple
See **Tuple**.

Nullary operation

Constant values in an algebraic specification are represented as *nullary operations*, that is as functions without (input) arguments. See also **Operation**.

OBJ

An executable algebraic specification language which has undergone a number of metamorphoses since the first implementation *OBJ0* was developed back in 1976.

Observer
See **Accessor operation**.

Operation

Let A be a nonempty set, then the n-ary operation *op* is a *function* from A^n to A and is written $op: A^n \to A$. This definition can be generalized to the situation where the *domain* is the Cartesian product of two or more sets. A *nullary* operation, $op_{nullary}: \to A$, corresponds to a constant value that is a member of the set A while a *unary* operation is a function from A into A, that is $op_{unary}: A \to A$. See also **Function**.

Order-sorted algebra (OSA)

An OSA is a many-sorted algebra in which a *partial ordering* exists among the carriers of the algebra which is interpreted as subset inclusion.

Parameterization

Many algebraic specification languages support the production of parameterized specifications. This provides a powerful tool for software design and production in that it promotes the reuse of specification components. New specifications can be constructed from existing specifications by instantiating parameters and transforming specification modules. In the present context, PROPS modules specify the syntactic and semantic properties that are demanded of an actual SPEC module in any meaningful instantiation.

Partial operation

An operation (or function) that is not defined for *all* values in its domain is said to be *partial*.

Partial ordering

A *partial ordering* over a set A is a relation that is reflexive and transitive but not symmetric. Commonly used symbols that denote particular partial orderings are $\leqslant$ and $\subseteq$.

Phylum

Another name for a *carrier* set. See also **Carrier**.

Place-holder

In most algebraic specification languages, operations can be represented using prefix, infix, postfix or mixfix forms. The position of the argument(s) for each form is denoted by a *place-holder* which is the underscore character _ in Axis.

Presentation

A *presentation* consists of a signature, Σ, together with a set of axioms E over that signature, so we can write the presentation as the tuple $<\Sigma, E>$. The set of all axioms (theorems) derivable under equational logic from the original set of axioms E is called the *closure* of E. A presentation $<\Sigma, E>$ together with the closure of E defines a *theory presentation*.

PROPS module

A PROPS module defines a collection of models that contain all the algebras which satisfy that module.

Quotient term algebra

The *quotient term algebra* or *quotient term structure* is derived from the *term algebra* by separating out all the equivalent terms, that is ground terms that can be shown to be equivalent using the axioms of the specification. The elements of the carrier set of a quotient term algebra therefore consist of the corresponding collection of equivalence classes. This algebra is initial. See also **Equivalence relation**.

Range

Given the operation op : s1 ... sn → s, the sort s corresponding to the result of the operation op is called the *range* or *value sort*. See also **Function**.

Rank

In OBJ, given the operation op : s1 s2 → s, the tuple < s1 s2 , s > is called the *rank* of the operation op. The rank therefore consists of the sequence of domain sorts followed by the range sort and is denoted in OBJ terminology by ⟨*arity, coarity*⟩. Note that the word *rank* is also used by some authors to denote the range sort of a nullary operation.

Reduced form

A *reduced form, term,* or *expression* is a ground term that consists of compositions of atomic constructors only. For the specification of natural numbers, terms such as zero, succ(zero), succ(succ(zero)) are examples of reduced forms.

Relation

Given two sets A and B, a *relation* from A into B is any subset of the Cartesian product $A \times B$.

Rewrite rules

A collection of axioms $L = R$ can be treated as a set of *rewrite rules* that specify how the left-hand side of any axiom can be rewritten to its corresponding right-hand side. For a set of rewrite rules, the symmetric equality operator $=$ is treated as a nonsymmetric, one-way (for example left to right) replacement operator.

Satisfaction

A class (family) of algebras $\mathscr{C}$ is said to *satisfy* a PROPS module P if $\mathscr{C}$ is contained in the class of algebras denoted by P. Roughly speaking, a SPEC module S satisfies a PROPS module P if the axioms of S imply the axioms of P.

Semantics

The *semantics* of the operations of an abstract data type defines their 'meaning' in the sense that it describes their behaviour (that is 'what they do'). In the algebraic approach to specification, the semantics of the operations is described by a collection of axioms (equations), each of which involves two or more of the operations.

Signature

The *signature*, Σ, of an algebraic specification consists of a collection of sort names together with a collection of operations whose domain and range sorts are drawn from this collection of sorts. The signature corresponds to the information contained in the SORTS, SUBSORT, and OPS components of a specification. The signature of an algebraic specification prescribes the *syntax* of the operations and determines the set of well-formed terms for each sort.

Σ-Algebra

Given a signature Σ, then any algebra that is denoted by that signature is called a Σ-algebra. Hence, a Σ-algebra is simply an interpretation of the signature Σ and so consists of a carrier A together with an interpretation over A of each operation symbol in Σ.

Sort

A *sort* or more precisely *sort identifier* is the name given to the symbolic sets of a specification. Sort identifiers are used in the signature component of a specification to denote the domains and ranges of the operations. Loosely speaking, sorts are the counterparts of data type identifier names, such as INTEGER and BOOLEAN in high-level programming languages.

SPEC Module

A SPEC module consists of a collection of sort names and operations defined over those sorts together with a collection of axioms that relate the operations. Unparameterized SPEC modules impose an *initial* interpretation whilst PROPS modules specify loose data types that can be used to instantiate a parameterized SPEC module.

Structural induction
This is a proof method based on mathematical induction in which the induction is on the syntactic structure of the terms of an algebraic specification.

Subsort
Often one set of data values contains or is contained within another set of values. For example, the set of natural numbers $\mathbb{N}$ is contained within the set of integers $\mathbb{Z}$. The corresponding concept at the specification level is that of *subsorts* and *supersorts*. If s1 is a subsort of s2, we write s1 < s2. Equivalently, s2 > s1 and we say that s2 is a supersort of s1.

Sufficient completeness
When a new data type is specified that uses existing abstract data types, the values of all syntactically legal terms (well-formed expressions) that can be constructed using the introduced operations of the new type should belong to *either* the new data type *or* be reducible by the axioms to values of the existing types. This property is known as *sufficient completeness*.

Supersort
See **Subsort**.

Term
A *term* or *expression* of an algebraic specification is well-formed if it is a constant (nullary operation), a variable, or an operation applied to the correct number of arguments, with each argument itself a well-formed term of the correct sort. The sort of a variable term is given by the sort identifier stated in the variable declaration, which for our language is the FORALL component of a specification.

Term algebra
A *term algebra* is an interpretation of a specification in which the carrier set of the algebra consists of the strings of symbols that denote all well-formed terms of the specification. This model always exists and has the advantage that we can treat and manipulate the strings of symbols that denote the sorts, operation names, and terms of the specification directly as a model in its own right.

Terminal semantics
See **Final semantics**.

Theory presentation
See **Presentation**.

Total operation
An operation (or function) that is defined for *all* values in its domain is said to be *total*.

Tuple
A *tuple* is an object $\langle x, y \rangle$ with two components x and y and their order is important. An *n-tuple* generalizes this idea to an object with n components.

Type(s) of interest

The principal sort (or sorts) that appear in the signature of an algebraic specification are sometimes referred to as *the type* or *types of interest*. For example, in the case of the specification Stack of Fig. 9.7, the types of interest are stack and ne–stack.

Variable-free term

See **Ground term**.

Variety

Given a signature Σ and a set of axioms E, the set of *all* algebras that are denoted by Σ *and* that satisfy E is called the *variety* over the presentation $\langle \Sigma, E \rangle$.

View

A SPEC module can often satisfy a PROPS module in more than one way. A *view* from a PROPS module P to a SPEC module S consists of a *mapping* from the sorts of P to the sorts of S together with a mapping from the operations of P to the operations of S that preserves the domain and range sorts of the operations.

AUTHOR INDEX

SUBJECT INDEX